GREAT POWER CLASHES ALONG THE MARITIME SILK ROAD

GREAT POWER CLASHES ALONG THE MARITIME SILK ROAD

Lessons from History to Shape Current Strategy

GRANT F. RHODE

Naval Institute Press
ANNAPOLIS, MARYLAND

Naval Institute Press
291 Wood Road
Annapolis, MD 21402

Library of Congress Cataloging-in-Publication Data
Names: Rhode, Grant F., author.
Title: Great power clashes along the maritime silk road : lessons from history to shape current strategy / Grant F. Rhode.
Description: Annapolis, Maryland : Naval Institute Press, [2023] | Includes bibliographical references and index.
Identifiers: LCCN 2023030032 (print) | LCCN 2023030033 (ebook) | ISBN 9781682478660 (hardcover) | ISBN 9781682478677 (ebook)
Subjects: LCSH: Naval battles–Eurasia–History. | Sea-power–Eurasia–History. | Geopolitics–Eurasia–History. | Balance of power. | Eurasia–History, Naval. | Eurasia–Foreign relations. | BISAC: HISTORY / Asia / General | HISTORY / Military / Strategy
Classification: LCC D27 .R47 2023 (print) | LCC D27 (ebook) | DDC 320.1/2095–dc23/eng/20230703
LC record available at https://lccn.loc.gov/2023030032
LC ebook record available at https://lccn.loc.gov/2023030033

∞ Print editions meet the requirements of ANSI/NISO z39.48–1992 (Permanence of Paper). Printed in the United States of America.

31 30 29 28 27 26 25 24 23 9 8 7 6 5 4 3 2 1
First printing

For Judy, Lauren, and Jamie

CONTENTS

ILLUSTRATIONS

CHARTS

MAPS

TABLES

PREFACE

> A good place to understand the present, and to ask questions about the future, is on the ground traveling as slowly as possible.
>
> —Robert Kaplan, *The Revenge of Geography*

When Rear Adm. Stephen B. Luce established the U.S. Naval War College in 1884, he declared that the college would be "a place of original research on all questions relating to war and the statesmanship connected with war, or the prevention of war." My aim in producing this study is to contribute to Luce's war and peace research agenda by providing historical hindsight that might help lead to foresight in statecraft, thereby assisting in the creation of policy options regarding Eurasia that are well-informed by the knowledge of precedents. The case studies included here allow a long look back, which I hope will lead to an enhanced ability for maritime strategists and other readers to see forward.

This book expands on Robert Kaplan's wise observation about travel on the ground through inclusion of travel by sea. Over the course of seven years, I explored the sites of the maritime case studies in this book in order to understand the past as well as to ask questions about the future. Through these explorations, I developed images of Eurasia's maritime past that I have shared in the case study narratives. The travels prompted me to reflect on the present as well as on the future. During an era when understanding the Indo-Pacific region is of increasing importance to the conduct of global affairs, this Eurasian maritime material seems particularly relevant.

We drove north along the coast road. The sun sparkled on the restless surface of the deep blue Arabian Sea to our east, illuminating the undulating buff and gray rock ridges to our west. The timeless landscape, unbroken by human settlement, allowed us to ponder the giant green turtles we had seen giving birth on the beach the night before at Ras al-Jinz. The turtles' nesting beach sits at the tip of Oman that juts into the Arabian Sea, a cape that creates a swirl of currents where from before recorded time the turtles have come ashore to lay their eggs in deep sand nests. We stopped in Sur with its ancient lagoon port, accessed by a narrow channel marked by three ancient lighthouses that must be lined up when approaching from the sea in order to avoid hitting the bar near the channel mouth. There we visited the still active yards where new dhows are built and old ones are repaired by skilled workers, most of whom are Indian. Later in our journey, we would find Yemeni boatbuilders in the yards of Kerala on the southwest coast of India, another indication of the cross-currents of maritime history in the Indian Ocean.

North of Sur, we stopped in Qalhat. There was not much there: a village, Bibi Maryam's tomb, and a silted-up harbor. We stopped because the Venetian merchant traveler Marco Polo had sailed into this now derelict harbor in the late thirteenth century. Polo was followed during the early fourteenth century by the Moroccan Islamic judge and traveler Ibn Battuta, who recorded his observations of the beautiful mosque that Bibi Maryam had built. Then the port was visited in the early fifteenth century by the venerated Chinese explorer Admiral Zheng He. During those centuries prior to devastation by an earthquake in the late fifteenth century and before the first Portuguese visit in 1507, Qalhat was a vibrant port on the ancient maritime silk road.

When I mentioned our visit in Oman to the commandant of the Indian Naval War College in Goa, his eyes lit up as he described the stark beauty of Oman precisely the way we had seen it. I lectured to his senior captains on current maritime affairs, but the commandant was most interested in hearing about our trip south from Mumbai along the Konkan coast of Maharashtra. We had visited the sea forts at Kolaba, Janjira, Suvarnadurg, Ratnadurg, and Vijaydurg, where the Maratha admiral Kanhoji Angre and his sons had successfully resisted the British using asymmetrical naval warfare tactics between 1699 and 1756. After hearing about the fascinating historical sites we had visited, he was intrigued as an Indian strategist by the details of Maratha grabs and gallivats marauding British East India Company cargo carriers in tactically successful asymmetric naval operations. His interest led to a tour of these historical sites by naval officers studying at the Indian Naval War College.

The broad Eurasian geographical scope of the maritime case studies that I researched brought me to many other absorbing sites, with opportunities for dozens of interviews with scholars, museum guides, military and diplomatic personnel, and local observers keen to share their maritime and cultural knowledge with interested outsiders. The following chapters elaborate my observations and thoughts on these Mediterranean Sea, Indian Ocean, and China Seas explorations.

INTRODUCTION

Great Power Clashes along the Maritime Silk Road

Cases and Modes of Explanation

The longer you can look back, the farther you can look forward.

—Winston Churchill

Global history is central to the foreign policy practice of Chinese president Xi Jinping and to the scholarly paradigm of Oxford historian Peter Frankopan. The history of the ancient silk roads has provided a model and rationale for China's Belt and Road Initiative. Intuitively grasping the power of historical metaphor, Xi wrapped existing Chinese globalization efforts into his 2013 vision for a re-creation of both the ancient Han and Tang Dynasty silk road land links through central Asia to Europe, and the Song and Ming Dynasty maritime silk road links through the China Seas and the Indian Ocean to South Asia, Arabia, and Africa. President Xi called his new land route program the "Silk Road Economic Belt," and the sea route program the "21st Century Maritime Silk Road." Originally named One Belt One Road (*yi dai yi lu*), the project subsequently has been relabeled the Belt and Road Initiative, or BRI.[1] During its first few years, the BRI has impacted great power competition by promising to invest trillions of dollars in infrastructure and other projects across Asia, Africa, Europe, and South America, albeit creating controversy, resulting in both positive and negative assessments.[2] With its broad application to economic, political, and strategic aspects of Chinese foreign relations, the BRI program has had an international presence, though its future remains uncertain, especially in the light of recent developments such as the Covid-19 pandemic and the Russian invasion of Ukraine.

In a very different scenario, Peter Frankopan has written compelling global history in his sweeping integrative work *The Silk Roads: A New History of the World*.[3] This substantial work by a Byzantine historian goes beyond Byzantium to explore patterns of human interconnection across Eurasia and beyond for the past two millennia. It is breathtaking in scope, breaking down silos of regional and national histories to understand broader patterns of global economic, political, and cultural connectivity. Using the core idea of the ancient silk roads, Frankopan traces the routes of ideas, religions, and trade across the globe.

Seeking to contribute to the maritime aspects of global history, as well as to the understanding of historical patterns that underlie discussions of Maritime Silk Road policy, this book fits along the continuum between the policy goals of Xi Jinping and the scholarly conception of Peter Frankopan. It seeks to interpret the past with a perspective toward policy implications for the present and the future. It asks how decision makers can use Eurasian maritime history to shape informed policy toward national strategy. Like Frankopan's scholarly approach, this work provides a broad sweep that breaks down traditional regional silos of historical study, although its time frame is one rather than the two millennia covered by Frankopan's *The Silk Roads*. The geographical scope is also more contained, with the outer limit of the Mediterranean in the west and the China Seas in the east, whereas Frankopan brings the Americas into his story. In addition, this book addresses maritime history rather than continental history, the primary focus of Frankopan's book. In its maritime perspective, this work partially overlaps with Frankopan's work and Xi's vision, because it concentrates on the history of the Maritime Silk Road rather than on the continental Silk Road Economic Belt.[4]

Cases of Great Power Clashes along the Premodern Maritime Silk Road

This book examines the past with the aim of developing an eye for the future. Contemporary practitioners of international relations, both military officers and diplomats, as well as those interested more generally in global strategic considerations, will find themselves thinking about the current period as they consider the past. This work provides an analysis of premodern maritime clashes along the Eurasian perimeter that offer examples of local or regional war reflecting the particular circumstances of time and place. As contemporary international relations studies of the Asia-Pacific region have expanded to address the Indo-Pacific region, this work is similarly wide-ranging, with clashes explored in the China Seas, the Indian Ocean, and the eastern Mediterranean Sea. These cases include the eleventh-century Chola invasion of Srivijaya, the thirteenth-century Mongol invasions of Japan and Southeast Asia, the early fifteenth-century Ming maritime expeditions to the Indian Ocean, the sixteenth-century Kunjali Marakkar resistance to the Portuguese on India's Malabar coast, the sixteenth-century rise and stall of the Ottoman navy in the Mediterranean and Arabian Seas, the late sixteenth-century invasions of Korea by Japanese samurai, the seventeenth-century late Ming wresting of Taiwan from the Dutch, and the eighteenth-century Maratha naval resistance to the British on India's Konkan coast.

During the premodern period, the largest global economies were the civilizations of India and China. Chart 1 illustrates that between 1 CE and 1000 CE, India (40 percent) and China (30 percent) accounted for about 70 percent of world GDP. Between 1000 CE and 1750 CE, the period reviewed in this book, India and China still accounted for 60 percent of world GDP, with China's GDP surpassing that of India. During the European colonial period 1750 CE to 1950 CE, China and India's combined share of GDP dropped precipitously to about 10 percent of world GDP. By 2017, China's rapid economic growth following Deng Xiaoping's reform and opening that began in 1979 helped China achieve a 20 percent share of world GDP. India grew to 10 percent of world GDP in the same period, reflecting for these two Asian giants an expansionary trend toward a larger share of world GDP. It may surprise many in the West, convinced by two centuries of economic dominance from 1750 to 1950, that shares in the global economy are beginning to look more like that of the premodern period. Thus an analysis of the premodern era is in order, especially with a focus on India and China, because they are aware of their dominant premodern history as a possible model for the future.

CHART 1
Shares of GDP, 1 CE to 2017 CE

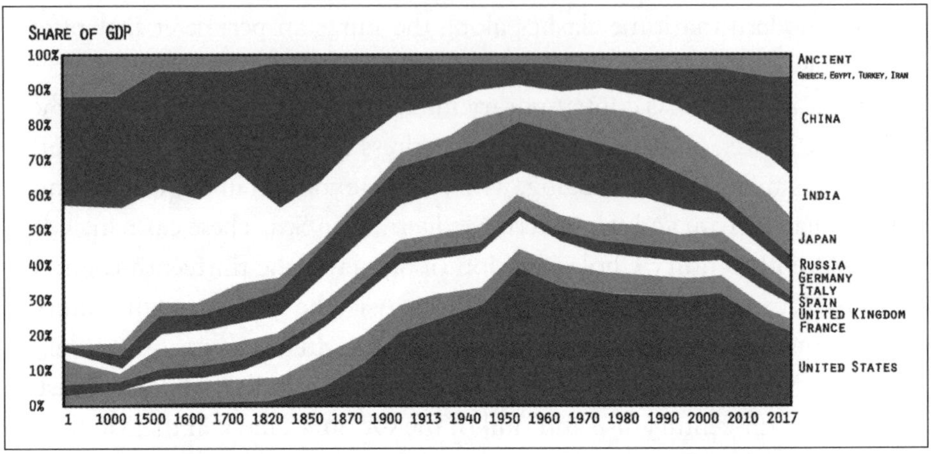

Created by Jamie Rhode, adapted from three articles by Derek Thompson, "The Economic History of the Last 2,000 Years in 1 Little Graph, Parts I, II, and III," in The Atlantic, *June 19–22, 2012. https://www.theatlantic.com/business/archive/2012/06/the -economic-history-of-the-last-2 -000-years-in-1-little-graph/258676/; updated through 2017, accessed May 31, 2022: https://www.visualcapitalist.com/2000-years-economic-history-one-chart/.*

The cases in this work, while not comprehensive histories, are intended to provide a chronologic and geographic range within which patterns during the ancient period may be assessed. The premodern maritime silk road included the ship connections from the China coast through the China Seas, into and across the Indian Ocean to India, Arabia, and Africa, and on through the Persian Gulf and Red Sea into the Mediterranean Sea. The term premodern is used to refer to the Age of Sail before the Age of Steam beginning in the nineteenth century. The early Age of Sail in Eurasia was a world of dhows and junks, rather than caravels and carracks that appeared with the Portuguese around 1500.

Eurasian maritime clashes during the Age of Steam beginning in the nineteenth century are also beyond the scope of this study. The opening of the Suez Canal, passages to India, the Opium Wars, and Perry's opening of Japan represent a fascinating and important period requiring the conversion of ports into coaling stations and other innovations. But, as in Mahan's work, the attempt here is to learn some timeless lessons from the Age of Sail. Mahan's focus was largely Euro-American, while this work's focus is Euro-Asian. Eurasian refers both to West Asian Ottoman incursions into Europe through the Mediterranean and also to the European powers' (Portuguese, Spanish, Dutch, French, and British) incursions into West, South, Southeast, and East Asia.

The eight case studies in this work represent a balanced survey in terms of the geography of Eurasian maritime clashes along the premodern Eurasian maritime silk road. The span of the case studies is represented on map I.1, which includes the Eurasian maritime perimeter from the Mediterranean island of Malta in the west to the Korea Strait island of Tsushima in the northeast.

During World War II, Yale scholar Nicholas Spykman theorized that the Eurasian rimlands would become the predominant theater of conflict in the post–World War II period. Current and potential conflicts in Mediterranean North Africa, Syria, Iraq, the Persian Gulf, the Gulf of Aden, the South and East China Seas, and Korea bear witness to Spykman's prescience. His predictions, however, should be understood within the long history of the Eurasian rimlands. This book examines deep roots of economic, geopolitical, cultural, and power-transition tensions

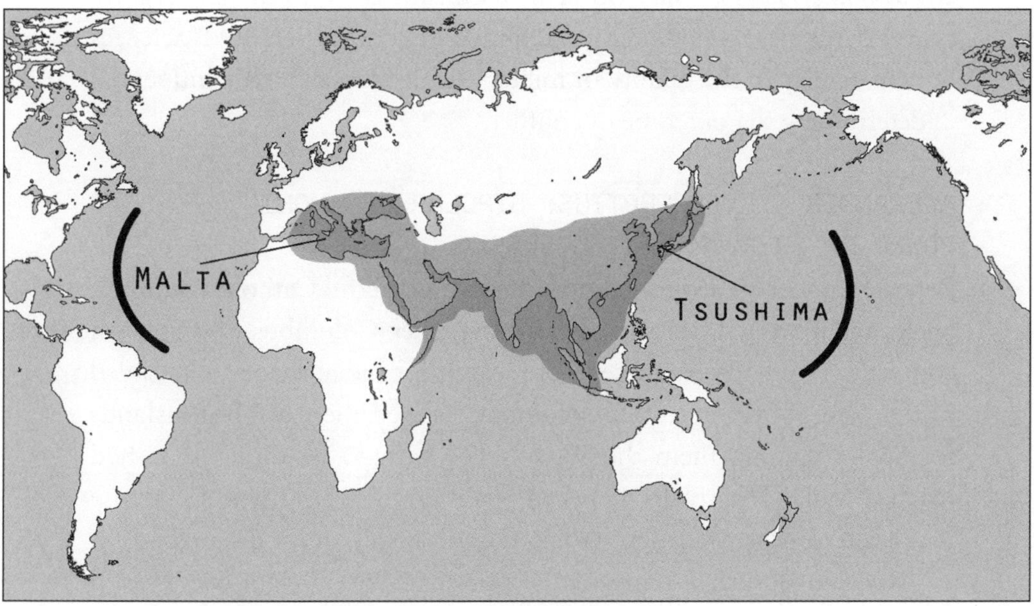

MAP I.1 Locational range of the case studies considered
Created by Jamie Rhode, adapted from Mountain High base map

in the Eurasian maritime rimlands that have resulted in repeated conflict over the centuries and that continue to be factors in international relations today. This work examines conflict between Asian powers, as well as between Asian and European powers, with varied explanations by historians and policy theorists.

Explanations for Great Power Clashes along the Premodern Maritime Silk Road

In order to consider these case studies in analytical terms, the application of relevant theoretical explanations for conflict will be examined. The following sections introduce legal, geoeconomic, geopolitical, cultural, and power-transition theorists. Each of the contending theories illuminates an understanding of the case studies, with varying degrees of explanatory power. Age of Discovery theorists include Pope Alexander VI and Hugo Grotius. Priority of economic explanations is provided by Alfred Thayer Mahan and Norman Angell. Relevant early twentieth-century geopolitical theorists include Halford Mackinder and Nicholas Spykman. More recently, Samuel Huntington gives priority to cultural/civilizational factors, while Graham Allison focuses on changing relative power dynamics to explain the likelihood of conflict. Jeremy Black sees human agency in the quality of military leadership as highly influential in determining the outcome of conflict.

ALEXANDER VI VS. GROTIUS: BIPOLAR HEGEMONIC POWER OR FREEDOM OF THE SEAS?

Pope Alexander VI arbitrated between two powerful Catholic countries, Spain and Portugal, shortly after Christopher Columbus, the Spanish competitor to the Portuguese in the search for India, successfully sailed to the New World in 1492. Columbus claimed the Caribbean islands for Spain, naming them the West Indies because he thought he had reached India. The rivalry between Spain and Portugal was so intense that a referee was needed regarding the ownership of his discoveries.

Rodrigo Borgia, a scion of the powerful Borgia clan, was elected pope in 1492, with rumors of using mules loaded with silver to buy papal votes. He took the name of Pope Alexander VI. Aside from his ruthless politics and controversy over his acknowledgment of having several children, he is generally considered to have been a competent and effective pope until he died in 1503. After Christopher Columbus returned from his voyage of discovery of the mistakenly named Indies in 1492, Alexander issued the papal bull *Inter Caetera* (Among Other Things) citing Columbus' discoveries on behalf of King Ferdinand and Queen Isabella of Spain and urging "the Catholic Faith and the Christian religion be exalted and be everywhere increased and spread." He delineated an unclear form of sovereignty for Spain in an area west of a longitude line defined in the decree: "[B]y drawing and establishing a line from Arctic Pole to the Antarctic pole, no matter whether the mainlands and islands, found and to be found, lie in the direction of India or toward any other quarter whatsoever, the said line to be one hundred leagues towards the west and south, as is aforesaid, from any of the islands commonly known as the Azores and Cape Verde; apostolic constitutions and ordinances and other decrees whatsoever to the contrary notwithstanding."[5]

Alexander VI effectively established a longitude line in the Atlantic, dividing the lands outside of Europe between Spain and Portugal. The line, with a modification farther to the west that was important to Portugal, became the basis for the 1494 Treaty of Tordesillas. With the modification, Portugal received the bulk of the bulge that became Brazil, which explains why Portuguese is spoken there, while Spanish became spoken in the remainder of South America. Thus, the globe was neatly divided into two spheres of influence, a solution that was satisfactory to both Spain and Portugal. The detail of drawing a longitude line in the Pacific Ocean, the other half of the line to complete the geographic definition of division of the globe, was delayed until the Treaty of Zaragoza in 1529.

Spain became preoccupied with its explorations and colonization of the Western Hemisphere, while the Portuguese had their hands full with their preoccupations in the Asian half of the world. Alexander VI was essentially the referee dividing the globe, creating a bipolar world division between two hegemonic powers with defined regions of influence, which Spain and Portugal took to mean sovereignty. As with most referees, Alexander's judgment was questioned, somewhat by Spain and Portugal, but extensively by other European powers who overwhelmingly rejected the pope's right to convey sovereignty over vast regions.

Hugo Grotius was one of the non-Catholic northern Europeans who objected strenuously to the Portuguese and Spanish assumptions of rights to sovereignty in the trade with India and with the Indies and China beyond. He was born in 1583 in the canal-laced village of Delft and is commemorated by a prominent bronze statue in the Market Square in front of the Delft Protestant Neiuwe Kerk (New Church, 1492), where he is entombed in the family mausoleum, with William of Orange and other members of the House of Orange nearby.[6] His learned father prepared him at age eleven in 1594 to enter the beautiful, quiet halls of Leiden University, which continues to be a bastion of learning about Asian subjects. A student and theorist of law, he was appointed advocate to The Hague in 1599, wrote *De Indis* (On the Indies) in 1604–5, became advocate general of Holland in 1607, and mayor of Rotterdam in 1609 at age twenty-six. Thus, Grotius was well-trained and well-placed to contribute to the flowering of the Dutch Golden Age, founded on the wealth generated by the Dutch East India Company, which had been established in 1602 as the first publicly traded stock company in the world. The company logo, consisting of the intertwined letters VOC, standing for the Vereenigde Oostindische Compagnie, can still be found carved in stone in many places in Asia, including over doors in the many Dutch forts in India, Sri Lanka, Malaysia, Indonesia, Taiwan, and Japan.

In 1609, Leiden University published Grotius' influential work *Mare Liberum* (The Free Sea), adapted from chapter 12 of *De Indis*. The work was commissioned as a defense of the Dutch East India Company's seizure in 1603 of the Portuguese carrack *Santa Catarina*. In this work, Grotius established in international law the concept of freedom of the seas, which continues to provide the basis for the international law of the sea today, as codified in UNCLOS, the United Nations Convention on the Law of the Sea, signed in 1982 and entered into force in 1994. At the time that he wrote *Mare Liberum*, Grotius was arguing against the Portuguese concept of *Mare Clausam* (The Closed Sea), which justified the Portuguese monopoly of high seas rights in the Indian Ocean. In *Mare Liberum*, Grotius begins by postulating that "By the Law of Nations navigation is free to all persons whatsoever."[7] He then systematically presented text arguments that the Portuguese had no right of sovereignty over the East Indies, to which the Dutch made voyages, by reason of discovery, papal donation, occupation, or prescription or custom. In further sections, he argued that "By the Law of Nations trade is free to all persons whatsoever" and that "The Portuguese prohibition of trade has no foundation in equity," and he concluded with a section beginning, "The Dutch must maintain their right of trade with the East Indies by peace, by treaty, or by war."[8] In developing this well-laid-out concept of the freedom of the seas for everyone, Grotius challenged the idea that the seas belonged only to Portugal and Spain.[9] Initially, the English challenged the idea *of mare liberum*, with John Selden arguing that England had sovereignty over the seas around the British Isles. Later this concept was modified to include only the distance that a cannon could fire from the mainland, a widely accepted basis for the three-nautical mile territorial sea limit, beyond which *mare liberum*, freedom on the high seas, prevailed. In the twentieth century, territorial sea limits were extended by UNCLOS to twelve nautical miles.

Grotius did not have a quiet life in Delft. In conflicts between civil and religious authorities, Grotius argued for the right of civil authorities to make university appointments, and he later drafted the edict of toleration. In 1619, Grotius was sentenced to life imprisonment for his secularist beliefs in the struggle between church and state, but he daringly escaped from his castle jail hidden in a book chest, an episode for which he is famous in Holland today. He lived in France for more than a decade, publishing *De jure belli ac pacis* (On the Law of Peace and War) in 1625, which developed an early theory of just war. This book is said to have been carried by the king of Sweden in his saddlebag when leading troops. After being appointed Swedish ambassador to

France, Grotius was shipwrecked when leaving Sweden. He made it to shore, dying shortly thereafter in 1645. Although persona non grata in Holland during his later life, his body was returned to Delft for its final resting place.

Even though he was forced to leave Holland in a chest in 1621, Grotius' work in his final two decades continued to justify Dutch expansionist aims overseas.[10] His legal contributions to disputes over herring fisheries in the North Sea and whaling near Spitzbergen supported Dutch arguments for freedom of the sea, legal disputes reminiscent of the Cod Wars between Iceland and the United Kingdom during the 1970s, as both of those seventeenth-century and twentieth-century cases had an impact on formulation of the law of the sea. He lobbied for and eventually saw legal appointments granted by the VOC to his younger brother Willem de Groot and to his second son Pieter de Groot in 1538 and 1644, respectively. In 1644, Pieter conducted himself with distinction in negotiating Dutch rights to cinnamon-producing areas in Sri Lanka following the Dutch capture of Galle from Portugal in 1640. Willem and Pieter were in absentia proxies for Grotius' ideas in the Netherlands during his period of exile, as they distinguished between Europe and the rest of the world.[11] Controversially, Grotius gave a free hand to Dutch sea captains to be thuggish in Asia, acting as VOC incipient states with military powers outside of Europe.[12]

MAHAN VS. ANGELL: SEA POWER ECONOMIC DOMINANCE OR ECONOMIC INTERDEPENDENCY?

Alfred Thayer Mahan, theorist of naval power, laid a foundation for understanding the need for sea power in relation to economic competition.[13] Mahan was born in 1840 during the premodern era of wooden sailing ships, short range guns, and signal flag communications, premodern technologies that characterize the case studies considered in this book. He died, however, in 1914, by which time naval technologies had evolved to include steel steamships powered by coal and oil; long-range armaments including guns, torpedoes, and airplanes; and electronic communications, including cable and radio. But Mahan's preoccupation was centered on exploring enduring underlying strategic principles that led to sea power dominance during earlier periods, rather than on technological advances. He wished to enlighten world leaders regarding naval strategy in modernized navies of the twentieth century, even though the examples he chose were primarily from the eighteenth century. His newly published work became highly influential on American president Theodore Roosevelt around 1900, as well as on Japan's Admiral Togo and on Germany's Kaiser Wilhelm.[14]

Mahan saw the oceans covering 80 percent of the globe as a continuous interconnected waterway used by all nations as a highway for trade. He began *The Influence of Sea Power* with the concept of the sea as a "wide common": "The first and most obvious light in which the sea presents itself from the political and social point of view is that of the great highway; or better, perhaps, of a wide common, over which men may pass in all directions, but on which some well-worn paths show that controlling reasons have led them to choose certain lines of travel rather than others. These lines of travel are called trade routes; and the reasons which have determined them are to be sought in the history of the world."[15]

Thus, Mahan's first principle of sea power involves the use of the sea to engage in trade between parties living on the shores of the seas. He understood the profound forces of economics better than other naval historians preoccupied with strategy and tactics.[16] Mahan's analysis, however, did not involve the history of trade, but rather the naval history of the protection of trade. In his analysis, a great sea trading nation must also be a nation committed to a strong navy to protect that trade: "The necessity of a navy, in the restricted sense of the word, springs, therefore, on the existence of a peaceful shipping, and disappears with it, except in the case of a nation which has aggressive tendencies and keeps up a navy merely as a branch of the military establishment."[17]

Mahan went on to enumerate and examine six principal conditions affecting the sea power of nations.[18] These include geographical position; physical conformation of the seaboard; extent of territory; number of population; character of the people; and character of the government.

Through this analysis of principal conditions Mahan identified countries likely to be successful developing sea power, such as Britain and the United States.

In terms of developing a prescription for naval development, Mahan argued for a robust navy based on the most powerful capital ships, and he argued against French concepts for development of cruisers built for long-distance commerce raiding and small torpedo boats built to attack enemy ships. In other words, he prioritized great naval power and an adequate budget for producing expensive capital ships. He succinctly summarized his point: "The vainest of all delusions is the expectation of bringing down an enemy by commerce-destroying alone."[19] He argued for the allocation of offensive ships rather than defensive forts. He regarded the Monroe Doctrine as virtually sacred and Dewey's victory in Manila Bay 1898 as vindication that the United States had invested in the right force structure. He did not look for a fair fight. He looked for dominance by overwhelming force. In Mahan's strategic script, prewar preparations included building the strongest naval forces and concentrating them, followed by offensive operations in enemy home waters to destroy or blockade the enemy's navy while convoy-protecting one's own merchant shipping. He advocated gaining victory by aggressively attacking and annihilating enemy forces and, where possible, forming coalitions to force the enemy to overextend by imposing a two-front problem on them, then forcing the war's termination by strangling the enemy's economy through blockade.

Mahan found the American Revolution to be the most interesting case regarding the British at sea, since this is the one situation where the British lost during the eighteenth century. He attributed this loss to several advantages held by the colonists. These included the logistical hardships imposed on Britain by the great distance of America from Britain, the colonists' proximity to each other, the character of the colonists, and the probable hostility of France and Spain to Britain when an alliance opportunity arose. Given these problems, Mahan thought that British arrogance led Britain to make a mistake in judgment by provoking war. According to the Barrington Plan, the British intended to blockade the entire American eastern seaboard from Canada to Florida, a particularly massive undertaking given other British commitments in Europe, the Caribbean, the Mediterranean, and the Indian Ocean. Following the American victory at Saratoga in October 1777, the French decided to recognize American independence in February 1778, and in April the French fleet sailed for America. Results at the battle of Newport in August 1778 left the British holding Rhode Island. The war see-sawed back and forth, as Spain declared war on England in June 1779, and Britain declared war on the Dutch in 1780. The naval balance of power in terms of battleships shifted from 52 French versus 66 British ships in 1778, to 138 French, Spanish, and Dutch allied ships to 94 British ships in 1781. Time and the accrual of allies changed American prospects such that the French prevented the British from resupplying Yorktown at the battle of the Chesapeake Capes, leading to Cornwallis' surrender at Yorktown in October 1781. Mahan pointed out that Washington acknowledged sea power as decisive to the American victory. It is worth noting that due to many commitments and inadequate budgeting, the British navy was less fit and maintained in the 1770s and early 1780s than it was when the British defeated the French in 1763, or than it was when the British defeated the French during the Napoleonic wars in the early nineteenth century.

Mahan provided an economic rationale for developing sea power capability for the protection of trade and commerce. Although he wrote during the modern Age of Steam, the examples he used to support his argument were from the Age of Sail, as are all the case studies in this book. The economic impetus toward conflict will be examined in our Eurasian cases. Mahan's case study of the American Revolution provides a model for describing how the greater sea power, Britain in this case, lost a war in a naval battle through a combination of overconfidence, overextension, and allied resistance, themes that occur in the premodern case studies considered in this book.

Norman Angell, like Mahan, wrote that economics was fundamental to international relations interactions. But unlike Mahan, he reached different conclusions about the role of the military regarding international relations. Born in England in 1872, Angell began studying at the

University of Geneva at age seventeen, where he developed the perspective that Europe was fraught with insoluble problems. After migrating to California and working first as a laborer and then as a journalist, he returned to Europe in 1898 and worked as a newspaper correspondent in Paris for more than a decade, writing an extended pamphlet in 1909, *Europe's Optical Illusion.* Angell argued that economic integration among European countries was so intertwined that war would be futile among them. Angell's 1909 pamphlet was issued as a book renamed *The Great Illusion* and was updated and reissued several times with the subtitle *A Study of the Relation of Military Power to National Advantage.*[20] Angell felt that countries would be economically rational and therefore see that building up armaments, including naval armaments, was a "great illusion" in the quest to maintain peace through military advantage. Angell moved back to England in 1914, where he joined the Labour Party and eventually was elected as a member of Parliament in 1929. Despite, or perhaps because of, World War I, Angell was widely read and popular for his ideas regarding maintaining peace through economic interdependency, and he received positive reviews from such figures as Sir John (Jacky) Fisher, the first sea lord of the Royal Navy (1904–1910). For his continued influence after the Great War, Angell was awarded the Nobel Peace Prize in 1933.

After several decades out of the public eye, Angell's argument is being reassessed by international relations practitioners and theorists, because he combined concepts of interdependence with modernity in the context of industrial economies, making an important contribution to theory.[21] Angell was viewed as a philosopher of war's disappointments, noting that war in the modern era seldom seemed to achieve the ends that motivated it. He underestimated the power of nationalism, a force Angell thought was declining but instead is resurgent. After both twentieth-century world wars, the victors had short growth spurts and the defeated had short declines, trends that were evened out within a decade. In 1977, Organski and Kugler called this the "phoenix factor," but it was a pattern Angell identified in his book in 1910.[22]

During the 1890s, the world was a globalized one, with large-scale international trade and investment, and powers engaged in arms races, especially the naval arms race between Britain and Germany. From Angell's point of view, the "great illusion" of military expansion helped lead to the devastation of World War I, followed shortly by World War II. Then, after decades of isolationist tendencies, the world reglobalized again and became more intertwined. Are we caught again in a "great illusion" that military competition will lead to peace? Some critics argue that Angell was right that military victors have more to lose than to gain during war.[23] Angell's interdependence theory seems to have done well in Europe for the most recent seventy years, but currently the ties of economic integration are fraying there, causing concerns about the future. Wars in other regions have kept happening since he wrote about *The Great Illusion* over a century ago. In short, the view that military conquest pays is a great illusion in Angell's reckoning, and he seems mostly correct in this assessment. But to hope that economic rationality will prevent war is also a great illusion, as emotions override rationality in many international relations episodes.

MACKINDER VS. SPYKMAN: EURASIAN HEARTLAND OR EURASIAN RIMLANDS?

Halford Mackinder obtained degrees in both natural science and history and engaged in debate as president of the Oxford Union in the early 1880s. By 1887, he was publishing on geographic subjects and was named reader in geography at the University of Oxford, where, as the pre-eminent geographer in Britain, he lectured twice a week in physical and historical geography. Mackinder's work subsequently influenced many American academics, including Nicholas Spykman, and academic policy practitioners, including Henry Kissinger and Zbigniew Brzezinski. Mackinder, in his 1904 essay "The Geographical Pivot of History," laid out his idea regarding a "pivot area" of Eurasia that today is aligned closely with the borders of Russia and which became better defined in his later work as the "Heartland."

Mackinder responded to Mahan's view of strategy by looking at "the seaman's point of view" in his classic 1919 work on geopolitics, *Democratic Ideals and Reality*.[24] He opened chapter III with an epigraph from Genesis central to Mahan's thinking: "And God said, Let the waters be gathered together in one place." Mackinder considered the world to be a great continuous sea, covering three-quarters of the surface. The Atlantic, Pacific, Indian, and Arctic Oceans surround the World Island of Europe/Asia/Africa, constituting two-twelfths of the earth's surface, and a secondary island including the North and South American peninsulas, constituting one-twelfth of it. Although he acknowledged the vast character of the sea on the globe, Mackinder's writings focused primarily on the two-twelfths coverage of the globe by the World Island. The center of the World Island was the Heartland, consisting of West Asia and East Europe. At the time that he wrote "The Pivot of History" in 1904,[25] Britain's navy was in control of three-quarters of the "margin of the Heartland,"[26] including the coasts of the Eurasian periphery in the Mediterranean Sea, Indian Ocean, and the China Seas/Western Pacific Ocean. He conceived of the Heartland as a potential mighty sea base that could oppose British sea power successfully in the future due to its population and resource base.[27] One of Mackinder's core formulations was tempered by American involvement that could tip the scales of the inevitability implied in Mackinder's memorable formulation:

> Who rules East Europe commands the Heartland;
> Who rules the Heartland commands the World-Island;
> He who rules the World-Island commands the World.[28]

Mackinder's key recommendation for peace during the First World War was the establishment of a series of seven buffer populations between Germany and Russia, with the purpose of preventing a united Heartland. The buffer populations included Poles, Bohemians (Czechs and Slovaks), Hungarians (Magyars), South Slavs (Serbians, Croatians, and Slovenes), Romanians, Bulgarians, and Greeks.[29] Writing in 1919, Mackinder showed great prescience for the future of this key border region between Russia and Germany. Stalin and Churchill acknowledged the importance of these border populations when they negotiated their secret percentages agreement regarding the postwar division of influence, with

Soviet influence to prevail in the north and the Western allies' influence to prevail toward the south of these regions. These populations and the changing states they occupied became the central contested frontier of the Cold War. More recently, since 2012 the same countries have joined China through the 16+1 platform, which comprises sixteen contiguous countries from Estonia in the north to Albania in the south, tied to China through economic, political, and cultural dialogue and agreements. Greece joined the group in 2019, while Lithuania withdrew in 2021. Mackinder certainly had a sharp eye for continental geopolitics, past, present, and future.

Mackinder wrapped up his geostrategic conclusion: "Thus far, we have been thinking of the rivalry of Empires from the point of view of strategical opportunities, and we have come to the conclusion that the World-Island and the Heartland are the final Geographical Realities in regard to sea-power and land-power, and that East Europe is essentially part of the Heartland."[30]

Thus, Mackinder was a continental geopolitical realist at the core. But he concluded his 1919 book with the thought that "you can only guide Humanity by the attraction of ideals," an idea similar to Joseph Nye's concept of soft power one hundred years later. In his final paragraph, Mackinder reminded his readers that neighborliness is the "only sure foundation of a happy citizenship."[31] At the end of World War I, he supported a Jewish national home in Palestine and a strong League of Nations. Thinking of the pre-eminent position of the Heartland, Mackinder asked the question, "Why should we not solve the problem of Constantinople by making that historic city the Washington of the League of Nations?"[32] Mackinder kept his mind open, favoring diplomatic solutions to seemingly intractable geopolitical problems.

Nicholas Spykman, Dutch born, studied in Delft and Cairo before completing his doctorate at Berkeley and teaching at Yale. He wrote during the 1930s and early 1940s, developing geopolitical ideas regarding possibilities for peace following World War II, reminiscent of Halford Mackinder positing concepts relevant to establishing peace following World War I. Spykman relabeled Mackinder's "inner crescent" surrounding the Heartland as the "rimlands," and he advanced the idea that this region was in fact more important to geopolitical stability than was the Heartland. He declared the famous Mackinder dictum regarding the Heartland and the World Island to be false, succinctly proposing a new formula:

> Who controls the rimland, rules Eurasia;
> who rules Eurasia controls the destinies of the world.[33]

In short, Spykman concluded that control of the Eurasian rimlands rather than the Eurasian Heartland was the key to the world's future. Spykman's work was influential. Isaiah Bowman, president of Johns Hopkins University, recommended that *America's Strategy in World Politics* (1942)[34] be read once a year by government officials responsible for policy. After Spykman passed away in 1943, his research assistant Helen Nicholl edited the maps and commentary related to Spykman's *America's Strategy in World Politics* and published the companion volume *The Geography of the Peace* (1944). In this work, Spykman stressed the function and importance of the rimland: "The rimland of the Eurasian landmass must be viewed as an intermediate region, situated as it is between the heartland and the marginal seas. It functions as a vast buffer zone of conflict between sea power and land power. Looking in both directions, it must function amphibiously and defend itself on land and sea. In the past, it has had to fight against the land power of the heartland and against the sea power of the off-shore islands of Great Britain and Japan. Its amphibious nature lies at the basis of its security problems."[35]

Spykman saw World War II as a conflict of the Eurasian rimland littorals, in which the objective was to prevent control of the rimlands by a single dominant power whose principles and ideals were opposed to Western civilization. Spykman's concept was pragmatic. In the first instance, he favored immediate peace following World War II rather than promising lasting peace, wanting to postpone the recurrence of conditions that could result in a Third World War. Although not obvious at the time, Spykman's view of China's power lying primarily in its coastal regions was prescient given China's desire and commitment to be a maritime power today. Spykman advocated leasing island bases in the Pacific to guarantee a balance of power in Eurasia. He recommended supporting both a strong postwar Germany and Japan as counterbalances to the Soviet Union and China. His geopolitical balance-of-power thinking as he looked forward to a new peace after the Second World War saw geographic factors continuing to operate: "Balanced power on the Eurasian Continent is one of the objectives for which we are fighting and the establishment of such an equilibrium and its preservation will be our objective when the fight is won. It will then be to the United States to continue to collaborate with any powers seeking to prevent the consolidation of the rimland regions."[36]

At the time of writing, Spykman felt that Russia and Great Britain were the two countries with which the United States should cooperate most closely in the postwar period. His analysis proposing a balance along the Eurasian rimland is equally penetrating today, even though power relations have changed such that China, India, and others are involved as balancing powers. Spykman's predilection for geographic determinism, as reflected in statements like "The foreign policy of a state must be examined, then, primarily in terms of the location of that state in the world," has been criticized for not including enough other factors, and for falling into "the dangerous trap of accepting geopolitics as the be-all and end-all of international relations."[37] In other words, despite Spykman's having developed a powerful geopolitical explanation for conflict in the Eurasian rimlands, other economic, cultural, and power transition factors must be analyzed in order to more fully understand both ancient and modern foreign policies of national actors involved.

The Pacific War made clear to Spykman that it was possible for war in this region to become large and general and could spread to Southeast Asia, Burma, and India. Events following World War II have proved Spykman to be visionary regarding his Eurasian rimlands theory. The regional wars and points of conflict since the end of the World War II have taken place in Northeast Asia (Korea), Southeast Asia (Vietnam), and in West Asia and the Mediterranean North Africa (Iraq, Syria, Libya). These locations create in an arc around the maritime perimeter of Eurasia from northeast to southeast and from West Asia on the edges of Eastern Europe and North Africa. In recent years, U.S. policymakers increasingly have expanded the conception of maritime geography from Pacific, to Asia-Pacific, to Indo-Pacific. In regions' conflicts, great powers have been involved, but they have not triggered world wars directly between the great powers. Korea and Vietnam were proxy wars of great powers, the United States and the Soviet Union. Afghanistan, Iraq, Libya, and Syria have experienced asymmetrical wars between radicalized Muslim minorities and Western greater powers.

Currently the United States and China are facing off over tensions in the East and South China Seas, although other smaller powers are involved as well. Limited clashes have broken out between China and Vietnam over the Paracels in 1974 and over Johnson and Fiery Cross reefs in 1988, between China and the Philippines over Mischief Reef in 1996 and over Scarborough Shoal in 2012. Larger conflicts have not occurred in these seas yet, but the tensions in these regions are complex and profound along the Eurasian maritime perimeter, the area that Spykman warned us to watch and seek control of tensions.

HUNTINGTON VS. ALLISON: CLASH OF CIVILIZATIONS OR POWER TRANSITION TRAPS?

Historian Samuel Huntington, writing during the 1990s in the aftermath of the Cold War when the threat of nuclear conflict between the United States and the Soviet Union had passed, assessed international politics in an attempt to understand from whence the next existential threat might come in the international system. With his deep historical perspective, he saw the likelihood that the values systems of these ancient civilizations which had been in conflict for centuries but were subdued during the period of Cold War crisis would resurface and become driving factors once again in international politics. His *Foreign Affairs* article "The Clash of Civilizations"[38] and subsequent book[39] are wide-ranging in their analysis of the possibilities for violent culture wars. Huntington presented his thesis in the second paragraph of his 1993 article: "It is my hypothesis that the fundamental source of conflict in this new world will not be primarily ideological or primarily economic. The great divisions of humankind and the dominating source of conflict will be cultural. Nation states will remain the most powerful actors in world affairs, but the principal conflicts of global politics will occur between nations and groups of different civilizations. The clash of civilizations will dominate global politics. The fault lines between civilizations will be the battle lines of the future."[40]

He defined civilizations in terms of the broadest possible cultural entities, encompassing discrete subgroups. They are defined by both common objective elements such as language, history, religion, customs, and institutions, and by subjective self-identification of people. He predicted that desecularization and the revival of religion would accompany the reassertion of civilizational frameworks, as seen in the Islamic world, or the reassertion of the Christian "fault line" originally established around 1500 through eastern Europe and the Balkans. In fact, Huntington saw the religious conflict between Western and Islamic civilizations occurring over the past thirteen hundred years as reappearing dramatically after a hiatus during the aftermath of the fall of the Ottomans in World War I and the conclusion of the Cold War in the 1990s. Additionally, he predicted that economic regionalism would reinforce civilizational consciousness, as seen in strengthening economic ties between China and Hong Kong, Taiwan, Singapore, and other overseas Chinese communities. The civilizations he included for analysis in his book were Western, Latin American, African, Islamic, Sinic, Hindu, Orthodox, Buddhist, and Japanese.[41] Of these, he saw two of them as the most likely to result in clashes with Western civilization, Islamic civilization and Sinic civilization, which he sometimes referred to as Confucian civilization.

During wars, Huntington suggested that states will tend to ally with their civilizational kin-countries. As an example, he pointed to the sympathy that Islamic countries tended to have for Iraq's Saddam Hussein as an Islamic strongman, even though they may not have agreed with his invasion of Kuwait. He suggested that the phrase "world community" is a euphemism to give legitimacy to actions of the West, and that an aspect of civilizational opposition is the development of "the West against the rest."[42] Huntington parsed the divisions in a much more complex fashion than this simple aphorism suggests, outlining cases not only where states with similar civilizations might ally, but also where states might be torn within by conflicting civilizational elements, Turkey being a classic case, where Western elements of secularization conflict with competing elements of traditional Islam. He suggested that Mexico might also be regarded as a torn state, as it has traditionally seen itself in opposition to the United States but recently has participated in the more Westernized concept of the North American Free Trade Area. A third significant torn country is Russia, conflicted between whether it is part of the West or part of a distinct Slavic-Orthodox civilization, a tension that has been operative in the past and continues to be.

Aside from the possibility that states with similar civilizational values could become allies, Huntington also looked at the possibility of civilizations becoming allies. He specifically considered the possibility of a Confucian-Islamic connection. The core of this arrangement would be military agreements and support between China and Iran and Pakistan, a civilizational bonding that now might become more profound with the development of China's Belt and Road Initiative, in spite of China's own internal preoccupations with limiting Islamic influence in its western provinces.

After reviewing the various permutations of civilizational alliances, Huntington concluded that the paramount axis of world politics would be the relations between "The West and the Rest" and that

> [i]n the short term it is clearly in the interest of the West to promote greater cooperation and unity within its own civilization, particularly between its European and North American components; to incorporate into the West societies in Eastern Europe and Latin America whose cultures are close to those of the West; to promote and maintain cooperative relations with Russia and Japan; to prevent escalation of local inter-civilization conflicts into major inter-civilization wars; to limit the expansion of the military strength of

> Confucian and Islamic states; to moderate the reduction of Western military capabilities and maintain military superiority in East and Southwest Asia; to exploit differences and conflicts among Confucian and Islamic states; to support in other civilizations groups sympathetic to Western values and interests; to strengthen international institutions that reflect and legitimate Western interests and values and to promote the involvement of non-Western states in those institutions.[43]

Huntington concludes his 1993 article with this thought:

> Hence the West will increasingly have to accommodate these non-Western modern civilizations whose power approaches that of the West but whose values and interests are significantly different from those of the West. This will require the West to maintain the economic and military power necessary to protect its interests in relation to these civilizations. It will also, however, require the West to develop a more profound understanding of the basic religious and philosophical assumptions underlying other civilizations and the ways in which people in those civilizations see their interests. It will require an effort to identify elements of commonality between Western and other civilizations. For the relevant future, there will be no universal civilization but instead a world of different civilizations, each of which will have to learn to coexist with the others.[44]

The final line of his 1996 book further developed the concept from his 1993 article and prescribed his thinking about international order based on civilizations by noting, "In the emerging era, clashes of civilization are the greatest threat to world peace, and an international order based on civilizations is the surest way to safeguard against war."[45]

In Huntington's map of world civilizations post-1990, it is graphically evident that the Islamic populations dominate the belt of the Eurasian rimlands in the current era. He began his section on Islam and the West[46] by arguing that fourteen hundred years of history illustrates that the West has struggled with Islam, not only with violent Islamic extremists. He then briefly reviews the key points of that history, including the period of Ottoman conflict with Christianity in the Mediterranean, one of the case studies included in this book. The cultural character of Huntington's argument diverges fundamentally from the geoeconomic and geopolitical explanations of Mahan, Angell, Mackinder, and Spykman.

Graham Allison emphasized power transition from one great power to another as an explanation for the source of conflict,[47] as opposed to geoeconomic or geopolitical explanations for conflict, or emphasis on differing civilizational values as a basis for conflict. In situations where a rising power confronts an established power, the seeds of conflict are planted and are likely to sprout. In fact, in his study of sixteen cases where a rising power confronted an established or status quo power between 1500 CE and the present, Allison found that twelve cases resulted in war. He called this high likelihood of war during power transition periods the Thucydides trap, based on the example of a rising Athens confronting an established Sparta during the Peloponnesian Wars in the fifth century BCE. He quoted Thucydides in translation, "It was the rise of Athens, and the fear that this instilled in Sparta, that made war inevitable." Allison took exception to the "inevitability" aspect of Thucydides' formulation, indicating that outcomes may not necessarily result in war, but they have done so in 75 percent of relevant cases over the past five hundred years, indicating that during power transition periods, the possibility of war is high, though it is not inevitable.

Through study of the 25 percent of cases that avoided war, the book provides cautionary information about how war might be avoided between the rising economic and military power of China and the established power of the United States during the twenty-first century. Two cases appear to be especially relevant for this analysis. The first case was the Anglo-American rivalry in the early twentieth century, in which Britain accommodated the United States by not directly challenging America in the Caribbean, and it was resolved eventually by Britain's accepting a role as a secondary great power. The second case is the U.S.-Soviet rivalry during the Cold War, which resulted in hot proxy wars in Korea and Vietnam but did not lead to a world war. The power transition rivalry was finally resolved by the economic collapse of the Soviet Union. Power-transition theory[48] suggests that matters become dangerous when the rising great power achieves 80 percent of the power of the established hegemonic power and does not resolve until it achieves 20 percent more power than the established power, as the United States did in relation to Britain, or fails in the attempt, as happened with the Soviet Union. The first case is one of accommodation, the second is one of confrontation. Policymakers face the dilemma of which model to follow. Allison hoped that his book would provoke something like "the four-year debate that ran from Kennan's long Telegram to Nitze's NSC-68 to shape what ultimately became America's Cold War strategy."[49]

Of the eight case studies in this book, one is included that Allison considers in his sixteen case studies: that of the rising power of the Ottoman Empire in relation to the ruling power of the Hapsburgs in the Mediterranean during the sixteenth century. Allison's power-transition explanation has relevance, but so do geostrategic, civilizational, and military leadership explanations, making the Ottoman case a valuable one for understanding the complexities of conflict along the Eurasian rimland, with some possible lessons for the twenty-first century.

Allison was clear that he attempted to make his study comprehensive regarding important power transitions between 1500 CE and the present.[50] But he invited suggestions of other possible case studies to supplement the sixteen cases considered in *Destined for War*.[51] Of the eight cases discussed in this book, the one that might be appropriate to include as a major post-1500 power transition clash in addition to the Ottoman case is the Imjin War of 1592–1598. During this conflict, a rising Japan, having militarily consolidated power at home under Hideyoshi, decided to attack a relatively declining Ming China via the Korean peninsula. Japan had greater success invading China during the 1930s, but, as Allison notes, became the loser in a power-transition war with the United States during the 1940s.

In a review article of Allison's book, John Maurer considered the Japan case in the 1930s compared to the China case eighty years later.[52] Maurer refers to a "Japanese Monroe Doctrine" leading up to the second Sino-Japanese War and the Pacific War during the 1930s, a point that Allison did not discuss. Whereas the American Monroe Doctrine succeeded in the Caribbean, the Japanese Monroe Doctrine failed in the Pacific. In relation to China treating the South China Sea as its own Caribbean, what are the lessons that both China and America should draw from these two earlier cases? China expert Ian Buruma feels that Allison, not a China expert, missed the mark on some details, but basically agrees that U.S. cultivation of an alliance strategy that contains China, reminiscent of the Cold War strategy of Kennan and Nitze, is the correct policy to pursue.[53] Allison's Thucydides trap thesis certainly points to the policy dilemmas faced by Japanese unifier Hideyoshi and by his opponent, Ming Dynasty emperor Wanli, who clashed in the Imjin War on the Korean Peninsula between 1592 and 1598.

BLACK: HUMAN AGENCY, THE IMPACT OF MILITARY LEADERSHIP

Historian Jeremy Black analyzed military leadership, positing that human agency in war matters at three levels: tactical, operational, and strategic.[54] He organized a group of scholars to assess military leaders from 600 BCE through 1950 CE in a long historical sweep, applying these three frameworks to consider dozens of key military leaders and their campaigns from all parts of the world.

At the tactical level, competent military leaders must demonstrate the ability to lead small groups with limited resources to accomplish discrete goals, such as capturing a hill, crossing a river, or securing a flank. They must inspire their troops, sustain morale, and promote unit cohesion through personal example and bravery. Many leaders of this type are needed in war. At the operational level, competent military leaders must successfully execute larger campaigns, requiring the movements of brigades and divisions. For operational leaders, tactical command abilities are essential experience, but the operational commander will likely be a step removed from personal interaction in the battle. In addition to experience in tactical command, operational commanders require skills of coordinating multiple forces, interpreting and reconciling conflicting information sources, providing clear communications to lower-level officers, and executing plans formulated at a higher level. At the strategic level, the interests of the state as defined by political aims are involved. Leadership often involves political perceptivity, whether leaders are of civilian or military background. In earlier times, political and military leadership was sometimes fused at the strategic level, as with Roman emperors, Turkish sultans, or European monarchs. Recent examples show more interaction of civilian and military leadership at the strategic level, such as the profiles of Churchill, Roosevelt, Stalin, and Hitler during World War II. Strategic leadership requires the broadest set of skills, including defining realizable goals, distributing resources between different campaign fronts, and ensuring support both domestically and with allies. These are the most complex and difficult leadership tasks. Civilian leaders may not understand military risk completely, and military leaders may struggle with realizable goals that require maintenance of domestic support or alliance coalitions.

In earlier times, what has been defined above as operational leadership may have been called strategic leadership, whereas what has been called strategic leadership above might be termed grand strategic leadership. Brief sketches of critical leaders are introduced in each of the case studies discussed in this book. The sketches are of operational naval leaders having varying degrees of influence in formulating aims for the wars in which they were involved. Black's historical examples included mostly army leaders, but he also included three major naval leaders: British admiral Nelson, Japanese admiral Togo, and American admiral Nimitz.[55] Since this work is about maritime conflicts, consideration of naval leadership is critical to analyzing the cases. Rajendra Chola of India, Tran Hung Dao of Vietnam, Zheng He of China, Kunjali Marakkar of India, Hayreddin Barbarossa of the Ottoman Empire, Yi Sun-sin of Korea, Koxinga of China, and Kanhoji Angre of India are the naval leaders discussed in this work. These names are not well known in the

West, but they are lionized in many parts of Asia, even as Horatio Nelson and Chester Nimitz are revered in the West and Togo Heihachiro is respected for leading Japan to victory against Russia in 1905.

Nelson, Togo, and Nimitz all achieved the ultimate in naval victories during their respective campaigns, although the outcomes of each of the wars in which they were involved relied on land operations that were tied significantly to war termination in each of their cases. Nevertheless, they each set extraordinarily high levels of naval achievement to which other naval leaders may be compared. Although this work does not attribute the flow of history primarily to the "Great Men in History" idea, it recognizes the role of human agency and the ability of military leaders to affect the outcome of battles and wars that have shaped the course of human events. Looking at specific powerful, effective, and colorful naval leaders across the range of these case studies allows better understanding of human agency in history.[56] Thus the role of leadership in Eurasian maritime conflicts, as well as the roles of geopolitics, civilizational values, and changing power relations, are included in this analysis.

While the role of naval leadership will be examined in each of the subsequent eight case studies, theories presented in this introduction will be discussed more systematically in relation to the case studies in the concluding chapter. An assessment of the relevance and relative importance of the various theories will be undertaken once the case study material has been presented.

ONE

Chola Maritime Expansion to the Ganges, Sri Lanka, and Srivijaya

Rajendra Chola, Eleventh Century

Early Indian Ocean Seafaring

The Indian subcontinent and Southeast Asia have been connected by maritime trade routes for two millennia. Testaments to the resulting relationships emerge from the archeological evidence and ancient structures found throughout this region. Carvings in stone of wooden trading ships that plied the "cinnamon route" across the Indian Ocean appear on the walls of Borobudur, the great Buddhist monument in central Java built during the early eighth century.[1] A replica of this ship that had been carved in stone was constructed and sailed in 2003–2004 from Indonesia to Madagascar and East Africa, reinforcing the understanding that these voyages were possible more than thirteen hundred years ago. Monuments influenced by Indian culture are widespread throughout Southeast Asia, indicating the extent of early Indian maritime contact and its impact on culture, religion, and economy in the region. Notable examples include the Cham monuments at My Son in Vietnam, the Khmer monuments at Angkor Wat and Angkor Thom in Cambodia, and the Buddhist and Hindu monuments at Borobudur and Prambanan in central Java. All these architectural wonders contain elaborately carved religious figures in stone, spectacular reminders of Indic influence in Southeast Asia over both an expansive geography and an extensive period of time. They also all include stone carvings of ships, documenting maritime sources of Indic inspiration.

India's Early Influence in the Indian Ocean

Indian historian and diplomat K. M. Panikkar provides a vivid word portrait of Indian Ocean geography that describes the ocean's distinctive character on the globe:

> For the most part its area is walled off on three sides by land, with the southern side of Asia forming a roof over it. The continent of Africa constitutes the western wall, while Burma, Malaya and the insular continuations protect the eastern side. The essential feature which differentiates the Indian Ocean from the Pacific and the Atlantic is not just the two sides, but the sub-continent of India which juts out far into the sea for a thousand miles to its tapering end at Cape Comorin. It is this geographical position of India that changes the character of the Indian Ocean.[2]

In the Indian Ocean, trade routes by sea were well-established during the millennium before the eleventh-century maritime expeditions of the Chola kingdom.[3] The Indian Ocean is bifurcated by Panikkar's "roof" into the western and eastern regions, each having its own complex trade routes and history. To the west, the Arabian Sea is at the southern foot of the Arabian Peninsula and east coast of Africa, while the Persian Gulf and Red Sea, the routes to the Mediterranean, funnel into it. To the east, the Bay of Bengal offers passage to continental Southeast Asia as it breaks up into the great 17,000-island archipelago of the East Indies, with outlet passages into the China Seas. After 1500, when Europeans arrived by sea into the Indian Ocean, the Portuguese and British ultimately controlled much of the west, north, and east of the Indian Ocean perimeter.

The winds across the Indian Ocean follow an annual pattern that made trade by sailing ship possible across the region. Every year prevailing winds blow from the southwest between May and October, bringing heavy rains to India and Southeast Asia. This is the wet season in Asia, and the term monsoon sometimes refers simply to the rainy season that accompanies the summer wet monsoon. The direction of the

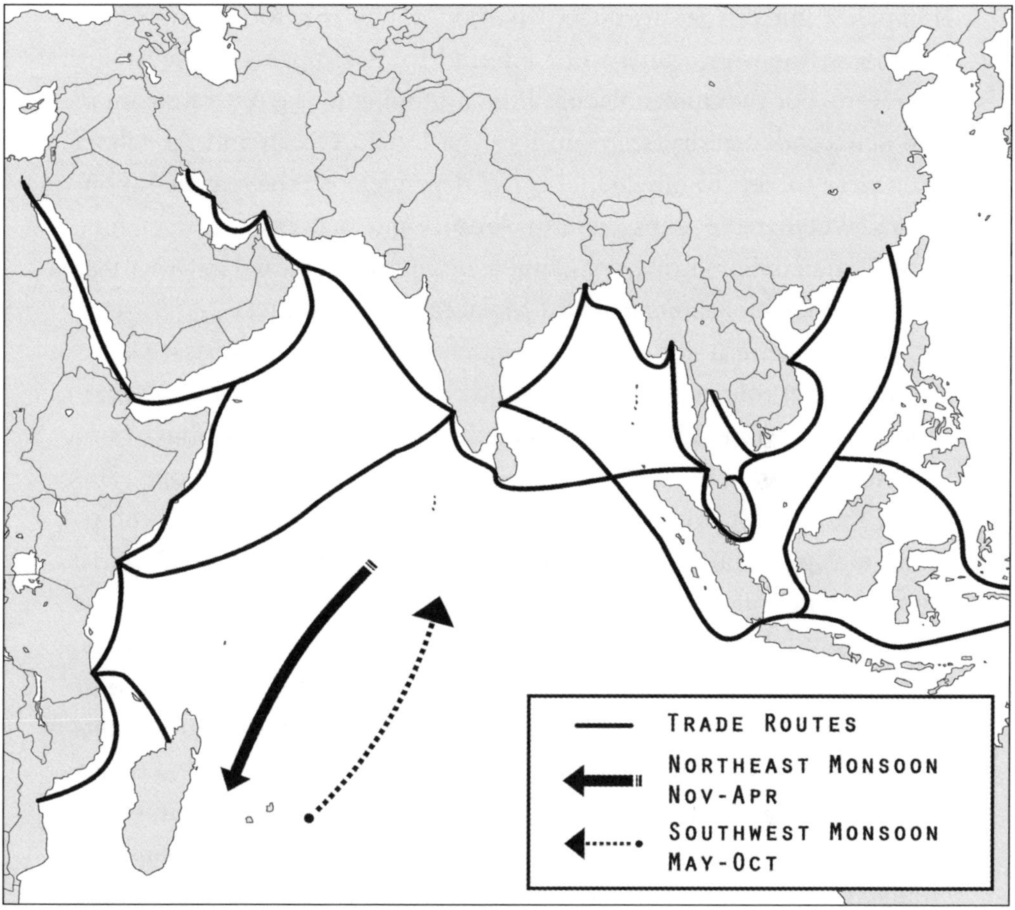

MAP 1.1 Indian Ocean trade routes, 500–1500 CE
Created by Jamie Rhode, adapted from Mountain High base map

prevailing winds switches reliably every year by 180 degrees, blowing from the northeast from November through April, which is sometimes called the dry monsoon. A first-century CE Greek sailing log, *The Periplus of the Erythraean Sea*,[4] describes the monsoons and attributes their discovery and importance to the Greek navigator Hippalus about a century earlier. Prior to Hippalus, Greek geography assumed that the coast of India stretched from east to west. Hippalus sailed east from the Red Sea using the southwest monsoon wind and discovered the north-south coast of western India, changing the parameters of geographical knowledge. Recognizing the monsoon wind pattern no doubt preceded

Hippalus, but due to his documentation of the monsoon pattern, the southwest monsoon came to be referred to as Hippalus in the sailing literature. For two millennia, until the beginning of the Age of Steam in the nineteenth century, ships in both the Indian Ocean and the China Seas were subject to directional travel dependent on the seasonal monsoons, whether the ships were of Arab origin that embarked in June from Oman to Sumatra, or of Chinese origin that departed in December from East China heading toward Malacca and on to India.

On the western side of the subcontinent, traders from Gujarat played an important role in the seafaring trade as long ago as the ancient Harappan civilization (2500–1700 BCE). The remains of docks have been found at Lothal in the modern state of Gujarat, dating from about 3700 BCE, the earliest archeological record of docks in the world.[5] Ships from that port connected the Harappan cities along the Indus River to coastal centers along what became known as the Arabian Sea, due to its proximity to the Arabian Peninsula and the sea trade pursued by Arabs. Alexander and his Greek cohorts returned by sea along this same coast in the fourth century BCE. The Greeks, Romans, Persians, and Omanis all traded with India through the Gulf of Oman, while Egypt and Africa traded through the Red Sea and from ports on the East African coast, including Mombasa and Malindi in Kenya. Following the beginning of Islam in the seventh century, Arab traders used their dhows to trade not only with India, but also to pursue trade through the Bay of Bengal and beyond the Indian Ocean all the way through the China Seas to Quanzhou on the Fujian coast of China. Indian Ocean spices were exchanged for Chinese silk and porcelain for many centuries on this early maritime silk road. The Chinese introduced the use of the compass, floating magnetic needles, to navigational practice by the eleventh century during the Song Dynasty, and possibly earlier.[6]

On the eastern side of the subcontinent, Indian influence spread through the Bay of Bengal in a wide-ranging arc from Burma through peninsular Southeast Asia and into the great island archipelago that became known as the Indies in recognition of Indian influence. Panikkar noted,

> The evidence of deep sea navigation of the Bay of Bengal long before the Christian era is even more convincing. The undoubted existence of prosperous Hindu colonies in Malaya, Sumatra, Java and even Annam in the first century A.D. and the continuous communication with Indonesia which the mother country maintained clearly show that the Bay of Bengal had also been mastered long before that time. This was entirely an Indian achievement. . . .
>
> These were not new, but established routes. Apart from coastal navigation it is now established that Kataha (Kedah) in Malaya was by this time a flourishing port of call for Indian sailors and the seat of a trading community, proving thereby that the crossing of the Bay between its widest points had been achieved long before that time.[7]

Indian movement into the region of the eastern Indian Ocean may have been motivated by trade and economic opportunities, but it was bolstered by sustained Indian influence in cultural and religious spheres. For example, the legacy of early Indian architecture is dispersed widely in both continental and insular Southeast Asia, often related to the ongoing practice of Hinduism and Buddhism. The first Indic-influenced kingdom of Southeast Asia, called Funan by the Chinese, was founded upon the marriage of an Indian Brahmin merchant prince, Kaundinya, and Soma, the daughter of a local Naga chieftain. The union took place when Soma led a band of pirates to attack Kaundinya's Indian merchant vessel in the Mekong delta.[8] Apparently impressed by each other during the incident, they married, and their descendants ruled Funan for many generations, establishing a bond with Indian culture and influence in that region that held for centuries. The royal families of the subsequent Cham and Khmer kingdoms in Vietnam and Cambodia, respectively, claimed descent from the Funan royal couple. Both cultures record different versions of the story in their inscriptions of their descent from the marriage of Kaundinya and Soma.

On Java, the Buddhist Sailendra Dynasty established an empire of the sea, and on Sumatra, a thalassocratic empire was founded by Srivijayan Buddhists.[9] By the tenth century CE, Sailendra and Srivijayan royalty intermarried, presenting a united and formidable challenge to any who wished to travel between the Indian Ocean and the China Seas.

Other Indic-influenced kingdoms[10] lay farther to the northwest, notably the Mon kingdom in what is now western Thailand and the Pagan kingdom in Burma. Dai Viet (northern Vietnam today) was north of Champa and south of China. These Indianized entities were referred to as kingdoms because they had royal leaders, usually with hereditary succession, creating a dynastic structure. These were not nation-states with clearly defined borders; they were what scholars have referred to as mandalas,[11] that is, regions of influence by kings at the center with decreasing influence at the soft borders where the mandala influence bled into adjacent kingdoms. Sometimes these entities are referred to as empires, since they included a group of smaller political entities under a supreme single authority. Thalassocracies will predominate in this analysis, particularly the relationship of Indianized Srivijaya to the Indianized states of the Sailendra, Cham, and Khmer, and finally Srivijaya's relationship with the Indian Chola state on the southeast of the Indian subcontinent.

Srivijaya developed hegemonic power in Southeast Asia, dominating the maritime realm in its region between the late seventh and early eleventh centuries. Its regional supremacy set the stage for subsequent conflict and defeat by the Chola Empire, which led to Srivijaya's decline in power by the mid-eleventh century. During its ascendency, Srivajaya became involved in close interactions and rivalries with the neighboring Sailendra on Java and with Champa and the Khmer on the Southeast Asian mainland. The predominant center of Srivijaya was in Palembang in southeast Sumatra, with a secondary power center in Kedah, located on the Malay Peninsula in what is now Malaysia near the Thai border. Srivijayan architecture was primarily of wood, so no architectural monuments survive from the great period of Srivijayan regional dominance, though text inscriptions in stone still exist. After Srivijaya's power diminished following defeat by the Chola and finally collapsed under the expanding power of Java's Majapahit Dynasty in the thirteenth and fourteenth centuries, the once regionally dominant kingdom was largely forgotten. In 1918, French historian George Coedes

TABLE 1.1
Chronology of Srivijaya and neighboring Southeast Asian Indianized states

Indianized Thalassocracies (sea powers)	Begin (CE)	End (CE)
Srivijaya	650	1377
Sailendra	850	1025
Indianized Tellurocracies (land powers)		
Champa	200	1832
Khmer	850	1436

pieced together enough information from local stone inscriptions and written records of Chinese travelers and Chola conquerors to postulate formally the existence of Srivijaya. Twentieth-century scholarship on the subject proliferated as further research expanded understanding of Srivajaya's significance.[12]

As an example of the importance of durable records in stone, thirty stone inscriptions from the seventh- to thirteenth-century Srivijayan period are now housed in Jakarta's National Museum of Indonesia, providing evidence in the Late Pallava Script (Old Malay) of the founding of the kingdom of Srivijaya, the victory of Srivijaya over all lands within its realm, and concomitant Buddhist religious ideas.[13] Chinese records are also important, beginning with those of the late seventh-century Chinese traveler Yijing (I-Tsing), who spent time studying Buddhism in Srivijaya both at the outset of a journey to India to attend the great Indian Buddhist center of learning at Nalanda, and at the culmination of his second journey to India as well. In his first visit, Yijing spent six months studying Sanskrit in Srivijaya in preparation for India, and on his second visit returning from India, he spent four years in Palembang translating Buddhist Sanskrit texts into Chinese, evidence of the importance of Srivijaya as a center of the expansion of Buddhism.[14] Yijing wrote two books about his observations, one on Buddhist doctrine and the other including biographies of fifty-six Chinese monks who traveled to India in the seventh century CE.[15] In the second book, he observed that Srivijaya was an important center of Buddhist learning and also that Srivijaya was expanding to become the hegemon of the region, having recently absorbed the competing kingdom of Jambi in southeastern Sumatra.

The Srivijayan story has been pieced together for posterity by archeologists and researchers, who note the empire's contribution to the expansion of Buddhism during this period. Patterns of trade, conflict, and conquest in this maritime region became well established, indicating that Srivijaya sustained lucrative trade agreements with China from the Tang through the Song dynasties. It also maintained religious, cultural, and trade links with the Buddhists of Bengal, as well as the Islamic Caliphate in Baghdad. Even though the Srivijayan core was centered around the Straits of Malacca and Sunda, Srivijayan navigators traveled widely and traded with Borneo, the Philippines, and Madagascar, as well as with what is now Eastern Indonesia, Indochina, China, and Bengal.

Eventually, by the thirteenth century, Srivijayan power was replaced by the Majapahit Empire on Java. Within Indonesia, current scholarship on Srivijaya has been well-received because it promotes national pride for Indonesian identity and a governing entity that existed prior to the colonial state of the Dutch East Indies. An example of contemporary Indonesian national pride in its ancient legacy is the establishment of a Srivijaya Archaeological Park southwest of Palembang city center.

Srivijaya successfully engaged in power rivalries with its Sailendra, Cham, and Khmer neighbors in insular and continental Southeast Asia. Meanwhile, the Sailendra clan became a Buddhist dynasty that established control over the central plain of Java and was notable for its great architectural achievement in building Borobudur, the world's largest Buddhist monument, on the Kedu Plain. With an enormous stone terrace reaching 150 feet tall and with 256 bell-shaped stupas and 400 statues of the Buddha, this imposing monument attracts hundreds of visitors every day. At dawn each morning, visitors and pilgrims gather to climb the monument and watch the sun rise between distant mountain peaks in this place of peace and reflection. On a lower terrace, a carved stone frieze portrays the life of the Buddha in great detail. In addition, there are ancient carved stone panels of ships that commemorate the Sailendra as a thalassocracy, ruling the region surrounding Java by sea. On the grounds near the monument, the Borobudur Ship Museum Samudra Raksa exhibits in numerous displays the ships that connected the Sailendra kingdom to the sea.

The mix of Hindu and Buddhist influence is prominent in central Java. Not far from Borobudur is the great Hindu monument Prambanan, which was founded after Borobudur in the ninth century, with its primary temple to Shiva and secondary temples to Brahma and Vishnu. The Sailendras were active promoters of Mahayana Buddhism with some interwoven Hindu elements, a common combination in the Indianized states of Southeast Asia. In addition to their sea trade, the Sailendra grew rice on the Kedu Plain. Initially competing with the Srivijayan kingdom, the Sailendra Buddhist royal family eventually intermarried with the Buddhist Srivijayans and came to dominate Srivijaya by the time the Chola raided the area in the eleventh century. Surprisingly, given the durable construction of Borobudur in Java, the Sailendra left no monuments for posterity in Sumatra.[16]

Aside from dominating Sumatra and Java, the Srivijayan culture extended its influence over the Malay Peninsula, most notably in Kedah, an area near the border of modern-day Malaysia and Thailand and beyond that to the east coast of contemporary Vietnam, making vassals of the Cham. Champa was a collection of smaller Cham polities that included what is now central and southern Vietnam from the second century until it was annexed by the Nguyen Dynasty emperor Minh Mang in 1832. The Indianization of the Cham is evident in the ruins of the former Cham capital at My Son near Danang. The buildings are mostly terra-cotta brick, but the elaborate Hindu figure carvings adorning the building are stone. Some Cham in the Mekong delta now wear white caps indicating Muslim identity, a pattern of changing religious affiliation that also developed among Malays along the Malacca Strait. To maintain their territory, the Cham fought against the Dai Viet to their north, against the powerful Khmer to their west, and against Srivijayan seafarers to their south.

The Rise and Expansion of the Chola Dynasty in India

An edict from the third century BCE during the Maurya Dynasty, the period of Ashoka, is the first datable reference to the Chola in South India. They were a people located in the Kaveri River Valley, with the river flowing east into the Bay of Bengal. Following this early evidence, however, a millennium of relative obscurity passed with occasional mentions in literature, including in the Greek *Periplus of the Erythaean Sea*, the source of information on the monsoon winds, which also contains notes on Chola ports and commerce in India in the first century CE. The Chola were successful in their battles with their Pallava neighbors to the north and their Pandya neighbors to the south, and they overpowered both in the mid-ninth century, though royal marriages still continued between the rival states. The Chola king Vijayalaya captured Thanjavur (Tanjore) in 850 CE, beginning the establishment of a Chola Empire with subservient states that lasted for more than four centuries until its final demise in 1279 CE. The Chola Empire lasted slightly longer that the Han Dynasty, the longest of the Chinese dynasties. Chola local rule before the establishment of the empire extended more than one thousand years.

Although smaller in geographic scope than India's Maurya Dynasty (322–180 BCE) or Mughal Dynasty (1526–1857), the Chola Dynasty created one of India's most splendid empires. It produced great achievements in architecture, literature, and sculpture, including many fine examples of graceful bronzes using the lost wax process. This productivity in many arenas provides evidence of and resulted from the Chola Dynasty's great success in political, commercial, military, and cultural domains. The Chola Dynasty was also a thalassocracy, an empire of the sea, whose core geographic location was in southeastern India immediately northwest of Sri Lanka. It became India's greatest overseas seafaring and naval power in the premodern period and generated widespread stimulus for India's commercial guilds. These guilds functioned not only in the subcontinent on the east and west coasts of India, but also in the

Maldive Islands, in Sri Lanka, and in the ports of Southeast Asia, including Sumatra and the Malay Peninsula, as well as in what is now Thailand and Vietnam, according to Tamil stone inscriptions found in these locations. On India's southwest coast, the Chola used the ports of Kerala and traded in the Maldives, but their primary overseas ventures were to the east in the Bay of Bengal and south to Southeast Asia. Regarding religion, the Chola were Hindus, as opposed to the Buddhist predilections of their Pandya and Pallava neighbors. Temples became centers of commercial activity as well as places of worship. Chola aesthetics also had an impact on art and architecture throughout Southeast Asia. For example, Chola temple design is thought to have influenced the great Prambanan temple complex near Borobudur in central Java. Overall, the dynasty successfully maintained peace, order, and prosperity at home, and extended its influence significantly abroad in an early Indian "look East" policy.

THE CHOLA NAVY

There were several important ports along the Coromandel eastern coast of India. The most significant of these was Nagapattinam, which became the home port for Chola expeditions to Sri Lanka and Southeast Asia. The Chola navy may have begun as a riverine force, as evidenced by dry docks that have been discovered in the Kaveri River basin near the river delta port of Nagapattinam. Eventually the Chola navy developed blue-water capability, in parallel with its commercial maritime growth toward the end of the ninth century. Consequently, important trade developed with the Tang Dynasty and even more so with the subsequent Song Dynasty in China, which also became a significant sea power.[17] The Chola sent at least four diplomatic missions to the Song Dynasty in China in 1014, 1020, 1033, and 1077, as recorded in both Chola inscriptions and Chinese annals.[18] Close diplomatic ties between the Chola and China facilitated the diffusion of technological innovations in both directions. These innovations included ships with watertight compartments in the hulls, the mariner's compass, and flamethrowers in naval combat. Scholars believe, however, that with the expansion of maritime trade activity in the region, up to one-third of the trade goods to China might have been lost to piracy. The Chola navy engaged heavily in anti-piracy operations.

Chola seafaring capabilities relied upon the quality of their ships and navigation skills. Well-built Chola ships manned with crews capable of ship handling and navigation provided the basis for the Chola navy, which was considered by some to have been the mightiest naval achievement of precolonial India. Indian scholars have determined that the Chola used ships with planking drilled and sewn together with vegetable fiber, similar to the construction techniques used in earlier boats, such as the Beliting wreck.[19] Chola vessels had square or rectangular sails and thus moved slower and less close to the wind than did later ships that used triangular lateen sails. For steerage, the Chola used dagger boards rather than rudders. Their navigational skills included acute observations of wind and wave circulation, currents, and drifts. They noted seasonal weather patterns that varied throughout the year. They used elements of celestial navigation, understood the rising time of the stars, and measured the height of stars above the horizon by using their hands. They developed efficient rhumb line sailing, the ability to sail a path with constant bearing as measured relative to true north, crossing all longitude meridians at the same angle.[20] In later centuries, capable Arab and Omani sailors studied Chola methods. The Chola also built lighthouses to notify sailors of hazards along the coast.[21] Although Indian sources mention that there were no European navies in the eleventh century that were capable of expeditions such as those that Rajendra undertook from India to Srivijaya, or the longer diplomatic missions to China by sea,[22] it is worth noting that Norse seafarers arrived at L'Anse aux Meadows in Newfoundland in the 1020s, the same decade that Rajendra Chola displaced the Srivijayans in Sumatra.

THE APEX OF CHOLA POWER: RAJARAJA CHOLA I AND RAJENDRA CHOLA I

The pinnacle of Chola power and influence occurred in the late tenth and early eleventh centuries CE during the reigns of Rajaraja Chola I (ruled 985–1014) and his son Rajendra Chola I (ruled 1014–1044).

Although Rajaraja[23] usually is considered to be the greatest of the Chola rulers, Rajendra is remembered as the greatest naval leader in early Indian history. Among Rajaraja's chief accomplishments were consolidating Chola power in south India, including Kerala, northern Sri Lanka, and part of the Maldives islands; establishing a competent navy; implementing a land survey in 1000 that reorganized the country; and building the great temple of Brihadisvara at the Chola capital in Thanjavur in 1010. After he died in 1014, Rajendra consolidated his father's legacy by extending Chola influence northeast to the Ganges River by defeating the Pala king in Bengal and assuming the title Gangaikondachola, "the Chola who conquered the Ganges." Rajendra also succeeded in conquering more of Sri Lanka and the Maldives; invading and subjugating the Srivijayan territories of Sumatra, Java, and the Malay Peninsula; exacting tribute from Thailand and the Khmer Kingdom; and building a new temple forty-five miles northeast of the Brihadisvara temple, which he named Gangaikonda Cholapurum in 1030. The Chola Dynasty continued as a powerful state for more than one hundred years after Rajendra's death in 1044. By the twelfth and thirteenth centuries, however, the Chola faced domestic resistance in the southern Indian subcontinent from the Western Chalukya Empire and the Pandyan Dynasty, which eventually replaced the Chola as the most powerful rulers in south India.

EARLY CHOLA CAMPAIGNS: SRI LANKA AND THE GANGES EXPEDITION

Although Rajaraja put his military effort primarily into consolidating control over the southern part of the Indian subcontinent, he also built a strong navy and used it in selective expansion operations. In 993, Rajaraja invaded Sri Lanka, sacking the capital at Anuradhapura and capturing the northern half of Sri Lanka. He established his capital at Polonnaruwa, where ruins of Chola architecture and extensive evidence of Chola occupation are found today. Inscriptions reflect a record of Rajaraja's powerful military that crossed the ocean in ships and destroyed the king of Lanka. Rajaraja also occupied much of the Maldives Islands through naval conquest and controlled the Bay of Bengal operating from the port of Nagapattinam.

Rajendra completed Rajaraja's conquest of northern Sri Lanka through a second invasion in 1017, in which he annexed the entire island after capturing the Sinhala king and taking him back to the Chola homeland. In 1019, Rajendra marched his forces northeast on the subcontinent beyond the borders of Rajaraja's territorial consolidations to the south. He reached the Bengali Pala kingdom at the delta of the Ganges River and defeated the Pala king. Subsequently, these northeastern territories gave tribute as subordinates to the Chola kingdom.

THE CHOLA EXPEDITIONS TO SRIVIJAYA

Under Rajaraja, relations with the Srivijayan kingdom in Sumatra had positive dimensions. Rajaraja granted land for the Srivijayans to build a Buddhist temple in 1005 at the Chola port in Nagapattinam, where Srivijayan ships traded goods from China. The Chola were Hindu, so this could have been perceived as an act of tolerance toward the Srivijayan Buddhists. There is evidence that the Srivijayans were paying tribute to the Chola rather than receiving tribute from them.[24] In 1016, the Srivijayans took control of the Sunda Strait between Sumatra and Java by defeating the Mataram kingdom in Java. Interpreting this as a Srivijayan-Song alliance, the Khmer king of Angkor gave gifts to the Chola around 1017 in an attempt to build a counterbalancing alliance between the Chola and the Khmer. There is evidence that in 1017, Rajendra sent a sent a brief expedition to Srivajaya, possibly for scouting reasons rather than for military purposes, and also potentially to warn Srivijaya to back away from attempting to exert regional control of trade and power relations. The warning appears to have gone unheeded. Rajendra also may have wished to explore continuing his successful expansionist vision.

Under Chola rule, Rajendra Chola consolidated an extensive portion of the southern Indian subcontinent and Sri Lanka and placed the northwest Bengal coast of India under Chola tributary influence. However, he was displeased with increasing restrictions being placed by the Srivijayans on Chola maritime trade with Southeast Asia and China. The Srivijayans had taken control of the Malacca and the Sunda Straits, the only two maritime pathways around Sumatra, the Srivijayan homeland.

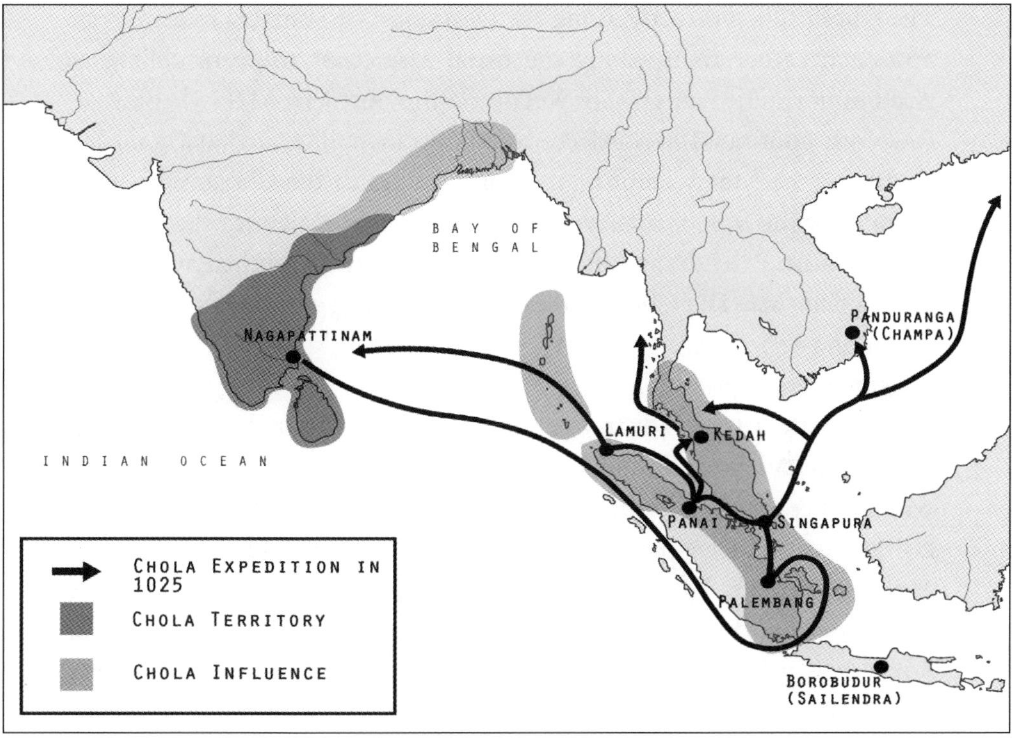

MAP 1.2 Chola expedition to Srivijaya in 1025
Adapted by Jamie Rhode from Paul Michael Munoz, Early Kingdoms of the Indonesian Archipelago and the Malay Peninsula *(Singapore: Editions Didier Millet, 2006), 162*

By controlling these two "choke points," the Srivijayans controlled the sea lanes of communication in their region. In particular, high tolls were placed on foreign ships traveling through the Malacca Strait. Maritime trade in the Indian Ocean had been relatively open and unobstructed for centuries. The Srivijayans practiced a naval trade monopoly, forcing vessels to call on their ports and pay tolls or risk being plundered. The Chola considered these to be Srivijayan acts of piracy. They objected to being held hostage by an opposing trade monopoly, given their commercial interests coupled with their naval strength. Thus, the Malacca Dilemma faced by the Chola was an early example of the Malacca Dilemma faced by China today.

In 1025, Rajendra Chola launched naval raids on the ports of Srivijaya in swift maneuvers that found the Srivijayans unprepared.[25]

The Chola sailed directly along the west coast of Sumatra in a surprise approach rather than taking the usual east coast route of calling at Aceh in northern Sumatra, or Kedah on the northern Malay Peninsula. Rajendra continued toward the Sunda Strait, while Srivijaya guarded Kedah on the Malay Peninsula. Javanese allies of the Chola, who were enemies of the Srivijayans, were pleased to assist Rajendra through the Sunda Strait. Palembang, the capital of Srivijaya in southeast Sumatra, was raided first. The Chola forces sacked the city, and the Royal Palace and monasteries were plundered. The Srivajayan king and much of his treasure were captured.

The Chola took advantage of the monsoon to sail swiftly northwest up the Malacca Strait, launching attacks on several ports along the way until reaching Kedah, which they conquered by using naval infantry against the defenders of the Kedah fort near the current Thailand/Malaysia border. This quick and violent raid resulted in major losses for Srivijaya and ended the Srivijayan maritime monopoly in the region. Srivijaya was left in confusion, leaderless, and greatly damaged. Despite the devastation, however, the Srivijayan sphere of political influence survived. The Chola, not seeking to govern so far from the center of their own power, did not install direct administration over Srivijaya.[26]

Gradually, the Chola guilds expanded their activities and increased their influence in Southeast Asia, paving the way for improved relations between the Chola and the Srivijayans. Nevertheless, Rajendra Chola's successful expedition had fragmented the ability of the Srivijayans to dominate the seas they had formerly controlled, leading to the decline and decimation of their empire. By controlling both sides of the Malacca Strait through their centers in Palembang and Kedah, the Srivijayans previously had a lock on control of the strait, but it was broken when Kedah and Palembang collapsed during Rajendra's Chola raid. Traditionally, the kingdoms on Java were often coequal rivals with Srivijaya for maritime supremacy over the Sunda Strait. Thus these rival Javanese kingdoms also were beneficiaries of the Cholas' restoration of freer maritime trade through the Sunda and Malacca Straits. Following the Chola victory, trade boomed for the Chinese Song merchants and for the Fatimid Caliphate that controlled Egypt and the Red Sea. Although there had been talk of a Chinese-Srivijayan alliance before the Chola raid, the Chinese appear to have been pleased with the demise of Srivijayan ability to extract excessive tolls on shipping in their home waters. By the end of the eleventh century, however, Chola power abroad began to ebb as focus on domestic involvements replaced focus on foreign operations.

MONUMENTAL LEGACIES: THE TEMPLES AT BRIHADISVARA AND GANGAIKONDACHOLAPURUM

Extensive eleventh-century inscriptions at Brihadisvara Temple, built by Rajaraja at his capital at Tanjore (then called Thanjavur) in thanksgiving for his many successes, provide a record of his many accomplishments. During his later years and before his death in 1014, Rajaraja shared power with his son Rajendra as a regent.[27]

After completing his conquests with the expeditions and raids on Srivijayan territory in Southeast Asia in 1025 and wishing to build an even more impressive monument than his father's Brihadisvara Temple, Rajendra constructed a new capital and temple in 1030 that he called Gangaikondacholapurum. Within the temple complex, a large well was built to contain holy water from the Ganges. The impressive Brihadisvara and Gangaikondacholapurum Temples are now UNESCO World Heritage Sites, along with the subsequently built Airavatesvara temple built by Rajaraja Chola II in the twelfth century. The carvings at this temple are even more refined that those at the earlier monuments to the Chola Empire and are proof of the accrued wealth of the Cholas during their prime.[28]

Conclusions from the Chola Maritime Experience

From a territorial perspective, the Chola did not appear to have attempted the establishment of permanent settlements in Sumatra, but they built a base in Sri Lanka at Polonnaruwa that was a Chola center of power for about sixty years. The legacy of the Chola in Southeast Asia lasted far longer than their few decades of physical presence. Evidence of Chola architectural and religious influence continues to be found in the region today.

Maritime Strategic and Tactical Lessons

The Chola maritime experience in the Bay of Bengal, the straits of the East Indies, and the South China Sea, accompanied by their significant landfalls and lingering influence in Sri Lanka, Sumatra, and the Malay Peninsula, are shrouded by the absence of evidence beyond temple complexes, inscriptions, and artistic traditions. Strategic, and tactical lessons, however, can be deduced from what remains of the archeological record of the Chola Empire in India, Sri Lanka, and Southeast Asia. Assessment of the case study material allows lessons to be drawn from several areas that help explain the prominence of the Chola as a sea power during the eleventh century.

LOCAL KNOWLEDGE OF NATURAL PHENOMENA

Chola knowledge of the maritime environment allowed them to be the greatest Indian sea power dynasty prior to Europeans arriving by sail in the Indian Ocean. The Chola knew and understood the seasonal monsoon wind patterns and accrued knowledge of currents in the Bay of Bengal through observations of wind and wave circulation, currents, and drifts. They also had studied the rising time of stars and measured their height above the horizon to guide their navigation practice, techniques that were borrowed later by Arab seafarers.

ADVANTAGES IN MILITARY TECHNOLOGY

The Chola led maritime technical innovation in the Indian Ocean, including the development of watertight compartments in their hull designs, use of a mariner's compass, and the creation of continuously shooting flamethrowers, which were especially useful in antipiracy operations. Using their knowledge of star movements, the Chola developed rhumb line sailing. On shore, the Chola built lighthouses to warn ships off dangerous shallow headlands. The square sails and dagger board steering of Chola warships were state-of-the-art until use of lateen sails that could point closer to the wind and that were combined successfully with central post rudders. The Chola sewed their wooden plank hulls together with vegetable fibers, eschewing the use of rusting iron nails. In these respects, Chola maritime technology exceeded that of other early Indian polities.

CONTINENTAL VS. MARITIME IDENTITIES

Of all the Indian dynasties, the Chola appear to have been the most attracted to the sea. Indeed, the Chola ventured out of their coastal waters across deep blue-water seas to conduct trade and to support that trade through military ventures requiring naval strength. Although not geographically the largest of the Indian dynasties, they developed a firm grip on the southeastern Indian subcontinent land mass. They developed land power as well as sea power through ports such as Nagapattinam and control of the coast as far northwest as the mouth of the Ganges. The Chola Dynasty is sometimes referred to as a thalassocracy, or a sea power state, though its capital cities lay inland away from the coast and its wealth derived from agriculture as well as ocean trade. That the great wealth of the dynasty derived from both revenue streams is apparent in the extensive and elaborately carved temple architecture of the capitals at Brihadisvara and Gangaikondacholapurum. As a sea power, the Chola state was able to compete with and conquer a true thalassocracy, Srivijaya, and at the same time defend itself against its main land rivals, the Chalukyas to the north and Pandyas to the south.

DEEPLY FELT NATIONAL IDENTITIES

Chola, Sinhalese, and Srivijayan identities played strong roles in the interactions between these parties in the eleventh century. Tamil was the language of the Cholas a millennium ago, and northern Tamil speakers in Sri Lanka are still connected in popular Sri Lankan imagination with the ancient Cholas. Symbols of these identities played a role in the Tamil separatist/Sri Lanka civil war between 1983 and 2009.[29]

MILITARY LEADERSHIP

Rajaraja and Rajendra, the Chola father-and-son team, effectively used their military prowess to create the power and influence apex of the

Chola Dynasty. At the same time, they were civilian kings who administered their lands in an orderly fashion and built great temple monuments at two separate capitals fifty miles apart from each other within the Chola kingdom. Rajaraja Chola was an effective warrior king who consolidated Chola power in southeast India from the time he assumed rule in 985 until his death in 1014. He made a successful foray to Sri Lanka, where he established Chola control during the middle of his reign. In order to do this, he established the beginnings of a Chola navy. During the last two years of his life, he shared power with his son Rajendra Chola, who expanded both the scope of Chola control in Sri Lanka and the Chola navy. Rajendra also extended Chola influence northwest to the mouth of the Ganges, and during the 1020s he focused on ending the trade control in the Malacca Strait exerted by the Srivijayan thalassocracy based in Sumatra with outposts on the Malay Peninsula. Rajendra's wily attack route along the south and west of Sumatra, rather than along the more usual sea route along the north and east coast, brought an effective element of surprise to the campaign that helped lead to Chola victory. Rajendra successfully eliminated the problem of piracy as well as the problem of the Malacca Dilemma, freedom of passage through the Malacca Strait, a problem that confronts China today.

RELATIVE POWER RELATIONS

The eleventh-century Cholas, at the peak of their power, had an economy that could support a navy and expeditions abroad. Locally strong though unsuspecting and unprepared, the Srivijayans' dominance over Palembang on Sumatra and Kedah on the Malay Peninsula was broken up by the Chola surprise attack. The Srivijayans never regained their earlier pre-eminent position as the maritime enforcer in the Malacca Strait. The Chola remained strong for about another century before their power declined.

ALLIANCE RELATIONS

The relations of the Cholas with the Javanese and the Kambujans were key to their long-distance success relating to their efforts to open up trade with China from the Indian Ocean into the China Seas. The relationships followed the ancient formula that "the enemy of my enemy is my friend." The Javanese and Kambujans struggled against the Srivijayans, and thus these kingdoms were natural allies for the Cholas, who also struggled against the Srivijayans. The need for navies to have friendly ports for both supply and shelter from storms was clearly foreseen by Rajendra Chola, who planned alliance relationships accordingly with the Javanese and Kambujans. Though the Srivijayans were nominally allied with the Chinese, the Chinese did not militarily oppose the Cholas when the Cholas attacked the Srivijayans.

RELATIONSHIP OF MARITIME ECONOMIC SUCCESS TO MARITIME MILITARY SUCCESS

The Cholas combined commercial savvy with military capability. The motivation for the creation of a navy had economic roots in their desire for free trade with China. Since the Malacca Strait trade was controlled by the Srivijayans, the Cholas acted to apply military force in order to enforce a free trade regime. This was not unlike the later Dutch concept of Mare Liberum, freedom of the seas. Thus Rajendra Chola's naval incursion to conquer Srivijaya in 1025 could be viewed as an early "freedom of the seas" operation because it reopened free trade through the Malacca Strait.

IMPORTANCE OF HISTORICAL AND CURRENT KNOWLEDGE

Buddhist and Hindu temples based on Indian religion and gods had been built in earlier centuries throughout Southeast Asia and were centers of economic as well as religious life. The Chola merchant guild system was able to operate effectively within the cultural context of these temple institutions largely because of the large body of shared historical and current knowledge. It can be surmised that because of this collaboration and knowledge, the Chola were familiar with the culture of the Indianized states in Southeast Asia, because the cultures of these states seem to have had parallel roots to Chola cultural roots.

Concluding Remarks: Looking Back, Leaning Forward

Following the expansion of Chola territory and power, first under Rajaraja Chola I and then more broadly under Rajendra Chola I, the Chola Dynasty remained stable for a century. Then it gradually declined in power until it was absorbed by the neighboring Pandyan Empire in 1279, the same year the Mongols defeated the Southern Song Dynasty in China and established the Yuan Dynasty. A century later, the Javanese Majapahits drove the remaining Sumatran Srivijayans north to Singapore, then subsequently to Malacca.[30] Before their final century of decline, the Chola Dynasty under Rajaraja Chola and Rajendra Chola established an empire to India's east in Sri Lanka and Southeast Asia. In today's terms, Chola policy would be called "Look East" and "Act East" policies, terms that India has used from 1990 to 2020 to provide a framework for developing its relations with Southeast Asia.

TWO

Limits on Mongol Maritime Expansion to Japan, Vietnam, and Java

Tran Hung Dao, Thirteenth Century

The Mongol Continental Vision Turns Maritime

After subjugating much of the Eurasian continent, the Mongols still had not satisfied their hegemonic plans, and they took to the seas between 1274 and 1293 in a series of expeditions to Japan, Annam, Champa, and Java to further their conquests.[1] During these two decades, the Mongols attempted to expand their huge land empire to encompass the substantial eastern maritime perimeter referred to now as the China Seas. These included enormous amphibious operations. For instance, two of their maritime operations, the attempted Mongol invasions of Japan in 1281 and of Annam in 1288, compete in scope and scale with the size of the World War II Normandy invasion of 1944. These invasions included massive amphibious sea crossings and landings involving 100,000 to 200,000 sailors and soldiers. These were serious expeditions in terms of resources, preparation, and commitment. The Normandy amphibious invasion, however, succeeded, while the Mongol maritime invasions failed to achieve their objectives. Why were the Mongols serially defeated at sea after their successive victories on land? This leads to a second important question: Under what conditions can a successful land power become a successful sea power, and does the Mongol failure at sea provide useful lessons to other land powers looking to take to the sea with the goal of expansion? This case study will examine the Mongol expeditions at sea in a search for answers to these questions.

Kamikaze, the "Divine Wind"

At the end of the second Mongol invasion of Japan in 1281, a great typhoon struck the Mongol fleet south of the island of Takashima in Kyushu, resulting in devastation of the fleet, forcing the return of fleet remnants to Korea.[2] Religious orders in Japan took credit for the Mongol defeat, saying that their prayers to the *kami*, Shinto gods, had been answered when the great wind, *kaze*, was sent by the *kami* to sink the Mongol fleet. Thus, the kamikaze, "divine wind," saved Japan from the Mongols.[3] Japanese samurai had organized a gritty defense against the Mongols during both the first and second invasion attempts, but the credit and consequent rewards following the conflict went more to religious orders than to samurai soldiers. Thus the kamikaze lodged for centuries in the Japanese imagination as the primary cause of the Mongol defeat.

As the tide of war turned against the Japanese in the Pacific during World War II and the American forces under Fleet Adm. Chester Nimitz pushed closer toward the Japanese home islands, the Japanese remembered how the divine wind had saved Japan from invasion during the thirteenth century. Between two and three thousand Japanese pilots volunteered to become the new "divine wind" to save Japan from invasion. Their kamikaze suicide missions sank or damaged 350 American ships, but this time the kamikaze were not enough to save Japan from occupation by outside forces. After the war, Admiral Nimitz said that prewar war-gaming had prepared him for every Japanese move in the Pacific, including the complex island-hopping campaigns, with one exception. He had not anticipated the kamikaze suicide missions, just as the Mongols had been unprepared for the kamikaze typhoon.

Because they were failures, the Mongol sea expeditions are less well remembered than the Mongol subjugation of almost five million square miles of Eurasian continent during less than seventy years between 1211 and 1279 under four generations of Mongol Khans. During the thirteenth century, the Mongols established the largest contiguous empire in world history, sweeping from their homeland in central Asia into Europe to their west and to the Pacific littoral to their east, bringing much of the Eurasian supercontinent under their control. No land power was able to oppose them for long. Genghis Khan (Chinggis Khan) established the empire beginning with eastern campaigns against the Jin in north China in 1211, then with western campaigns against central Asians and Persians. He passed away in 1227, and was buried in an unmarked grave in Mongolia per his own request. After Genghis Khan's death, the Mongols were led by Genghis's son Ogodei, who completed subjugation of the Jin Dynasty north of the Yangzi River. The Jin had driven the Chinese Song Dynasty south of the Yangzi a century earlier in 1127. This action split the former Song Dynasty into two approximately equal halves, with the Jurchen Jin Dynasty in the north and the Southern Song Dynasty in the south. The Mongols subjugated the Jin under Ogodei in 1234, but it took them another forty-five years to subdue the Southern Song Dynasty. In the intervening years, Ogodei consolidated Russia, Poland, and Hungary under Mongol control, but he died in 1242 before taking Vienna. Genghis' grandson Mongke succeeded Ogodei. Mongke Khan's great achievement was overseeing the fall of Baghdad in 1258 before he died in 1259. He was replaced in 1260 by Kubilai, another grandson of Genghis. Kubilai became Great Khan in the East and established Eurasian Pax Mongolica by maintaining security ties with the khanates to the west.[4]

Korea's Historic Place in Asian Geopolitics

For many centuries, Korea has occupied contested geopolitical space between its more powerful neighbors, China and Japan. During the fourth through seventh centuries, the Korean peninsula was divided into three kingdoms that allied at different times with either China or Japan, and sometimes with each other in a two against one alliance structure. Even during this early period, there was division and competition on the peninsula, as well as outside great power involvement. These same issues haunt Korea today. Variants of this pattern took place not only during the thirteenth-century Mongol period, the subject of this case study, but also during the 1590s Imjin War invasions of Korea by the Japanese, the Sino-Japanese War of 1894–1895, the Russo-Japanese War of 1904–1905, the Sino-Japanese War of 1931–1945, the Korean

War of 1951–1953, and the Cold War and post–Cold War aftermath. This history is about the changing map of Korea over centuries. While the map has changed, patterns have repeated as divisions on the peninsula have been marked by invasion routes of great powers, often with tragic consequences for the Koreans.

ANCIENT PATTERN: THE KOREAN THREE KINGDOMS PERIOD

Between about 50 BCE and 668 CE, three kingdoms governed the Korean peninsula: Goguryeo in the north, Baekche in the southwest, and Silla in the southeast. There was also a smaller state in the region of present-day Busan, Gaya (Mimana in Japanese).[5] The relationship between these political entities was dynamic and complex. Mimana and Baekche usually were allied to Japan through tributary relations, and Silla tended to be allied with China. Goguryeo preferred to be independent when possible, but it often entered into alliances for strategic reasons. This was typical of a general pattern in which alliance dynamics changed to accommodate present circumstances convenient to the parties. Korea's Three Kingdoms period and its aftermath includes configurations and reconfigurations of political entities on the peninsula for many centuries, as well as invasions of the peninsula as a corridor between the greater powers of China and Japan.

In 562, Silla annexed Mimana, thereby pushing Japan off of the peninsula. Japan sought to repossess this territory from Silla, in spite of the latter's strong relations with China. In terms of balance-of-power relations, for the next one hundred years China cultivated relations with Silla, while Japan cultivated relations with Baekche and Goguryeo, under the principle that "the enemy of my enemy is my friend." For instance, Sui emperor Yang invaded Goguryeo in 612, using ships built along the Yangzi. He defeated the Goguryeo fleet, but not its land forces. The competition increased after the establishment of the Tang Dynasty in China in 618. Japan armed Goguryeo and Baekche, then all three collaborated to invade Silla in 642. China's relations with Goguryeo and Baekche deteriorated when their navies interfered with China's Silla trade. China entered the conflict, deploying four hundred warships built in Jiangxi in 644 by Chinese emperor Tang Taizong. Taizong's strategy was to attack Liaodong to draw out Goguryeo, then surprise Goguryeo with a strike by sea, then moving on to the Goguryeo capital Pyongyang. The Chinese naval force arrived, so Goguryeo did not send all of its troops to Liaodong, across the Yalu River border with China. Winter bogged down the Chinese army, and they were forced to retreat in this first invasion attempt.[6]

A second invasion was planned for the following year, with the burden on Jiang-nan, the shipbuilding area south of the Yangzi River. Again, preparations went too late in the season and winter prevented a successful invasion. In 648, China planned a third invasion, but when Emperor Taizong died, the invasion was canceled. Tang Taizong never fully defeated Goguryeo, but occupied parts of it, saving Silla from attack by Goguryeo for over a decade. In 660, the new Tang emperor, Tang Gaozong, developed an alternate strategy to attack Goguryeo, deciding to strike Baekche instead. Silla would strike Baekche by land, while China would strike it by sea, thereby gripping Baekche in a vise from both sides. Baekche fell quickly, prompting the Chinese navy to put Pyongyang in Goguryeo under siege. The Chinese navy lifted the siege in winter, by now a familiar constraint on Chinese operations on the Korean peninsula. In 663, China was back on the Korean peninsula and subdued the recalcitrant Baekche. In October 663, the Chinese navy defeated the Japanese fleet decisively at Kibol Island in the Baek River. Almost one thousand years passed between Japan's Battle of Baek River defeat in 663 and Hideyoshi's invasion of Korea in 1592. This defeat of early Yamato Japan is considered to be the greatest military defeat of Japan during that millennium. The victory at the mouth of the Baek River is thought to be the "apogee of Tang naval activities."[7]

In 668, after a five-year war, China and Silla defeated Goguryeo as well, leading to the capture of Pyongyang. The Chinese administered eastern Korea as a province for the subsequent period. The Later or Unified Silla Dynasty became the ascendant kingdom on the Korean peninsula from 668 to 935, occupying much of the same territory that South Korea does today. When the Mongols arrived on the Korean peninsula in the thirteenth century, Korea again became the subject of great power intrusion. This time the intrusion was by the Mongols, a power from central Asia that subjugated China and then attempted to subjugate Japan, coercing Korea to assist in this effort.

MONGOL SUBJUGATION OF KOREA

The Mongols under Ogedei invaded Korea in 1231 before the Jin Dynasty was finally subdued in 1234, three decades before the Mongols entered Song territory at Xiangyang. The Mongols, however, were unable to overthrow the Korean king, because he took refuge with his court on Ganghwa Island in the estuary of the Korean Han River as it exits to the Yellow Sea west of Seoul. The Mongols had such little sea capability at the time that they could not cross the approximately one-half mile of water to the island. Despite fierce infighting between pro- and anti-Mongol factions, the Koreans resisted the Mongols until 1270, when the royal family invited the Mongols to overthrow the hard-line anti-Mongol faction. Goryeo, the Korean kingdom at the time, had its palace site in exile on Gangwha Island between 1232 and 1270, a site that still exists. When the Goryeo king partnered with the Mongols, the Korean rebels fled to Jeju Island. In 1273, the Mongols allied with the Koreans through the marriage of the Korean crown prince to Kubilai Khan's daughter. The rebels on Jeju Island ended their resistance, and the island subsequently became a pasture for Mongol horses. Unfortunately for the Koreans, within a year the Mongols had humiliated the Korean king by commandeering ships and sailors for an expedition to Japan to push their ambitions forward, even though they had just broken into Song territory with their 1273 victory at Xiangyang. They would learn a lot from the Song navy during the next few years, but also would learn from the Korean navy as they crossed the Strait of Tsushima during their first invasion of Japan during 1274.[8]

Mongol Invasions of Japan

Although it had taken forty years for the Mongols to subjugate Korea between 1230 and 1270, Kubilai Khan wasted no time in pushing Mongol influence beyond the East Asian littoral to include the Japanese islands. Already in 1266, Kubilai had composed a letter to the Kamakura *bakufu* feudal government sent through Dazaifu in Kyushu. The letter arrived in 1268 and received a mixed response. On the one hand, the letter spoke of friendly relations without resort to arms. On the other hand, it referred to Kubilai as the "master of the universe" and equated Japan to Goryeo/Korea, people described as subjects. The Japanese took a prudent course and instructed Kyushu lords to prepare a defense against a Mongol incursion. Receiving no reply, Kubilai ordered some ships to be built, yet continued to send unanswered letters.[9]

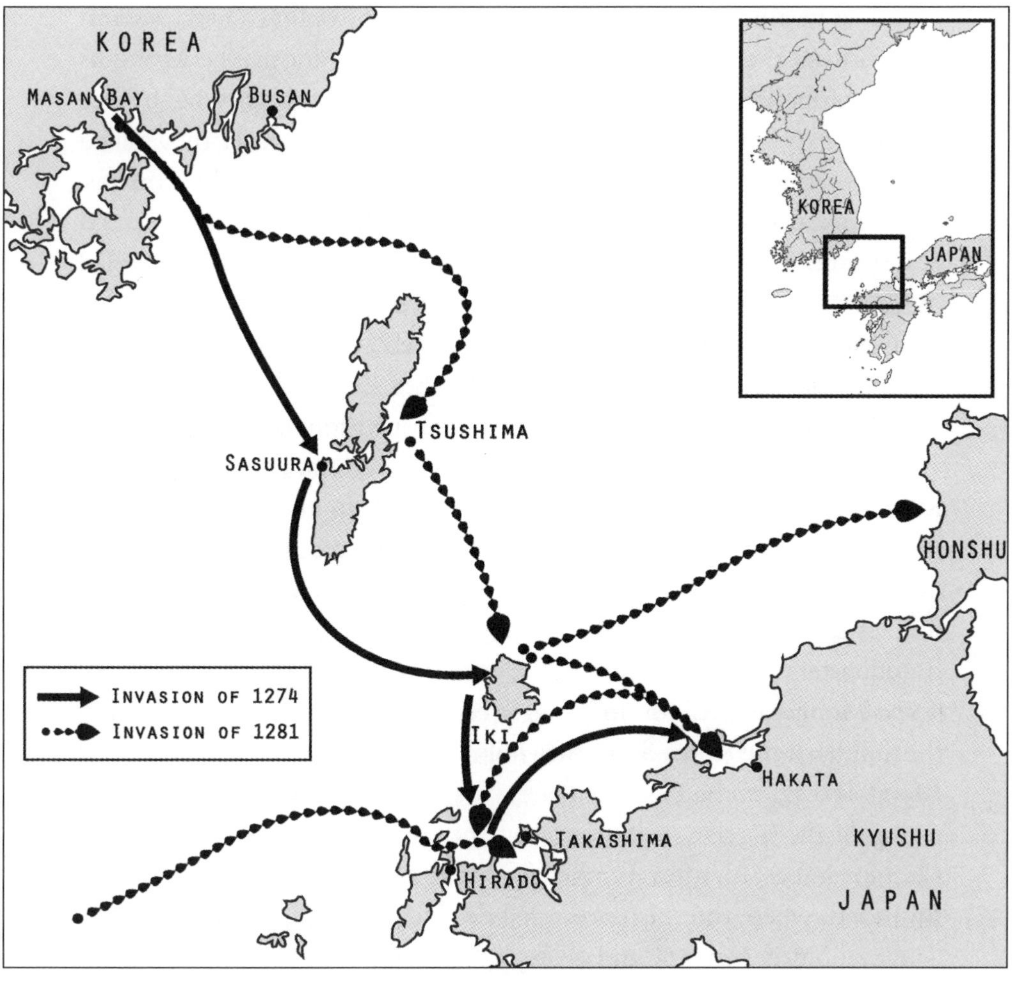

MAP 2.1 Mongol invasions of Japan, 1274 and 1281
Adapted by Jamie Rhode from Stephen Turnbull, The Mongol Invasions of Japan 1274 and 1281 *(Oxford: Osprey, 2010), 34, 56*

FIRST MONGOL INVASION OF JAPAN, 1274

The first Mongol invasion of Kyushu, the southern main island of Japan, was unsuccessful. In hindsight, the Mongols learned that the Japanese resistance was stronger than expected, perhaps because Mongol intelligence appeared to have been faulty about preparations that began after letters had been received from Kubilai Khan. Daizaifu, the administrative capital of Kyushu, did not fall easily. Rather, the Mongol's ammunition and food supplies were exhausted just as they reached their primary engagement, leading to the failure of the siege of Hakata Bay. Aside from lack of planning for adequate supplies, crossing the sea had its own perils, including weather, as well as the challenge of confronting a fierce enemy.

Without the benefit of these hindsight observations, the Mongols began shipbuilding specifically for the expedition in February 1274. Since Mongol expertise was horse warfare, not naval warfare, they relied heavily on the experienced shipbuilding and sailing skills of the Koreans. The expeditionary force included 900 ships, 30,500 combatants, and 6,700 sailors and oarsmen.[10] The Mongol expedition leaders included Hong Dagu and Liu Feng. The first expedition may have been intended as a Mongol reconnaissance mission, which would explain its short duration of about a month during November 1274.

The Mongols originally scheduled their invasion to begin in August 1274, during the reliable southwest monsoon season. Unexpectedly, the Korean king died in July and the funeral was held in October, delaying the departure of the invading forces until after the funeral, when less favorable northeast monsoon winds prevailed. Thus the expedition did not set sail from Korea's Masan Bay, where the Mongols had a fort headquarters for their eastern army, until November 2.[11] On November 4, the Mongol expedition forces arrived in Tsushima, the large island in the middle of the Korea Strait fifty miles from the Korean peninsula. The Mongols overran the Japanese defensive forces, who were under the leadership of the So clan, at Sasuura on the southwest coast of Tsushima. On November 13, after another fifty-mile sail, the Mongols arrived at Iki Island, where they also prevailed despite strong Japanese resistance. The combined Mongol and Korean fleet sailed on to Hakata Bay at present-day Fukuoka, arriving on November 18.

The Mongol goal was to capture Dazaifu, about nine miles inland and east of Hakata Bay. It only took a day for the Mongol forces to reach Dazaifu, but despite the Mongols' use of fearsome exploding artillery shells, the Japanese samurai forces at Mizuki Castle, an ancient fortress near Dazaifu, strongly resisted and repelled them. Suffering from an exhausted supply of incendiary missiles, the Mongols withdrew to the beach at Hakata Bay, and while passing the Hakozaki Shrine burned it down. They boarded their ships in the harbor that night. A raging gale with heavy rain drove a number of the Mongol ships onto the shore. In the morning, the Japanese witnessed the Mongol fleet departing Hakata Bay and executed about two hundred Mongol stragglers. The Mongol fleet arrived back at Happo Bay in Korea about one week later.[12] An estimated one-third of the expeditionary party had been lost during the first invasion.

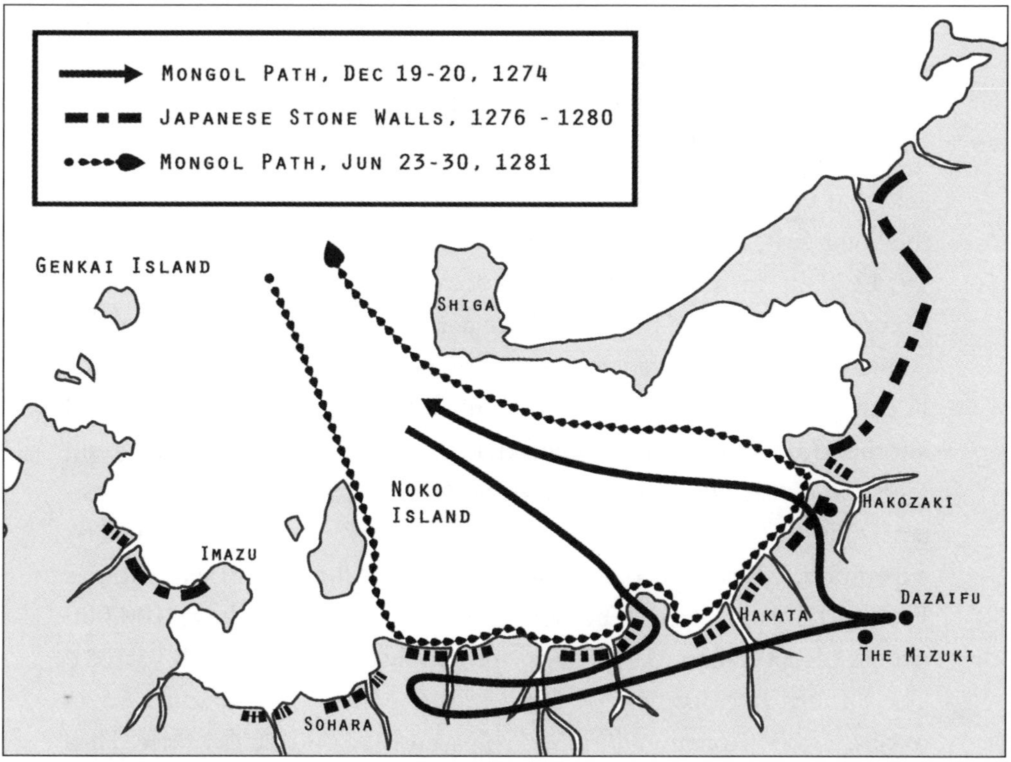

MAP 2.2 Hakata Bay battles, 1274 and 1281
Adapted by Jamie Rhode from Turnbull, The Mongol Invasions of Japan, *57*

A larger expedition force with more personnel and supplies would be needed for a second invasion. Meanwhile, the Mongols had not yet defeated the Southern Song Dynasty. Defeating the Song would take priority, both to allow the Mongols to concentrate more force on Japan, but also to co-opt the substantial Song sea power into the second invasion of Japan. While the Mongols focused on defeating the Song during these intervening years, the Japanese on Kyushu were also busy in anticipation of another Mongol invasion attempt. Beginning in 1276, they built over twelve miles of high stone walls along the beach at Hakata Bay. The walls were sheer stone, ten to thirteen feet high, and facing the bay, with graduated ramping behind so the samurai could ride their horses to the top, firing their arrows and slashing their *katana* down on the Mongols arriving on the beach from their ships. The value of these walls, remnants of which still exist, became apparent during the second Mongol invasion of Japan.

SECOND MONGOL INVASION OF JAPAN, 1281

Following the first Mongol invasion of Japan in 1274, Japan executed Mongol envoys sent by Kubilai Khan to negotiate in 1275 and 1277, acts that cried out for Mongol revenge. Following the final demise of the Song navy and the drowning of the Song child emperor on March 19, 1279, at Yashan, Kubilai Khan decided to launch his second invasion of Japan, despite hearing advice against it from some of his senior councilors.[13] He ordered 600 ships to be built in Quanzhou on the Fujian coast and 900 ships to be built in Korea. In 1280, he ordered another 3,000 ships and mobilized 100,000 men. This time he would send two divisions, a Southern Division from eastern China, and an Eastern Division from Korea. The preparations dwarfed those of the first expedition, which had been about the size of the second expedition's Eastern Division alone. The Southern Division was to have 100,000 troops, 65,000 sailors, 3,500 ships, and supply of 500,000 piculs of rice.[14] The Eastern Division was to have 15,000 Mongol, Han, and Korean troops, 17,000 Korean sailors, 900 ships, and 123,560 piculs of rice. Thus the joint expedition would total more than 200,000 men and 4,400 ships. Since the winds were not favorable for the Southern Division to sail to Happo in Korea to rendezvous with the Eastern Division, the two divisions planned to meet at Iki Island, a short distance from the northwest coast of Kyushu. As with the first invasion, the initial goal would be to take the Kyushu administrative center of Dazaifu, about nine miles inland from Hakata Bay.

The Mongol Eastern Division sailed from Happo Bay on May 21, 1281, and was delayed on Koje Island off the Korean coast by a storm before arriving on Tsushima on June 8. As had happened during the first invasion, the Tsushima islanders under the So clan resisted in bloody fighting but were again overwhelmed. Japanese captives told the Mongols that the shores of Hakata Bay were undefended. Iki Island was captured a week later on June 13. Without waiting for the larger Southern Division that was due to arrive in July, the Eastern Division arrived in Hakata Bay on June 22. The Mongols fired *huopao*, incendiary bombs, at the shore for two days before landing. When the Mongols stormed the beaches from the ships, Japanese samurai standing on top of the walls forced the Mongols to remain on the narrow strip of beach between the shore and the walls. Japanese reinforcements were added as necessary from the inland regions of Kyushu. Having believed the misinformation that Hakata Bay was lightly defended, the Mongols were unprepared for the rigorous defense. Fierce but indecisive fighting took place for a week with no Mongol advances beyond the strip of beach along the bay. This time the Mongols did not make it to Dazaifu as they had during the first invasion. Mongol ships in the bay formed a ring to repel smaller, more agile Japanese attack craft. By June 30, the Mongol Eastern Division was suffering from spoiled food and bad water as well as many losses in their unsuccessful fight for Hakata Bay. The division commanders decided to retreat to Iki Island to wait for the larger Southern Division.

The Southern Division fleet was delayed by the death of Mongol commander Alaqa. Under the new leadership of Fan Wenhu and Ataqui, a segment of the fleet arrived at Iki on July 10, but the bulk of it arrived at Hirado beginning on July 16.[15] Japanese attacks prevented the two parts of the fleet from meeting at Hirado and Iki, as fearsome samurai bands boarded the Mongols' ships when not repulsed by incendiary bombs. After three weeks of inconclusive sea battles with intermittent delays, the Southern Division fleet left Hirado to sail for Takashima Island, while the Eastern Division fleet left Iki to rendezvous with them in Imari Bay south of Takashima. The intent of the combined fleet was to land along the shore of Imari Bay, which was unprotected by the high stone walls that had been built along the shores of Hakata Bay thirty-one miles to the east. As the fleets arrived in the bay south of Takashima beginning on August 16, the weather deteriorated. The wind and tides became ferocious as a great typhoon, the kamikaze divine wind, struck from the southwest, driving hundreds of ships against the southern shore of Takashima. Other ships crashed together, the stronger Korean ships surviving better than the larger, less well-constructed Mongol ships built in Fujian province of southeast China. Estimates of loss of life from the storm ran as high as 70 to 80 percent. On August 20, Mongol commander Fan Wenhu sailed away with a small fleet, leaving at least 100,000 behind. Japanese mop-up operations were reported to have killed 20,000–30,000 shipwrecked stragglers, primarily Mongols, Koreans, and Jurchens from Manchuria. The Japanese forces reputedly spared former Song troops, as the Song had previously had good relations with Japan. Fan Wenhu was convicted at a Mongol court martial for abandoning the invasion scene. From this time forward, the myth of invincibility of the Japanese islands, because of the intervention of the kamikaze divine wind, began to grow in Japan.

In spite of the horrific losses during the second invasion attempt of Japan, Kubilai Khan remained convinced until his death in 1294 that the Mongols could subjugate Japan. In fact, he even worried that the Japanese would invade the mainland if he did not finish the job of conquering Japan. He planned to invade Japan again during 1283 but delayed in order to concentrate on Southeast Asian invasion operations against Champa and Annam. The loss to Annam in 1285 prompted him to cancel invasion plans for Japan in August 1286.

The Japanese defense was more effective than the Mongol offense, and the weather was a significant factor. Because the Mongols were more vulnerable to natural disaster due to their extended amphibious operation, the typhoon winds affected them negatively much more than they affected the Japanese. Aside from the devastation caused by the typhoon, the Mongols had several recurring military problems that inhibited their naval success. The subjugated Song boatbuilders may have built lower quality ships than required for the demanding Japan expeditions. The Japanese were fierce fighters and built effective defensive walls, enabling them to repel the Mongol forces. In addition, they also improved their *katana* long swords so they could penetrate Mongol leather armor. The Mongol side suffered from dissension within the ranks due to combining their own nonseafaring Mongol horsemen with seafaring Chinese and Koreans. In addition, rushed shipbuilding contracts and graft likely contributed to the Mongol invasion failures. Thus, despite sustained efforts for twenty years, Kubilai Khan was unsuccessful at sea in northeast Asia against the Japanese.

Mongol Invasions of Southeast Asia

After the Mongols began their three-decade-long conquest of Korea in northeast Asia, they turned to the sea in Southeast Asia. Ultimately, the Mongols lost their southern sea campaigns as they had in Japan. The great Mongol continental power was again frustrated as it attempted to become a maritime power.

MONGOL INVASIONS OF ANNAM AND CHAMPA: 1258, 1285, AND 1288

In 1257–1258, fifteen years before completing the conquest of Korea and their first invasion of Japan in 1274, the Mongols attempted an invasion of Annam, now northern Vietnam, by land through Yunnan. By 1266, Annam agreed to allow the Mongol emperor to be its overlord but refused to obey the "Six Duties" to which the Koreans had agreed that same year. These duties required the subject ruler to pay homage to the khan, to give their sons or brothers to the Mongol ruler as hostages, to submit to a census, to supply provisions and men to the khan's army, to submit revenue records to the khan, and to give administrative authority to a resident Mongol general. Thus, Annam's vassalage to the Mongols was nominal compared to Korea's and would remain so until after the Song were finally defeated in 1279, notwithstanding the clear Mongol interest in subduing areas south of the former Song Empire in Southeast Asia in the 1250s and 1260s.

During the 1270s Kubilai Khan's eye fell upon Champa, a sea-facing region further south along the coast of Vietnam that would make a good base for Mongol Southern Sea expeditions. The Cham, however, were pro-Song and would not submit to Mongol demands, even imprisoning Mongol envoys sailing toward the South Seas. Following the Mongol success in defeating the Song in 1279 and their failure in their second expedition to Japan in 1281, a Mongol fleet sailed to Qui Nhon in late 1283. The Cham capital of Vijaya near Qui Nhon fell to the Mongols. Cham King Indravarman escaped to the mountains, and a cat-and-mouse game ensued as the Cham engaged in selective ambush insurrections against the Mongols. Eventually, the Cham king said he would acknowledge Kubilai Khan's suzerainty but would not send tribute, again a partial submission similar to that of the Annamese further north. The Mongols decided that they would again rely on their land-based offensive tactics. They organized a massive land invasion of Annam all the way through to Champa in order to control both land and port access to the South Seas. This major Mongol invasion began in 1285 and had a degree of success, even though the Annamese and Cham were supported by remnants of Song loyalists who had fled south after their defeat in 1279. In fact, after the Mongols reached Champa, they were pushed back to Hanoi in Annam by Annamese and Song forces. The Mongol fleet managed to patrol the coasts of Annam and Champa effectively during this period.

Fearing an invasion of southwest China by Annamese forces even more than an invasion by the Japanese in the northeast, Kubilai Khan organized 94,000 troops and five hundred ships to invade Annam in a larger expedition in 1285. After quelling a rebellion in Manchuria, the Mongol army marched for Guangxi in southwest China in October 1287. The fleet sailed in December at the same time that the Mongol army crossed the border by land. The army took Hanoi in February but suffered from a lack of grain because the supply ships were driven back to Hainan Island in southern China. In April 1288, the fleet returned under the Mongol commander Omar. It had some initial successes in Haiphong Harbor but ran into disaster as it attempted to sail up the Bach Dang River toward Hanoi.

Tran Hung Dao Led Vietnam's Defeat of the Mongols

The history of Vietnamese resistance to those who have controlled China and pushed south to subdue Vietnam is remembered through commemoration of a series of heroes who were successful in their resistance efforts. For instance, in modern-day Hanoi, there is a temple to the Trung sisters, Trung Trac and Trung Nhi, Vietnamese women warriors who rode elephants into battle in 40 CE to drive back the Han Chinese for three years during a long period of Chinese domination over Vietnam.[16] Mongol invasions of Dai Viet, northern Vietnam, were repulsed by the Vietnamese military hero Tran Hung Dao. He is commemorated on the shores of Hoan Kiem Lake in northeast Hanoi and is noted especially for defeating the Mongol navy at the Battle of Bach Dang River in 1288. In southeast Hanoi, a major park and memorial commemorates the 1788 victory of Vietnamese general Nguyen Hue over the invading Manchu, after which he became Emperor Quang Trung. All these monuments have been refurbished in recent years as symbols of Vietnam's spirit of independence in the face of unrelenting pressures from the north.

Of all these figures, Tran Hung Dao is perhaps the most revered, if the number of statues and memorials to his memory scattered throughout Vietnam are to be taken as a token of esteem. Certainly, the monumental statue of Tran Hung Dao at the roundabout in Ho Chi Minh City (Saigon) indicates that his reputation spreads far beyond the area of his military resistance to the Mongols in northern Vietnam, then known as Dai Viet. His story is a remarkable one, worth looking at in more detail.

Originally from a princely family, Tran Hung Dao was appointed commander-in-chief of Dai Viet forces preceding Kubilai Khan's authorization of the Mongol invasion during the mid-1280s. He was a popular leader who reached out to all Vietnamese, and his call for national unity was heeded. They unified behind him in a scorched earth guerrilla war against the Mongols who had come pouring into the Red River valley at the border with China. Although the Mongols captured Hanoi, Tran's counteroffensive drove them back into China in 1285. After this defeat, the Mongols regrouped for another invasion of Vietnam instead of again invading Japan. In 1287, Kubilai Khan sent approximately 500,000 troops to south China to conquer Vietnam with overwhelming force. The Mongol land forces were split into two columns under the command of Toghan and Aruq, with a third force, the sea fleet, under the command of Omar. In a pattern similar to the previous invasion three years earlier, Vietnamese guerrilla forces fell back as the Mongols took the capital in Hanoi. This time, the Vietnamese were unable to push the more numerous Mongol forces back into China by land. Instead, Tran Hung Dao used a clever naval strategy to challenge the Mongols, and he ultimately defeated them with a surprising naval tactic.

The massive Mongol fleet included six hundred battle junks and a junk convoy carrying 70,000 tons of food supplies. It sailed from Canton (Guangzhou) in south China. Southwest of Hainan Island, the fleet sailed into Halong Bay, a virtual sea river protected from storms by dramatic limestone islands leading to the mouth of the Bach Dang River passage and on to inland Hanoi. It was here that Tran Hung Dao planned his trap for the Mongol fleet. As in Japan, the Vietnamese ships were small compared to the Mongol ships, so a type of asymmetrical tactic was required. Tran Hung Dao cut long poles from tree trunks, pointed the ends with iron tips, and stored them in caves in the limestone islands of the bay. As the Mongol fleet approached, his troops planted the poles in the mud between the islands of the Bach River estuary at low tide, with the points facing upriver. As the Mongol ships approached, a decoy group of Vietnamese ships lured the Mongols ships upriver at high tide. As the tide changed, thousands of smaller Vietnamese ships appeared from behind the river islands, many of them blazing fireships. The Mongols ships turned back in retreat, but were caught on the now exposed pointed pilings, with the fireships setting blaze to the Mongol fleet. Meanwhile, the Vietnamese attacked from the front, the rear, and the flank. About four hundred Mongol junks sank, and hundreds of thousands of Mongols were killed.[17] Omar was taken prisoner. Through this victory, the Vietnamese felt not only had they saved themselves from Mongol domination, but also that Japan and other parts of Southeast Asia were saved, as the devastation of the Mongol force was extreme and the Mongol defeat at the Bach Dang River had crippled their ability to attempt other invasions.

The Mongol fleet's disastrous defeat eliminated the Mongol army's source of food supplies, and the Mongol army was thus forced to retreat from Vietnam, as was the Mongol navy, which was crippled by the capture of Omar by the Annamese. This event ended the third and final Mongol invasion of Annam. The Annamese king refused to kowtow to Kubilai Khan in the Mongol capital. Instead, he compromised by sending a golden statue to Kubilai who accepted the statue but refused to accept Omar's return. Instead, Kubilai executed Omar.

Tran Hung Dao is remembered in Vietnam for his remarkable strategic and tactical success against the Mongols. Moreover, his strategic theories of guerrilla and asymmetrical war provided a model for communist guerrilla warfare in the twentieth century, including his emphasis on mass mobilization of the entire Vietnamese population. His proclamation for national unity and his book on military strategy became much-used classics during the Indo-China Wars between 1946 and 1975, as rural temples to him proliferated in the countryside.

In fact, Tran Hung Dao's tactic of using log spikes to defeat the Mongol navy was a rhyme of history that the Mongols should have studied before they sailed up the Bach Dang River in 1288. Three hundred fifty years earlier, in 938, Vietnamese commander Ngo Quyen effectively used a similar log spike tactic to repel the Chinese at the mouth of the Bach Dang River, even then considered to be Vietnam's "Sea Gate with a vital location."[18] The Chinese had gained effective suzerainty over Vietnam for almost a millennium following the collapse of the Trung Sisters' resistance in 43 CE. Ngo Quyen broke Chinese suzerainty 900 years later, with his Bach Dang River naval tactic, subsequently to be repeated by Tran Hung Dao in 1288. Thus, Ngo Quyen earned his title as the "Founding Father of national restoration." His tactics also were studied during the Vietnam's twentieth-century wars, emphasizing his focus on "swift attack, quick victory."

In summary, Ngo Quyen's tactic in 938 was again used successfully by Tran Hung Dao in 1288. Hidden stakes were placed in the Bach Dang River estuary to impale Chinese and Mongol ships, respectively, on the falling tide. During the two battles, the stakes were placed in different locations, as shown in Map 2.3 of the two battles. Following defeat at the Battle of Bach Dang River, Kubilai Khan never again attempted to invade Annam or Champa, but he still aspired to control maritime Southeast Asia. Before he died in 1294, Kubilai sent an expedition to Java that failed in its attempt to conquer lands by way of the sea. Thus the power of the charismatic leader's intentions passed away along with him.

MONGOL SUPPORT FOR MARITIME COMMERCE

During the Yuan Dynasty, the Mongol dynasty of China between 1279 and 1368, businessmen held an honored place, and trade was encouraged. Quanzhou had extensive trade links to Southeast Asia and the Indian Ocean, and it became the commercial capital of Asia and the center of the Mongol trade empire. The export of Chinese goods was encouraged while high tariffs limited imports, although Arab traders who specialized in gold and pearls thronged the city, building both mosques and cemeteries that still exist. Motivation for the Mongol invasions of Japan appears to have been driven by a desire for wealth,

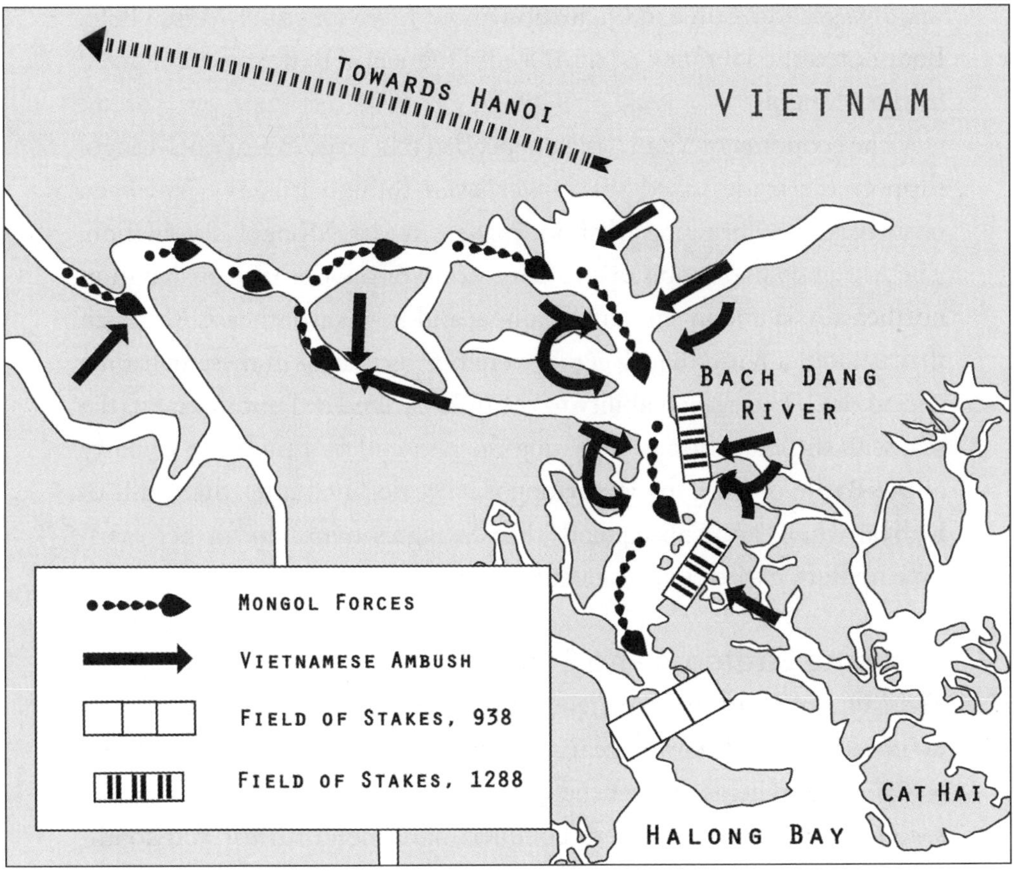

MAP 2.3 Battles of Bach Dang River, 938 and 1288
Adapted by Jamie Rhode from Some Historic Battles in Vietnam *(Vietnam: The Gioi Publishers, 2013), 2, 38*

especially gold and pearls. After the failed second invasion attempt, brisk trade continued between Japan and Mongol-occupied Korea, even as the Mongols contemplated a third invasion.[19]

It is worth noting that two medieval travelers made important observations about Mongol connections with the sea, especially in relation to trade. Venetian Marco Polo served Kubilai Khan during the course of his travels. Although he traveled overland through central Asia to China, he returned by sea, accompanying a Persian wedding party by ship from Quanzhou to the Persian Gulf, then on to the Mediterranean. Moroccan Ibn Battuta served as a judge in Delhi before traveling on to China by sea, also spending time in Quanzhou about fifty years after Marco Polo. Both noted the vibrancy of trade with Quanzhou that was encouraged by the Mongols.

The economy of Yuan China depended to a large extent on Mongol support for trade-based sea power, even though its navy had been unsuccessful in bringing offshore powers under Mongol domination. The Mongols had ambitions to control maritime domains in Japan in northeast Asia and in Annam, Champa, and Java in southeast. Although they created a navy, the Mongols were not successful in these maritime endeavors. Their fabled ability to conquer by land did not extend to the sea, with the exception of defeating the remainder of the Song Dynasty at the Battle of Yashan. The Mongol navy declined after the death of Kubilai Khan, and subsequently, the Mongols made no further maritime military expeditions to northeast or southeast Asia.[20]

Maritime Strategic and Tactical Lessons

The Mongol maritime experience demonstrates that great land powers do not inevitably become great sea powers. Assessment of Mongol case study material helps answer the question of why the Mongols were not successful in their attempts to conquer maritime northeast and southeast Asia.

LOCAL KNOWLEDGE OF NATURAL PHENOMENA

Successful naval campaigns require local knowledge of tides, currents, winds, and weather, as well as coastal configurations, water depths, and obstruction locations. These phenomena are the maritime equivalents of terrain and weather, the importance of which Sunzi noted in his classic of military strategy translated as *The Art of War*.[21] Although the Mongols relied to a certain extent on the local knowledge of Korean sailors in their employ, they were not familiar with the typhoon season, nor with the appropriate caution that should be exercised in relation to it. Also, the shallowness of water in the Hakata and Imari Bays was a condition known to the Japanese but not to the Mongols. The smaller, faster Japanese boats were more suited to moving easily in these shallow waters where there was little room for maneuver. The Mongols did not make a strategic decision to avoid insurmountable natural odds involved with typhoons, nor did they have a tactical plan to find a "hurricane hole" to attempt to ride out storms. The results were devastating, as the Mongols lost the bulk of their fleet to storm damage, and tens of thousands of their soldiers were set adrift to be slaughtered on the beaches by the Japanese.

ADVANTAGES IN MILITARY TECHNOLOGY

Superior military technology can be decisive, both historically and today. The Mongols successfully used trebuchet catapults, a new naval technology, on the rivers of western China by placing them on their vessels, but they were unable to use them in their overseas expeditions, as tossing sea conditions were unlike placid river conditions. They wrought havoc on the Japanese with their *huopao*, incendiary shells memorialized by the Japanese in the Mongol Scrolls. The super-strong and sharp samurai *katana*, the finest sword blades in the world, prompted improvements to Mongol leather armor to cope with them. Once the Japanese built their defensive walls near Hakata Bay in 1275, developing ramps from the back side so they could ride their horses to the top of the walls and fight down against the Mongols, they were in a superior defensive position to repel the Mongols using both their swords and bows. The Mongols had no offensive technology to combat this defense. Although they brought some horses by sea in an attempt to use their famed equine techniques, they did not work on the wall-lined beach. Mongol tactics of speed and mobility that had been successful across the plains of Eurasia did not couple well with amphibious operations. They literally got in over their heads.

CONTINENTAL VS. MARITIME IDENTITIES

Great power continental and maritime pressures to expand have existed in East Asia for two millennia. Periodically, forces from China have pushed toward the Japanese islands, and Japanese forces have pushed toward the continent. During the late nineteenth century, American naval strategist Alfred Thayer Mahan identified six key elements of sea power: geographical position, physical conformation, extent of territory, size of the population, character of the people, and character of the government.[22] These six traits overall fit Japan better than they fit China, even as they fit Britain as an island nation better than they fit France or Germany as continental powers, albeit with coastlines. For a continental power, co-opting established navies by conquest appears not to be an effective way to become a maritime power. The Mongols co-opted the Song and Korean navies, but with limited results. At the very least, the Mongols attempted to do too much in the maritime realm, and too fast.

DEEPLY FELT NATIONAL IDENTITIES

Asian identities are deeply felt and have affected international relations both historically and in the present era. The same was true during the Mongol period. For example, Annam and Champa had profound national interests in opposing expansive Chinese hegemonic objectives in Asia from the time of the Trung sisters' resistance in 40 CE. Likewise, the Vietnamese thwarted Mongol incursions into Vietnam and organized significant national resistance to the Mongols similar to Vietnamese national resistance to the French and Americans in the twentieth century. Korean and Song national identity affiliations also were impediments to smooth Mongol operations. Even though the Mongols co-opted Song and Korean forces to work in their invasion expeditions, Song loyalists tended to defect to the Cham or Annamese when they were able to exercise their preference, and many Koreans were happy to see the Mongols lose to the Japanese in their hope of throwing off the Mongol yoke from Korea. Although the Mongols had been successful enough maintaining control among disparate peoples on the continent, it proved more difficult to do so in the maritime environment, where they were less expert.

MILITARY LEADERSHIP

Capable and wise military leaders can make a critical difference in the success or failure of a military campaign, whether on land or at sea. Military leadership may lead to a variety of outcomes, but the "genius" of the particular military leader involved, according to Clausewitz, provides intangible power to shape the outcome of military events. [23] A case in point is Dai Viet's Tran Hung Dao. His long military experience with the Mongols gave him tools to succeed. He was able to motivate his countrymen in spite of tremendous odds against them in terms of both Mongol numbers and ferocity. Realizing that food supply was essential for Mongol success, he organized a scorched-earth policy to limit local agricultural products from falling into Mongol hands. And more importantly, he decided to prohibit the column of Mongol grain supply ships from reaching the two columns of Mongol soldiers in the Hanoi region. His tactical brilliance in sinking the Mongol fleet in the Bach Dang River estuary in 1288 is a story still revered by the Vietnamese today.

On the Mongol side of military leadership, Kubilai Khan had surprising success against the Song, overthrowing its dynasty and establishing the Yuan Dynasty in its place. He juggled campaigns concurrently in China, Korea and Japan, and Southeast Asia. Although he might have stretched Mongol forces such that their maritime campaigns failed, he never gave up his dream of maritime dominance. Instead, his death resulted in the cancellation of further Mongol maritime expeditions in both northeast and southeast Asia. Without Kubilai's leadership, the Mongols lost both the will and ability to pursue further conquests at sea.

RELATIVE POWER RELATIONS

Preponderant power does not necessarily lead to military victory. Aside from shrewd strategic and tactical practice playing key roles, chance and luck are factors in the outcome of war, according to Clausewitz.[24] In the case of the overwhelming force that the Mongols brought to Japan in the two-pronged Southern and Eastern Naval Divisions, the death of a commander delayed the larger Southern force, an interruption that led to the demise of the fleet in a devastating typhoon. It appears that the Mongols were overconfident about winning their battles in northeast and southeast Asia, based on their almost unbroken record of success on the continent. They may have confused preponderant power at sea with preponderant power on land, whereas the two are very different in terms of necessary experience, skills, and technology. Korean states on the peninsula did not have the preponderant power that China and Japan have had during their peak periods of power. As a result, the pattern of Korea's divisions and subservience has been clearly shown both during the Three Kingdoms and Mongol periods. This pattern has continued to the present day.

ALLIANCE RELATIONS

The Japanese had significant outposts in Tsushima and Iki with feudal lords loyal to Japan, but they had no external allies on which to rely. Having no allies, but having internal unity of purpose, mitigated Japan's isolation. On the other side, the Mongols had allies, relying on Korean and Song ships and sailors. But neither the Koreans nor the Song supported the Mongols out of free choice; they both served the Mongols because they had been forced into submission by them. Korean politics were divided between those who supported the royal Mongol/Korean marriage between one of Kubilai Khan's daughters and King Chungnyeol of Goryeo, and those Koreans who wished to continue to oppose the Mongols. Thus Korean sentiments about the Mongols ranged along a spectrum of compliance and resistance. Meanwhile, the Song who escaped south after their defeat at Yamen in 1279 were sympathetic to and supported the resistance of the Annamese and Cham to the Mongols. Those Song who were co-opted by the Mongols to build a fleet and sail with the Mongols most likely also had divided sympathies. The Annamese and Cham may have had internal dissension but were natural allies against the Mongols. The Annamese were pleased to accept help from the disenfranchised Song who fled south after being defeated in China. Thus alliance relations during the Mongol invasion period were a varying factor, weaker in the cases of Japan's lack of alliances and the Mongol's weak alliances with the Koreans and the Song, and stronger in the case of Annam's alliances with the Cham and Song.

RELATIONSHIP OF MARITIME ECONOMIC SUCCESS TO MARITIME MILITARY SUCCESS

Mongol maritime trade flourished in Southeast Asia and the Indian Ocean for a brief period, even though Mongol maritime military success was limited to the China coast. The accounts by Marco Polo and Ibn Battuta about the market of Quanzhou, the greatest of the Mongol merchant ports, were glowing. In this regard, the Mongols were following both the tradition of the free ocean trade that had existed for more than a thousand years in the Indian Ocean, as well as the tradition of their promotion of trade and business along the silk roads crossing the Mongol heartland. Mongol sea trade, however, was not sustained by ongoing concomitant Mongol naval power, and it faded within a few short decades. European trading in later centuries was more closely linked to naval power, including the successive trade and naval patterns of the Portuguese, Spanish, Dutch, and English. But the Mongols largely followed the peaceful, nonmilitarized, pre-European pattern of Asian sea trade.

IMPORTANCE OF HISTORICAL AND CURRENT KNOWLEDGE

The Mongols would have been more cautious on the Bach Dang River in 1288 if they had been familiar with the lesson of the Chinese defeat in the same location in 938. This is a cautionary tale about studying the history of a region before becoming involved militarily. Certainly, Tran Hung Dao knew the history, so he simply re-created a plan that had worked before and correctly assumed that the Mongols would not be familiar with the 350-year-old story in the remote Bach Dang River. In a similar fashion, Japanese admiral Togo established the model of a successful sneak attack on Port Arthur in 1904. In 1941, Japanese admiral Yamamoto oversaw the sneak attack on Pearl Harbor, which was modeled after the Port Arthur attack. The lack of preparedness by the United States was possibly less forgivable than the lack of preparedness by the Mongols, since the earlier event had taken place within living memory, only thirty-seven years before. As Sunzi said, "Know the enemy, know yourself; your victory will never be endangered. Know the ground, know the weather; your victory will then be total."[25] Sun Tzu was cautioning not only about knowing the history and psychology of one's opponent for strategic advantage, but also knowing about current intelligence to gain tactical advantage. The Mongol record is thin in this regard, so few lessons can be drawn for the Mongol case study about the use of intelligence procedures. Sunzi was a proponent of deception as well as intelligence collection. Misinformation given to the Mongols on Tsushima that Japanese forces in Hakata Bay were unprepared led to the Mongols being unpleasantly surprised when they were confronted by unsurmountable walls on the Hakata Bay beaches.

LIMITS ON MONGOL EXPANSION AT SEA

Most Westerners are aware of the highly significant amphibious invasion that took place in Normandy in 1944, known as Operation Overlord by the American, English, and Canadian troops. On D-Day, June 6, 1944, between 130,000 and 150,000 troops landed on the Normandy beaches after following various routes across the approximately one-hundred-mile-wide English Channel. After securing the landing area, these initial Allied troops were followed by many more in the ensuing days and months, as Axis opponents were forced into retreat. The Normandy landing was successful and led to the Allied victory in World War II.

Fewer Westerners are aware that a similar size Mongol invasion of Kyushu of approximately 200,000 troops took place in 1281 across the one-hundred-mile-wide Korea Strait, or that a Mongol invasion force of well over 100,000 troops in 500 ships attacked Vietnam at the Bach Dang River in Halong Bay in 1288. The Mongol amphibious landings in Japan and Vietnam were unsuccessful, leading back to the questions raised at the beginning of this case study: Why were the Mongols serially defeated at sea subsequent to their successive victories on land? Under what conditions can a successful land power become a successful sea power, and does the Mongol failure at sea provide useful lessons to other land powers looking to take to the sea with the goal of expansion?

Notwithstanding that the Mongols had no substantial rival and were able to deploy overwhelming military power with their horse-mounted cavalry, the Mongols suffered significant defeats at sea based on their lack of knowledge of ships, the sea, and seamanship. They sailed during the typhoon season and did not have safe harbors in mind if and when severe storms arose. In terms of amphibious landings in Kyushu, the horses they brought were of little help, especially during the second invasion, when the Mongols were faced with tall walls that the Japanese had built between the 1274 and 1281 invasions. The seas were too rough to deploy the catapults they had used during their riverine entry to China. Thus, the Mongols were forced out of Hakata Bay to await the larger fleet reinforcement from the Southern Division. Communication between Mongol fleets was difficult, and coordination was poor, with increasing danger from limited supplies and possible weather changes. Although the Japanese ships were smaller than the Mongol ships built by the Koreans and the Song, they were mobile and allowed successful asymmetrical naval operations in the shallow Hakata and Imari Bays. The Japanese were on "death ground," defending their native soil, which added a national fervor to the samurai skill set. Similar logic held in relation to the Vietnamese resistance to the Mongols, and Tran Hung Dao's military leadership added the deciding edge to Vietnamese maritime resistance to the Mongols.

Both the Japan and Vietnam cases show that weaker powers can stand up to preponderant power when they have home advantage with short supply lines and a united response. The Japanese lacked external allies, while the Mongols had problematic allies, relying on Korean and Song ships and sailors although neither the Koreans nor Song supported the Mongols out of free choice or conviction. The Vietnamese/Annamese had more cohesive alliance relations with the Cham and Song who fled south of the Chinese border, which presented a more formidable opposition to the Mongols. The Mongols suffered from a lack of both historical and contemporary maritime intelligence, which led them into carelessness with the weather in Japan and with the tides, coupled with a clever asymmetric Dai Viet adversary in the Bach Dang River near Hanoi. All of these factors limited Mongol expansion at sea.

Becoming a successful maritime power is a complex process that must address the many aspects where failure can take place. Building maritime power and capability differs, and strength in one arena does not guarantee strength in the other. Patience is required to learn the ways of maritime power, which takes decades to understand and implement. Moreover, a successful land power must have significant sea frontage to become a sea power. The Mongols only brought the major portion of the Chinese coast under their control when they defeated the Song at sea in 1279. Yet they had already attempted to invade Champa in 1258 and Japan in 1274. The Mongols clearly moved too quickly in thinking they could become the major Asian sea power while having so little experience of the sea and so little access to it. Thus the Mongols provide a cautionary tale to land powers seeking to become sea powers. Sea power has distinct parameters that must be studied and developed systematically, with care, time, and patience. With the hubris of inexperience, the Mongols attempted too much at sea, too quickly.

Although the Mongol amphibious landings in Japan and Vietnam were unsuccessful, they have left a residue of historic consciousness about vulnerability to invasion. These episodes of northeast and southeast Asian maritime history are part of the fabric of Asian historic consciousness. Although the Mongol maritime case may seem far away from European and American concerns, the saving of the Japanese islands by the divine wind is still commemorated in a song sung by Japanese adults and children alike.[26] In a southeast Asian echo of the Mongol invasion event, statues of Tran Hung Dao are omnipresent in Vietnam. The relevance of these cases of Mongol maritime invasion in northeast and southeast Asia continues to express itself in song and sculpture, indicating that the Mongol maritime invasions echo in memory and thus continue to deserve attention and study.

THREE

Early Ming Voyages to the Western Ocean

Zheng He, Fifteenth Century

Early Ming Wooden Shipbuilding and Zheng He's Voyages

During the early Ming Dynasty between 1405 and 1433, with the blessing of Emperor Yongle and his grandson Emperor Xuande, Admiral Zheng He (1371–1433) led seven huge maritime expeditions from eastern China into the Western Ocean, what is known today as the Indian Ocean. Each expedition included about two hundred ships and 30,000 sailors, soldiers, and support staff.

The largest of the ships, the treasure ships, carried gifts and returned with tributes from leaders in foreign lands, and were built in the Longjiang shipyard in Nanjing. The yard contained seven large dry docks that could be filled using water gates connected to the Yangzi River to float the massive wooden hulls. Three of the shipyard docks have been excavated, and the shipyard area is now a park with large pools in dock locations, as well as a museum displaying excavated artifacts and bronze reproductions of early maps that tell Zheng He's story. It is not a remote narrative from ancient history. Within China, the story of Zheng He has become a parable about the nature of current Chinese interaction with the wider world. Chinese accounts portray Zheng He as one who, despite being a naval military figure, treated those he met on his voyages with respect, not violence or economic exploitation. These expeditions are seen as an example of China's "Peaceful Rise" into world affairs, a term that recently has been borrowed from the early Ming period and used to describe the opening up of China to the world from the Deng Xiaoping era to the present. Notwithstanding the controversies about the use of the term Peaceful Rise for China's modern expansion of global influence and also about the size of Zheng He's ships, his voyages are impressive maritime endeavors, and the clashes that occurred during these expeditions warrant consideration and inclusion in this analysis.

ZHENG HE'S SHIPS AND FLEET

Many consider Zheng He to have sailed the largest wooden ships ever built, recording that they were over 400 feet long.[1] The standard Ming history, the *Ming Shi*, describes the ships as forty-four *zhang* long by eighteen *zhang* wide. Since a *zhang* is about ten feet long, Zheng He's largest ships would have been more than 400 feet long—modern aircraft carriers are only about twice as long as this—truly an impressive feat of engineering and construction capability. No nautical archeological evidence exists to verify the size of Zheng He's ships, except for a rudder post excavated in 1962 at the Longjiang shipyard in Nanjing, from which a ship of 400-plus feet has been extrapolated by making assumptions based on extant Chinese wooden ships.[2] Aside from this one piece of available archeological evidence, literary sources such as the *Ming Shi* and other early accounts are the basis for the 400-foot estimate.

Other scholars argue that Zheng He's ships were in the 200-foot-long range, similar to Lord Nelson's flagship HMS *Victory* preserved in Portsmouth Harbor, UK, which is 227 feet long.[3] It has been estimated that the *Victory* consumed six thousand trees. At 225 feet, each ship would have used a similar amount of timber. At 400 feet or more, each treasure ship would have consumed many times that number of trees.

The replica of the Zheng He treasure ship in the shipyard dry dock in Nanjing is about the same length as *Victory*, just over 200 feet long. The case made for the shorter ship length includes displacement and crew size calculations, alternate assumptions about the rudder post, and, most significantly, engineering arguments that European ships were limited to about 200 feet because of longitudinal strength issues, namely, that they relied on a keel made of a single piece of oak, very difficult to find at more than 200 feet. European shipwrights believed it was not possible to build longer wooden ships than this. These longitudinal strength issues would have confronted Chinese shipbuilders as well. It is possible, however, that the longitudinal strength issues might have been solved through the use of structural bracing and a keel-less design, relying on ship wall strength and transverse bulkheads inside rather than a keel for structural strength. Those giving credence to this design argument conclude that, "The evidence indicates that Zheng He's largest ships may well have been the largest wooden sailing ships ever constructed."[4] Unless conclusive archeological evidence of a hull or bracing is found, however, the debate is likely to continue about the length of Zheng He's ships.

Regarding the speed and maneuverability of Zheng He's ships, the sail area to displacement ratio was not high, despite the largest of these ships having nine masts with twelve sails. This ratio likely limited the speed of the treasure ships to two to three knots with a following wind. Expedition planning for the ships had to rely on knowledge of the changing seasonal direction of the monsoon winds, as the ships could not point closely toward the wind.

Despite controversies over size and structure, all agree that these ships were very large and undoubtedly highly impressive when they arrived in a formation spread out like the wings of a bird arriving at ports in Vietnam, Sumatra, Malaya, Sri Lanka, India, Arabia, and eastern Africa. Zheng He's voyages were the pinnacle of China's maritime accomplishments before the twentieth century. Zheng He arrived in Calicut on the west coast of India in 1408, ninety years before Vasco da Gama arrived in Calicut from Portugal in 1498. A bigger question than the size of Zheng He's vessels is why China did not become the dominant sea power in the Indian Ocean rather than the Portuguese, who arrived later and in far smaller ships and numbers. Scholars continue to debate this question. But it seems that the failure to become dominant over the long term did not result from maritime capability, but from priorities in Chinese dynastic policy. Navies are expensive. Threatened from the north and west by Manchu and Mongol raiders, the Ming Confucian treasury officials, always in conflict with palace eunuchs such as Zheng He, allocated funds to combat these immediate northern threats by land rather than allocating resources for the necessary refurbishing that a massive wooden fleet would require after three decades of use, particularly as it faced an unthreatening south.

Cycles of Chinese Sea Power and Records before the Ming Dynasty

Scholar Lo Jung-pang theorizes that Chinese sea power occurred in three cycles of about five hundred years each before the modern era, and a similar cycle may be beginning now.[5] The three cycles occurred during the Qin and Han Dynasties (221 BCE–220 CE), the Sui and Tang Dynasties (581–960 CE), and then during the Southern Song, Yuan, and Ming Dynasties (1127–1450 CE). Lo's book, especially important for accounts of the Mongols in the case study preceding this one, also discusses in some detail the maritime capabilities of the preceding Southern Song and the following early Ming. The work provides a context for the extensive historical maritime involvement of the Chinese, before touching briefly on the voyages of Zheng He during the early Ming period, which he considers as having been toward the end of the third cycle of Chinese sea power. The case studies in this book about the Imjin and Sino-Dutch Wars, however, indicate that there was considerable Chinese sea power still in place during the middle and late Ming periods, suggesting that the third cycle of Chinese sea power had not ended completely during the early Ming voyages of Zheng He.[6]

TRANSITION FROM YUAN DYNASTY TO MING DYNASTY

During the medieval period, the Indian Ocean was a two-way maritime thoroughfare between the Mediterranean and the China Seas. The early Ming maritime voyages traveled from east to west before returning home and were reminiscent of expeditions from west to east by the Venetian traveler Marco Polo and the Moroccan traveler Ibn Batutta. Though land and sea travel across this great expanse had taken place many centuries previously, the thirteenth- and fourteenth-century chronicles of Marco Polo's and Ibn Battuta's travels during the Yuan Dynasty created a detailed and fascinating record of Eurasia during this period. An equally revealing record was created by the early Ming fifteenth-century accounts of Zheng He's voyages by his travel companion and chronicler, Ma Huan, narratives that are central when describing details of Zheng He's voyages.

The Yuan Dynasty of Mongol rule was short-lived compared to the preceding Tang (618–906) and Song (960–1279) Dynasties, and the following Ming (1368–1644) and Qing (1644–1912) Dynasties, lasting less than a century from its founding in 1279 by the great Mongol leader Kubilai Khan to its demise in 1368. Following Kubilai's death in 1294, successor khans (rulers) were less powerful and had relatively brief periods of governance. For example, four separate khans ruled during the 1320s. Chinese secret societies developed with the goal of toppling the Mongols and re-establishing the Song Dynasty. One of the societies, an offshoot of the White Lotus Buddhist sect called the Red Turbans to reflect their garb, plotted armed rebellion during the 1350s. Zhu Yuanzhang, a Buddhist mendicant, eventually won both land battles and a huge naval battle at Lake Poyang against a rival force in 1363, taking control of central China. In early 1368, Zhu proclaimed himself as the Emperor Taizu of a new dynasty, and by summer he had driven the Mongols out of their capital at Dadu, now Beijing. Subsequently, Zhu Yuanzhang established a firm foundation for the Ming Dynasty. His son Zhu Di, the Yongle emperor,[7] took the throne in 1402 after he staged a coup against his nephew Zhu Yunwen, the Jianwen emperor, who had taken control of power briefly between 1398 and 1402 after the death of Zhu Yuanzhang.

Early Ming Voyages to the Western Ocean

Emperor Yongle was the primary patron for Zheng He's voyages and authorized protégé's first six voyages between 1405 and 1421 before his death in 1424. Zheng He's final seventh voyage was authorized by Yongle's grandson, Emperor Xuande, in 1433.

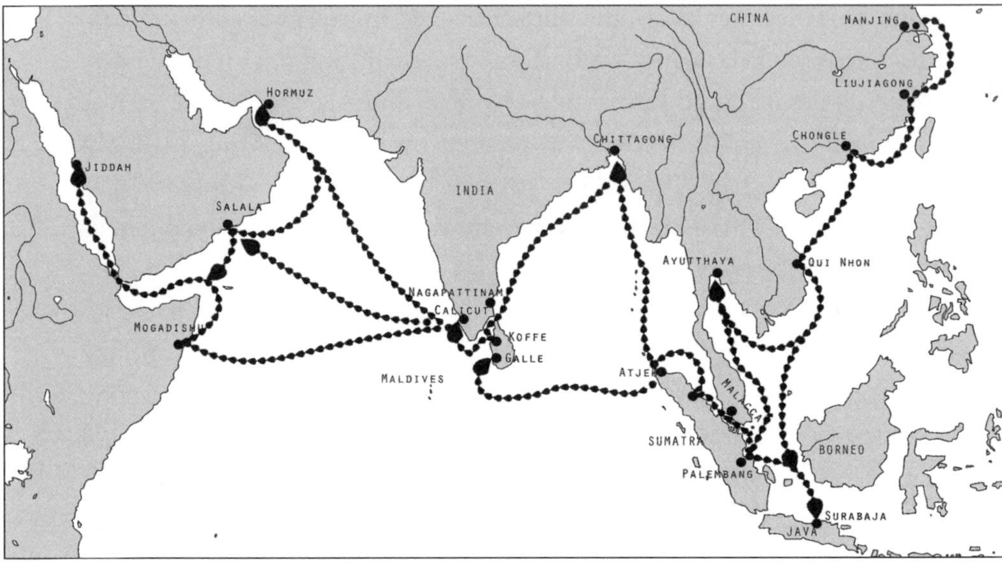

MAP 3.1 Schematic routes of Zheng He's voyages, 1405–1433
Adapted by Jamie Rhode from Louise Levathes, When China Ruled the Seas: The Treasure Fleet at the Dragon Throne, 1405–1433 *(Oxford: Oxford University Press, 1994), 10–11*

ZHENG HE'S SEVEN EXPEDITIONS

Zheng He made seven official maritime voyages on behalf of the Ming emperor and conducted at least one solo mission as well.[8] There is uncertainty about Emperor Yongle's motives for sponsoring these maritime missions, which could have been to develop commerce with Southeast Asia and India; to extend China's power and prestige to foreign lands; to find Zhu Yunwen, the Jianwen emperor who had fled after Yongle usurped his throne; or to collect tribute gifts from abroad. The first two motives seem to be the most convincing. Yongle saw China as the central polity in the world and thought that suzerainty as ruler should be recognized by other peoples. The fleets he conceived and authorized to be built to achieve his trade and power objectives consisted of both warships and treasure ships to deliver gifts and return with tribute. He gave the orders to Zheng He while the early Ming capital city was situated in Nanjing, though later in Yongle's reign the capital was moved to Beijing. The larger ships of the fleet were built in the Longjiang shipyards in Nanjing, but many of the other ships were built in Fujian Province, the maritime center of shipbuilding during the earlier Song

Dynasty. The large treasure ships sailed out of the Yangzi River from Nan-jing to Fujian to join the rest of the fleet at Changle near Fuzhou in Fujian, where Zheng He took command of the fleets.

A stone marker in Changle inscribed with accounts of the voyages remains an important record of Zheng He and his expeditions, as many of the official Ming records were destroyed by Qing Dynasty officials when the Ming Dynasty fell in 1644.[9] Only two other stone markers inscribed with records of Zheng He's voyages are known. One was located at Liujiagang[10] near Nanjing, and the third one, the only one found outside of China, was discovered at Galle[11] on the south coast of Sri Lanka. It now is on display at the National Museum in Colombo. Although Zheng He's voyages varied in composition and specific destinations, all seven involved expeditionary forces of between 20,000 and 30,000 people, and they plied routes connecting China and India with many other Eurasian ports of call.

Zheng He's biography in the *Ming Shi*, the official dynastic history of the Ming Dynasty prepared during the succeeding Qing Dynasty, provides a succinct summary of each of the seven voyages and a specific list of the three dozen countries Zheng He visited over the course of three decades. The biography was written by a Qing official and thus reflected the prevalent disdain toward the Ming. It noted, for instance, that "The goods and treasures without name that he acquired were too many to be accounted for, yet they did not make up for the wasteful expenditures of the Middle Kingdom."[12]

A summary of key features of each of the voyages follows, including, for some of the voyages described herein, the *Ming Shi* list of locations visited by Zheng He's fleet. These illustrate the geographic range of these voyages and the familiarity Zheng He had with the peoples and places across Eurasia, which ultimately made possible the projection of China's power during this period.

FIRST VOYAGE (1406–1407)

- Zheng He visited Java, Sumatra, the Malay Peninsula, and India.
- The Majapahit, a Hindu thalassocracy based on Java, had stopped sending tribute to China. While Zheng He's forces were in Java, the

king of Tumapel, a vassal to Majapahit in east Java, "accidentally" killed 170 of Zheng He's men. Tumapel paid 10,000 taels of gold in compensation, without response by the Majapahit Empire.

- The fleet sailed to Calicut in India and erected a stone monument, though its location currently is unknown.
- Zheng He encountered resistance from Chinese pirates led by Chen Yi in Palembang, Sumatra, on his return. He burned ten of their ships and took seven captives.
- Zheng He decided that he would use Malacca on the Malay Peninsula as a forward base for subsequent Ming voyages. He elevated Malacca's status and appointed the chief of Malacca as king. He dispatched smaller squadrons to explore other places in the region, then they reconnoitered in Malacca for the return to China.

SECOND VOYAGE (1407–1409)

- Zheng He sailed with his fleet to Malacca.
- Chang Ch'ien, one of Zheng He's deputies, sailed part of the fleet to Brunei, where he told its king that he would no longer have to pay forty catties of refined camphor to Majapahit.
- A Chinese name was given to the principal mountain and a stone marker was erected.
- The other part of the fleet sailed to Ceylon (Sri Lanka) where Zheng He erected a stone stele in three languages claiming Chinese suzerainty[13] over the island.

THIRD VOYAGE (1409–1411)

- Zheng He's fleet expanded to 27,000 men in 48 ships.
- The fleet was divided into squadrons, and each was given a unique destination. One squadron sailed to the Liuqiu (Ryukyu) Islands, and another visited what is now the Philippines. Other locations visited included Champa (Vietnam); Cambodia; Karimata, Gelam Island, Java, Janggala, Palembang, Sumudra, Aru, Achin, and Bras Island (Indonesia); Tamaing (Burma); Malacca, Pahang, and Lankasuka (Malaysia); Pule Condore, Maldives; Nicobar, Kaulam, Cochin, La-sa (Lar), and Bengala (India); Ceylon (Sri Lanka); Hormuz, Dzufar,

Aden, Mecca and Brawa (Persian Gulf, Red Sea, and Arabia); and Mogadishu (on the African east coast).

- The squadron under Zheng He's personal command was returning from the Red Sea ports when it came under attack by 50,000 Singhalese troops commanded by Alagakkonara, the king of Ceylon, whom Zheng He captured and brought back to Nanjing. Zheng He's forces replaced the Singhalese king with a docile prince willing to acknowledge overlordship of the Chinese emperor Yongle.

FOURTH VOYAGE (1413–1415)

- The fleet visited Malacca and then proceeded to Champa, Sunda, Pahang, and Kelantan (Malaysia), crossed the Bay of Bengal to Calicut, Lambri, and Cochin in South India, and then continued to the Maldives and Hormuz.
- On the return voyage, Zheng He intervened in the internal affairs of Achin (Aceh) in northern Sumatra, where Sekander had usurped the throne. He was taken to Nanjing in chains by Zheng He's forces and executed by Yongle.

FIFTH VOYAGE (1417–1419)

- The fleet visited Malacca, Champa, Sumadra, Java, Pahang, Palembang, Calicut, Ceylon, Lambri, La-sa (Lar), Cochin, Maldives, Aden, Hormuz, Malinde, Mogadishu, and Brawa.
- A mountain in the south Indian state of Cochin was given a Chinese name, providing evidence of China's influence through these recurrent voyages and port visits.

SIXTH VOYAGE (1421–1422)

- This voyage included what were by now routine and relatively uneventful calls at Malacca, Aru, Calicut, Lambri, Ceylon, Maldives, La-sa (Lar), Cambay, Aden, Mogadishu, Dzufar, and Brawa.
- British naval officer Gavin Menzies has asserted that a squadron of this expedition sailed around Africa's Cape of Good Hope, proceeding to the Caribbean and beyond to points north including Newport, Rhode Island. He claims that a still-existing stone tower in

Newport was erected by these forces and modeled on the Quanzhou, Fujian, lighthouse. His theory that Zheng He's expedition discovered the New World in 1421, seventy-one years before Columbus, has not convinced many scholars.[14]

ZHENG HE'S MISSION WITHOUT A FLEET (1424)

- Zheng He sailed alone without an accompanying fleet on a mission to Palembang to appoint a successor to deceased governor Shi Jinqing, his son (or daughter according to Ma Huan) Shi chi-sun.
- Emperor Yongle had died by the time Zheng He returned to China. The new emperor, Hongxi, the son of Yongle, was advised by Minister Xia Yuanji to discontinue Zheng He's expeditions to the "Western Ocean." The capital had been moved from Nanjing to Beijing in 1420, and Zheng He had been appointed the commander of the Nanjing garrison. Hongxi died in 1425 after ruling for one year, and Yongle's grandson Xuande succeeded him. Emperor Xuande was cautious, waiting until after Xia Yuanji died in 1430 before issuing a decree commanding Zheng He go to sea again for his seventh and final voyage.

SEVENTH VOYAGE (1431–1433)

- The 27,550-man fleet, similar in size to earlier expedition fleets, visited Siam, Palembang, Malacca, Aru, Cochin, Calicut, Ceylon, Lambri, La-sa, Cambay, Maldives, Hormuz, Aden, Dzufar, Mecca, Mogadishu, Brawa, and Juba.
- In Siam, the Chinese envoy strongly protested to the king of Siam for interfering with the ambassador of Malacca to China.
- Some sources assert that Zheng He perished at sea off the coast of Calicut in 1433. Other accounts affirm that he returned to Nanjing and passed away in 1435.

MA HUAN

Three of Zheng He's voyages were chronicled by Ma Huan (1380–1460), who had joined for these three voyages. His fifteenth-century account is a resource that allows an understanding of the routes taken and ports visited by Zheng He. Ma Huan was born in Zhejiang Province. Although Ma is a common Chinese Muslim surname, he was not born a Muslim but converted to Islam when he was young and learned Arabic as well as Chinese. He traveled with Zheng He on his fourth, sixth, and seventh voyages and completed an account now available in translation of all three expeditions called "The Overall Survey of the Ocean's Shores" (*Yingyai Shenglan*) in 1451, nine years before his death.[15] Many hand-copied and printed copies of his work circulated during both the Ming and Qing Dynasties. Ma Huan's account is a primary source on the history of the Ming Dynasty, Southeast Asia, and India of that period, as well as of naval/maritime exploration. Aside from recording the extensive and complex geography of the expedition routes, Ma Huan also made important observations about the politics, economy, local customs, weather conditions, environment, and punishment methods for criminals of the many places the fleet visited. During the seventh voyage, several Muslims on the expedition went with Ma Huan on a pilgrimage to Mecca. Given his route to Mecca, it is likely he visited Oman and Aden on this final voyage.[16]

Ma Huan described many places in great detail, including Malacca, Calicut, and Mecca. Ma Huan referred to Mecca as the country of the square, a reference to the Ka'ba or "cube house." He was part of a squadron that had traveled from Calicut to Mecca separately from the main fleet, which had sailed on to Hormuz. Ma Huan reported that the journey took three moons, or 2,500 sea miles, about 26 sea miles per day, which translates approximately to 1 knot. He noted the religious nature of the people, commenting that they followed religious law in marriages and funeral rites, that they were "stalwart and fine-looking," and that they spoke Arabic. Although some analysts fault the details of his description of buildings and distances, his description of the tomb of Ismail near the Ka'ba as made of green stone parallels that of Ibn Battuta a century earlier. Ma Huan also mentioned that Medina is a day away, although it is actually three hundred miles north of Mecca, or a caravan distance of ten days away. Seven men were appointed by the eunuch Hung Pao, one of Zheng He's commanders, to make the journey from Calicut to Mecca, then back to Beijing. The seven brought gifts of porcelain and other articles to those in Mecca, and returned to the capital Beijing with an accurate representation of the "Heavenly Hall" (the Ka'ba). They were accompanied by envoys from Mecca bearing local gifts to convey to the emperor's court. The visit to Mecca must have had a special meaning for Ma Huan and his fellow Muslim travelers. Although also a Muslim from birth himself, Zheng He left no record of having been part of this pilgrimage to Mecca on this or any of his other voyages.

MALACCA: PARAMESWARA AND A WESTERN OCEAN FORWARD BASE

Zheng He visited Malacca during his first voyage and set up there what was essentially a forward base for all of his subsequent expeditions. Malacca was strategically located as a port of call for Zheng He's fleets as they sailed through the strait between the west coast of the Malay Peninsula and the east coast of Sumatra. Although Malacca is a sleepy town now compared to its apex as a trade port during the fifteenth century, memories of Zheng He have been reinforced by exhibits in three museums that document the complex history of the region. In the early fifteenth-century period, the supreme leader of Malacca was Parameswara. Descended from Sumatran Srivijayan nobility, Parameswara was attacked by the Javanese Majapahit, so he moved to today's Singapore, formerly called Temasek, and established himself as the Buddhist Raja of Singapura. In 1398, Majapahit attacked Singapura, and Parameswara sought a safe haven farther north along the coast. Resting against a tree, he was amused to see a small mouse deer kick his hunting dog down the bank and into the river. He took this as a good omen for the spot where he sat, and thus decided to create a settlement in that location, which became Malacca.

Parameswara was ensconced in Malacca when Zheng He arrived on his first voyage in 1405. Zheng He built a relationship with Parameswara, who granted him permission to build warehouses on the north bank of the Malacca River near where it flowed into the strait connecting the China Seas with the Indian Ocean. Parameswara agreed to a tributary relationship with China, and in return gained a powerful Chinese friend who shielded him from the predations of stronger local kings in Siam and Java. An important moment arrived in 1409 when Parameswara married a Muslim woman, after which the ruling class began converting to Islam, although Parameswara maintained his titles as both a Buddhist raja and a Muslim sultan. In 1411, Parameswara, together with his wife, son, and a royal party of 540 individuals traveled to China with Zheng He. Parameswara paid homage to the Yongle emperor, who acknowledged him as the rightful ruler of Malacca and gave him a seal, silk, and a yellow umbrella. In 1414, it was reported in the Chinese chronicles that Parameswara had died at about age seventy. The strong tributary relationship between China and Malacca, however, remained intact. Malacca became the major trading entrepôt in the region, surpassing Calicut during the fifteenth century before the Portuguese arrived in 1511. It prospered, attracting Muslim traders from throughout the world, and it became an Islamic center that facilitated the dissemination of Islam throughout the region.

As a Muslim, Zheng He likely was sympathetic to the expanding Muslim influence in Malacca. What was immediately more important to him, however, was the ability to use the area granted to him in Malacca for developing warehouse space that he could use for both distributing gifts and collecting tribute, as well as to stock the immense supplies necessary to provide the logistical base for subsequent massive fleet operations.

The Cheng Ho Cultural Museum in Malacca is devoted specifically to Zheng He and his voyages. The building itself sits in the *guanchang* "warehouse" area, on a site of about ten acres that served as a logistical forward base for Zheng He's voyages.[17] There are references to lesser *guanchang* bases in Samudera, Calicut, and Hormuz, but the Malacca *guanchang* appears to have been the most important due to its strategic location at the southern end of the Malacca Strait. In fact, it served as the chief trading and navigational base for Zheng He outside of China. Excavations in the Malacca *guanchang* area have located several wells of Chinese design from the early Ming period, although competing theories exist for exactly what stood on the site six hundred years ago and whether there are other locations in and around Malacca that might have been used for warehouses. The evidence is strong that Malacca can claim to be the most lustrous of the pearls in the "string of pearls" that were Zheng He's primary ports of call in the Indian Ocean.

CONFLICTS IN PALEMBANG, SRI LANKA, AND ACEH

In today's Chinese narrative, Zheng He's voyages have been interpreted as a model of benign interaction with countries and peoples of the China Seas and Indian Ocean. Popular enthusiasm in China for the public celebration of his journeys developed in 2005 around the six hundredth anniversary of Zheng He's first voyage. The anniversary was perceived as a chance to show how the historical example of Zheng He could be seen as a model for China's "Peaceful Rise" in the twenty-first century. In July 2004, Xu Zu-Yuan, the vice minister of communications for the People's Republic of China,[18] stated, "These were thus friendly diplomatic activities. During the overall course of the seven voyages to the Western Ocean, Zheng He did not occupy a single piece of land, establish any fortress, or seize any wealth from other countries. In the commercial and trade activities, he adopted the practice of giving more than he received, and thus he was welcomed and lauded by the people of the various countries along his routes."

But several incidents during the voyages, as well as the very nature of the fleet and expeditions, may contradict the perception that these voyages were entirely peaceful. Aside from the "shock and awe" visual impact that Zheng He's flotilla must have had when arriving at ports throughout Asia, Zheng He's fleet consisted of a large number of ships, some of them huge by any standard, carrying many thousands of soldiers capable of defending the fleet or violently confronting any land forces that opposed their landing parties. Accounts of the voyages describe several violent encounters, including armed conflicts in Palembang in southeast Sumatra, in Kotte near Colombo in Sri Lanka, and in Aceh in northwest Sumatra.[19]

In 1407, upon arriving in Palembang Old Port during the return portion of his first voyage, Zheng He quelled a plot by Chen Zuyi, a local Chinese ruler described in the accounts as a pirate, to attack his maritime army. During this altercation, Ming records list five thousand of Chen's men killed, ten of his ships burnt, and seven ships captured. Zheng He apprehended Chen Zuyi and two others and brought them to China, where they were beheaded.[20] Due to the large number of Chinese from Fujian and Guangdong in Sumatra, Geoff Wade argued that the Palembang clash was a "pacification superintendency;" in other words, a proto-colonial arrangement in which Zheng He replaced the insurrectionist Chen Zuyi with a local superintendent appointed as the local ruler to represent the Ming state. According to this perspective, by removing Chen Zuyi, Zheng He was involved in an internal Chinese police action rather than an attack on a foreign entity.

In 1411, after arriving in Sri Lanka on his third expedition, Zheng He encountered armed resistance by Alagakkonara, the king of Ceylon, who attacked the Chinese forces with about 50,000 Sinhalese troops.[21] Zheng He organized a military invasion of the royal city of Kotte, destroyed the military opposition, and captured the king and members of his family. A few ancient red rock walls of Kotte are still visible southeast of Colombo, spurring recollection of this history. Zheng He took Alagakkonara and family back to the Ming court in Nanjing. Emperor Yongle appointed a Sinhalese official who had accompanied Alagakkonara as the new king of Ceylon as "a puppet ruler to replace the king," a clear regime change strategy.[22]

On his fourth voyage in 1415, Zheng He intervened in a civil war in Samudera, located in Aceh on Sumatra.[23] Sekander had usurped the throne of a Samudera king sympathetic to the Ming, so once again Zheng He's forces became involved in a regime change operation. Sekander was brought to Nanjing in chains and executed. Wade again provides a point of view skeptical of the entirely peaceful intent of Zheng He's voyages. "Again we see an instance of the maritime expedition acting mainly as a military force in an attempt to impose a 'Pax Ming' on what we now know as Southeast Asia and the Indian Ocean."[24] This action, as all of these examples illustrate, contradicts the diplomatic narrative now advanced by the People's Republic of China that espouses

Ming history as the precedent for China's modern posture of noninterference in the affairs of other states. Although Zheng He's seven expeditions had peaceful objectives, these three examples show that Zheng He and the early Ming were not averse to engaging in military options and violence when it suited their purposes. Other examples of violence during the expeditions include conflict in Java in 1407, in Burma in 1409, and a record that the men of Cathay "inflicted no small slaughter on the people of Calicut."[25] Moreover, the deployment of such a large fleet over such a large expanse of time and geography had a dimension of "gunboat diplomacy" that cannot be ignored. Thus, using the precedent of Zheng He and his voyages as a historical example of China's current peaceful international intentions is an argument that has significant qualifications.

Life and Legacy of Zheng He

In addition to the preceding review of Zheng He's seven voyages, the following provides details regarding Zheng He's background, important influences in his life, how he came to be entrusted with leading the early Ming maritime program, and what legacy he left behind.

FAMILY BACKGROUND, TRAINING, AND SERVICE

Zheng He, originally named Ma He, was born in 1371 into a Muslim family whose ancestors had served the Mongols in China's southwest Yunnan Province. His birth came three years after the founding of the Ming Dynasty by Zhu Yuanzhang, the Hongwu emperor. An illustrious ancestor (Sayyid Ajjal Shams al-Din Omar) had been governor of Yunnan during the early Mongol Yuan Dynasty. The family took the Sinicized name Ma, which was often used by Chinese Muslims as a link to the name Muhammad. Both Ma He's grandfather and father were *hajji*, which meant they had made the pilgrimage to Mecca. The Ming conquest of Yunnan took place in 1381, more than a decade after it had founded its capital in Nanjing in 1368. Ma He's father Ma Hajji was killed in the struggle, but his son was captured. His punishment for being the offspring of an enemy, typical for captured young males in that period, was castration. When his health recovered from the ordeal, Ma He was sent to serve in the household of Zhu Di, the prince of Yan, who later became the Yongle emperor in 1402. In the period before he became emperor, Zhu Di came to trust Ma He and made sure he had a good education, unusual for eunuchs, who were more often considered to be untrustworthy. During his service in the prince's household, the Muslim Ma was given the Buddhist name of Sanbao, which reflected an aspect of Zhu Di's traditional Chinese embrace of Buddhism, Confucianism, and Daoism.

Zhu Di trained Ma He through his twenties in military matters. After the founder of the Ming Dynasty, Emperor Hongwu, died in 1398, a struggle for succession ensued. Zhu Di, brother of Hongwu, opposed his nephew, Hongwu's son, taking the Ming throne. The nephew became the Jianwen emperor for four years until he was deposed by Zhu Di, who became the third Ming emperor Yongle. Ma He's involvement in this struggle included successfully defending the Zhenglunba Reservoir in Beiping in 1399, and he assisted Zhu Di in capturing the capital Nanjing in 1402.[26] In 1404, the Yongle emperor bestowed the name Zheng on Ma He in perpetuity because of his loyalty and successful defense of the Zhenglunba Reservoir. A year later, Yongle ordered Zheng He to set out on the first of his expeditions to the Western Ocean. During the period of his voyages, Zheng He was given the titles grand director and later chief envoy. In 1431, his title *sanbao taijian* combined his informal Buddhist name Sanbao with the title of grand director.

The circumstances of Zheng He's death remain obscure. Some believe he died during his final voyage and was buried at sea in 1433 near Calicut in India, though others believe he returned to China before passing away. There is a tomb for Zheng He near the Longjiang shipyards in Nanjing, with a museum that focuses on his expeditions rather than presenting a personal biography.

END OF THE EARLY MING EXPEDITIONS AND THEIR LEGACY

By the end of the seventh voyage in 1433, Zheng He had achieved an unprecedented, thirty-year-long period of hegemony for the Ming state in the maritime domain of the China Seas and Indian Ocean. He had brought back more than forty envoys with tribute gifts to the Ming emperor, as well as prisoners such as insurgent Chen Zuyi and King Alagakkonara of Sri Lanka. He had helped anoint Parameswara as king of Malacca and established a forward base for his Western Ocean operations in the *guanchang* on the north bank of the Malacca River. He protected Malacca from the kings of Siam (Thailand) and Majapahit on Java, two of the strongest states in the region, which were unable to challenge China in the South China Sea and he set up a Chinese governor in Palembang.

With the death of Zheng He and the failure of the Ming emperors to support expeditions after 1433, China's maritime influence in the Western Ocean diminished, as the attention of the throne turned to quelling the Mongols on the northwestern border and expanding the Great Wall, depleting any funds that could have been allocated for naval purposes. Ming influence in the China Seas, however, continued well into the seventeenth century through the maritime operations of many traders. These included the family of Zheng Zhilong and his son Zheng Chenggong, who created a business empire that competed successfully with the Portuguese and Dutch from Japan to Java and even extended the influence of Ming Dynasty remnants in southern China after the Qing had taken control of the north.

The legacy of Zheng He was largely forgotten during the Qing Dynasty, which destroyed many of the Ming records, until reformist intellectual Liang Qichao published a *Biography of Our Homeland's Great Navigator, Zheng He* in 1904. Of greater recent significance, the modern-day government of the People's Republic of China has used the life and legacy of Zheng He as a symbol of China's successful maritime history. Chinese president Xi Jinping referred to Zheng He as a precedent and role model for China's Maritime Silk Road in 2013 when he announced his signature foreign policy, the Belt and Road Initiative (BRI). Portrayed as a peaceful emissary, images of Zheng He appear in many of the Eurasian places that Zheng He visited six centuries ago, from the mosque in Surabaya to the train station in Mombassa.

Conclusions from the Early Ming Maritime Experience

This section includes observations on the nature of the early Ming maritime experience, a survey of lessons that may be taken from study of this historical episode, and a comment on the relevance of Zheng He's voyages to Chinese policy in the twenty-first century.

PEACEFUL INTERACTION, COLONIALISM, OR VIOLENCE?

During the three-decade period of Zheng He's voyages, the early Ming state exerted maritime hegemony over the China Seas and Indian Ocean, the region referred to today as the Indo-Pacific. Zheng He employed a variety of techniques to interact with local leaders and their people, including peaceful outreach, proto-colonial submission, and violent conflict, demonstrating a range of possible policy options open to a hegemonic power. From an analytical point of view, Zheng He exercised all three of these options successfully as the situations and conditions warranted to achieve the empire's objectives. Most analysts agree that these were primarily to expand China's central position in the world order by developing tributary relations with the coastal polities of the time along the China Seas and Indian Ocean, thereby supplementing longstanding tributary relationships with Korea, the Ryukyu kingdom, and Vietnam.[27]

The expeditions were successful: envoys were brought back to Nanjing from about three dozen places bearing tribute for the Ming emperor. Some believe that Yongle most loved the tributary giraffe brought back from East Africa, a possible incarnation of the mythical *qilin*, a legendary creature said to appear with the arrival of illustrious Chinese leaders. On the voyages, records indicate that the bulk of interactions followed a pattern of largely cooperative dealings between local leaders and Zheng He and his subordinate envoys, including several other fellow eunuchs. These relationships produced a steady stream of tributary envoys who arrived in Nanjing bearing gifts for the emperor from Eurasian and African places where Zheng He had visited and established ties.

The accounts of Zheng He's voyages, however, also provide examples of proto-colonial hierarchical relationships. Zheng He's appointment of a governor in Palembang and in Luzon, areas where large numbers of Chinese settlers lived, has been interpreted by some scholars as examples of colonial-style practices later followed by the Portuguese, Spanish, Dutch, British, and French European powers when they arrived in subsequent centuries to Asia after the early Ming period of Zheng He's voyages. In a more subtle exertion of control, Zheng He ensured Malacca's security vis-à-vis other regional entities by inserting the power of the Ming state between Malacca and the nearby kingdoms of Ayutthaya in Siam and Majapahit in Java. This action put Malacca in the position of a highly compliant tributary state, reminiscent of China's relationship over the centuries with Korea. Although China did not administer Malacca directly as it did Palembang, it controlled Malacca's destiny by securing its foreign relations. This made it difficult for Malacca to be anything but highly cooperative with regard to Zheng He's need for a logistical staging base through the creation and use of a large *guanchang* warehouse area occupying part of central Malacca. Thus, implicit coercion through proto-colonial relationship building was a component of Zheng He's toolkit beyond creating mutually beneficial peaceful relationships.

When the options for mutually beneficial interactions or proto-colonial relationships failed, Zheng He resorted to violent means when necessary to achieve the objectives of the Ming Empire. The clash with, consequent capture of, and execution of Chen Zuyi in Palembang precluded Chen's domination of the Malacca Strait in 1407. Similarly, the conflicts with Alagakkonara resulted in his capture and regime change in Ceylon in 1411. The intervention in a civil war in Aceh resulted in the capture and execution of Sekander in 1415. There are a number of other examples of Zheng He's use of military violence during the voyages as well, although these incidents were fewer in number than the many peaceful encounters.

Maritime Strategic and Tactical Lessons

The early Ming voyages of Zheng He are instructive in providing useful lessons for understanding premodern Eurasian maritime history.

LOCAL KNOWLEDGE OF NATURAL PHENOMENA

The early Ming fleets relied on extensive maritime knowledge and skills accrued during the Southern Song period when southeastern China began a cycle of sea power that continued into the Ming period. Each of Zheng He's voyages began in the month of December, with the knowledge that this was the beginning of the northeast monsoon season, which would take the fleets through the China Seas and into the Western Ocean. Typically, they would spend a year in the Indian Ocean before returning on the second summer southwest monsoon that would push the fleet back to China, completing a pattern of two-year voyage cycles.

ADVANTAGES IN MILITARY TECHNOLOGY

China's ships were seaworthy with their internal separate bulkhead compartments, and Chinese navigation skills, honed with the use of charts and compass, were well developed. The ships were not fast, having limited sail area compared to their large hull displacements, but that gave them the advantage of carrying large numbers of troops and supplies. Zheng He's military encounters during his voyages primarily were land encounters rather than naval encounters, so the large numbers of troops carried on the ships were a major advantage that allowed the Ming to prevail in any clashes that occurred.

CONTINENTAL VS. MARITIME IDENTITIES

These voyages provide evidence that during the early Ming period Emperor Yongle undertook serious study of China as a hybrid land and sea power. With a historical legacy for its continental empire, China was better known as a land power. Zheng He, as Yongle's maritime emissary, developed the precedent for China to become a maritime power. Thus Yongle was successful during his lifetime in developing China as a hybrid land and sea power. China's ability to successfully project power by land and by sea during the Ming period is an example today, as it was based upon the confluence of national leadership, vision, and will and was combined with the allocation of appropriate talent to both the continental and maritime domains.

DEEPLY FELT NATIONAL IDENTITIES

Although Zheng He's family antecedents had served the previous Mongol administration with distinction, Zheng He appears to have developed a thorough Ming identity through his special relationship with Zhu Di, who became the supreme representative of the Ming as the Emperor Yongle. It was, however, a complex identity, which may have helped him understand and relate to those he met across his far-flung maritime voyages. Zheng He's Muslim identity allowed him to understand and relate to the communities in Malaya, Java, and Sumatra that were experiencing a transition to Islam. It was also useful in communicating with Muslims in Ceylon, as well as in Arabia and East Africa. Zheng He's Buddhist identity helped in connecting with cultural currents in Ceylon and India, and his Taoist inclinations through the worship of Mazu firmly bonded him to the community of Chinese sailors, especially those from Fujian and Guangdong, who were the most numerous Chinese sailors in the China Seas all the way south to Java and Sumatra.

MILITARY LEADERSHIP

Zheng He was a highly capable military commander who proved his worth, ability, loyalty, and close working relationship with Zhu Di, the Yongle emperor, during his campaign to seize the throne from his nephew. The emperor provided the means for Zheng He to bring overwhelming force on all of the expeditions to the Western Oceans, which, along with competent command, ensured that Zheng He prevailed in the armed clashes that took place during the expeditions.

RELATIVE POWER RELATIONS

With his enormous fleets, Zheng He was able to project overwhelming force on all of his expeditions to the Western Oceans. The Ming allocated sufficient resources to equip Zheng He with a preponderance of ships, manpower, and supplies that demonstrated to all those along the voyage routes the strength and will of the Yongle emperor. This substantial fleet infrastructure was complemented by Zheng He's competence and the trust that the emperor had in him. Thus, Zheng He was well-positioned to prevail in both peaceful interactions and armed clashes that took place during his expeditions. Zheng He had no significant losses in military and nonmilitary encounters during his voyages.

ALLIANCE RELATIONS

Zheng He established a symbiotic working relationship with Parameswara, the king of Malacca. He provided security for Malacca against stronger local powers in Siam and Java, while Malacca provided what amounted to a forward logistical base at the entry to the Western Ocean for these early Ming expeditions. The relationship worked smoothly with mutual benefit throughout the entire period of the voyages.

RELATIONSHIP OF MARITIME ECONOMIC SUCCESS TO MARITIME MILITARY SUCCESS

From the Ming side, a primary motivation for Zheng He's voyages was driven by the desire for recognition of the Chinese emperor's preeminence. Yongle desired receiving tribute as a symbol of China's centrality in the world order, which may have outweighed the economic rationality of comparative advantage in trade. Dozens of envoys came to Nanjing with Zheng He bearing tribute, indicating the success of the voyages in relation to the tributary motivation. In the end, the cost of the voyages after Zheng He's death may have contributed to their cancellation, as the state treasury was reallocated to military operations to fight the Mongols and Manchus in the north.

IMPORTANCE OF HISTORICAL AND CURRENT KNOWLEDGE

The routes and viability of trade through the China Seas and across the Indian Ocean were historically well-known to Ming seafarers. The extensive use of these routes has been noted in the earlier accounts of the Cholas, the Song, and the Mongols. A great deal of knowledge continued to be developed with each of Zheng He's voyages, especially as he sent squadrons to gather knowledge in separate corners of the island archipelagoes, as well as to differing ports of the Bay of Bengal and the Arabian Sea.

LEANING FORWARD: THE MARITIME SILK ROAD PARABLE

Of the case studies considered in this book, the early Ming case of Zheng He is the best known both within China and globally. Chinese reflect on the life and legacy of Zheng He today as an example of China's place in the world, especially in the maritime context. President Xi Jinping announced the inception of his plan to model twenty-first-century Chinese foreign policy on the model of, and as the resurrection of, ancient land and sea silk roads, with Zheng He as a central example from the fifteenth century.

Zheng He's voyages may be seen as a parable for China's current BRI policy stance toward projecting its naval power in the twenty-first century. The complexity of Zheng He's differing relationships with the dozens of entities he encountered on his voyages—varying from peaceful to proto-colonial to violent—can be likened to the range of responses to China's BRI program, which are also complex. Thus far, the first years of China's BRI policy have been characterized by peaceful interactions and occasionally by proto-colonial relationships. But Chinese military capability and inherent options are growing quickly, and it remains to be seen whether military violence may occur in Eurasia along the routes of the BRI. China's potential hegemonic power has been expanding rapidly, but an important difference from the time of Zheng He is that China now has to contemplate interaction with the United States and its global hegemonic power. Zheng He and the early Ming exerted hegemonic force without a peer competitor, as European powers had not arrived on the scene. Consideration of Zheng He's fifteenth-century voyages as a parable to provoke thought regarding China's twenty-first-century Maritime Silk Road is useful and stimulating for maritime strategists.

FOUR

Kunjali Marakkar Naval Resistance to the Portuguese on the Malabar Coast

Kunjali Marakkar, Sixteenth Century

The Arabian Sea before the Europeans: Calicut as the Center of Trade

The Mishkal Mosque, one of three mosques in an active Muslim neighborhood in Calicut (Kozhikode) on the Malabar coast of India, is about 600 years old. It was founded in the fourteenth century by a renowned trader and shipowner, Nakhuda Mishkal, from Yemen. The other two mosques, 900 and 1,100 years old respectively, also were founded by Yemenis involved in the Arabian Sea trade. Notices at the Miskhal Mosque indicate that the mosque was designed and built by skilled craftsmen in the traditional architectural style of the region. It was partially destroyed by the Portuguese commander Alfonso Albuquerque on January 3, 1510. The zamorin (Calicut's Hindu ruler) was cordial with Muslims at the time and donated wood to make necessary mosque repairs. Both local and foreign students still study at the Mishkal Mosque today.

Why and how did these Muslims settle in Calicut, more than a thousand miles of open sea away from their homes in the Arabian Peninsula? The Arab merchant impulse included sea as well as land trade, and the Arab traders came in search of Indian spices with sailing craft designed and built for open water. The hull planks of Arab dhows were traditionally sewn together with vegetable fiber rather than fastened with metal.[1]

Over time, the sailors learned to use the monsoons winds to cross the Arabian Sea, reducing the passage to a direct one thousand miles of blue water, rather than the two-thousand-mile coastal journey north along the coasts of Persia and India.

The Indians embraced trade with the Arab merchants wholeheartedly. At the time the Arabs arrived, the Indian subcontinent was ruled by a variety of local rulers, the most powerful of whom on the west coast of India was the zamorin of Calicut. He encouraged all trade, including with the Arabs from the west and with the Chinese and others from the east. For a sustainable fee, the zamorin encouraged them to come to Calicut to conduct their business, and he supplied factory space for the traders. Calicut became the central trading depot in the Indian Ocean. Peaceable, open trade benefited all. Europeans, most usually Venetians, participated in this trade, mainly to obtain spices, most notably Malabar pepper. They followed combined sea and land routes through the Mediterranean and then through Arab lands to the Indian Ocean.[2]

Calicut was not the only port on the Malabar coast. Cochin (Kochi), about 118 miles south of Calicut, began to develop as a port in the late fourteenth century, because Muziris, the main port on that segment of the coast, had been destroyed in 1341 by a natural disaster involving an earthquake and floods.

The Portuguese Arrival in the Indian Ocean

While most southern Europeans on the north shore of the Mediterranean Sea spent the fifteenth century focused on the rising power of the Ottomans in the eastern Mediterranean, the Portuguese concentrated instead on developing sailing technology to use the Atlantic Ocean as a route around Africa to get to the riches of India. Once there, the Portuguese thought they would ally with the legendary Christian king Prester John to obtain his support in lands where Muslim Arabs and Ottomans already had a continental foothold. The sea route from Portugal around Africa to India, however, was a difficult one that took many decades to develop.

HENRY THE NAVIGATOR AND THE SEA ROAD TO THE INDIAN OCEAN

During the fifteenth century, Henry the Navigator guided the Portuguese effort to find their way to India. The wind and the currents of the Atlantic made it difficult to get around the bulge of Africa's west coast. In fact, Portuguese ships had to sail west all the way to South America, then back east to Africa to get around the Cape of Good Hope.[3] Gradually, the Portuguese made their way down the west coast of Africa, sailing with the currents all the way to Brazil before finding the reverse gyre currents to take them back to southern Africa. Henry's explorers had found Cape Verde in 1444 and Cape Palmas on the bulge of Africa in 1460. In the ensuing decades after Henry's death, they made it to Principe and Sao Tome in 1471, and to the mouth of the Congo River in 1483. Finally, Bartolomeu Dias zigzagged west and then east through Antarctic latitudes to make it in 1488 around the Stormy Cape, renamed the Cape of Good Hope. The stepping-off point into the Indian Ocean from southern Africa was reached seven decades after the first early foray to Madeira, culminating in a remarkable effort in the history of exploration.

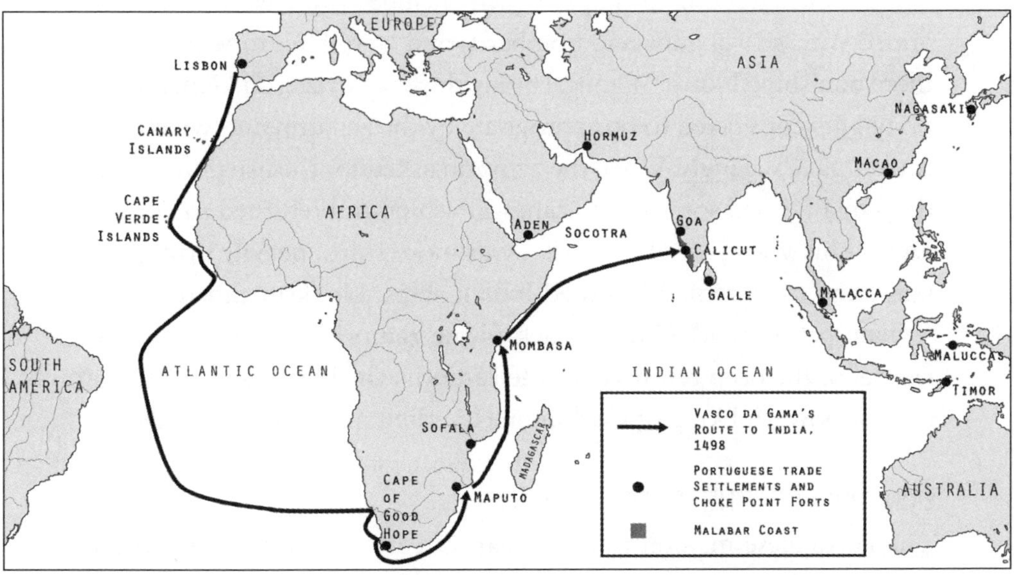

MAP 4.1 Portuguese entry into the Indian Ocean and locations of choke-point control
Adapted by Jamie Rhode from Roger Crowley, Conquerors: How Portugal Forged the First Global Empire *(New York: Random House, 2015), xiv–xv*

Vasco da Gama did not leave Portugal to follow in Dias' wake until 1497. Going beyond Dias, he sailed around the Cape of Good Hope, north along the east coast of Africa, and finally across the Arabian Sea to reach Calicut on the Malabar coast of India in May 1498. Although da Gama arrived later in Calicut than Columbus arrived in what he called the Indies, his advantage was that he actually had arrived in India. The Portuguese were new to the Indian Ocean and wanted to be part of the well-established sea trade there. Da Gama was unsuccessful in establishing a trade treaty with the zamorin of Calicut in his first voyage, as was Cabral during the second Portuguese voyage in 1500. Instead, Cabral established a factory trading entrepôt in the Kingdom of Cochin on the Malabar coast to the south of Calicut. Da Gama returned on his second voyage, the third Portuguese expedition, in 1502.[4]

The record is clear that the peaceful maritime relations of the Arabian Sea became conflictual with the advent of the Portuguese, for they rejected the rules of trade interaction that had been established for centuries by the traders operating in Calicut and other smaller ports along the Malabar coast. Moreover, the Portuguese had the upper hand in terms of size and strength of ships, which included caravels and carracks armed with swivel guns and bombards and were built to withstand the more punishing North Atlantic. During the first voyage, da Gama did not bring gifts considered to be appropriate by the zamorin and which other traders gave willingly. When the zamorin asked for the usual trading fee, da Gama burned some of the zamorin's ships and returned to Portugal. During his voyage, Cabral came with more ships, heavily armed with guns, and captured and burned Indian ships. He dismembered Indian seamen before sending them back to the zamorin. Nevertheless, being careful of the deep resources of the zamorin, the Portuguese allied with the less powerful king of Cochin one hundred miles south of Calicut.

CONTROL OF THE SPICE TRADE

The Portuguese mission to the Indian Ocean was motivated predominantly by the search for spices, although the religious ideology of the Catholic Church was also an incentive for the voyages. In the search for Christian allies and converts, Vasco da Gama and other Portuguese explorers hoped to find the legendary Christian king Prester John, rumored at that time to be the king of Abyssinia. King Manuel I of Portugal had expelled the Muslim minority from Portugal in 1496, and the need for Christian allies in the Indian Ocean, where trade was controlled by Muslims, was regarded as a high priority. When da Gama arrived in Calicut, he was aware that Muslim traders controlled the port. Initially, he thought the Hindu zamorin might be a Christian king following unknown Eastern practices. There was, however, no mistaking the Muslims, making the development of trading practices more difficult.

Although religious ideology played a role in Portuguese motivations, the spice trade was predominant. Europeans had acquired a taste for spices from the east, most prominently black pepper from Malabar. It drove the spice trade in the Indian Ocean, even as silver and sugar became the trade drivers in the Pacific and Atlantic Oceans, respectively. For two centuries, Venice had controlled the supply of Asian spices into the European market through its maritime dominance in the eastern Mediterranean. From there, Venice maintained links to Arab and Ottoman waterways through the Red Sea and Persian Gulf that tied into the great Indian Ocean trading network. By circling around Africa by 1500, Portugal established a second route to the Indian Ocean, one it hoped would lead to a Portuguese monopoly over the spice trade in their competition with Venetian and Muslim traders.

What became the Portuguese trade war with Muslims in the Indian Ocean was all the more virulent because of the intense religious divide between them. The zamorin of Calicut sat geographically at the center of the Indian Ocean trade routes connecting to Aden, the entrepôt for the Arab world and Europe, and to Quanzhou, the entrepôt serving China. The zamorin was religiously tolerant and accepted participants of all religions into the trade, whether they be Hindu, Muslim, Christian, or Jew. There was order and organization in his port, and for a modest fee, open trade had led to general prosperity. From the moment the Portuguese arrived in Calicut, their refusal to participate in the zamorin's trade system and their outright attacks on Muslim sea traders led to ongoing conflict, notwithstanding the accumulation of twenty rooms of pepper worth "a very great sum," a volume not surpassed until 1517, at India House in Lisbon.[5]

Despite their impressive maritime skills, unparalleled ship technology, and strategic genius controlling the choke points of the Indian Ocean, which thereby created a "Portuguese Lake," the Portuguese were unable to impose a monopoly on the pepper trade in the Indian Ocean. They never came close to achieving a monopoly; they only controlled about 10 percent of the pepper trade at the peak of Portuguese power.[6] Two major factors thwarted Portuguese pepper trade ambitions. Complexities in the trading system involved both the Malabar economy in which the Por-tuguese sought to buy pepper and the larger distribution networks throughout the Arabian Sea and Bay of Bengal. The Hindu zamorin's navy, competently commanded by four generations of Muslim Kunjali Marakkar, also created problems for the Portuguese.

The structure of the pepper trade had several levels of complexity, all of which were difficult for the Portuguese to control.[7] On the Malabar coast, largely today's state of Kerala, the pepper trade included three levels of business involvement: inland producers of pepper, middlemen who bought and warehoused the pepper away from the coast, and those who ran the port markets. The Portuguese were unable to establish relations to buy directly from the pepper growers, so they had to rely on the warehouse middlemen who sold in the ports to the highest bidders. Outside Calicut, the Portuguese had more presence in Cochin and Cannanore, where they had factories to store pepper for shipment to Europe. Finding an effective business position within the structure of producers, warehousers, and port purchasers was a challenge for the Portuguese. As port purchasers, they were not in the best position to establish a monopoly.

Another level of complexity beyond the trading business on the Malabar coast involved competing markets. Aside from European interest in pepper, the spice was in high demand in both the Chinese and Middle Eastern markets, with the Chinese buying about twice as much as the Arabs. The Portuguese wanted to purchase below market prices, so Malabar pepper suppliers preferred to sell Arab and Chinese traders because they were willing to pay higher prices. Other pepper supplies increasingly became available outside of Malabar, especially from Sumatra and Java, but the taste quality was not as high as Malabar pepper. Although the market price was higher for Malabar pepper, the Portuguese wanted the higher quality for lower prices, an approach that was unsuccessful in local markets.

A third level of complexity was found in the alternate routes established by the pepper traders in Malabar. For Middle Eastern markets, Malabar traders established strong ties with Gujarati merchants, bringing them pepper by varied land and sea routes. For Chinese markets, they established a "back door" route, shipping pepper east through the pass at Munnar in the Western Ghat mountains, then loading the pepper on ships at Nagapattinam and other east coast ports on the Coromandel coast. From there, these traders avoided Portuguese ships as they crossed the Bay of Bengal.

Thus, from the perspective of business strategy, the Malabar pepper traders found a variety of ways to work around Portuguese efforts to establish a pepper monopoly in the Indian Ocean. These strategies were based on Muslim mercantile networks that were well-established and flexible. Early efforts to resist the Portuguese on the sea, both in Malabar and farther north on the Indian Konkan coast and Gujarat, were unsuccessful from about 1500 to 1520. Naval resistance to the Portuguese along the Malabar coast, however, strengthened from 1520 to 1600, when the zamorin of Calicut employed a family of Muslim seafarers known as the Kunjali Marakkar, the "dear Ali sea captains." For four generations, they became the admirals of the zamorin's navy, limiting the Portuguese pepper trade to about 10 percent of the Malabar crop. The Portuguese were unable to do business with Muslim merchants, nor were they able to accomplish their goals by naval force.

Despite the negative assessment of Portuguese naval effectiveness on the Indian coast during the sixteenth century, Portugal's early successes at Kochi and Diu are important to understand, because these initial unsuccessful Indian confrontations with the Portuguese pointed the way toward more successful guerrilla naval warfare later in the century.

BATTLES AT KOCHI, CHAUL, AND DIU

In his seminal essay "India and the India Ocean: An Essay of the Influence of Sea Power on Indian History" (1945), historian and diplomat K. M. Panikkar states, "Judged from results, the battle off Cochin in 1503, and the engagement off Diu in 1509 are among most significant events in Indian history . . . they are fundamentally more important than Plassey (1756) or Buxar (1764) for the future history of India."[8] Panikkar posits that supremacy in the Indian Ocean passed to Portugal with these battles, although Indians more successfully contested coastal sea control for the remainder of the sixteenth century.

Regarding the battle in 1503 off Cochin (Kochi), Panikkar summarized that the battle was tactically indecisive because Kassim's Calicut navy with its small fast boats could not pursue da Gama's high-sea fleet. "Though the honours of the battle off Cochin (1503) lay with the Calicut navy, the failure of Kassim to force a decision when he had the superiority was disastrous, as it showed to the Portuguese the essential weakness of the Zamorin's sea power."[9] Other accounts relying on logs of Portuguese voyages indicate that the Indian forces were routed in this engagement and that the results were less inconclusive than Panikkar suggests.[10] This battle was an early demonstration, perhaps the first recorded, of a turning point in naval history through the Portuguese application of a single battle line of ships coupled with the use of artillery broadsides. The battle also demonstrated the importance of maintaining the "weather gauge," that is, taking a position between enemy ships and the wind. The battle took place during Vasco da Gama's second expedition to India. The Calicut navy commanded by Khoja Kassim was reinforced by an Egyptian squadron commanded by Khoja Amber. With their superior ship numbers consisting of smaller craft, the Indo-Egyptian forces planned to attack the Portuguese fleet as it headed north from Cochin toward Calicut on its way to Cananore. The Indo-Egyptian force anticipated that their boarding parties would overwhelm the Portuguese craft and crews, then burn and sink the Portuguese fleet. It planned to follow the ancient naval formula of "ram, board, and fight," a variant of land warfare that was the logical alternative prior to the advent of naval artillery pieces. The Portuguese fleet included two squadrons. The one commanded by Vincent Sodre consisted of smaller, faster caravels with lateen sails recently installed for maneuverability after the long square-sail voyage from Portugal. The second squadron, commanded by Vasco da Gama, included heavier carracks with their larger guns. Sailing position would be important. Fortunately for the Portuguese, the wind that day was from the east off the land. The Portuguese caravels, with their premier sailing ability to point toward the wind, were in the lead. It was the best position possible to hug the shore and keep the Indo-Egyptian fleet to seawards, where the Portuguese ships could issue broadsides that would keep off boarders and allow the heavier broadsides of the following carracks to devastate the more numerous local navy ships.

During this 1503 battle, the winds during January blew from the northeast.[11] The more easterly the winds, the better sea traction that the two Portuguese sea squadrons would have maintained. Sodre led with five caravels and three naus. Da Gama followed with the heavier carracks farther out to sea. Although outnumbered in terms of vessels, Sodre and da Gama held the "weather gauge" during the encounter by coming as close to shore as they could sail. By staying upwind, they had plenty of wind in their sails for maneuverability when they wished to bear down on their Indian opponents. Although the Portuguese were outnumbered by as many as ten ships to one, their heavier, stronger ships armed with swivel guns and bombards were superior in armament to the Indian ships. The guns kept the Indians far enough away so they could not board. None of the Portuguese ships were lost, although Indian arrows killed swivel gunners and left Portuguese ships looking like they were covered in porcupine quills. Dozens of Indian ships were sunk. Sodre captured several ships, towed them to Calicut, and set them on fire. Unlike Panikkar's more neutral summary of the battle, Padfield's summary is as follows: "It was a massacre rather than a battle, but it should stand out in naval history as the first recorded sea battle fought to a pre-arranged pattern as a stand-off artillery action by squadrons sailing in close-hauled line ahead."[12]

Following the Portuguese victory near Cochin in January 1503, the Portuguese finally suffered their first naval defeat in the Indian Ocean at Chaul, just south of present-day Mumbai, in March 1508. A substantial Muslim fleet from Mamluk Egypt had sailed to India to assist in removing Portuguese interference in traditional Indian Ocean trade routes. The fleet had been built near Suez with timber from the Black Sea, but the fleet was much reduced because half of the timber had been intercepted en route by the Knights of St. John in Rhodes. On his way south along the Indian coast to join forces with the zamorin of Calicut, Egyptian commander Hussein al-Kurdi heard news of Portuguese ships in the river mouth at Chaul. He caught the three Portuguese ships and five caravels at anchor in constricted quarters. The Portuguese squadron was commanded by Lorenzo de Almeida, son of the Portuguese viceroy in India, Francisco de Almeida. Trapped in the river, Lorenzo resisted boarding parties by using artillery broadsides for three days until his men were exhausted. The Egyptians were reinforced by arriving Gujaratis. Lorenzo died tied to the mast with a broken leg, expecting no mercy.[13] Although victorious, Hussein's Egyptian fleet was discouraged by the intense Portuguese resistance and the heavy damage sustained during the battle. It sailed to Diu in Gujarat for repairs.

The Portuguese viceroy, who had lost his son in the battle, vowed revenge. He exacted it eleven months later when he was victorious in a subsequent military victory at Diu. Combined forces of Gujaratis, Egyptians, Venetians, and the zamorin gathered in Diu, one of the key ports on the spice trade route. Diu had access to both the Persian Gulf and the Red Sea. Unbeknownst to the zamorin and the Egyptian and Venetian forces, the Portuguese viceroy Almeida had recruited the king of Gujarat's governor in Diu, Malik Ayyaz, who deprived Hussein's navy of his supplies.[14] Nevertheless, Hussein fought back when Almeida arrived in February 1509. A major sea battle ensued that some have compared to Lepanto or Trafalgar. In fierce fighting, the Portuguese navy won the day. Gujarati governor Malik Ayyaz returned the prisoners taken at Chaul in 1503 well-dressed and well-fed. Almeida allowed him to maintain his governorship of Diu fort, since it was expensive to maintain, and allowed him a trade agreement as well. The Portuguese later sought a fort at Diu, but this acquisition was postponed until Malik Ayyaz was no longer governor. Meanwhile, Mamluk captives were hanged, torn to pieces, and tied across cannon mouths in retaliation for the death of the Portuguese viceroy's son. Hussein fled to Egypt on horseback, disgusted by the treachery of the sultan of Gujarat. Zamorin forces returned to Calicut. After the victory at Diu, supremacy on the sea was left to the Portuguese. Although the Ottomans returned to attempt to capture Diu in 1538, again unsuccessfully, historical consensus considers the 1509 Portuguese victory at Diu to have been an essential turning point in the overall exercise of Portuguese control over the important sea lanes of the Indian Ocean.

INDIAN OCEAN CHOKE POINTS AND THE *CARTAZ*

In the wake of Almeida's return to Portugal, the framework for Portuguese success in the Indian Ocean was honed by Afonso de Albuquerque, who established control of the key choke points to the Red Sea and the Persian Gulf in 1507 at the islands of Socotra and Hormuz, respectively. Unable to conquer Calicut, he established Goa as the center of Portu-guese rule and administration in 1510, and then conquered the key choke point of Malacca in 1511, ensuring the ability to control trade between India, the East Indies, China, and Japan.[15] Thus, the Indian Ocean became a Portuguese-controlled sea. Portugal dominated the southwest entry to the Indian Ocean through the strait between Mozambique and Madagascar, the northwest passages through the Red Sea and Persian Gulf, and the southeast exit to the China Seas at Malacca. Portuguese control established within the first decade after their arrival lasted for more than a century before Dutch and English pressure began to make inroads into the Indian Ocean. During the period of successful exclusion of other Europeans, the Portuguese continued to struggle for the entire sixteenth century to gain clear domination against Indian forces for control of the west coast of India and the spice trade. One of the reasons Indian and Arab traders who had operated in the Arabian Sea for centuries opposed the Portuguese presence was that they instituted a toll system on merchant shipping known as *cartaz*.

Cartaz was a maritime trade license issued by the Portuguese allowing merchant ships to trade in the Indian Ocean in exchange for part of their profits. Rates varied but were in the range of twenty percent. The system was instituted in 1502, at the time of da Gama's second voyage to India, and remained in place until the mid-eighteenth century. In theory, paying *cartaz* to the Portuguese gave protection to merchants against pirates and rival states. Its main purpose from the Portuguese perspective was to direct trade toward Portuguese ports such as Goa, Hormuz, and Malacca so that the Portuguese could maintain a monopoly on the spice trade. Muslim, Hindu, and Malay merchant ships risked losing their cargo or being sunk if they were caught without *cartaz* do umentation.[16] In fact, many local traders felt that the Portuguese permit system did not afford safety to them, reporting that Portuguese patrol caravels attacked vessels whether they had permits or not.[17] Also, because the permits required the declaration of freight and destination, trading captains were fearful that the information would be passed on to pirates.

The Hindu Zamorin's Muslim Admirals: Kunjali Marakkar

The Hindu zamorin of Calicut, the most powerful local ruler on the Malabar coast between the twelfth and eighteenth centuries, continued to remain powerful on land and developed the ability to control coastal waters through employing a series of Muslim admirals known as the Kunjali Marakkar. Four Kunjali Marakkar fought the Portuguese successively from 1520 through 1600, with many notable successes. Kunjali Marakkar is a title rather than the name of each individual who held the title, and it means "dear Ali sea captain" in Malayalam, the language of the Malabar coast. The inclusion of Ali in the term of address clearly indicates the Muslim background of these sea captains.

Sometimes the four Kunjali Marakkar are referred to individually as Kunjali I, Kunjali II, Kunjali III, and Kunjali IV. They are also known by their given names as well, Kutty Ahmed Ali (1520–1531), Kutty Pokker Ali (1531–1571), Pattu Marakkar (1571–1595), and Muhammed Ali Marakkar (1595–1600). After the failed early sixteenth-century sea battles with the Portuguese, these leaders of resistance adopted a guerrilla

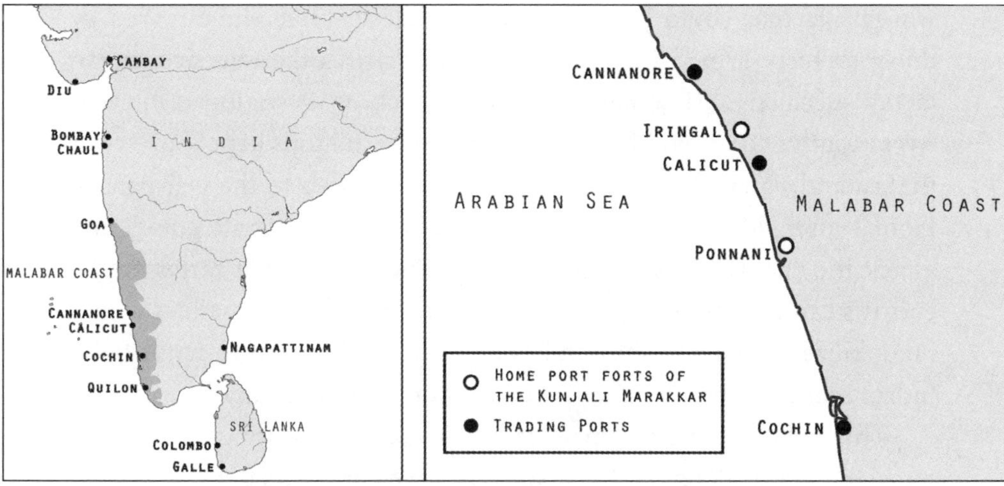

MAP 4.2 Malabar coast ports and Kunjali Marakkar sites of activity
Created by Jamie Rhode, adapted from Mountain High base map

form of naval warfare, since the power relationship with the Portuguese navy was asymmetrical. In many cases, the resistance was highly effective.

A museum and memorial have been preserved at the location of the last coastal fort held by the Kunjali Marakkar at Iringal, about eighteen miles north of Calicut. The last standing building of the fort houses the museum near the protected water passage from where the Kunjali sent forth their raids.[18] Inscriptions on the memorial stele in the garden summarize key contributions of each of these commanders.

KUNJALI I: KUTTY AHMED ALI (1520–1531)

> *The first of the Kunhali Marakkars, systematically tormented the Portuguese with his "padaes," or small fast rowing craft.*[19]

Compared to the smaller, faster, shallower draft *padae* or *paroe* of the Malabar coast, Portuguese caravels and carracks/naus were larger and slower and had deeper drafts. Thus the sailors serving the zamorin under the direction of the Kunjali Marakkar had some advantages in coastal waters, which included shallow estuaries and thick clumps of mangrove swamps in which the Indian boats could hide before striking Portuguese ships passing along the coast. Kunjali I constructed fast war-*paroes* that could be navigated in shallow water while rowed by thirty to forty armed men. Nambiar summarizes the effective Indian tactics succinctly: "[H]e had hundreds of such boats stationed in every river mouth and creek. His main station on the hilltops kept watch over the sea and signaled the movement of enemy vessels to the war-paroes. Flotilla after flotilla would then streak out from different points and attack the enemy. These small boats presented a difficult target to the enemy's cannon. By setting fire to the sails and tackles the sailors would immobilize the enemy ship and board her. In the hand-to-hand fight, Indian seamen generally gave no quarter nor asked for any."[20]

This pattern of asymmetrical guerrilla tactics appears to have remained in use along the Malabar coast for eighty years until the demise of Kunjali IV. Sometimes the tactics resulted in victories, sometimes in losses, and sometimes with inconclusive results. But the Malabar natives' ability to maintain resistance for many decades indicates that the Portuguese were unable to subjugate the Indians in coastal engagements along the coast, although the Indians were unable to compete with the Portuguese navy in offshore deeper water. However, concerns about Kunjali Marakkar raids along the coast, the Portuguese had to convoy their merchantmen with armed ships, reducing their volume of trade. As the Portuguese put it, "Calicut greatly oppressed us with their *paroes*."[21] Albuquerque complained to the king that his ship did not dare to sail from Cannanore to Cochin. The interdiction of Portuguese trade from Calicut was successful. In addition to attacking Portuguese ships, Kunjali I also successfully escorted and protected Indian and Arab ships carrying trade merchandise. In 1523, Kunjali I freighted eight ships with pepper and dispatched them with forty escorts to the Red Sea while the Portuguese looked on, thus demonstrating that Portuguese interdiction of Indian trade was not completely successful during this period.[22]

In 1524, Vasco da Gama returned to India with the goal of ensuring that his forces operating out of Goa did a more thorough job controlling the coast. A number of inconclusive naval battles were fought between Goa and Calicut, with the Portuguese under De Souza finally achieving a pair of victories off Cannanore and Goa. The new zamorin declared war and attacked the Portuguese fort in Calicut. The Portuguese commander, Menezes, attacked the zamorin's shipping at Ponnani. Kunjali I stealthily entered the port at Cochin, burned the Portuguese vessels, and returned to Calicut safely. In 1526, Menezes died of wounds received at Beypore on the north bank of the river six miles south of Calicut. Sampayo succeeded Menezes and had greater success in 1528, destroying a good part of Kunjali I's fleet. Nevertheless, later that year, the Indians counterattacked in an attempt to bottle the Portuguese up in the river mouth at Chetwai, destroying Portuguese ships and massacring the crew.[23]

Despite the back-and-forth nature of the Calicut-Goa sea battles, Kunjali interdiction of trade between Cochin and Goa was so effective by the end of the decade that the Portuguese administration in Goa complained to the king in 1530 that "the principal reason that we have no pepper is because the coast is not well protected and it is taken to Mecca, Diu and elsewhere."[24] In addition to protecting the trade on the west coast of India, Kunjali I also went as far as Ceylon to oppose the Portuguese. The Portuguese had established a fort at Colombo in Ceylon in 1510. The zamorin helped the Ceylonese king of Lanka in a campaign to expel the Portuguese from Ceylon and reduce the fortress with the help of his navy. The Portuguese were forced to evacuate their fortress in 1524 for a period of time until a civil war occurred in the 1530s. Clearly, by the time Kunjali I passed away in 1531, he had established a pattern of successful resistance to the Portuguese.

KUNJALI II: KUTTY POKKER ALI (1531–1571)

Continued to battle the Portuguese, overwhelming many a commander such as Viceroy Martin Alphonso Miranda.

Portuguese opposition to the zamorin's trade in the Arabian Sea turned some of Calicut's focus to the eastern trade with Pegu (Burma), Malacca, China, and especially Ceylon, the Lanka Kingdom. In the Lanka civil war that developed during the 1530s, the zamorin backed Mayadunne, the brother of the Lankan king, who asked the Portuguese for assistance. In 1536, the zamorin sent a large expeditionary force led by Kunjali II to assist, but Mayadunne capitulated. The zamorin's navy received the news early enough to avoid defeat but resolved to fight the Portuguese on the seas. In 1537, a large zamorin fleet sailed from the Malabar port of Ponnani with eight thousand soldiers, including one thousand *arquebusiers* and four hundred pieces of artillery. The fleet captured Portuguese ships on the way, including the *San Pedro*, which had made an unrivaled twenty-two voyages to India. With the approach of the Calicut fleet, Mayadunne overcame his remorse and declared war once again on his brother the king, who again asked the Portuguese for assistance. Portuguese commander De Souza sailed speedily toward Ceylon but turned back to Cochin to equip his fleet more strongly once he heard of the strength of the Calicut occupation of Ceylon. The zamorin's forces thought the Portuguese fleet was destined for Diu in Gujarat, so they were not prepared in Ceylon when De Souza arrived with a powerful fleet. The Portuguese were victorious in the subsequent engagement, and they sent trophy presents taken during the victory to the raja of Cochin, archenemy of the zamorin of Calicut.[25] Kunjali II lost a great deal of wealth in this encounter. The king of Ceylon offered a large loan to the Portuguese toward the expenses of the fleet, but the loan was never repaid. Mayadunne was repentant and made peace with his brother the king until the king's son married, ruining Mayadunne's chance at succession. Mayadunne once again called on the zamorin for help. Accounts vary regarding the subsequent disastrous campaign for Mayadunne and the zamorin. P. E. Pieris, Ceylon historian, records "The truth will never be known" regarding the final events of treachery that removed the zamorin and Kunjali from Ceylon for the duration of the century. At the same time that the collapse of Mayadunne and Calicut opposition in Ceylon took place, the Portuguese won the battle of Diu in Gujarat in 1538 against combined Egyptian, Ottoman, and Indian forces. The zamorin died brokenhearted in 1540.[26]

Despite the defeats in Ceylon and Gujarat, Kunjali II is regarded highly by some as the most outstanding of the four Kunjalis due to his success incontinuing the naval war for control of the sea trade on the Malabar coast, where he achieved a string of important victories. Between 1564 and 1566, Kunjali II's forces avenged the death of a

Mopla sailor by blockading Cannanore and interdicting communications with Goa, successfully enough that the Portuguese sued for peace and Kunjali II's esteem rose. At Chaliyam in 1566, the Calicut navy captured Portuguese ships and a thousand veteran sailors. In 1569, Kunjali's fleet took Mangalore, setting fire to Portuguese warehouses without losing a single ship. In 1570, Kunjali II performed the remarkable feat of sailing past the Portuguese under cover of night into Chaul, remaining for twenty days fighting and doing much damage, before escaping again in the night. Kunjali II died in 1571 in a sea battle off Cannanore in a fight with fifty Portuguese galliots.[27] Despite the distant losses in Ceylon to the east of India and Gujarat to the northwest, Kunjali II's efforts achieved success for the zamorin along the southwest coast of India.

KUNJALI III: PATTU MARAKKAR (1571–1595)

Sustained a prolonged resistance to the Portuguese, destroyed the Portuguese fort at Chaliyamand, and built the Kunhali fort at Iringal.

The legacy of protecting the Malabar coast for the zamorin continued during the 1570s with control of the zamorin's navy under Kunjali III. In 1571, the zamorin's forces under Kunjali III took the Portuguese fort at Chaliyam, on the river in Calicut, and destroyed it. The zamorin allowed the Portuguese to embark without molestation, but the Portuguese governor in Goa, De Menezes, was furious about the loss of the Chaliyam fort and executed the commander of the lost fort, De Castro, in Goa's marketplace.[28] With this auspicious start at Chaliyam, the zamorin's navy, led by Kunjali III, established control along the Malabar coast during the 1570s. Kunjali III's cousin, Captain Kutty Moosa, had mastery along the eastern Coromandel coast.

In 1580, Portugal united with Spain for a period of sixty years. In 1584, the Portuguese made enemies of their ally Cochin by forcing the raja of Cochin to allow them to manage the customhouse, rousing the people of Cochin to revolt. A few English and Dutch seafarers began to arrive on the west coast, giving Indian seamen help to fight the Portuguese. Kunjali III feared that the weak zamorin at the time would grant the Portuguese the right to build a fort at Ponnani south of Calicut, so he asked the zamorin for permission to build a fort on the peninsula at the mouth of the Kotta River north of Calicut. He was able to build a strong fort, Kotta, in that location, which is now called Iringal. He had anchorage for his fleet there before the Portuguese were able to establish their fort at Ponnani in 1586. The zamorin gave permission for this construction, as Kunjali had feared. From Kotta, Kunjali III attacked the Portuguese, taking many ships that were richly laden with cargo. During this period united with Spain, Portugal was distracted from the Indian Ocean due to the failure of the Spanish Armada in 1588. Although the Calicut navy continued to inflict losses on the Portuguese, the zamorin allowed the establishment of a Portuguese factory in Calicut. Relations grew tense between the Kunjali Marakkar and the zamorin, and estrangement began to set in. The results of this estrangement would lead to the downfall of the Kunjali Marakkar during the naval leadership period of Kunjali IV.

KUNJALI IV: MUHAMMED ALI MARAKKAR (1595–1600)

An innovative commander, was captured treacherously by the Portuguese and put to death. This brought down the curtains on the Marakkar era, a period of remarkable naval ascendancy in the history of the Malabar coast.

Kunjali IV was a nephew of Kunjali III. During the sixteenth century, there were fifteen zamorin kings of Calicut, although there were only four Kunjali, admirals of the zamorin. Thus Kunjali tended to serve multiple zamorins and may have been more experienced than the leaders they served as evidenced by the length of their careers.[29] During the eighth decade of successive Kunjali service to the zamorins, the relationship between Kunjali IV and the zamorin broke down.[30] Although achieving some successes, such as capturing a treasure ship from China within sight of Goa, Kunjali IV began acting more on his own, calling himself the king of Kotta. The stage was set for a final bloody scene between the zamorin and his estranged admiral.

In 1597, Francisco da Gama, the grandson of the discoverer of the sea route to India, Vasco da Gama, arrived to take the position of viceroy in Goa. His most important task was to attack Kunjali IV. The Dutch became a thorn in his side when they began to make their first appearances on the Malabar coast. The viceroy began tedious negotiations with the zamorin, who was reluctant to come out openly against Kunjali IV, because both Muslims and Hindus respected him and considered him a national hero. The zamorin made untenable demands of the Portuguese and waited for a sign of contrition from Kunjali IV to determine which alli-ance option to pursue. Kunjali IV seemed convinced of his invincibility and insulted the zamorin by cutting off the tail of one of his royal elephants.[31] Thoroughly angered, the zamorin offered the Portuguese viceroy the aid of land forces in a war against the rebellious Kunjali IV. He prepared an army of 20,000 and marched on the Kunjali fort at Kotta, cutting off communication between the fort and the mainland by organizing troops in a semicircle from the town to the shore. The Portuguese blockaded Kotta from the sea.

The siege went on for three months until a zamorin and Portuguese joint attack took place against Kunjali IV's forces in March 1599. Although he anticipated the direction of the attack, Kunjali IV was at a disadvantage at sea because his light craft had no chance against heavy ships in confined space. Additionally, many of his vessels were scattered on other assignments. Due to the land blockade Kunjali IV could not summon reinforcements to Kotta.

But all was not smooth on the opposite side either. The alliance between the Portuguese and the zamorin became tense. When the zamorin asked the Portuguese for assistance, the Portuguese commander, being suspicious, demanded hostages, an outrageous demand from the zamorin's point of view, because he was a sworn ally to the Portuguese. Nevertheless, the zamorin suppressed his anger and sent six high-ranking men.

The zamorin and the Portuguese attacked Kunjali IV's forces by land and sea. The Kunjali forces resisted with skill and tenacity. After the first day of fighting on March 5, 1599, in which there were heavy losses on both sides without the fort being taken, Portuguese morale was much diminished, especially when news of the unsuccessful capture of the fort disaster reached Goa on March 15. Kunjali IV was proud of his victory and described himself the "Expeller of the Portuguese" and "Defender of the Faithful" in an appeal to attract all Muslims. The Portuguese renewed the blockade during the ensuing months, and Kunjali IV lost men through attrition who had been resupplying the fort with food and water.

In December 1599, the Portuguese assembled a renewed fleet under the leadership of the capable commander Furtado and requested to meet with the zamorin. The zamorin suggested that once the power of the Portuguese armada was seen, he would convince Kunjali IV to capitulate on the condition that his life and those of all the Muslims with him would be spared. The Portuguese continued to build the strength of their fleet until February 1600. The Kunjali's forces inside the fort had been reduced to about eight hundred, with scarce provisions. In March, bitter fighting ensued, with the Portuguese forces pounding the fort with artillery and Furtado and Kunjali IV personally rallying their men. Furtado continued the attack despite orders from Goa to desist. Kunjali IV reopened negotiations only with the zamorin, offering rich presents in exchange for leniency. They agreed that Kunjali IV would surrender to no one but the zamorin, and that his life and the lives of his men would be spared. The Portuguese were his enemy, but the zamorin was his king, and Kunjali IV asked to be pardoned for his offense. During negotiations, a final attack on the fort took place on March 7, 1600. The zamorin wanted Kunjali IV's surrender but not his death, but Furtado wanted both. The zamorin received Kunjali IV's surrender on March 17 based on the agreement between the zamorin and the Kunjali. Kunjali IV, accompanied by principal officer Chinali, a Malaccan Chinese who had become his main confidant, presented his sword to the zamorin. Kunjali IV was immediately seized by Furtado. A scuffle ensued over the treachery, but the Portuguese prevailed. The fort was razed, and the treasure hunt began for Kunjali IV's fortune. Kunjali IV was brought to the gloomy Tronco prison in Goa, where he was imprisoned along with Chinali and forty other Mopla captives.

His sentence was to be beheaded and quartered, a fate he faced with "great dignity and courage which won the respect of his pitiless foes." Kunjali's quartered body was displayed on the beach, and his salted head was sent to Cannanore and stuck on a standard to terrorize the Muslims. Thus the largely successful resistance of the four Kunjali Marakkar to the Portu-guese came to an end.

How successful were the Kunjali Marakkar in their resistance to the Portuguese? Although not effective in distant places such as Gujarat and Ceylon, the Calicut navy's efforts along the Malabar coast were successful. Malabar was the main supplier of high-quality pepper during the sixteenth century, and the Portuguese desire to monopolize the Malabar pepper trade was never realized. For centuries Muslim mercantile networks had controlled the pepper trade both to Europe and to China. Portuguese trading post reports at the end of the sixteenth century concluded that they had bought a mere ten percent of Malabar's pepper production. Thus, despite their ultimate defeat, the efforts of the Kunjali Marakkar to break the Portuguese attempts at trade monopoly along the Malabar coast were successful.[32]

How did the zamorin's Calicut brown-water navy succeed in controlling the bulk of the pepper trade during the sixteenth century in the face of a much stronger Portuguese blue-water navy? The answer lies in the largely successful asymmetric naval tactics employed by the Kunjali Marakkar between the beginning of the Kunjali I's command of the zamorin navy in 1520 and its demise in 1598, when the zamorin allied with the Portuguese. These tactics worked close to home on the Malabar coast, where wind, water, tide, water depths, and estuary conditions were all well-known by the experienced Muslim sailors of the coast. The approach was much less effective in distant places like Gujarat and Ceylon, supply lines were stretched, reinforcements were not readily available, and local conditions were less well-known. The Kunjali Marakkar led a type of naval guerrilla war that appears to be an example of "Peoples War at Sea" as defined and described much later in Chinese military literature. The Indians were pioneers at this type of warfare.[33]

Several tributes to the Kunjali Marakkar have been issued in recent years. In 2000, on the four hundredth anniversary of the end of the Marakkars, India issued a stamp in honor of the great admirals who wrote a heroic chapter in India's maritime history that shows: "[T]he *war-paroe*, a small craft used by the Kunjalis, which, manned by 30–40 men each, could be rowed through lagoons and narrow waters. Several of these crafts were deployed at strategic points and they would emerge from small creeks and inconspicuous estuaries, attack the Portuguese ships at will, inflict heavy damage and casualties by setting fire to their sails and get back into the safety of shallow waters. In these guerrilla raids, the Marakkars had shown remarkable prowess."[34]

Other tributes include naming the marine college of the University of Cochin University of Science and Technology as the Kunjali Marakkar School of Marine Engineering, as well as releasing dramatic films celebrating the achievements of the Kunjali Marakkar.[35]

Reflections on the Kunjali Marakkar Maritime Experience

Although Muslim traders by background, the four generations of Kunjali Marakkar who became the commanders of the zamorin's navy transferred their sea skills into military action against the Portuguese who sought to dominate the Malabar coast of India and establish a monopoly in the pepper trade. The Portuguese prevailed in early sea battles north of Cochin in 1503 and later at Diu in 1509, following the first Portuguese loss at Chaul in 1508, where they had inflicted heavy casualties on their Arab and Indian opponents. The zamorin learned from these defeats and appointed the Kunjali Marakkar to oppose the Portuguese. The Kunjali Marakkar were successful in asymmetrical naval warfare tactics along the Malabar coast for eighty years.

Maritime Strategic and Tactical Lessons

Useful lessons can be learned from a review of the case study material on the maritime interactions of the Portuguese and Indians during the sixteenth century, and specifically how the Kunjali Marakkar managed their successful naval resistance to the Portuguese on the west coast of India within their home waters.

LOCAL KNOWLEDGE OF NATURAL PHENOMENA

While the Portuguese understood and were experienced blue-water sailors, the Kunjali Marakkar had greater knowledge of the details of the Malabar coast, including rivers, estuaries, and water depths. They knew the sources of fresh water and could supply their sailors with provisions. This local knowledge allowed the Kunjali Marakkar to conduct successful asymmetrical naval war between 1520 and 1600. Until the Portuguese gained experience in the Indian Ocean, local sailors also understood better the storm systems, including the annual alternation of monsoon winds from the southwest during the summer to northeast during the winter.

ADVANTAGES IN MILITARY TECHNOLOGY

By the sixteenth century, the Portuguese had developed their carracks and caravels with substantial military capability. These ships were the world's best sailing ships at that time in terms of seaworthiness, especially in deep water, heavy weather, and offshore conditions. Caravels were sailed to the Indian Ocean using square sails, which were then swapped for lateen sails for better maneuverability in naval encounters. Lateen sails allowed caravels to point closer to the wind than the ships of their opponents, a clear advantage for a commander trying to gain a superior position against a naval opponent. The Portuguese also had developed efficient bombards and swivel guns to change the nature of naval warfare from "ram, board, fight" hand-to-hand combat, based on the model of land warfare, to the use of broadside cannon artillery technique to win fights at sea from a distance. There is little mention of broadside cannon technique used in Europe before 1500, but clear records of it are available from the Battle of Cochin in 1503. Thus the Portuguese had an advantage in both ship design and armament over opponents in the Indian Ocean. The asymmetrical advantages the Kunjali Marakkar developed included superior numbers when properly used and protected. Their tactics included attacking along the coast in low-wind situations when the rowed canoes and *proas* could attack the sterns of Portuguese ships where there was little protection by guns. Using swarm techniques of fierce boarding attacks, the larger Portuguese ships could be overwhelmed, including not only overcoming the crews but also disabling the ships through slashing the rigging with straight swords, dismasting, and setting fires.

CONTINENTAL VS. MARITIME IDENTITIES

As a small country on the maritime perimeter of Europe, Portugal spent the fifteenth century exploring the Atlantic Ocean while attempting to find a maritime route around Africa to India. By the time the Portuguese arrived in India, they had developed a profound maritime identity. Portugal was too small to compete by land on the European continent, but by 1500 it had the sea skills, the ship technology, and the pope's blessing to place any part of the world to the east of the Treaty of Tordesillas longitude line under its dominion. When the Portuguese arrived in the Indian Ocean, peaceful trade had been taking place there for centuries. The most active seafaring people in the Indian Ocean were the Arab traders, although Zheng He's huge fleets had only retreated from the Indian Ocean a few decades before the Portuguese arrived. It was less than a lifetime between 1433, when Zheng He possibly died off Calicut, and 1498, when Vasco da Gama arrived at Calicut. During this period, however, the *kala pani*, the Hindu prohibition against traveling on the sea and crossing the black water, appears to have been strong. Over the many centuries of trade between India and the Arabian Peninsula, many Muslims had settled along the Malabar coast, their coastal residential neighborhoods providing a buffer for Hindus living comfortably removed from contact with the water. As seafarers, the Muslims not only engaged in the open trade promoted by the Hindu zamorin of Calicut, but also became the zamorin's keepers of order upon the sea. Thus it was a reasonable progression for some of these Muslim seafarers to become the maritime military when the Portuguese arrived and refused to participate in the standard operating procedures for trade that had long been in place under the zamorin's rule. The Portuguese had a strongly developed maritime identity. The Hindus did not, but they relied with confidence on the maritime identity and capabilities of the Muslims who had lived in their communities for centuries. The family of the Kunjali Marakkars emerged as the naval leaders willing and able to represent the zamorin of Calicut when he was confronted by Portuguese maritime threats.

DEEPLY FELT NATIONAL IDENTITIES

Although smaller in numbers than the Indians they encountered, the Portuguese keenly felt their bond to each other. The Indians had more disparate, localized identities. During the sixteenth-century period of Portuguese interaction with the Kunjali Marakkar, there was some concentration of power with the zamorin's rule in Calicut, but there was opposition from other local rulers, most notably by the king of Cochin, who was pleased to ally with the Portuguese to fight against the zamorin and his Kunjali Marakkar naval forces. Thus, the intense Portuguese self-identification coupled with their ability to identify and exploit fragmentation in Indian society helped them to succeed militarily.

MILITARY LEADERSHIP

Alfonso Albuquerque demonstrated strategic genius by identifying the choke points guarding entry to the Indian Ocean and establishing his program to control them. The strength of the Kunjali Marakkar lay in their grasp of tactics that worked in smaller-scale environments. The greatest of the asymmetrical naval tacticians were Kunjali II and Kunjali III, who pioneered asymmetrical tactics that were successful over a sixty-four-year period between 1531 and 1595. An example was the destruction of the Portuguese fort in Calicut by Kunjali III and the establishment of the Kunjali fort Kotte in Iringal, in an estuary that was both defensible and ideal for carrying out sudden coastal raids.

RELATIVE POWER RELATIONS

The Portuguese had superior sea power with their ships and guns, but their longevity in the Indian Ocean depended on their establishing a series of forts around the Indian Ocean perimeter under Albuquerque's direction. Socotra, Hormuz (including both the Persian and Omani sides of the strait), Goa, and Malacca were all keys to Indian Ocean control, and Diu was added later. In general, the Portuguese succeeded in dominating the sea lanes, except in the important area of local control in Malabar, where they were successfully contested by the Kunjali Marakkar. Once they were victorious over the Kunjali Marrakar in 1600, the Portuguese maintained military control through their superior sea power until the Dutch and English arrived in the mid-seventeenth century. In the case of the Portuguese, however, naval supremacy did not lead to the overwhelming trade dominance they sought, as Muslim trading networks still managed to ship and sell the largest proportion of spice in the Indian Ocean during the sixteenth century.

ALLIANCE RELATIONS

The zamorin of Calicut maintained positive alliance relations with the Gujaratis, except when the Gujarati leader treacherously changed sides and supported the Portuguese, as happened at Diu in 1509. He also maintained good relations with the Egyptians under Mamluk rule and was able to develop positive relations with the Ottomans after they had defeated the Mamluks in 1517. Joint military operations with these allies were less successful than joint attempts to control the spice trading routes through the Persian Gulf and the Red Sea. After Albuquerque abandoned Socotra in 1511 and was unable to dominate Aden, the Red Sea became the main conduit in the Indian Ocean where the Portuguese monopoly over the spice trade was siphoned off. The Portuguese had no major allies around the perimeter of the Arabian Sea, but rather focused on local allies in Malabar. They successfully established relations with the king of Cochin, building a trading factory there, and supported the Cochin king in his rivalry with the zamorin of Calicut. The Portuguese also successfully established a base in Cannanore. Late in the sixteenth century, when the zamorin of Calicut felt that the Kunjali Marakkar was becoming too independent, he allied with the

Portuguese, leading to the final demise of the Kunjali IV in 1600. Thus, ally relations were important for both sides and played out in a variety of ways over the course of the sixteenth century.

RELATIONSHIP OF MARITIME ECONOMIC SUCCESS TO MARITIME MILITARY SUCCESS

Although unable to drive the Portuguese from the west coast of India, the Kunjali Marakkar succeeded in limiting the ports controlled by the Portuguese, most significantly to their Indian Ocean headquarters in Goa. Kunjali III destroyed the Portuguese fort in Calicut, the largest of the trading towns on the Malabar coast. Before the sixteenth century, the Venetians had controlled the spice trade by working with Arab middlemen who brought Indian Ocean spices to the Mediterranean for European consumption via the Red Sea and the Persian Gulf. The Portuguese desire was to monopolize the spice trade with Europe through its alternate route sailing around Africa. On the military front, the Portuguese were strategically successful, establishing overall control of the Indian Ocean though command of the choke points at the Madagascar Strait, at the mouths of the Red Sea and Persian Gulf, and at the Malacca Strait. On the economic front, Kunjali harassment of the Portuguese on the coast of India was successful. The Portuguese never monopolized the spice trade, but instead were only able to control at most about 10 percent of the pepper trade. The Kunjali ensured that much of the pepper and other spice trade continued through the Muslim community over the traditional routes by way of the Red Sea and Persian Gulf.

IMPORTANCE OF HISTORICAL AND CURRENT KNOWLEDGE

Prior to the arrival of the Portuguese, the Arabian Sea had been a trading area with relatively little conflict for about fifteen hundred years going back to the Roman period. Thus there was little precedent for the Indian Ocean traders to consult with each other when the Portuguese arrived with the intent to control trade by force. The use of current intelligence when available, however, was important for both sides. With such information, Muslim trade networks sidestepped and frustrated

Portuguese trading efforts and maintained the ability to move spices north along the Arabian Sea coast and east to the coastal ports of the Bay of Bengal. Through their warehouses and local alliances at Cochin and Cannanore, the Portuguese had local information sources to compete with the zamorin of Calicut. The value of special local relationships that the Portuguese created was demonstrated by Viceroy Almeida's alliance with the sultan of Gujarat in 1509, whose treachery, from the point of view of the zamorin and the Mamluk and Venetian forces opposed to the Portuguese forces in Diu, led to the ensuing Portuguese domination of Indian Ocean sea lanes.

SUCCESSFUL DEVELOPMENT OF ASYMMETRICAL NAVAL WARFARE TACTICS

The major lesson for residents of Malabar from the losses in 1503 and 1509 was that direct fleet-to-fleet action against the Portuguese would result in failure, even when the Portuguese were heavily outnumbered, as at Cochin. The guns of the Portuguese were far more powerful and the sailing ability of the caravels was superior. The Portuguese had also learned how to use the advantages of both ships and guns together by developing stand-off artillery action while sailing in line. By 1520, the Kunjali Marakkar had developed guerrilla naval techniques using quick raids on Portuguese trade convoys from protected bays and tidal mangrove estuaries. Their ships were smaller but were capable of avoiding devastating broadsides if they approached the trading ships from the stern and did not try to take on a large fleet. Thus their disruptive effect on Portuguese trade was significant, particularly from the 1520s to 1600 following initial defeats during the first two decades of the century.

FIVE

Limits on the Ottoman Navy in the Mediterranean Sea

Hayreddin Barbarossa, Sixteenth Century

Ottoman Rise and Maritime Theaters

The saga of the Ottomans at sea during the sixteenth century is one of high drama. The Ottoman Empire is remembered primarily as a land power, yet it was mostly due to sea power during the reign of Sultan Suleiman the Magnificent (1520–1566) that the Ottomans curbed European influence on the western flank of Constantinople in the Mediterranean Sea. During this period Ottoman naval activity flourished in two maritime theaters with varying degrees of success, to the west in the Mediterranean Sea and its Aegean and Ionian subseas, and to the east in the Indian Ocean and its Red Sea and Persian Gulf subseas to the north and south of the Arabian Peninsula.[1]

The Ottoman Empire spanned from the late 1200s through the early 1900s. In a broad sweep, Ottoman history can be categorized in several phases from the rise of the empire beginning in 1299 and culminating in the capture of Constantinople in 1453; the expansion and peak of the empire with the siege of Malta in 1565; stagnation of the empire beginning with the naval loss at Lepanto in 1571 and continuing until Greek independence in the 1820s; decline of the empire from then until World War I; and the defeat and subsequent breakup of the empire following the Great War. The focus here is on the early expansion period through the aftermath of the Ottoman defeat at Lepanto.

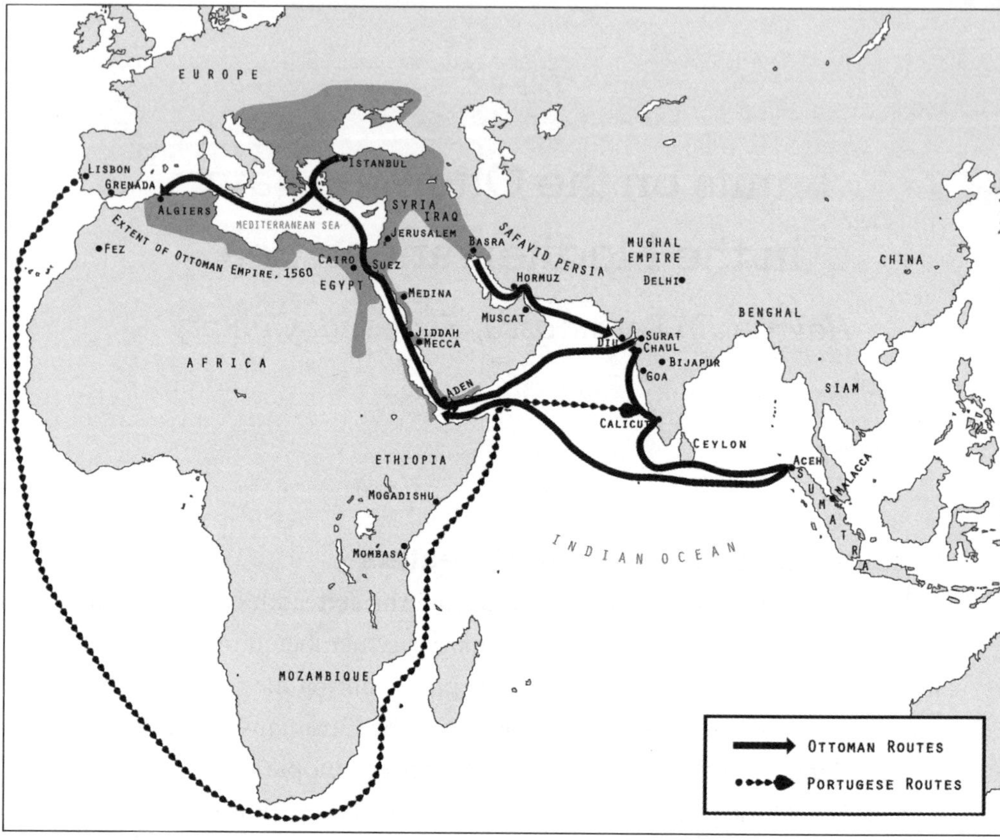

MAP 5.1 Ottoman maritime theaters, circa 1560, the Mediterranean Sea and Indian Ocean. *Adapted by Jamie Rhode from Giancarlo Casale,* The Ottoman Age of Exploration *(Oxford: Oxford University Press, 2010), 136*

The exercise of naval power simultaneously in its two theaters of maritime operation characterized Ottoman history during the sixteenth century, with its peak by the 1570s. Rather than going into immediate decline, however, Ottoman expansion stalled for another two centuries. Thus the story of Ottoman naval power following its 1571 defeat in the battle of Lepanto is a narrative of naval power stagnation rather than outright decline.[2] Ottoman power at sea had grown steadily from 1453 when Mehmed II conquered Constantinople. After a series of smaller Ottoman naval successes against Venice in the late fifteenth century, Suleiman successfully besieged Rhodes, defeating the Knights of St. John in 1522 and taking control of the sea lane between Constantinople and Alexandria. The Barbarossa brothers—highly successful maritime operators of the period—seized and ruled the North African coast between 1500 and 1520. Suleiman appointed younger brother Hayreddin Barbarossa as Ottoman grand admiral in 1532. Barbarossa reconstructed the Ottoman fleet and defeated the Holy League naval alliance at Preveza in 1538, the most significant Ottoman naval victory. Even after Barbarossa passed away quietly in his palace on the Bosphorus in 1546, Ottoman naval conquests continued for another two decades.

After a century of rise, Ottoman sea power stalled in Malta in 1565, its first failure in the Mediterranean. The stall was sealed six years later in 1571 when the Holy League decisively defeated the Ottoman navy at Lepanto, not far from the site of the earlier Ottoman victory at Preveza. Although the Ottomans continued to fight for another two centuries, essentially maintaining their territories, this was a stalemate period during which Ottoman naval expansion was substantially over, ended in the Mediterranean by the Christian alliance and in the Indian Ocean through Portuguese domination by sail power.

Suleiman's reign neatly defined the great period of Ottoman naval expansion. His rule began in 1520, a year before the successful Ottoman siege at Rhodes, and it ended a year after the failed Ottoman siege of Malta in 1566. Suleiman was present at Rhodes, but not at Malta. In the Indian Ocean during Suleiman's reign, Ottoman commanders had been active but less successful during the first half of the sixteenth century. Despite winning earlier victories as commander of the Indian Ocean fleet at Aden in 1548 and at Muscat in 1552, Piri Reis, the greatest Ottoman cartographer of this era, was executed in Egypt in 1553 for his failure to support the governor of Basra. Piyale Pasha made out considerably better in the Mediterranean Sea than did Piri Reis in the Indian Ocean. Piyali had won at Djerba off Tunis in 1560, lost at Malta in 1565, but won again at Chios in 1566. He became the first Ottoman admiral to be promoted to vizier in 1568 and was appointed head of the Ottoman navy following its defeat at the battle of Lepanto in 1571. Such were the vagaries of Ottoman naval command.

OTTOMAN WARSHIPS

It is clear that the Ottoman galleys were unable to compete successfully with the Portuguese caravels and carracks in the blue-water environment of the Arabian Sea. But in the Mediterranean, the Ottoman galleys, galleasses, and galliots squared off successfully against the galleys of Venice, Genoa, the Knights of St. John, and the Spanish on many occasions. The rowed galleys were an ancient technology not substantially different from the galleys used by the Greeks and the Romans in the Mediterranean two thousand years earlier. Variants to galleys used in the Mediterranean came to be known as galleasses and galliots. A galleass was larger than most galleys and was a rowed ship with three lateen-rigged masts, used between the fifteenth and eighteenth centuries.[3] Galliots were small, swift galleys of shallow draft used to get underneath the oars of larger galleys to disrupt their ability to maneuver. Although galleys had sails, oars were their primary source of power for forward motion over the water. They had the advantage of moving without wind. If, however, the wind was against a galley in an engagement, it was at a disadvantage to an opposing galley bearing down upon it with the help of the wind.

Portuguese caravels of the fifteenth to seventeenth centuries were small, fast sailing ships with lateen sail rigs that had good maneuverability due to their ability to sail relatively close to the wind. Portuguese carracks, sometimes called *nao*, were three- or four-masted sailing ships developed in the Mediterranean in the fifteenth century. They had a high, rounded stern with an aftcastle and a forecastle and bowsprit at the stem. They were square-rigged on the foremast and mainmast, and lateen-rigged on the mizzenmast. Square rigging limited the range in which the carrack could sail forward against the wind. These Portuguese developments pioneered the Age of Sail, which proved their worth in supporting Portuguese naval domination of the Indian Ocean. Ottoman galley technology could not successfully compete with Portugal's sailing ships, which were better able to dominate the open, blue-water environment of the Indian Ocean.

The Ottoman Navy in the Mediterranean Sea

Though their scope was limited, naval forces were involved during the fall of Constantinople to the Ottomans in 1453. While the Ottomans had more than 50,000 land troops, they had fewer than one hundred ships at Constantinople. The Byzantines pulled a chain across their galley harbor off the Bosphorus, the Golden Horn, to limit access from the sea, as well as to protect their remaining two dozen ships. The naval component was relatively unimportant during the fifty-three-day land siege of the city, but the location of Constantinople, modern Istanbul, on the main Bosphorus channel between the Mediterranean and Black Seas, clearly marked the looming importance of sea trade and a powerful navy for the Ottomans. Venetian and Genoese sailors assisted in the Byzantine defense of the city's walls, setting the stage for their opposition to the Ottomans in the postsiege period.

From the thirteenth through fifteenth centuries, Venice and Genoa were the great maritime trading powers competing in the Mediterranean. On the military front, the Knights of St. John had been driven from Jerusalem in 1187 after engaging in a holy war with Muslim forces during the Crusades.[4] Subsequently the Knights were driven from Acre on the Levant coast in 1291 and found a home on the island of Rhodes, just off the Anatolian coast, by seizing it from the Byzantine Empire in 1310. Meanwhile, by the fifteenth century, the Hapsburg and papal naval forces had come onto the scene in the western Mediterranean, where the Genoese held power, while in the eastern Mediterranean , the Venetians had control. With the Ottoman victory at Constantinople in 1453 and sub-sequent expansion of their landholdings, the importance of sea trade and sea power became apparent. In their quest for expansion, Ottoman naval forces directly confronted the sea power capabilities of the Knights of St. John and of Venice, the established sea powers in the eastern Med-iterranean. Although the Venetians were initially amenable to diplomatic and trade pact solutions, frictions soon developed and two Ottoman-Venetian wars broke out during the late fifteenth century.

Venice, in particular, presented a challenge to Ottoman hegemony in the Mediterranean. Beginning in the thirteenth century, Venice had developed an extensive maritime empire, including many island and coastal possessions in the Adriatic, Ionian, and Aegean Seas. Many imposing Venetian forts from this period still sit on the hills and islands of the harbors they controlled, including Methoni, Coroni, Monemvasia, and Nafplio in the Peloponnese.[5] After the Ottoman success at Constantinople, the Venetians developed peaceful trade relations with the Ottomans until disputes ignited raiding on both sides. The conflict was finally settled through the 1479 Treaty of Constantinople, which, most importantly, confirmed Ottoman control of the substantial Aegean island of Negroponte, which it had captured in 1470.

Peace reigned for twenty years before the next Ottoman-Venetian War broke out in 1499. At the battle of Zonchio in 1499, cannons were used on board ships for the first time.[6] The Ottoman admiral Kemal Reis deployed about eighty-five galleys and galliots compared with about sixty-five of the Venetian commander Antonio Grimani. Kemal Reis' greater forces prevailed in this conflict. Despite the loss, Grimani subsequently became doge of Venice in 1521 for two years. Shortly after this conflict, in 1500, the battle of Modon, near Pylos and the island of Sapienza, resulted in anOttoman victory again by Kemal Reis. During these battles, Methoni and Coroni, the "two eyes of the Republic" of Venice and Venice's earliest possessions in Greece, were lost to the Ottomans. Despite regaining the important island of Kefalonia, the Venetians sought peace and recognized Ottoman gains in 1503.

Because Venice preferred coexistence and trade with the Ottomans, they settled amicably after the first Ottoman-Venetian War, and again after the second war, with peace lasting from 1503 until 1537. Following the battle of Preveza in 1538, with tragic results for Venice, a long peace was again established between 1540 and 1570, up to the battle of Lepanto. Both the naval battles of Preveza (1538) and Lepanto (1571) are detailed below, chronologically interspersed with discussions of the siege of Rhodes (1522) and the siege of Malta (1565). These four events form the core of the narrative of the rise of the Ottoman navy in the Mediterranean at Rhodes and Preveza, the stalemated crest of Ottoman naval power at Malta, and the Ottoman loss at Lepanto signaling that Ottoman naval power was no longer invincible in the Mediterranean.

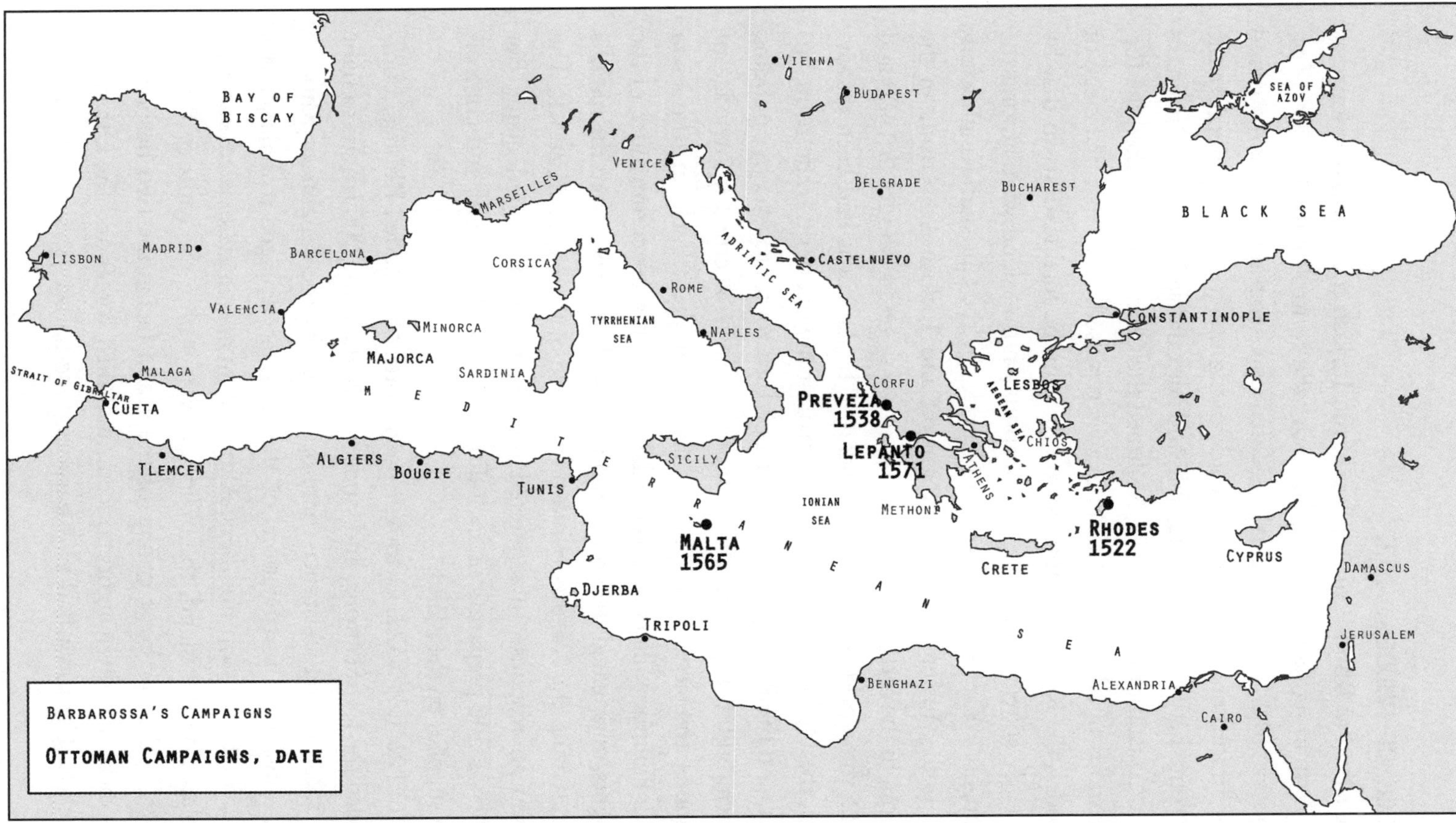

MAP 5.2 Barbarossa's Mediterranean world and key Mediterranean battles
Adapted by Jamie Rhode from Roger Crowley, Empires of the Sea: The Siege of Malta, the Battle of Lepanto, and the Contest for the Center of the World *(New York: Random House, 2008), xviii–xvix*

SIEGE OF RHODES, 1522

The island of Rhodes, nine miles off the Turkish coast, was developed as a Christian settlement that came under the control of the Knights of St. John in 1310. The strategically located and geographically large island was important for controlling trade along the coast, most notably the sea route between Constantinople and Alexandria.[7] After the Ottomans took Constantinople in 1453, Mehmed the Conqueror attacked the fortifications of Rhodes in 1480 but was repulsed. After this first siege of Rhodes, the Knights continued to build up the fortifications so that by the early sixteenth century, fortifications on the island were among the strongest in the region. Control of Rhodes by the Christian Knights limited both Muslim Ottoman expansion and Turkish-Arab trade in the region. In the forty years between the two sieges at Rhodes in 1480 and 1522, the world changed dramatically. The Americas had been discovered, the Ottomans had taken control of the overland trade routes to Asia, and the Portuguese had developed sea routes to Asia by rounding Africa. Sultan Suleiman the Magnificent, with accrued knowledge of cannons and siege tactics, personally led another attack on Rhodes in 1522. Philippe Villiers de L'Isle Adam, grand master commander of the Knights, anticipated the attack and requested assistance from the nations representing the Knights based on the size of the expected attack. The European response to requested reinforcements was inadequate, but Villiers made preparations including chaining the harbor and controlling supplies on the island.[8]

In late July 1522, Ottoman naval forces blockaded Rhodes, bombarded the fortifications, and landed more than 100,000 troops to fight the 7,000-strong resistance force organized by the Knights of Rhodes. The substantial fortifications of the Knights managed to balance the differential in troop numbers. Although smaller forts existed in several places on the island, the main fort was within the walls of Rhodes Town in the northeast corner of the island facing the two harbors. It was there that the Knights concentrated their forces and the Ottomans attacked. The town had two harbors. One harbor was used for galley warships and the other was designated for commercial ships. The enclosed walls included about a half mile of harbor front and a mile and a half of wall protection against surrounding lands.[9] The Knights organized themselves according to eight linguistic, groups based on the European lands from which the Knights came.[10] Each langue had its own inn within the walls of Rhodes Town, and the defending Knights spoke the corresponding language of their respective region. Each langue defended a specific section, called a post, of the town walls. The walls were twenty to forty feet high, interspersed with taller towers and gates. Protection of the northern wall section along the waterfront was the responsibility of the post of France. Moving counterclockwise to the west were the posts of Germany, Auvergne, and Aragon (Spain). The bridge over the moat at the post of Germany led to the Grand Master's Palace. The post of England, defending the southern flank of the city, included a double wall with a double moat. The posts of Provence and Italy defended the eastern walls leading back to the harbor front. The harbor mouth itself was protected by a chain boom. Although heavily constructed, the walls were built on soil. Ottoman tactics included bringing miners and sappers, combat engineers, to tunnel under the walls, while the Knights' grand master brought the accomplished Venetian engineer Gabriele Tadini from Crete to countermine the Ottoman tunnels.[11] The fortifications were strong, but over the course of four months, Ottoman sappers were successful in causing some of the walls to collapse, most notably a thirty-foot section in the southernmost post of England.

By November 1522, the Knights' food and gunpowder supplies were running low and the struggle to combat the Ottomans, who were pouring through breached walls, became untenable. After much soul searching and consultation, Grand Master Villiers accepted Suleiman's terms of surrender in December 1522, and his forces left Rhodes on January 1, 1523. Suleiman's victory resulted in Ottoman expansion into the areas around Rhodes, including the ability to secure the surrounding seas and control trade in the eastern Mediterranean. The Knights were forced to the west, where they resettled on Malta in the central Mediterranean, beginning in 1530, after temporary stays in Italy and France.[12] The

Knights maintained their dream of returning to Rhodes until their loss at Tripoli on the northern coast of Africa in 1551. Strategically, they had lost their large fortress island of Rhodes, with its verdant hills and control of trade in the eastern Mediterranean, and exchanged it for the smaller, rocky island of Malta, located at a strategic choke point with good harbors in the central Mediterranean.

NAVAL BATTLE OF PREVEZA, 1538

The dominant Ottoman naval figure opposing European forces during the 1520s through the mid-1540s was Hayreddin Barbarossa. His string of important victories set the stage for a naval showdown between the Ottoman and the Christian powers in the Mediterranean. In early 1538, Pope Paul III assembled a Holy League alliance consisting of forces from the Papacy, Spain, Genoa, Venice, and Malta to respond to Barbarossa. The league assembled a fleet of about 170 galleys and smaller ships near Corfu in the Ionian Sea. Marco Grimani led the papal fleet, Vincenzo Cappello led the Venetian fleet, and Andrea Doria, placed in overall command of the league forces, led the Spanish-Genoese fleet.

After ravaging Crete in early 1538, Barbarossa left Kos in the Aegean Sea for Preveza, capturing Kefalonia on the way. At the suggestion of his lieutenant, Sinan Reis, Barbarossa left troops at the fortress in Actium, on the southern shore of the mouth the Ambracian Gulf opposite Preveza, thus maintaining an artillery position to keep the league fleet offshore.[13]

Doria's ships struggled against winds driving them toward the hostile shore, and instead they sailed south toward the island of Lefkada. They anchored and decided to attack Barbarossa the next day, on Sep-tember 28, 1538. They were surprised by Ottoman ships headed for them at dawn. The Ottoman fleet led by Barbarossa was smaller, about 120 ships compared with the league's 300, but they were fast, maneuverable, and hugged the shoreline, thereby controlling it. Doria took hours to weigh anchor, although pressed by Grimani and Cappello, who thought Doria's caution was unwarranted. The fleets engaged in the Gulf of Arta near Preveza, where early lack of wind favored the Ottomans.

When the wind rose, Doria tried unsuccessfully to draw the Ottomans out to sea, stringing out his fleet along the west coast of Lefkada, with the Venetians in the rear, including a large, heavily armed galleon. The Ottomans swarmed the Venetian galleon with smaller galleys but were unable to take it, although they captured and sank other Holy League vessels. During the day, the Ottomans lost no ships but suffered ship damage and casualties, including four hundred dead and eight hundred wounded. Holy League losses were much greater, including thirteen ships sunk or burned, thirty-six ships captured, and three thousand prisoners taken. Andrea Doria had a favorable wind and retreated to Corfu, infamously extinguishing his stern lanterns to avoid detection, in spite of pleas from his papal, Venetian, and Maltese commanders to continue the fight. Some historians speculate that Doria did not wish to risk the Spanish-Genoese ships, many of which were his personal vessels, and preferred to sacrifice his long-time rivals, the Venetians.

The battle was both a tactical victory for the Ottomans as well as a resounding strategic success. The victory at Preveza led to two additional decades of Ottoman supremacy in the Mediterranean based on fear of Ottoman invincibility at sea. Charles V's disastrous loss of his fleet in storms off Algiers in 1541 compounded problems for the Europeans in the sixteenth-century naval equation in the Mediterranean. Following Barbarossa's death in 1546, Ottoman naval pre-eminence continued with significant victories at the battles of Ponza, an island near Naples, in 1552 under the Ottoman commander Dragut; and at Djerba, an island off Tunisia, in 1560 under the Ottoman commander Piyali. Both commanders were subsequently involved in Ottoman leadership during the siege of Malta. Despite the momentum of the rise of Ottoman sea power to this point in the sixteenth century, Ottoman naval pre-eminence was about to be stalled at Malta in 1565 and stalemated at Lepanto in 1571.

SIEGE OF MALTA, 1565

In early September 1565, Ottoman admiral Piyali Pasha commanded his galleys to set sail from Malta's St. Paul's Bay to begin a one-thousand-mile retreat to Constantinople. Three thousand Ottoman bodies floated in the bay, remnants of the bloody final battle of the siege that had brought the Ottomans to Malta to fight the Knights of St. John four months earlier. Had the Ottomans been successful in taking Malta, the history of Europe might have been different. Strategically located in the middle of the Mediterranean, Malta likely would have been the Ottoman stepping stone to Sicily and beyond, as it was for the Allies during World War II. Piyali's retreat moved the course of history in a different direction.

Returning to the beginning of the siege in Malta, Suleiman the Magnificent kept an eye on the Knights as they resettled on the strategically located island of Malta in 1530. Situated in the center of the constricted waist of the Mediterranean, the Knights on Malta were in position to control maritime traffic between the eastern and western halves of the Mediterranean Sea. With Ottoman naval power ascending progressively through victories at Rhodes in 1522, Preveza in 1538, and Djerba in 1560, the Ottomans perceived the Knights' control of Malta as an impediment to further development of their maritime power.[14]

Jean Parisot de La Valette became grand master of the Knights in 1557. He had been a young soldier who fought for the Knights during the siege of Rhodes and subsequently was captured and served as a galley slave to Barbary corsairs before escaping and rising to command the Knight's fleet of galleys and finally to appointment as grand master. On Malta, he commanded between 6,000 and 8,500 troops, approximately the same number that had defended Rhodes. Troop cohesion was bound by common Christian faith, except for the five hundred or so galley slaves. Although they spoke a Semitic language similar to some forms of Arabic, the Maltese were mostly Christian, and they supported the Knights loyally during the siege.

Estimates regarding the Ottoman invading force that targeted Malta vary between 20,000 and 50,000 troops, depending on whether the estimate includes only troops sent from Constantinople, or also includes North African corsairs and troops from the western side of the Ottoman Empire. Some sources assume 30,000 troops, including 6,000 Janissaries, plus galley slaves. In any event, the number of Ottoman troops at Malta was fewer than the number deployed at the siege of Rhodes.[15]

The fortifications of Malta, although solid, were less substantial than those on Rhodes. Malta is considerably smaller than Rhodes, with an area of 95 square miles versus Rhodes' 540 square miles, suggesting the rationale for a smaller landing force. Mobilization across a greater distance at sea also was a limiting factor on the size of the Ottoman force deployed on Malta.

In May 1565, initially unopposed Ottoman landings took place south of the fortified areas of Malta's protected harbors on the east side of the island. Fort Saint Elmo was built on the promontory between two long harbor inlets, Marsamuscetto to the north and Grand Harbor to the south. Two other fortresses were built in the southwest part of Grand Harbor, Saint Angelo on Birgu peninsula, and Saint Michael on Senglea peninsula. The Ottomans calculated that Fort Saint Elmo was the key defense structure protecting the Marsamuscetto harbor that Admiral Piyale wished to use as his base for the siege. Whether or not this sequence was the best strategy, the Ottomans attacked Saint Elmo first, believing it would fall within a few days. The Knights held out for much longer than expected, encouraged by Grand Master La Valette's offers of money and wine in addition to appealing to their more profound sense of duty. Taking the fort from the Knights took a month, during which the Ottomans lost half of their Janissary force.

Whereas the Knights' leadership was unified in the person of La Valette, Ottoman leadership was divided by Sultan Suleiman, who appointed separate land force leadership under General Mustapha Pasha and naval force leadership under Admiral Piyali, and with both advised to take counsel from Barbarossa's protégé and successor, Dragut. Dragut died of wounds on the day Saint Elmo was taken. Disputes about strategy continued between Mustapha and Piyali until the Ottomans returned to Constantinople at the end of the siege.

After taking Fort Saint Elmo, the Ottomans continued to press against the other two forts during July. The Knights had summoned reinforcements from other parts of Europe, including a relief force that was assembling in Sicily. The Ottomans breached the walls of the forts in August, seeming to doom the Christian position, in spite of the Knights' grand master appearing on the walls to inspire the defenders. But the

Ottomans hesitated at a critical moment: when the Christian cavalry from the interior town of Mdina appeared and sacked their base camp, the Ottomans mistook these troops for the Christian relief force from Sicily and stopped their attack. In early September, when the actual relief force arrived, the Ottoman leadership overestimated the relief force size and withdrew, first to St. Paul's Bay in northeast Malta, where a bloody battle took place, and from there to Constantinople by sea. The loss of Dragut's wisdom was sorely felt. La Valette's focused siege defense proved more effective than the divided offensive strategies of Mustapha and Piyali.

The siege of Malta instilled fear of Ottoman expansion as far away as England, providing a rationale for cohesive Christian action in the face of Ottoman expansionary pressure. The successful defense of Malta by the Knights demonstrated that the Ottomans were not invincible and could be stopped. The siege of Malta was a strategic victory for the Christian Europeans because it halted forty years of progressive Mediterranean expansion led by the rise of the Ottoman navy.

NAVAL BATTLE OF LEPANTO, 1571

The battle of Lepanto plays an important role in the history of naval warfare as it is taught in the West. This decisive sea battle took place on October 7, 1571. Christian and Ottoman naval forces faced each other again, as they had at Preveza in 1538, this time about seventy miles south of Preveza and thirty miles west of Lepanto near the island of Oxia.[16] The battle is notable for being the last substantial naval engagement in the West to be fought between rowed vessels. It involved more than four hundred warships, making it the largest naval battle in the Mediterranean since classical times.

Several Catholic maritime states representing the Holy League provided more than two hundred galleys and six galleasses commanded by Admiral Don Juan of Austria. Holy League participants came from Venice, which provided more than half the warships, along with Austria, Genoa, Malta, the Papal States, Savoy, and Spain including Naples and Sicily. The Ottoman fleet commanded by Ali Pasha consisted of more than two hundred galleys and more than forty galliots. Each side had about 30,000 soldiers and 40,000–50,000 sailors and oarsmen. There was rough parity between numbers of ships and men, but the Holy League held the edge in guns, with more than 1,800, compared with 750 for the Ottomans.

Before the battle of Lepanto, the Holy League Christian coalition had been organized by Pope Pius V to protect the Venetian colony of Famagusta on Cyprus, which had come under Ottoman siege after the fall of Nicosia to the Ottomans in 1570. Despite these papal efforts, in August 1571, the Famagusta Venetians surrendered after being told that they could leave Cyprus. But after losing about 50,000 men during the siege, the Ottoman commander, Mustafa Pasha, broke his word, imprisoned the Venetians, beheaded some officers, and flayed alive the Venetian fortress commander Marco Antonio Bragadin. During July and August 1571, the Holy League fleet gathered at Messina in Sicily and was blessed by the pope. Upon receiving news of the fall of Famagusta and torture of Bragadin, the fleet crossed the Adriatic in spite of internal dissent among league members resulting from the competitive positions taken by Spain, Genoa, and Venice. Despite bad weather, the fleet reached Kefalonia. On October 7, the Holy League fleet sailed east toward the Gulf of Patras, where they encountered the Ottoman fleet. Both sides decided to engage near Oxia Island and Scrofa Point on the north side of the Gulf of Patras as it flows into the Ionian Sea. From the time they sighted each other at dawn, it took about six hours for the two fleets to array themselves in battle formation. Two great battle lines were set up on a north-south axis.[17]

The Holy League fleet organized itself south of Oxia Island in a battle line facing east. The Christian Center Division was commanded by Austrian admiral Don Juan with more than sixty galleys.[18] He was flanked to the north by Left Division commander Venetian Agostino Barbarigo with about fifty-five galleys, and to the south by Right Division commander, Genoese Giovanni Andrea Doria also with about fifty-five galleys.[19] A reserve division stayed behind the battle line to assist where needed. The six larger galleasses with heavy guns were positioned in front of the battle line to lead the charge and wreak damage before the fleets fully engaged.

To the east, the Ottoman Center Division was commanded by Ali Pasha with more than ninety galleys. He was flanked to the north by Right Division commander Mehmet Sirocco with about fifty-five galleys, and to the south by Left Division commander Uluch Ali with about sixty-five galleys. The Ottomans kept a small division in reserve for reinforcement but had no galleasses to lead the charge. They did employ some smaller galliots to row in under the oars of opposing galleys to disrupt their rowing ability. Thus set up, the two battle lines were about evenly matched in numbers, although the Christians maintained a substantial reserve reinforcement division to supplement any of the forward line divisions that appeared to be failing and had six larger, heavily armed galleasses leading their forward line. Before the battle, Ali Pasha is reputed to have promised liberty to his rowing slaves if the battle was won. Don Juan told his rowing slaves that there was no paradise for cowards, but he released them from their chains. Don Juan's approach proved to have a later tactical advantage.

At the start of the battle, the wind was behind the Ottomans, and the Christians feared that contact would be made before the battle line was formed. But the wind shifted to favor the Christians just before noon, allowing assigned positions to be reached before contact. The Christian galleasses opened fire to confuse the lead Ottoman galleys. On the northern end of the line nearest the shore, the ships of Christian Barbarigo and Ottoman Sirocco made contact. Barbarigo attempted to stay close to shore to keep Sirocco from surrounding him, but Sirocco still inserted galleys, some which ran aground. The Scrofa Point sandbar was likely more submerged than it is today. The galleys formed a continuous platform for hand-to-hand combat in which both fleet commanders were killed. Meanwhile, Christian galley slaves broke free on the Ottoman ships and turned the battle in favor of the Christian side. In the center of the line, the flagships and their fleets clashed, allowing Spanish infantry and Ottoman Janissaries to fight hand to hand. Ottoman forces broke up their forward attack line to go around the six heavily armed Venetian galleasses and were in relative disarray by the time they reached the Holy League divisions. Nevertheless, the Christian flagship was nearly taken before reinforcements arrived and killed Ali Pasha and the entire Ottoman flagship crew. The Holy League banner was raised on the Ottoman flagship, breaking the morale of the Ottoman galleys. On the southern end of the line, Ottoman Uluch Ali got the better of Doria, who had sailed too far south to avoid being flanked. Uluch Ali attacked the center rather than pursue Doria, nearly shifting momentum back to the Ottomans. Ultimately, the Christian reserve squadron forced Uluch Ali to retreat, leaving victory to the Holy League navy. Mop-up operations continued until the evening, as Ottoman Janissaries continued fighting to the last.

Holy League losses for the one-day battle at Lepanto were heavy, but Ottoman casualties were three times as high, and the proportional loss of ships was even higher. Approximately 7,500 Christian soldiers and sailors died in the battle, about 10 percent of those involved. On the Ottoman side, approximately 20,000 were killed, wounded, or captured, 25 to 30 percent of those involved, and 12,000 Christian slaves, mostly rowers, were freed. The Holy League lost 17 ships, while 50 Ottoman ships were sunk and 137 were captured.

It was a devastating naval loss for the Ottomans. It ended their maritime dominance in the eastern Mediterranean and thus their expansionary capability. In spite of this, the Holy League failed to regain any of the territories previously lost to the Ottomans, and the Ottomans, due to their formidable land forces and administrative infrastructure, did not lose any territory despite losing control of the eastern Mediterranean.

The Ottomans continued to be a status quo power in the region with firm administrative control, albeit less expansionary, for another two centuries. The loss at Lepanto marked the beginning of a period of stagnation for the Ottomans rather than a period of direct decline. After Lepanto, the Ottomans quickly rebuilt their navy, but with inferior ships and crews. Meanwhile, cracks in the Holy League widened, and the united Christian fleet failed to sail together in 1573, indicating the end of a Holy League opposed to the Ottomans. Cyprus remained with the Ottomans in the treaty of that year, and Venice resumed trade negotiations rather than return to war with the Ottomans, a peace that lasted until the 1645 Cretan War.

The Ottoman Navy in the Indian Ocean

While the Ottomans fought European Christians in rowed galleys in the Mediterranean Sea during the sixteenth century, they began a parallel campaign against the Arabs and the Portuguese in the Red Sea, the Persian Gulf, and the Arabian Sea. There were substantial differences facing the Ottomans in the divergent maritime theaters of the Mediterranean Sea and the Indian Ocean. To the west, the Ottomans sought to solidify control of their land empire in Anatolia, Syria, North Africa, and southeastern Europe adjacent to the Mediterranean Sea. To the east, the Ottomans sought to control the coastlines of the Red Sea and the Persian Gulf, and also to challenge Portuguese influence in the Arabian Sea. The Ottoman Indian Ocean maritime theater was more defensive, whereas the Mediterranean maritime theater required a more aggressive, offensive posture.

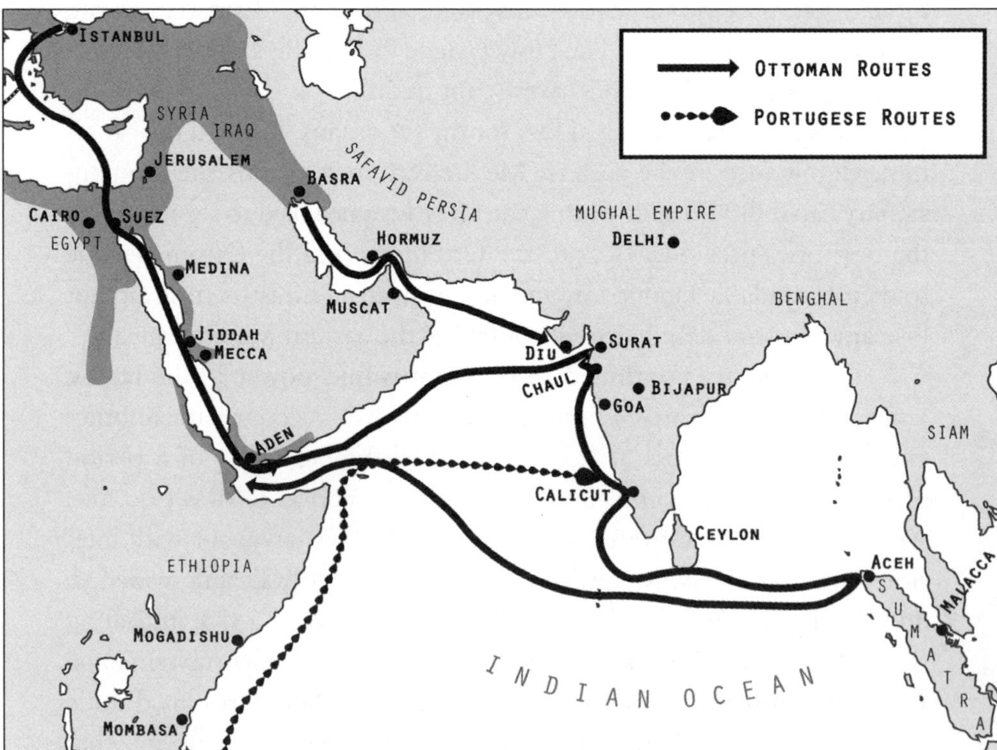

MAP 5.3 Indian Ocean maritime theater
Adapted by Jamie Rhode from Casale, The Ottoman Age of Exploration, *81*

This case study focuses on the Ottomans in the Mediterranean, but Map 5.3 notes the routes of Ottomans in the Indian Ocean during the sixteenth century for comparative reference. During this period, the Ottomans had less success against the Portuguese than they did against the Holy League. Portuguese caravels and carracks were built for open seas and had an advantage over Ottoman galleys in the broad reaches of the Indian Ocean.

Hayreddin Barbarossa: Revered Ottoman Admiral

In a highly competitive maritime environment, Barbarossa was the Mediterranean's most successful naval commander during the last quarter-century of his life. Barbarossa, "Redbeard" in Italian, adopted the colorful name from his elder brother Oruc when he was killed by the Spanish following a siege in 1518 at Tlemcen near the Algerian-Moroccan border.[20] The brothers, Oruc and Khizr, both to be called Barbarossa, were born and raised along with two other brothers in the northeast Aegean Sea on the island of Lesbos, by their Muslim Albanian father, a potter and merchant, and their Greek Christian mother.[21] The sons took to the sea early as part of their father's trade but subsequently turned to a life of plunder at sea that was tempered by a broader vision of becoming established potentates on the north African coast. Although born in the eastern Mediterranean, the brothers eventually built their power base in the western Mediterranean. After the death of his older brother Oruc, younger brother Khizr eventually reasserted Ottoman power in the eastern Mediterranean. In addition to being given the honorific title Hayreddin,[22] "best of the faith," he was appointed by Suleiman the Magnificent in 1533 to be the *kapudan-i derya*, grand admiral, of the Ottoman navy, as well as *beylerbey*, governor general, of North Africa. As grand admiral, he had both the vision and logistical genius to build a great navy in shipyards he developed in Consta-ntinople. He successfully brought many islands formerly under Venetian control into Ottoman administration. The battle of Preveza in 1538 was his greatest naval success. In this battle, the Ottoman navy defeated the combined Spanish, papal, Malta, Genoa, and Venice naval forces of the Holy

League. The subsequent twenty-five years were the pinnacle of Ottoman naval ascendancy in the Mediterranean, which lasted twenty years after Barbarossa's passing in 1546. It was also the greatest period of Ottoman ascendancy on land under Suleiman the Magnificent. At the time of his death, Hayreddin Barbarossa was known appropriately in Constantinople as "The King of the Sea." Although the Portuguese and Spanish with their sailing ships were becoming dominant in the broad oceans by the mid-sixteenth century, to be followed in the seventeenth century by the Dutch and the English, Barbarossa controlled both the western and eastern Mediterranean during the mid-sixteenth century with his rowed galleys supplemented by sail power.

A physical description of Khizr/Hayreddin Barbarossa suggests that he was an imposing leader. "His stature was advantageous; his Mien portly and majestick; well-proportioned and robust; very hairy, with a Beard extremely bushy; his Brows and Eye-lashes remarkably long and thick; Before his Hair turned grey and hoary, it was a bright Auburn; so that the Surname Barbarossa, or Red-Beard, was conferred on him, rather to preserve the memory of his Brother Aruj, than from any Title he had to that Appellation."[23]

BAND OF BROTHERS' FAMILY CULTURE

Oruc Reis,[24] the original Ottoman Barbarossa,[25] was elder brother and mentor to Khizr, Hayreddin Barbarossa. Oruc, a linguistic polymath, spoke Italian, Spanish, French, Greek, and Arabic. He became a successful seaman, learning the trade by commanding ships carrying pottery from his father's business in Lesbos to other Mediterranean ports. He was wounded and captured by the Knights of St. John based at Rhodes during the 1490s and served time as a galley slave on *Our Lady of the Conception*,[26] the ship that captured him. The experience left him with no love for Christians and galvanized his sense of mission to defeat naval opponents. After achieving freedom again, probably through ransom payment, Oruc made the island of Djerba his base in 1503, where he was accompanied by Khizr. He became known as Baba Oruc, father

Oruc, by the thousands of Morisco and Jewish refugees he brought from Spain to North Africa, especially in the campaigns between 1504 and 1510, such as the raids into Calabria in 1505 and Liguria in 1507.[27] He came to be called Barbarossa because of his red beard, and perhaps also as a corruption of the sobriquet Baba Oruc. By 1510, Oruc was one of the richest men in the Mediterranean. After 1510, he continued to conduct successful raids, but these were coupled with some setbacks as well. He lost his left arm in a battle in 1512 at Bougie, east of Algiers, which he replaced with a silver prosthetic, resulting in his being known as "silver arm" as well as "red beard."

Oruc developed a reputation as an aggressive, tactically brilliant commander. After he became ruler of Algiers in 1516, he offered the city to Ottoman sultan Selim I. Selim appointed him *bey* (governor) of Algiers and *beylerbey* (governor general) of the western Mediterranean in 1517, transitioning him from a private operator into a respected government official shortly before his death. After Oruc died in battle at Tlemcen in 1518, his younger brother Khizr, who had served with him for two decades, took over his career, responsibilities, and the name Barbarossa. He carried forward Oruc's fearsome reputation through continued tactical successes but added to them greater strategic vision. Oruc and Khizr had two brothers who campaigned with them, Ilyas and Ishak, both of whom died in battle.[28]

KHIZR TAKES THE HELM

Following Oruc's death and adoption of his feared name Barbarossa in 1519, Khizr consolidated control around Algiers and was recognized by Sultan Suleiman the Magnificent as the *beylerbey* of Algiers.[29] Despite official Ottoman navy reversals against combined Genoese/Spanish forces led by the Genoese commander Andrea Doria, Barbarossa had a string of substantial successes in the western Mediterranean. These included recapturing Tlemcen in 1518, raiding Toulon in 1519, raiding the Balearic Islands in 1521, and assisting Kurtoglu, the Ottoman commander at Rhodes, to participate in the successful siege of 1522. He also raided Sardinia in 1525, Calabria in 1526, and many Italian and Spanish ports in 1527. Ever more feared, in 1529 Barbarossa captured the Spanish fort on Penon, which controlled the Algerian coast, and attacked the coast of Spain, freeing 70,000 Moriscos, Spanish Muslims who had converted to Catholicism. In 1530, he raided Sicily, Provence, Liguria, Sardinia, and the Balearics. In 1531, he repulsed Andrea Doria's attempt to retake Penon de Velez de la Gomera on the Moroccan coast, sank a ship of the Maltese Knights near Messina, and raided the coast of Spain.

In 1532, Andrea Doria captured Coron, Patras, and Lepanto, which the sultan recaptured, but this made Suleiman realize the need for a powerful sea commander. Barbarossa's record over the past decade made him the prime candidate, so in 1533 the sultan summoned Barbarossa to Constantinople to take control of the Ottoman navy and defeat all of its enemies. He bestowed two important titles on Barbarossa, *kapudan-i derya* (grand admiral) of the Ottoman navy and *beylerbey* (governor general) of North Africa and gave him governing powers in the provinces of Rhodes, Euboea, and Chios, all in the Aegean. No longer a corsair working on the western fringes of the Ottoman Empire, Barbarossa continued his maritime career for more than two decades as the chief naval officer of the Ottoman Empire, with substantial fiefdoms in North Africa and the Aegean.[30]

Barbarossa established naval dominance with naval missions to France in 1533 and 1534, in which the French sought assistance against the Hapsburgs. He also carried out major raids along the Tunisian and Italian coasts, capturing Tunis in 1535 and attacking Naples in 1536, although he was unsuccessful in his siege of the Venetian stronghold on Corfu. During 1537, Barbarossa captured Otranto and many Aegean and Ionian islands that belonged to the Republic of Venice, including Syros, Aegina, Ios, Paros, Tinos, Karpathos, Kasos, and Naxos. In 1538, he led the Ottoman navy to destroy Venetian Crete. Then in September, Barbarossa proceeded to his most important naval victory at Preveza in the Ionian Sea. This substantial fleet engagement cemented Barbarossa's reputation as the chief naval commander of the mid-sixteenth-century Mediterranean.

CONSOLIDATION OF MARITIME CONTROL IN THE MEDITERRANEAN

After the 1538 victory at Preveza, Barbarossa continued to expand Ottoman control in the Mediterranean by capturing many islands from the Christians, including Skiathos, Skyros, and Andros and recapturing Castelnuovo and Risan in present-day Montenegro. Venice signed a treaty to recognize Ottoman territorial gains in 1540 and paid 300,000 gold ducats in indemnity. In a 1540 attempt to win over his archrival on the sea, Hapsburg emperor Charles V offered to make Barbarossa his admiral-in-chief and ruler of Spain's territories in North Africa. When Barbarossa spurned the offer, Charles V attacked Algiers in 1541, but much of his fleet was grounded in violent storms during October and November, and the Christian fleet was forced to withdraw in December. Charles lost so many troops that Christian slaves were reportedly sold in Algiers for an onion per head. Barbarossa carried on by confirming his alliance with the French and continued successful raids in Italy, Sardinia, Majorca, and Minorca. He also met with Andrea Doria in Genoa to free his captured commander Dragut.[31] In 1545, he retired in Istanbul, built a palace on the Bosphorus, appointed his son Hasan Pasha as his successor in Algiers, and dictated his memoirs in five handwritten volumes now kept at the Topkapi Palace. Barbarossa died peacefully in his Bosphorus palace in 1546.

In spite of his recognition by the sultan as admiral-in-chief, Barbarossa had opponents within the Ottoman power structure. He was regarded as a corsair by Ottoman commanders who had gone through the conventional Ottoman ranks, and his appointment thus engendered jealousy by other competent commanders, such as Sinan Reis. Although Grand Vizier Ibrahim recommended that Barbarossa be elevated to the rank of lead admiral, Barbarossa had differences with him as well. Most notably, Ibrahim was more sympathetic to Venice than was Hayreddin since Ibrahim's family roots were in Venice.

Not only did Barbarossa have opposition within the ranks of the Ottoman commanders, he also faced overwhelming opposition from his European enemies. After successfully taking Tunis from Muley Hassan in 1534, he only had a small force there when Charles V came to Muley Hassan's assistance in the spring of 1535. In one of his rare losses, Barbarossa's troops were driven from Tunis. His commanders urged him to return to Constantinople to request reinforcements to face the forces of Charles V on an equal footing. Rejecting this advice, he led his forces to Minorca, laying waste to dominions of Charles V and taking six thousand slaves. Following this successful aggressive counterattack, Barbarossa asked his commanders, "What think you then is this not better than going to the Levant?"[32]

LEGACY

Was Barbarossa an outlaw pirate or a distinguished naval commander? The answer depends on the part of his career being considered and on the point of view of the person making the judgment. He has been called the "greatest pirate in history" as well as the most distinguished admiral of the mid-sixteenth century.[33] Khizr's career moved progressively from being a seaman on his father's ship transporting pottery between the 1490s and the early 1500s, to reuniting with his brother Oruc after the latter's release from incarceration at Bodrum by the Knights of St. John, to plundering the Knights' merchant ships, to establishing a fiefdom at Algiers recognized by the Ottoman sultan beginning in 1517, to being appointed admiral-in-chief of Sultan Suleiman the Magnificent's fleet from 1533 until his death in 1546.

Although Suleiman might have been a less effective tactician than his predecessor Selim I, the peak of Ottoman power and the territory of the empire was attained during Suleiman's reign. Sultan Suleiman made what appears to have been a strategic mistake when in 1541 he dismissed Grand Vizier Ibrahim, a man who supported Ottoman naval strength. Suleiman instead concentrated on land battles in Hungary and so was insufficiently prepared to ensure victory two decades after Barbarossa's death at the siege of Malta in 1565, which began the decline of Ottoman naval power in the Mediterranean. On the role of Barbarossa during Suleiman's reign, Bradford opines, "If the years 1538 until the death of Sultan Suleiman in 1566 were the most glorious in the history of the Ottoman Empire, it was largely due to Kheir-ed-Din."[34]

By appointing Barbarossa admiral of the fleet in 1533, Suleiman set the stage for a quantum leap in Ottoman dominance at sea. Barbarossa was a planner who worked carefully and diligently. "The supremacy of Turkey at sea dates from Kheir-ed-Din's first winter in the dockyards of this city. . . . Barbarossa was continually in the arsenal where he did both eat and drink to lose no time. . . . Inspiring his men with his marvelous energy, he laid out sixty-one galleys during the winter, and was able to take to the sea with a fleet of eighty-four vessels in the spring."[35] Thus Grand Vizier Ibrahim's statement in his recommendation to appoint Barbarossa, "We have set our hand on a veritable man of the sea," was fully justified.

During Barbarossa's lifetime, French, Spanish, and British opinion recognized Barbarossa's talent and accomplishment, although later scholarship demeaned him as a pirate. The Ottomans, however, never forgot him, as they said upon his death, "The King of the Sea is dead." His tomb and monument on the shore of the Bosphorus in the Besiktas section of Istanbul near where his ships anchored and where he built his retirement palace has been a place of pilgrimage and honor since his death. In subsequent centuries Ottoman and Turkish navies have conducted ceremonies and offerings at his tomb before major expeditions.

Reflections on the Ottoman Naval Experience

A comparison of the sieges of Rhodes and Malta and the naval battles of Preveza and Lepanto, is useful to understanding why the outcome of these clashes were so consequential to the history of the Mediterranean region.

QUESTIONS ARISING FROM THE OTTOMAN NAVAL RISE AND STALL IN THE SIXTEENTH CENTURY

Why did the Ottomans drive the Knights from Rhodes in 1521 but fail to drive the Knights from Malta in 1565? Table 5.1 compares the sieges of Rhodes and Malta. Primary factors leading to Ottoman success at Rhodes and failure at Malta were unity of command, short supply lines of communication, and the imposition of an effective naval blockade at

Rhodes, while at Malta there was divided command structure, long supply lines of communication, and an ineffective naval blockade. Secondary factors were related to relative imperviousness of fortifications, numbers of forces, seasonal conditions, and relief force availability.

Why did the Ottomans succeed in the naval Battle of Preveza but not at the naval Battle of Lepanto? Table 5.2 compares the naval battles of Preveza and Lepanto. Primary factors leading to Ottoman success at Preveza were unity of command and ability to choose the moment of battle with favorable conditions, while at Lepanto the Holy League had more unified command structure and superior technology with its six galleasses.

These comparisons demonstrate the sixteenth-century rise and stall of Ottoman naval power in the eastern Mediterranean, with success during the reign of Barbarossa and inability to expand Ottoman naval power thereafter.

TABLE 5.1
Comparison of Ottoman actions in the sieges of Rhodes (1522) and Malta (1565)

Aspect	Rhodes	Malta
Leadership	Suleiman consolidated leadership	Mustapha, Piyali, Dragut Divided leadership
Geography	300 miles from Constantinople Close to Ottoman shore	1,000 miles from Constantinople Far from Ottoman shore
Knights' fortifications	On soil: tunneling option	On rock: no tunneling option
Crop potential	Verdant	Barren
Ottoman land forces	100,000 troops	40,000 troops
Knights land forces	8,000	8,000
Navy	Effective blockade	Ineffective blockade
Knights' relief force	Never arrived	Arrived (late)
Siege period	Aug–Dec 1522: Suleiman committed to the end	May–Sep 1565: Leaders not committed to winter
Result	Ottoman tactical and strategic victory	Holy League tactical and strategic victory

TABLE 5.2
Comparison of Ottoman actions in the battles of Preveza (1538) and Lepanto (1571)

Aspect	Preveza	Lepanto
Leadership	Holy League: divided under A Doria Ottoman: unified under Barbarossa	Holy League: unified under Don Juan Ottoman: divided
Geography	Ottoman control port and foray out	Ottoman control port and foray out
Fleet compositions	Slightly larger Holy League fleet	Approx. equal # of ships
Technology	Similar on both sides	Holy League: Galleass advantage Holy League: had twice as many cannon
Weather	Shifting winds	Shifting winds
Battle period	1 day: Sep 28, 1538	1 day: Oct 7, 1571
Result	Ottoman victory	Holy League victory
Aftermath	Continued Ottoman naval expansion until 1565	Ottoman naval power stalemated

Maritime Strategic and Tactical Lessons

The successes and failures of the Ottoman navy during the sixteenth century provide useful lessons about maritime strategy and tactics.

LOCAL KNOWLEDGE OF NATURAL PHENOMENA

Currents and tides in the Mediterranean are relatively mild compared to most oceans of the world. Tides average about one to one and half feet, with variance from a few inches in a place with a flat coastline such as Algiers to almost three feet in Trieste at the head of the Adriatic funnel. This pales in comparison to tides of about five feet in Busan and Hong Kong, eight feet in Malacca, ten feet in Bombay, or the monster forty-five-foot tides at the head of the Bay of Fundy funnel. Winds, however, are a significant factor in the Mediterranean. For instance, the famed annual *meltemi* north wind that blows into the Saronic Gulf (milder) and Aegean Sea (wilder) during the summer can be either a sailor's delight or nightmare when it rises to 7–8 on the Beaufort scale (thirty to seventy knots). The early winter storms in the Mediterranean put cautious sailors in retreat during that season. In general, the Ottomans responded better to the storms than did the Hapsburg fleet. Barbarossa knew well the north African storm season, but Charles V got caught by storms and lost 150 ships and 17,000 men off the coast of Algiers in late October 1541. The Ottoman navy retreated from Malta in 1565, cutting short its siege of the island, in order to get back to the Constantinople docks before the early winter storms struck. They lost the siege, but saved the fleet, a tradeoff to be pondered for relative value.

ADVANTAGES IN MILITARY TECHNOLOGY

Venetians controlled the eastern Mediterranean Sea for about three hundred years from 1200 to 1500. They extended their trading routes from the Mediterranean to the Black Sea ports connected to the Asian land-based "silk road," and to the Persian Gulf and Red Sea ports connecting to the sea-based Asian maritime "silk road." The Ottomans became fierce competitors with the Venetians in the late fifteenth century and soon were able to build galleys to the high standards set by the Venetians. Galleys, with their combination of oar and sail power, were well-suited to controlling the Mediterranean, where ports were always within a day or two of shore and where provisions were easily accessible for the massive crews needed to keep a rowed galley properly staffed. While Ottoman ship technology did not significantly surpass that of their Mediterranean competitors, it was adequate to win sea control, especially after Barbarossa rebuilt the Ottoman naval shipyards in Constantinople during the 1530s.

In the Indian Ocean, the Ottoman story was different. In those waters, the Ottoman galleys could not compete with the blue-water sailing capacity of the Portuguese caravels and carracks. Blocked from the Mediterranean by their Spanish neighbors, the Portuguese conceived the idea of sailing through the Atlantic rather than through the Mediterranean to get to the riches of trade with India, the Spice Islands, and China. It took decades of constant effort by the Portuguese to develop the blue-water sailing ships that had the strength and agility to be effective against the currents and winds of the South Atlantic, before they finally made it to the Indian Ocean in 1498, six years after the Spanish arrived in the Americas. In the Indian Ocean, the Ottoman brown-water galleys were unable to compete with the Portuguese blue-water sailing vessels. Thus the Ottoman navy never had the success in the Indian Ocean that it had in the Mediterranean.

CONTINENTAL VS. MARITIME IDENTITIES

The Ottomans fundamentally saw themselves as a land power. They controlled the sea by controlling the land. This worked in the Mediterranean Sea, the Red Sea, and the Persian Gulf, but it did not work in the broader expanses of the Indian Ocean. On the maritime front, the Ottoman navy became approximately coequal to the Mediterranean navies of the Hapsburgs, the Italian city-states, and the island-based Knights. Meanwhile, during the fifteenth century, Portugal had developed a true maritime identity with fewer continental aspirations. Their maritime identity eventually overshadowed the Ottoman continental identity in the Indian Ocean, where the broad ocean expanses did not allow the Ottomans to control the sea by controlling the land.

DEEPLY FELT NATIONAL IDENTITIES

Clashes between the Ottomans and Europeans were less about identity with national place and more about identity with religion. The wars were reminiscent of the Crusades in many ways. Catholic Christianity united several national powers of Europe into the Holy League to fight the Muslim Ottomans. Each side enslaved the other. Muslims served as galley slaves on Christian ships, and Christians served as galley slaves on Ottoman ships. Naval commanders on each side rose to their positions of command from their earlier roles as slaves on the opposite side's galley benches. Such memories stoked the bitterness of response during conflict. The connection with the Crusades for the Knights of St. John was direct. They had arrived on Rhodes after being expelled from Jerusalem and Acre in the thirteenth century. The sieges of Rhodes and

Malta were similar to the earlier Crusade sieges in the Holy Land. For instance, although Venice and Genoa were profound rivals in their trading competition and in setting up their outpost forts in the eastern Mediterranean and Black Seas, they came together under the banner of the Holy League to fight the Ottomans, albeit with strains in their alliance. Their common Christianity took precedence over their proud city-state identities.

MILITARY LEADERSHIP

Suleiman the Magnificent made a good choice by offering Hayreddin Barbarossa the post of admiral of the Ottoman fleet. With his many years under the tutelage of his elder brother, the original Barbarossa, the younger Barbarossa built further upon his maritime skills, people skills, and organizational skills, as well as reinforcing the ferocity and single-mindedness of his capable sibling. Although opposed by some who were jealous of his rapid rise coming from outside the Ottoman navy, Barbarossa's vision and discipline in improving the shipyards and his record of winning naval battles brought him acceptance, and then veneration. Barbarossa's archrival in the Mediterranean was Andrea Doria of Genoa. The rivalry of these two naval commanders came to a head in 1538 when Andrea Doria led the Holy League force south along the Adriatic, where Barbarossa had gathered his fleet in the mouth of the Gulf of Ambracia, the same spot where Octavian had vanquished the combined forces of Marc Antony and Cleopatra in the naval battle of Actium in 31 BCE. Barbarossa refused to be lured from the defensible port of Preveza into battle with the larger Holy League force until the wind changed in the Ottomans' favor and he was able to successfully attack the Venetian rearguard of the Holy League ship column, which had begun to move away, with Andrea Doria protecting his ships from Genoa at the head of the column. With this victory, Barbarossa established himself as the greatest commander in the Mediterranean. He remained so until his death in 1546, under peaceful circumstances in his villa on the Bosphorus. Subsequent Ottoman naval commanders could not match his nearly perfect record. He is still venerated by the modern Turkish navy as the greatest naval national hero. In August 2019, the Turkish navy fleet returning from the largest naval drill in its history enlivened a dormant Turkish maritime tradition by saluting the tomb of Barbaros Hayreddin Pasha as they sailed past the tomb's location in Besiktas on the western bank of the Bosphorus.[36]

RELATIVE POWER RELATIONS

Ottoman power rose quickly during the fifteenth century, leading to the fall of Constantinople in 1453. The Ottomans then sought to expand more broadly both to the east and to the west. The Ottoman rise included expansion into the eastern Mediterranean during the siege of Rhodes in 1521 and the battle of Preveza in 1538. The rise was stalled at the siege of Malta in 1565 and the battle of Lepanto in 1571. Despite the stall of its maritime expansion, Ottoman presence continued in the eastern Mediterranean with a similar footprint for more than two centuries until its demise as the "sick man of Europe," beginning with the Greek war of independence during the 1820s and culminating with the subsequent Ottoman collapse in the twentieth century during World War I.

ALLIANCE RELATIONS

The Ottomans failed to develop successful alliances in the Mediterranean. Instead of allying with Barbarossa as the governor of North Africa, Suleiman the Magnificent hired Barbarossa directly to be commander of his Navy. This "external hire" upset those who had been in longer service in the Ottoman navy, but Barbarossa was able to prevail by force of both personality and capability. Control of the Red Sea came to the Ottomans as a result of their conquering the Mamluks by land in Egypt, then controlling the Red Sea ports to keep out the Portuguese. In the broader Indian Ocean theater, the Ottoman navy attempted to fight alongside the navies of the Indian states of Gujarat and Kerala as allies to drive the Portuguese out of the Indian Ocean. This alliance had flaws that were exploitable, such as at the siege of Diu in 1538, and the combination of alliance flaws and Portuguese naval technological superiority in ships and guns which limited Ottoman naval success in the Indian Ocean. The single Ottoman force in the Mediterranean faced at least five naval foes: the Venetians, the Genoese, the Knights of St. John first on Rhodes and then on Malta, the papal naval force, and the Hapsburg navy, mostly Spanish, commanded by Charles V. The Ottoman navy was successful against all these other navies individually, including the powerful Venetians. In response, the pope pulled together a Holy League alliance of all five of these navies to oppose the Ottomans and challenge the Ottoman navy under Barbarossa's command at Preveza in 1538, with the Holy League navy commanded by Andrea Doria of Genoa. The Holy League alliance had fatal flaws in its unity, with Andrea Doria letting the Venetians take damage from the Ottomans while he sailed off in the lead to save his Genoese ships for another day. Thirty-three years later, however, the same group of naval partners in the Holy League faced off against the Ottoman navy at Lepanto in 1571. This time, Holy League commander Don Juan, appointed by Charles V, held together his forces and decisively defeated the Ottoman navy. This sequence demonstrates that alliances may be effective, but they must work together without flaws of disunity, even if the alliance partners have differing goals and suspicions of each other.

RELATIONSHIP OF MARITIME ECONOMIC SUCCESS TO MARITIME MILITARY SUCCESS

For both the Europeans and the Ottomans, trade was important, and naval capability reinforced the ability to trade. Between the thirteenth and fifteenth centuries, Venice grew wealthy beyond all other Europeans through trade supported by its armed ships and many forts in the eastern Mediterranean and Black Seas. Following the fall of Constantinople, the Ottomans began to compete with the Venetians, capturing Venetian forts to control the trade routes. Other forces, including the Genoese and the Knights of St. John, also became competitive targets for expanding Ottoman trade. Notably, the Knights controlled the trade route between Constantinople and Alexandria from their heavily fortified position on Rhodes. This trade route constriction was so important to Ottoman trade that Sultan Suleiman the Magnificent personally led the Ottoman siege of Rhodes in 1521. Ottoman success during this siege allowed for much more open trade for the Ottomans in the eastern Mediterranean. Thus maritime economic success was linked to maritime military success through the control of trade routes, whether by Ottoman or European navies.

IMPORTANCE OF HISTORICAL AND CURRENT KNOWLEDGE

Knowledge of the world expanded rapidly during the fifteenth and sixteenth centuries. Cartography became a key discipline for all naval powers. The Portuguese were well known for guarding their wide-ranging information gathering about sea travel, and this "information is power" approach gave them a competitive edge for a century. The Ottomans, however, also developed sea charts of great detail and value, most notably in Admiral Piri Reis' charts of the Mediterranean. His map of the three-island Malta archipelago established not only the relative layout of the islands to each other, but also the harbor details that became so critical during the siege of Malta. Piri Reis also sought and obtained the maps of Columbus, enabling him to create a world atlas that included not only Asia, but also Europe, Africa, the bulge of South America, the Caribbean Islands, and the Atlantic Ocean. Both the Ottomans and Europeans developed and used new sources of information effectively in their competition.

LIMITS ON THE RISE OF THE OTTOMAN NAVY

The rise of the Ottoman navy to support continental ambitions was quick and initially effective in the Mediterranean between the late fifteenth century and mid-sixteenth century, the high point of Ottoman naval dominance. After that, European naval power in the Mediterranean stalemated the Ottoman naval rise.

SIX

Japan's Thwarted Maritime Invasions of Korea

Yi Sun-sin, Sixteenth Century

Japan Develops Continental Ambitions

The late sixteenth century was a period of dynamic tension in northeast Asia. After two hundred years of strength and consolidation, China's Ming Dynasty (1368–1644) had reached a period of stability, albeit with some worrying signs of decline. Japan, however, had worked its way through a long period of internal civil war. This "warring states" period (Sengoku Jidai 1467–1600)[1] in Japan was similar to China's warring states period (475–221 BCE) before it was united by Qin Shi Huang into the first of China's great dynasties, the Qin, in 221 BCE.[2]

UNIFICATION OF JAPAN

The dramatic unification of Japan during the later sixteenth century was led by Oda Nobunaga, then by his retainer and successor, Toyotomi Hideyoshi. By 1591, three of the main islands of Japan—Honshu, Shikoku, and Kyushu—were completely ruled by Hideyoshi, as was the southern tip of the northernmost fourth main island, Hokkaido. Aboriginal Ainu controlled the rest of Hokkaido, while the Ryukyu Islands remained under the rule of the Okinawan king in Naha. Importantly, the large island in the middle of the Korea Strait, Tsushima, was under the control of the So clan who paid homage to Hideyoshi.

Hideyoshi's unification was not entirely stable following his death in 1598. This stabilization was completed by another of Nobunaga's retainers, Tokugawa Ieyasu. His victory at the Battle of Sekigahara in 1600 led to two and a half centuries of stable Tokugawa rule in Japan.

During Hideyoshi's later years, Japan developed expansionist aims and challenged China during the Imjin War in a classic case of a power transition struggle between a rising power and a status quo power, in this case between a rising Japan and a status quo Ming Dynasty China in its later phases.

Besides desiring to end the civil wars among Japan's feudal lords (*daimyo*) and consolidating power under his command, Hideyoshi also set larger goals. His dream was continental, including dominance over China, with an eye toward Southeast Asia and India as well. Not completely understanding Korea's position as a tributary state to China, Hideyoshi assumed that Korea would side with Japan once his troops arrived in Korea. Additionally, he anticipated that the troops would not only be joined by Korean forces, but that Koreans would feed and house Japanese troops. Explanations for why Hideyoshi decided to invade the continent include a "lebensraum" theory in which Japan sought agricultural supply, much like Germany sought grain from Russia during the twentieth century. Another theory is the "excess samurai" theory. Once Japan's warring states civil war was concluded, where would samurai go to win prizes of war? The possible answer to this dilemma was expansion from east to west onto the Asian continent.

KOREA, ONCE AGAIN AT THE CENTER

The Joseon (Choson) Dynasty ruled Korea for more than five hundred years between 1392 and 1910. This dynasty was the longest period of unified rule on the Korean peninsula, although the Joseon Dynasty recognized Chinese suzerainty and paid tribute to China. Japan had last attempted a naval invasion of Korea in 663 during the three kingdoms period. Japan supported the kingdom of Baekche on the southwest side of the peninsula in a struggle against the southeast kingdom of Silla, which was supported by allied China. After the disastrous naval loss at the mouth of the Baekgang River on the coast of Baekche in 663, Japan did not invade Korea again until Hideyoshi's invasion attempt in 1592, 929 years later. During this millennium, apart from the attempted Mongol invasions of Japan in 1274 and 1281, Japan lived in relative maritime isolation, trading with Korea and China through So clan intermediaries in Tsushima and playing a role in piracy in the China Seas. Having experienced the Mongol invasions, Japan feared the possibility of invasions by Koreans or Chinese. Hideyoshi thought he could prevent this possibility by defeating and controlling China. As in the past, Korea was a "shrimp between whales," and would suffer during the sixteenth century as it had in the sixth and thirteenth centuries, since it was once again the nexus and corridor for great power rivalry between Japan and China.

The Imjin War, First and Second Japanese Invasions

Within one year of achieving peace at home in the Japanese main islands in 1591, Hideyoshi began his attempted conquest of China. He himself never set foot on the Asian mainland, and his forces never made it further than Pyongyang in northern Korea. Nevertheless, over the course of eight years, Korea was a battleground between the greater powers of Japan and China.

Hideyoshi's dream of conquest was ultimately thwarted on the Korean peninsula through the support of Chinese armies coming to the aid of the Korean resistance forces. Simultaneously, in the maritime realm off the peninsula's south coast, the Japanese navy was defeated by the Korean navy led by Korean admiral Yi Sun-sin.

The three phases of the Imjin War were marked by the first Japanese invasion of Korea beginning in May 1592, a negotiation period beginning in August 1593, and a second Japanese invasion beginning in September 1597. The war ended with the Japanese evacuation of Busan in December 1598. Hideyoshi died in September 1598, prior to the final evacuation. In the aftermath of the first two Japanese invasions, Hideyoshi's contemplated third invasion of Korea never took place.

MAP 6.1 Routes of Japanese invasions of Korea, 1592 and 1597
Adapted by Jamie Rhode from Stephen Turnbull, The Samurai Invasion of Korea 1592–1598 *(Oxford: Osprey, 2008), 25, 76*

FIRST JAPANESE INVASION, 1592–1593

In May 1592, Hideyoshi sent approximately 158,800 troops into Korea and was successful in taking the port of Busan before advancing through Seoul to Pyongyang by the end of July 1592. While Japanese success on land took place between May and July, between June and August, Korean admiral Yi Sun-sin defeated Japanese naval forces in a series of battles on Korea's south coast. In February 1593, after quelling a rebellion in western China, Ming Chinese troops finally retook Pyongyang from the Japanese. The Chinese army and the Korean irregular monk and volunteer army drove the Japanese back to Busan by July 1593. Busan became a coastal Japanese enclave where little fighting took place for the next four years until the second invasion in 1597. Following is a more detailed review of the Japanese capture of Busan and the route north to Pyongyang, naval engagements on the south coast, and a review of the Japanese retreat south from Pyongyang to Busan.

After his final internal battles to unify Kyushu with the rest of Japan and before invading Korea, Hideyoshi prepared his invasion force in Kyushu. He surrounded Hizen-Nagoya Castle, overlooking Tsushima Strait and purpose-built for the invasion, with the camps of more than one hundred of his *daimyo* retainers. Hideyoshi personally entertained his troops at this castle location, playing the lead role in a series of Noh plays. After assembling at Nagoya Castle, Japanese troops sailed by way of Iki Island to the island of Tsushima, halfway across the Korea Strait between northwest Kyushu and Busan on the southeast corner of the Korean peninsula. His troops built another staging fort, Shimizuyama Castle, near Izuhara port on the southeast coast of Tsushima. Tsushima had been a home port and refuge for *wako*, pirates who had ravaged the coasts of Korea and China for most of the sixteenth century prior to Hideyoshi's invasions. In fact, the *wako* raids were relevant experience for confronting the state-to-state Japanese invasion since some of the Japanese invaders had backgrounds as *wako*. The Japanese So clan ruled Tsushima as feudal lords from the thirteenth until the late nineteenth century. Hideyoshi had reconfirmed the clan's possession of the island in 1587. Japanese commander Konishi Yukinaga's daughter married the head of the So clan, consolidating Japanese clan relations in support of the invasion.[3]

There was little Korean naval resistance to the Japanese when they arrived in spacious Busan harbor on May 24, 1592. At Busan, local Korean naval commander Won Gyun was ineffective. Korean army chief Chong Bal resisted courageously at the Busanjin fort until his forces were overwhelmed and Chong Bal, dressed in distinctive black armor, was shot dead.[4]

The Japanese army was divided into nine divisions, of which the First and Second Divisions were the lead and most important. The First Division was commanded by Konishi Yukinaga, and the Second Division was commanded by Kato Kiyomasa. Yukinaga was a baptized Christian, while Kato was a devout follower of Nichiren Buddhism.[5] This religious divide made cooperation between the two leaders difficult. For the most part they stayed out of each other's way during the first six months of the invasion, as Yukinaga led the central peninsula thrust to Seoul and Pyongyang, and Kiyomasa secured the east coast and northeast region, protecting the Japanese invaders from flanking maneuvers.

The First Division led by Yukinaga began its rapid march north toward Seoul by taking the mountain fortress of Dongnae,[6] followed by Yangsan, Miryang, Daegu, Sangju, and Ch'ungju, two-thirds of the way to Seoul.[7] Each of these were easy victories for the First Division, which was provided flank protection by the Second and Third Divisions to the east and west respectively. By June 10, eighteen days after arrival in Busan, the Japanese army reached the capital in Seoul. Shocked by the rapid advance of the Japanese, King Sonjo of Korea fled to Pyongyang, leaving the occupation of Seoul to the Japanese. Due to the rapid advance of the Japanese, some in the Ming court suspiciously wondered if the Koreans had given up their tributary relationship with China and were assisting the Japanese, even though the Koreans had called on the Chinese for help. The Japanese, however, were slowed down in their march north for almost a month, encountering Korean resistance and not knowing where to cross the wide Imjin River northwest of Seoul.[8]

Once across the river, the road to Pyongyang proved lightly defended, and the Japanese forces occupied the city on July 24. King Sonjo fled once again, this time to the Yalu River on the border with China. Thus, in summary, the Japanese army swiftly invaded and captured Busan (May 23), Seoul (June 10), and Pyongyang (July 24) in a virtual blitzkrieg, stalled only briefly by the barrier created by the Imjin River. The Japanese thrust toward China, however, was confounded by logistical lines broken by the actions of the Korean navy, which was conducting its own blitzkrieg on the south coast, effectively severing Japan's ability to supply men, weapons, and provisions to its army divisions desiring to move on to China. Korean superiority in the maritime arena was decisive in limiting the ultimate effectiveness of the Japanese invasion.

KOREAN NAVAL RESISTANCE DURING THE FIRST INVASION AND THE TURTLE SHIPS

Busan naval commander Won Gyun proved unable to defend the port of Busan when the Japanese arrived there in May 1592. Subsequently, Yi Sun-sin, destined to become revered for his seminal role in Korean history, was chosen to command the important central section of the south coast. By June, he was ready to oppose Japanese naval activity along the intensely indented coastline, full of deep inlets, peninsulas, and islands. Six major Korean naval victories took place in rapid succession. These included the battles at Okpo (June 16), Sachon (July 8), Dangpo (July 10), Danghangpo (July 13), Hansando (August 14), and Angolpo (August 16). Thus, while the Japanese army quickly marched up the peninsula, the Korean navy decisively secured the south coast and established a blockade, preventing Japanese resupply of their army.

At Okpo, twenty-four Korean warships surprised a larger Japanese fleet, sinking twenty-six ships on the first day and eleven ships on the second day. No Korean ships were lost in these encounters. Three weeks later at Sachon, Admiral Yi turned as if to flee the Japanese fleet on an ebb tide, only to successfully lure the Japanese out so they could be attacked by his turtle ship, known as a *geobukseon*, a heavily armored ship with ramming capability, heavy guns, and metal cladding plates with spikes on the deck to repel the fearsome samurai boarders, known for their ability in hand-to-hand combat. It was the first time Admiral Yi used this innovative type of ship, which he had developed in the period immediately preceding the war. At Sachon, all of the Japanese ships were sunk, although Yi was slightly wounded by a bullet. In quick succession after the Okpo and Sachon victories, Yi used a turtle ship to decimate the Japanese fleets at Dangpo and Danghangpo, where almost all of the Japanese ships that engaged in battle were sunk. The Korean fleet main force was made up of *panokseon*, conventional warships similar to those of the Japanese. Following the initial use at Sachon, the *panokseon* ships were led into battle by up to three *geobukseon*, the armored turtle ships that Yi had developed. This was the pattern for the remaining naval battles during the first invasion of 1592–1593.

Why were Admiral Yi and the Korean navy so successful in this early series of battles? Yi developed and implemented an effective attack formula using surprise, subterfuge, superior knowledge of coastal geography and sea conditions, and superior technology in ships and guns. This effective formula was supplemented by superior naval leadership. Yi Sun-sin was a capable, flexible commander, known for being bold, decisive, and fearless. Thus, under Yi's leadership, the naval war on the south coast began with four clear victories, soon to be followed within a month by Yi's greatest naval battle victory at Hansando.

Hideyoshi, hearing of the Japanese naval defeats leading up to the battle at Hansando, ordered that Yi be destroyed. Japanese admiral Wakizaka Yasuhara, famous for his successes in Japan's inland sea, led eighty-six ships into the protected Gyonnaeryang Strait north of Hansan Island. Yi sent six ships ahead to lure out the Japanese fleet from the protected strait into open water. Incautiously, Wakizaka did not wait for reinforcements. Yi met the Japanese fleet with a "crane's wing formation," which engulfed and sank almost the entire Japanese fleet. Three turtle ships took the lead from the center of the formation.

Wakizaka barely escaped. Yi chased the few remaining ships to Angolpo, where he engulfed another Japanese fleet in his crane's wing formation, again wreaking havoc with the devastating core of turtle ships.

Hideyoshi's command to destroy Yi Sun-sin could not have gone further awry. These six naval victories effectively cut off and isolated Konishi Yukinaga's forces in Pyongyang from adequate resupply.

A week after the Korean victory at Hansando, Chinese began to arrive in northern Korea to fight against the Japanese advance. During late August 1592, Chinese commander Zu Chengxun unsuccessfully attacked Konishi Yukinaga's Japanese land forces in Pyongyang, while Kato Kiyomasa won a battle at Songjin in far northeast Korea. Zu's unexpected defeat awoke China's leaders in Beijing to the real possibility of Japan's invasion reaching China. During September, Korean irregular forces, consisting of 1,500 "warrior monks," captured the granary center at Ch'ongju from the Japanese, an unexpected but morale-building victory. This Korean irregular army was defeated later in the month at Kumsan, but in November the Koreans successfully defended Jinju from a major Japanese attack, causing deep embarrassment for the Japanese generals and great fury on the part of Hideyoshi. This fury was used against the Koreans at Jinju eight months later when the Japanese took the walled city during a bloody second siege.

Early in 1593, substantial Chinese forces began arriving under the leadership of General Li Rusong, following the quelling of a rebellion in the far western province of Ningxia. Li patiently began the siege to oust the Japanese from Pyongyang in early February 1593, after waiting until the ground had frozen so that he could move his artillery pieces. Against the 15,000 Japanese in Pyongyang, Li brought 43,000 Chinese soldiers and about 10,000 Koreans.[9] Under intense siege pressure, the Japanese were forced to retreat east across the frozen Taedong River, many suffering from severe frostbite. The momentum of Japan's first invasion of Korea had been turned by their failure to hold Pyongyang. It took just over a week for the Japanese to retreat to Seoul, with the Chinese and Korean army in hot pursuit. Ultimately, the Japanese retreat ended in Busan six months later.

During the period that the Japanese held Seoul, two major battles were fought outside the city. These were at Pyokjeyek, a Japanese victory, and at Haengju, a Korean victory. As a Japanese victory, Pyokjeyek is lauded in Japanese sources as a battle in which the Chinese general Li Rusong was driven north in disgrace following his victory during the earlier siege of Pyongyang. The victory in this large battle brought but minor relief to the Japanese. Korean general Gwon Yul set up defenses in the ruined castle of Haengju on a hill overlooking the Han River eight miles northwest of Seoul. The Japanese general who won the battle of Pyokjeyek, Ukita Hideie, targeted Haengju as his next victory, leading his 30,000 troops against Gwon Yul's 2,300 defenders at the Haengju fortress. Japanese forces marching slowly up the hill were clear targets for the Korean artillery and fire wagons. Miraculously, during nine Japanese attacks, the Korean defenders, with the support of women and children in the fort, prevailed by inflicting 10,000 casualties on the Japanese, according to Korean sources. Haengju is now remembered as one of the three great Korean victories of the Imjin War not requiring Chinese assistance, along with Hansando and Jinju. The Haengju victory in March gave new life to General Li Rusong, despondent after his loss at Pyokjeyek in February. He returned to assist with the siege of Seoul, where about 50,000 Japanese troops remained of the more than 150,000 that had invaded Korea ten months earlier. The two battles at Pyokjeyek and Haengju had the effect of canceling each other out. The battles were followed by a partial siege truce, broken on both sides, until the Japanese evacuated Seoul by crossing the Nakdong River, leaving the Chinese and Koreans to liberate Seoul on May 19, 1593.

The Japanese fury of the first invasion, however, was not yet over. On their way south in July 1593, the Japanese revisited Jinju for a second siege at the site of their humiliating loss during the first siege of Jinju in November 1592. Ukita Hideie, the victorious Japanese general at Pyokjeyek, pulled together 90,000 Japanese troops from north and south, the greatest concentration during the war, to oppose about 60,000 Koreans in the Jinju fort overlooking the Nam River. Although Ukita Hideie led the overall battle plan calling for surrounding the Jinju fortress to prevent reinforcements from reaching it, most of the other Japanese divisional commanders were also there, including Konishi Yukinaga and Kato Kiyomasa. The Japanese generals were determined that Hideyoshi would have his revenge after the failed first siege of Jinju. Despite heroism on both sides, including that of the Korean courtesan Nongae, who leapt off the castle wall dragging a Japanese commander to his death, 20,000 Korean heads were taken and the Nam River ran red with Korean blood. For the Japanese who had their greatest victory here along with that at Pyokjeyek, the results were Pyrrhic. Knowing that Chinese and Korean reinforcements were pouring down the peninsula to confront them, the Japanese continued their retreat to Busan, where by June 1593, they reached the safety of their *wajo* fortresses.[10] Many of the invaders returned to Japan, while some remained to garrison the Busan perimeter *wajo* for the next four years until 1597. Inconclusive peace negotiations took place during the following period while Hideyoshi organized the return of a second invasion force.

NEGOTIATIONS INTERLUDE, 1594–1596

During the period of relative quiet between mid-1593 and mid-1597, some Japanese, perhaps 50,000, remained in the Busan perimeter area on the Korean peninsula, much like the Japanese had done in the same region known as Mimana during the seventh century. During the eighteen-month period of the first invasion, the Japanese had taken over and revived earlier Korean fortifications as well as built new fortresses they called *wajo* in southeastern Korea around Busan. *Wajo* were built with heavy stone bases in the Japanese style, more complicated and more effective than the Korean fortresses that the Japanese had easily overcome at the beginning of the first invasion. About eighteen of these were built along the southeast Korean coast from Seosaengpo fortress in Ulsan, thirty-one miles northeast of Busan, to Geoje Island, thirty miles southwest of Busan. Four of the *wajo* protected Busan harbor itself.[11] The southeast coast *wajo* were strong positions successfully defended by a few thousand Japanese during the period until the second invasion in 1597, at which point they became safe arrival points for the second invasion armies.

During this interim period, each side submitted settlement terms to the other side, but a peace agreement remained elusive. The terms were far apart and irreconcilable, leading ultimately to the second round of military conflict in 1597–1598.

In spite of agreement on some demands from each side, the points of disagreement prevented the establishment of a lasting peace. The crux of the matter was a disagreement over territory. Japan wanted a foothold in southeastern Korea, which they partially had during the negotiating phase while holding Busan and the southeastern *wajo* defensive positions. China and Korea wanted Japan completely off the peninsula. Unhappy with the deadlocked negotiations, Hideyoshi organized and sent forth a second invasion force, which left Japan in 1597, again using Tsushima Island as a stepping stone to the Korean peninsula.

SECOND JAPANESE INVASION, 1597–1598

Fighting resumed in 1597 when Hideyoshi put approximately 141,000 Japanese troops back on the Korean peninsula. The second invasion drive northward in 1597 was less successful than the 1592 invasion. The Japanese army was unable to get north as far as Seoul. In fact, rather than heading directly for Seoul as they had during the first invasion, Japanese forces headed further west rather than north, meeting opposing Chinese and Korean troops at Namwon, a fortified town sitting on a plain among mountains. The decision to hold this position was made by Chinese general Yang Yuan, in opposition to Korean counsel to establish a defensive position on higher ground. Japanese commander Ukita Hideie, veteran of the Pyokjeyek and Jinju Japanese victories, led the Japanese attack on Namwon on a clear moonlit night following rain. The first attack was repulsed, but a second attack four days later was successful. So many heads were taken by the Japanese that they took noses instead, which were shipped back to Japan and eventually were buried in the misnamed Mimizuka "Ear Mound" in Kyoto. By capturing Namwon in brutal fashion, the Japanese had secured a piece of territory outside the scope of what they had captured during the first invasion.

From Namwon the Japanese armies marched north through Jeonju toward Chiksan. Realizing that Seoul once again was being threatened, Chinese and Korean troops rushed to mass together north of Chiksan to meet the Japanese forces that were traveling northward. In a large, tactically indecisive battle on October 17, 1597, the Japanese held Chiksan but were unable to push directly on toward Seoul. They used Chiksan as a base to prepare for an assault on Seoul as they awaited reinforcements, but Chinese and Korean forces were encouraged by keeping the Japanese from advancing directly toward Seoul. Japanese reinforcement forces never arrived, as Admiral Yi Sun-sin effectively cut off the sea reinforcement route at the battle of Myeongnyang on October 26, 1597. Chiksan thus was the farthest north that the Japanese penetrated during the second invasion, leaving Seoul and Pyongyang safe from capture, much to the chagrin of Hideyoshi.

During the second invasion, the Japanese built more *wajo* to the northeast and west of the contained group of *wajo* that they used to control the area around Busan during the years between invasions. Following the stalemate at Chiksan, many of the Japanese fell back to these defensive posts, including the three important ones at Ulsan, Sunchon, and Sachon. In late January 1598, Ulsan northeast of Busan became the site of the largest siege raised against a Japanese-held *wajo*. Chinese troops unsuccessfully tried to scale the carefully constructed high stone walls built to protect the base of the Ulsan *wajo*. Lacking a well, the Japanese defenders were parched by the time a huge relief army of Japanese reinforcements was sent to finally dispel the Chinese attackers. Despite the successful defense, Japanese commanders began to understand that holding territory by way of *wajo* defenses was going to be costly and difficult over time. The other major *wajo* defensive struggles at Sachon and Sunchon later during 1598 were also held by the Japanese at high cost. These were to the east and west, respectively, of the final naval battle of Noryang, following Hideyoshi's unexpected death. Before discussing the battle of Noryang, the earlier naval encounters of Japan's second invasion attempt will be reviewed.

NAVAL RESISTANCE DURING THE SECOND INVASION AND CHINA-KOREA NAVAL ALLIANCE RELATIONS

During the second Japanese invasion, Admiral Yi Sun-sin defeated the Japanese at the battle of Myeongnyang in 1597 and was subsequently joined by Ming naval forces in 1598 in an alliance to fight Japan's naval forces. Due to envy and political intrigue, Admiral Yi had been demoted during the period between Japanese invasions. He was replaced by Admiral Won Gyun, who was swiftly defeated at Chilcheonryang when the Japanese second invasion began in 1597. The king asked Yi to take over command of the navy with the few Korean ships remaining. Yi agreed to return to his naval leadership, even though the Korean fleet was greatly outnumbered. Japan had several hundred ships, compared to the twelve Korean ships remaining after the Chilcheonryang disaster. Surprisingly, Yi won the battle of Myeongnyang in October 1597, using his twelve ships against a Japanese naval force of more than one hundred ships. He took advantage of his local knowledge of the tidal current in the strait, which flows at a rate of up to thirteen knots. Yi exhorted his men: "If you seek to live you will die; if you do not worry about death, you will live." No Korean ships were lost, while the Japanese fleet was devastated. The result of this battle on the southwest corner of Korea limited Japanese naval movements to the south coast and prevented Japanese from supplying their troops from the west coast of Korea.

Meanwhile, Ming naval forces were preparing to join the Korean naval forces. Chinese army land forces had been important, even decisive, during the first invasion by Japan in 1592–1593. They had not allowed Japanese forces to penetrate China and had driven them south from Pyongyang in February 1593 and all the way back to Busan by July 1593. Would a China-Korea naval alliance be as successful as the China-Korea land alliance?

The Ming developed and maintained a strong coastal naval defense during the sixteenth century. Coastal defense capability was effective in combatting the grand scale of *wako* piracy that ravaged the Chinese coast, especially in Zhejiang and Fujian. Through this effort, Ming shipbuilding capacity and naval leadership remained formidable 160 years after Zheng He's final voyage.

Zhang Wei, the Chinese grand secretary favoring war with Japan, was supported by Ming Emperor Wanli. He won the court struggle to oppose the Japanese in Korea. He calculated the cash needed and allocated funds for 100 large ships and 10,000 men. The best Ming ships were built in the south, where these were to be constructed. To staff the ships, he assigned many experienced sailors from Fujian Province, as well as some fierce aboriginals from the southwest, and he appointed veteran naval officer and firearms expert Admiral Chen Lin to head the Ming navy.

Chen Lin was a native of the southeast maritime province of Guangdong. He was experienced in antipiracy efforts and the use of heavy guns on the southeast coast of China. After facing a mutiny in 1583, he was reappointed in 1592 but was subsequently sacked in 1593 for trying to bribe the minister of war. He was reinstated in 1596 to quell a rebellion in southwest China, where he was involved in land battles rather than sea battles and used his own money to pay troops. Through this action, he won the attention of the court and was appointed to head the Ming navy in the war against Japan during its second phase. Deng Zilong was appointed second in command. When he arrived in Korea at Dongjak on the Han River in Seoul in May 1598, Chen laughed at the Korean troops for their lack of discipline. Through such actions, he came to be regarded by the Koreans as rude, arrogant, and avaricious. After all, the Korean navy had succeeded in defeating the Japanese navy on its own under Yi's leadership during the first Japanese invasion in the summer of 1592 and had severely defeated the Japanese again at Myeongnyang in autumn 1597, even though greatly outnumbered. Potential cracks in the Chinese-Korean naval alliance became apparent even during this earliest interaction on the west coast of Korea before the alliance partners saw action together. Nevertheless, Chen Lin led a substantial Chinese naval force of 21,000 men and 500 ships, although most of his ships were smaller than the Korean ships. He moved some of his men to the heavier Korean ships.

Admiral Chen Lin arrived on Kogum Island, about midway between the preceding great battles of Hansando and Myeongnyang, on August

17, 1598, and joined forces with Admiral Yi Sun-sin. Compared to Japanese naval leaders, Chen and Yi were both experienced naval commanders, although the Koreans continued to be unconvinced by Chen's character and ability. The Chinese army commander Liu Ting thought Chen was boastful about capturing pirates. Rumors arose, such as that Yi gave Chen forty of seventy heads to send to King Sonjo to save Chen's face for his sailors shirking in raids on Japanese. A month after Chen's arrival without subsequent major naval encounters, Japanese leader Toyotomi Hideyoshi died unexpectedly on September 18, 1598. The Japanese kept his death secret for a while, as the Japanese Council of Five Elders planned a retreat from Korea. Meanwhile, tensions heightened between Chen and Yi because Chen wanted to negotiate a Japanese withdrawal, while Yi wanted to avenge 185,000 Korean heads taken by the Japanese forces during the course of the war.

The Japanese *wajo* in Sunchon was defended by Konishi Yukinaga, the lead Japanese commander in both the 1592 and 1597 invasion attempts. The allied Korean and Chinese leaders decided to attack Yukinaga's fort by both land and sea. The land attack was to be organized by Liu Ting, commander of the Chinese Western Army by his establishing a land siege line north of Sunchon. Sea attack was to be undertaken by Admirals Yi and Chen, establishing a floating siege line that included Yi's forces plus one thousand Chinese vessels.

Initially, Liu's forces attacked the fort with cloud ladders and siege engines, but they were repelled. Allied Korean and Chinese ships were also repelled by the turn of tide. Yi's misgivings about attacking close to shore at night were validated when more than thirty of Chen's ships were grounded on a falling tide. Nineteen vessels were lost. Yi provided rear support and rescued Chen personally. In spite of these initial losses in the siege of the Sunchon fort, a sea blockade was established at Sunchon, preventing supply of the fort or escape from the fort by sea. The nearest source of Japanese support for Yukinaga at Sunchon was from the port of Sachon, firmly in Japanese control, thirty-five miles to the east.

Admiral Yi refused to negotiate with Konishi Yukinaga to lift the blockade, wanting the Japanese to pay a high price, whereas the

Japanese wished to withdraw with minimal losses following the death of Hideyoshi. Chinese commanders Liu Ting and Chen Lin were more amenable to the idea of allowing a Japanese retreat, having had fewer losses and seeing an opportunity to recognize victory in the Japanese retreat without incurring further losses. In secret negotiations, Konishi reputedly offered Chen hogs and barrels of wine, prompting the Koreans to accuse the Chinese of being willing to settle for "2 pigs and 2 bottles of wine." Instead of maintaining the blockade, Chen suggested a raid on Namhae Island. Yi was furious that Chen wanted to take the heads of Koreans whom Chen called "collaborators." Yi wondered what kind of alliance was this, where there was no trust based on the ongoing resistance and price paid by Koreans. One of Konishi's boats escaped through Chen's porous blockade to rally reinforcements for Konishi from Sachon. At Sachon, five hundred Japanese ships gathered to run the Sunchon blockade and free Konishi, thus setting the stage for "the most famous military engagement in Korean history," the battle of Noryang.[12]

The Japanese fleet from Sachon, commanded by Shimazu Yoshihiro, passed through Noryang Strait north of Namhae Island. The Japanese were met by three Choson-Ming allied squadrons led by Yi on the left, Chen in the center, and Deng on the right. Chen was first to engage. He was defended by Deng, who subsequently died in battle. Then Chen was rescued by Yi. Overall, the results were devastating for the Japanese, with two hundred ships sunk and one hundred ships captured. Although the Japanese were decisively defeated at Noryang, the distraction of the battle allowed Konishi Yukinaga to escape from Sunchon, possibly with the complicity of Liu Ting. Yi Sun-sin was shot and died on the deck of his flagship at the end of the Noryang battle in circumstances similar to Nelson at Trafalgar two hundred years later. His death was kept secret by his son and nephew, who were on deck with him at the time. After brief interment in Noryang, his body was brought to Kogum Island, then to its final resting place near his family home in Asan. In the end, Yi was honored as "Minister of Loyal Valor," in spite of his fall from grace between the invasions. After the defeat at Noryang, the Japanese retreated to Busan, then evacuated by sailing to Japan on December 24, 1598, with only fifty of the five hundred ships they had brought to Korea.

King Sonjo of Korea hosted a feast of honor for Chinese naval commander Chen Lin, who was given higher military honors than Chinese army commander Liu Ting. Deng Zilong, second in naval command, was honored posthumously as well. Emperor Wanli distributed 100,000 silver liang as rewards in spite of court critiques that commanders had received enough in Japanese bribes. Hearing such critiques from his advisors, Wanli dismissed them. Wanli lectured the Koreans to adopt methods as military farmers, so that they would not have to rely on the treasury for foodstuffs. The Koreans began the painful process of rebuilding their country following the devastation of the two Japanese invasions.

An assessment of the Ming navy during the Imjin War shows that sixteenth-century naval technology improved due to intensive trade and antipiracy operations. Firearms had improved, which especially gave an edge to the Chinese and Koreans over the Japanese. In spite of financial pressure on the Ming government, funds were allocated for the Korean expedition to repulse the Japanese. Quality ships and sailors were allocated to the campaign. Nevertheless, the overall Chinese naval record during the Imjin War was shallow with mixed results. The Chinese participated in naval campaigns only for the final few months of the war, between August and December 1598.

In terms of naval leadership, Yi Sun-sin overshadowed Chen Lin in spite of the latter's claims and bluster. Even though the Chinese supplied many ships, Korea provided the heaviest front-line vessels. Chinese naval commanders demonstrated a preference for negotiating rather than fighting. Yi Sun-sin might well have been successful at Sunchon and Noryang without Chinese help, based on his record up to that time. Nevertheless, the Chinese land forces turned the Japanese forces back in Korea, achieving the Korean objective, but also, more importantly to the Chinese, achieving their own objective of preventing Japanese forces from making their way onto Chinese soil.

Within four decades of the end of the Imjin War, Japan instituted its seclusion policy of *sakoku* during the late 1630s, and the Ming Dynasty collapsed in China with the Manchu Qing occupation of Beijing in 1644. China and Japan did not go to war again for three hundred years until the Sino-Japanese War of 1894–1895. Unsurprisingly, given the patterns of the past, the root causes of this late nineteenth-century war and its battlegrounds once again lay in Korea.

Life and Legacy of Yi Sun-sin

Following Japan's first unsuccessful invasion of Korea in 1592–1593, Korean admiral Yi Sun-sin was appointed naval commander (*tonjesa*) of the Three Provinces in recognition of his key role in defeating the Japanese at sea. In the period of negotiation before the second Japanese invasion of Korea, Yi lived on Hansan Island between July 1593 and February 1597. Trained as a scholar as well as a warrior, Yi reflected carefully and wrote beautifully. In a painting in which Yi is depicted in his study on Hansando beneath the moonlight, he is writing a poem called "Song of Hansan Island":

> A night when moon lights brightened Hansan Island
> Sitting in solitude on the watchtower
> Wearing a long sword at my side
> Tormented by deep concerns
> Sudden sound of a flute
> Consoles my sorrow[13]

The Imjin War (1592–1598), well-known in Asia but less studied in the West, was a major conflict similar in size to the huge clashes in Europe taking place during the sixteenth century between the Ottomans and the European powers. In 1592 and 1597, Japan sent two invasion forces of 150,000 soldiers into Korea. These were remarkable amphibious achievements, yet the Japanese navy could not stand up to the Korean navy and its leadership under Admiral Yi Sun-sin. More than 200,000 Koreans, military and civilian, died during the war.[14] With the help of China, Japan was ultimately repulsed. About 35,000 Chinese and 80,000 Japanese also died during the war. These death totals are about twice the totals from both sides from the American War of Independence.[15] If it is possible for Americans to imagine, Yi Sun-sin may be a greater hero in the minds of Koreans than George Washington is in the minds of Americans. The British navy had been unsuccessful in blockading the American coast during the American War of Independence. By contrast, Yi Sun-sin led the Korean navy in a successful blockade of the Korean coast during both the first and second Japanese invasion attempts, preventing the Japanese samurai invaders from resupplying men or material as their forces moved north on the Korean peninsula.

IMJIN WAR LEADERSHIP, WAR DIARIES

When the first Japanese invasion of Korea began in May 1592, Yi Sun-sin was not in Busan when the Japanese arrived. Although the Korean forces resisted bravely at Busanjin, they were quickly overrun, and their commander, Chong Bal, was killed in the initial fighting. The invading samurai armies faced little resistance in spite of a few fierce skirmishes. They moved quickly north up the peninsula to take Seoul in June and Pyongyang in July. Yi Sun-sin, however, was determined during this early period of the conflict to hold the south coast of Korea through naval actions. Control of the south coast would prevent the Japanese navy from supplying by sea reinforcements and equipment to the rapidly moving Japanese armies in the north, whose goal was to subdue Korea before invading China. He succeeded in this objective with a string of naval victories beginning at Okpo and culminating in his famous "crane's wing" victory at Hansando, in which he outflanked and engulfed the main Japanese naval force using three turtle ships. His string of naval victories continued in smaller battles until the Japanese were driven back to the perimeter around Busan during the summer of 1593.

Yi Sun-sin bottled up the Japanese fleet in Busan for the subsequent period of peace negotiations, which took place between 1594 and 1596. He was not a proponent of the peace talks, believing that Hideyoshi's intractable position to occupy the southern provinces of Korea was clearly unacceptable to the Korean notion of sovereignty. When the Japanese ships left Busan in 1594, he struck and defeated them in sea battles, consolidating the fearsome impression the Japanese had of the dominating Korean admiral. After it became clear that the peace talks would

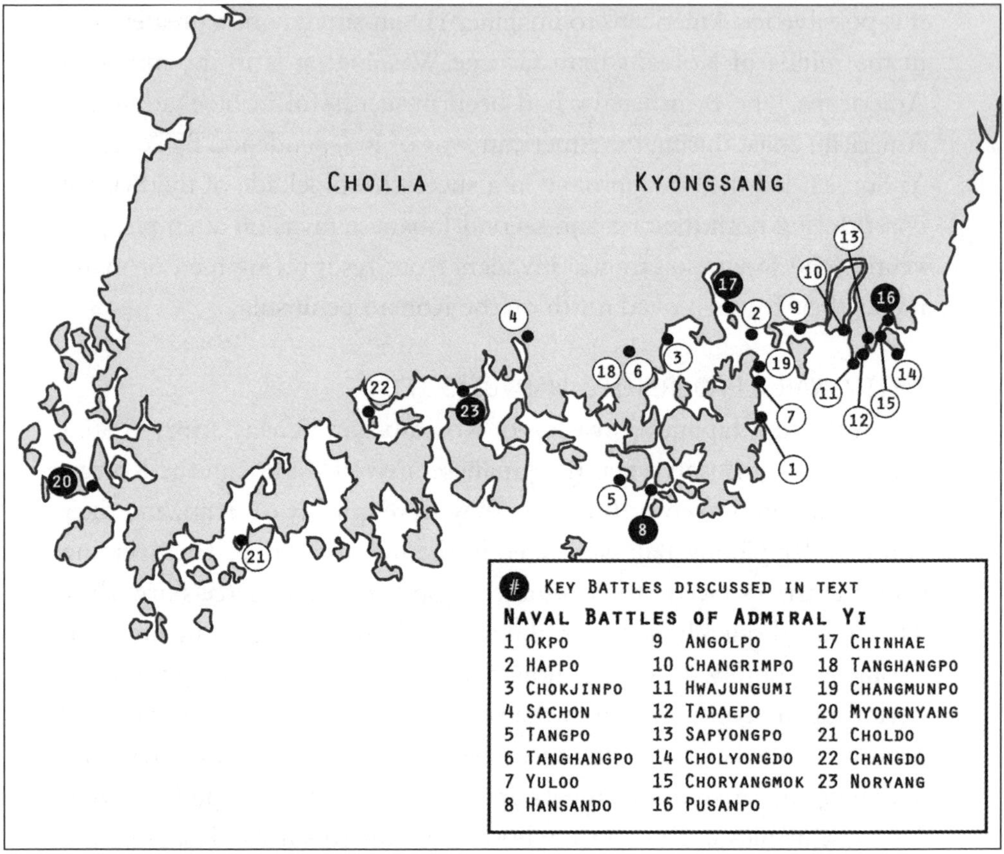

MAP 6.2 Sites of Yi Sun-sin's twenty-three naval victories, 1592–1598
Adapted by Jamie Rhode from Admiral Yi Sun-sin: A Brief Overview of the Life and Achievements. *Korean Spirit and Culture Promotion Project (Seoul: Samjun Munhwasa, 2nd edition, 2010), 82–83*

fail, political intrigue and rivalry put Yi in a difficult position. Yi did not ingratiate himself to King Sonjo or Chief Commander Gwon Yul, who had won the important land battle at Haengju on the heights above the Han River near Seoul. These leaders were open to listening to charges brought against him by naval rivals.

In 1597, a Japanese double agent sent by Konishi Yukinaga infiltrated the Korean armed forces and won the confidence of the Korean king and chief general Gwon Yul. When the agent provided information that the Japanese were arriving by a certain route, and that Yi Sun-sin should attack the Japanese, Yi declined to lead the expedition, as he did not trust the Japanese informer and knew that the proposed battle site was strewn with shallow rocks. He suspected other misinformation as well about timing of Japanese reinforcements. The king and general fired Yi as supreme naval commander for insubordination and disloyalty, not understanding Yi's caution. They put Won Gyun in his place, although Won Gyun had been unable to effectively counter the Japanese when they arrived in Busan at the beginning of the first invasion. At the beginning of the second invasion, Won Gyun fell into the Japanese trap and lost 122 of 134 ships in a devastating battle against 1,000 Japanese ships at Chilchonnyang. After Won Gyun failed in his effort to thwart the Japanese, the king and commander approached Yi, who was working as a demoted deckhand. Yi agreed to be reinstated as supreme naval commander and was given the remaining twelve Korean ships as his naval force. In spite of the impossible odds against him, Yi agreed to resume his role as savior of the country. He determined that he must stop the Japanese from sailing up the west coast to the Han River into Seoul. Thus he moved his small force to the southwest corner of Korea to a defensive spot where he could take advantage of the tides rushing between the mainland and Jindo Island. Here he miraculously won the battle of Myeongnyang, previously described, and later the battle of Noryang, where he died in battle with his final words "Cover me with a shield. The battle is in an urgent state now. Never let the sailors know that I am dead."[16]

Aside from these three best-known victories won by Yi Sun-sin at Hansando, Myeongnyang, and Noryang, he won an additional twenty naval engagements during the Imjin War without losing a single naval battle. Sixteen of these battles took place during the first Japanese invasion in 1592–1593, three occurred during the period of negotiation in 1594, and the final four took place during the second invasion in 1597–1598. These second invasion victories followed the loss of most of the navy while it was under the command of Won Gyun at Chilchonnyang in July 1597.

Yi Sun-sin kept a diary that documented his daily involvement in the Imjin War. It contains much fascinating material. He quoted Sunzi, the great Chinese military sage, "Knowing yourself and knowing the enemy is the surest way to secure success in a hundred battles."[17]

Judging by the many statues commemorating Yi throughout Korea, the replica turtle ships in museums, and the recent movie about his success at Myeongnyang, Yi Sun-sin is revered by the Korean people to this day. He is known as a great example of character, having sustained himself through two devastating demotions and facing down impossible battle odds with courage and tenacity against the Japanese, a larger, powerful foe. In the years after his death, Yi was awarded several posthumous titles including ranks as high as vice minister and prime minister. The title Chungmugong, "Lord of Valour," is often used for him at places of commemoration. It is remarkable that the greatest of Japanese naval heroes, Admiral Togo Heihachiro, who sank the Russian Baltic fleet at Tsushima in 1905, acknowledged the greatest of Korean admirals above the greatest of British admirals. He declared, "You may compare me with Lord Nelson, but not with Yi Sun-sin. Next to him, I am only a petty officer." Nelson indeed had a great record of naval victories, winning all but one of his naval battles. He was defeated only at Santa Cruz de Tenerife in 1797, losing not only the battle but also his right arm. Like Yi Sun-sin more than two hundred years earlier at Noryang in 1598, Horatio Nelson was shot on deck and died at Trafalgar in 1805. Both Noryang and Trafalgar were key naval victories in the history of their respective countries. Nelson is remembered atop the great column at Trafalgar Square in London, while Yi is remembered in the great statue at the Gwanghwamun Plaza in Seoul, illuminated at night with colored fountains representing his twelve ships at Myeongyang and twenty-three naval victories without defeat. Although less well known outside Asia than Nelson and Togo, Yi's naval legacy is unsurpassed in Asian memory.

Conclusions from the Imjin War Experience

The Korean peninsula has occupied a critical place in East Asian geopolitics for two thousand years. It sits at the nexus of continental China and insular Japan. The strait between Korea and Japan has been the location of important amphibious operations over the course of many centuries. These include the seventh-century failed Japanese attack on Baekgang, the failed thirteenth-century Mongol invasions of Japan, and

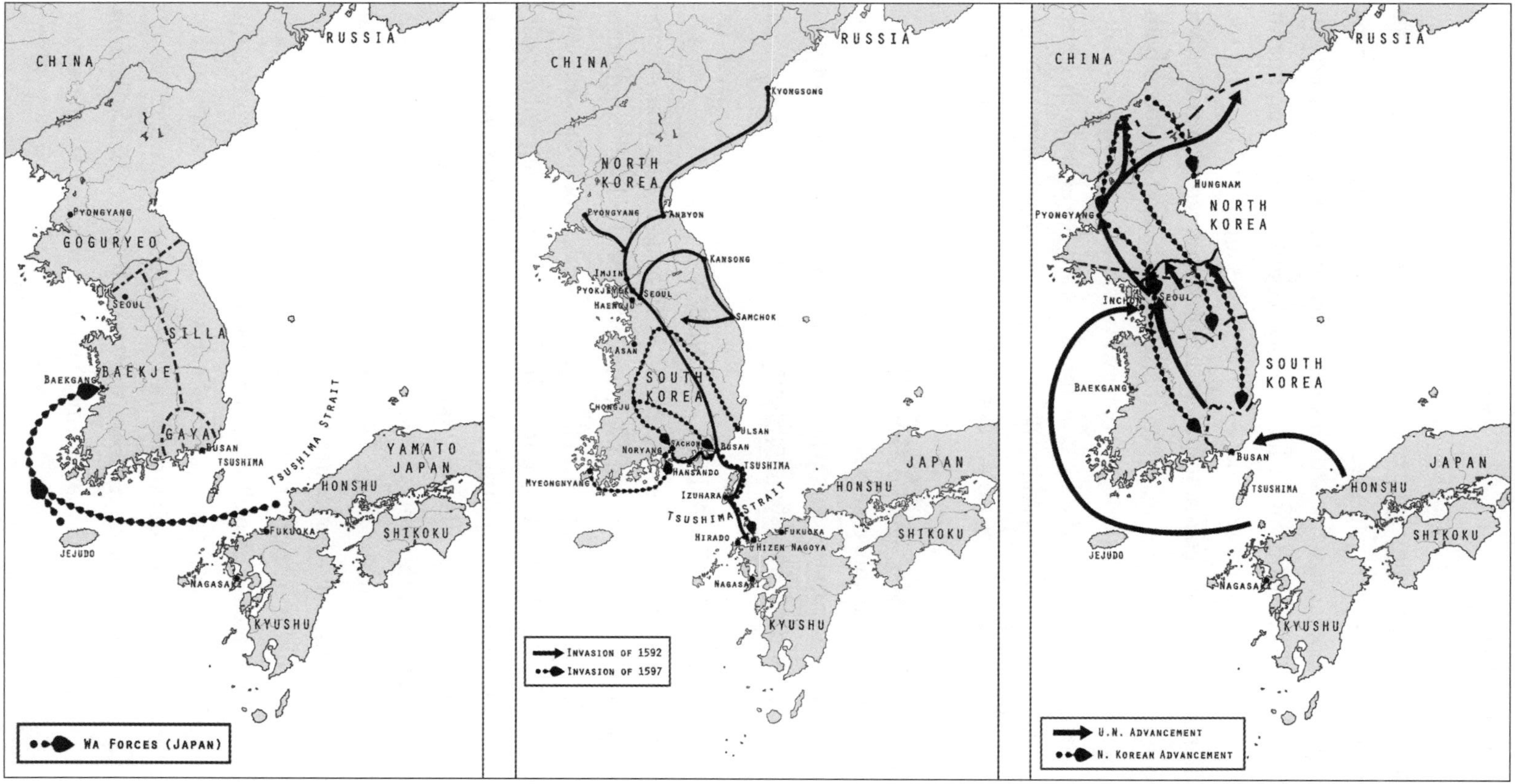

MAP 6.3 Korea: Seventh, sixteenth, and twentieth centuries
Adapted by Jamie Rhode from Edwin O. Reischauer and John K. Fairbank, East Asia: The Great Tradition *(Boston: Houghton Mifflin Company, 1958), 407, from Turnbull,* The Samurai Invasion of Korea, *25, 76, and from a map at the Korean War cemetery in Busan, Republic of Korea. Map 6.3c schematic routes created by author*

the failed sixteenth-century Japanese invasions of Korea. These cases all support "The stopping power of water."[18] Douglas MacArthur was temporarily more successful with his amphibious landing at Inchon in 1951. But this ended up much like the successful samurai landing at Busan in 1592. The land war maps of the 1590s and the 1950s on the Korean peninsula look remarkably alike: troop movements up and down the peninsula, a "Busan perimeter" established for a period of time in both cases, problems with battle during the bitter winters, and Chinese troops making decisive entry into battle by crossing the Yalu River in both cases. Political strategists and decision makers are wise to consider this history before formulating military policy in relation to the Korean peninsula.

Maritime Strategic and Tactical Lessons

Several lessons from this case study explain why the Japanese failed to prevail against their opponents when they crossed the sea into Korea in their strategy to use it as a steppingstone to China.

LOCAL KNOWLEDGE OF NATURAL PHENOMENA

Aside from his keen tactical sense, Admiral Yi Sun-sin's central advantage over Hideyoshi's navy was his knowledge of the local conditions of the south coast of Korea. At Hansando, he understood the necessity of drawing the Japanese fleet out from their constricted, defensible position in the Gyonnaeryang Strait into the open water off Hansando, where his "crane's wing" flanking tactic could be effective. More dramatic than the use of this knowledge was Yi's knowledge and use of the thirteen-knot tidal current in the Uldolmok, the "roaring current," that flows through the Myeongnyang Strait between Jindo and the mainland on the southwest corner of Korea. Although his ships were outnumbered by a factor of well over ten to one, Yi was able to use the current to bear down on the Japanese fleet with his twelve ships, and at the same time to use the constriction of the narrow channel to ensure that there were never more Japanese ships able to enter the battle than he had in the channel at the same time. Yi had to lure the Japanese fleet all the way across the south coast of Korea to make use of the roaring currents in the Myeongnyang Strait. That he knew the place with the right conditions for success, and his ability to choose that place and use it, led to one of the most remarkable naval victories ever achieved.

ADVANTAGES IN MILITARY TECHNOLOGY

Yi Sun-sin launched his first turtle boat the day before the Japanese entered Busan Harbor in the first invasion in 1592. Thus he was aware of the danger of the Japanese before they arrived and developed a new technology to be ready when battle was necessary. The most fearsome aspects of the Japanese navy were samurai riflemen using arquebuses and subsequent samurai boarding parties, which gained access due to the Japanese tactic of gripping enemy ships with grappling hooks. Yi won his first battles in 1592 without use of the turtle ships, which demonstrated naval competence, but he did not destroy entire Japanese fleets until he inserted one to three turtle ships in the middle of his own fleet. He softened up the Japanese fleet with heavy cannon fire from a distance beyond arquebus range, then rammed Japanese ships with his more heavily built turtle ships, repelling Japanese boarding parties with the spike armor covering his upper decks.

Yi's technological edge was effective during the first Japanese invasion. Unfortunately, he had no turtle ships during the second invasion, as he had only the twelve ships remaining in the Korean fleet to defeat the Japanese during the second invasion. After defeating the Japanese at Myeongnyang in 1597, he rebuilt the Korean fleet during the winter of 1597–1598, but he did not have time to build more turtle ships. Korean naval victories during the second invasion were attributed more to tactical decisions regarding choosing advantageous sites for battles, and in the final battles to the naval alliance with China.

CONTINENTAL VS. MARITIME IDENTITIES

Although Japan was an island nation, it chose not to develop a seafaring navy after its defeat in 663 by the combined forces of China and the Korean kingdom of Silla. This situation held until Hideyoshi decided to undertake an amphibious invasion of Korea in 1592. In the three centuries prior to the Imjin War, *wako* pirates controlled much of the coast of Korea and China and wreaked havoc both on merchant shipping and on coastal towns. Many considered these pirates to be Japanese. Some were Japanese, but the *wako* actually consisted of a mix of ethnic Japanese, Chinese, and Koreans. *Wako* were incorporated into Hideyoshi's invading forces, bringing experienced seafaring skills to the invasion force despite Japan's lack of national naval program. As an archipelagic nation, would Japan ever become a continental power? It did not do so during the Imjin War, taking a beating from the Korean navy. A major lesson from the Imjin War for Japan was that if it was to become a serious power in Asia, it had to become a maritime power capable of controlling the seas. Japan tucked that lesson away for three hundred years following the late sixteenth-century losses during the Imjin War. In the late nineteenth century, Japan observed the power of the British navy on the China coast during the Opium Wars and the power of the American steam navy under Commodore Perry when it sailed into Tokyo Bay uncontested in 1853. Young Japanese were sent abroad to learn naval arts. Heihachiro Togo was one of these early students of the British navy. He studied naval matters for seven years on the Thames in London and walked the decks of Nelson's flagship *Victory* in Portsmouth. Later, after he had sunk the Russian Baltic fleet in the strait of Tsushima in 1905 in one of history's greatest naval victories, he compared himself favorably to Nelson, but as a shadow compared to Yi's naval acumen. Despite his modesty when comparing himself to Yi, with Togo's sinking of the Russian fleet, Japan arrived as a maritime power. Admiral Togo took his inspiration from Admiral Yi, the greatest of the Eastern admirals, even more than from Admiral Nelson, the greatest of the Western admirals.

DEEPLY FELT NATIONAL IDENTITIES

The impact of the Imjin War on Korea was profound compared to the impacts on either China or Japan. During the war, about a third of the population of the Korean peninsula was lost due to battle, starvation, and disease. Korean identity became tied into its sense of opposition to Japan, much as the Vietnamese identity became tied to its opposition to China during the Mongol and earlier Chinese invasions. Korean army commanders against the Japanese, such as Chong Bal and Gwon Yul, continue to be celebrated with major statue commemorations in Busan and Haengju. The greatest images of national hero identity are the many statues and commemorations of Yi Sun-sin throughout the country. Yi's memorials were built up during the strongman rule of South Korean president Park Chung-hee during the 1970s. It was during this period that the shrine commemorating Yi at his family home in Asan was redeveloped and opened to the public.[19] For President Park, the restoration of Yi's shrine and his memory during the 1970s was an exercise in profound patriotic nationalism. By restoring Yi's memory, Park hoped to raise himself in the national consciousness as an exercise in patriotic history. This was not the first time in twentieth-century Asia when an Asian leader built a current sense of national pride on the foundation of association with an earlier national hero.

Another type of shrine that defines Korean national memory in opposition to Japan is that of a *mimizuka*, an "ear mound" containing ears or noses from Koreans and Ming Chinese killed during the Imjin War. One of these memorial mounds can be found in Sachon, a battle site on the south coast of Korea. Another *mimizuka* may be found in Kyoto next to the Shinto Toyokuni Shrine honoring Hideyoshi. This mound is said to enshrine the noses or ears of more than 38,000 Koreans killed during the Imjin War. The *mimizuka* in Kyoto is mostly visited by Koreans in Japan and is avoided by other tourists. In such a role, it is a symbol of the "history wars" between Korea and Japan, and a touchstone of Korean national identity.

MILITARY LEADERSHIP

The military leadership of Yi Sun-sin was arguably a deciding factor in the outcome of the Imjin War, in which the Japanese were forced back from the Asian mainland to their home islands of Tsushima and Kyushu. Admiral Yi's record of twenty-three consecutive naval victories without defeat between 1592 and 1598 qualifies him as one of the outstanding admirals of global naval history. His character is celebrated as much in Korea as is his military genius. If George Washington could not tell a lie about cutting down the cherry tree, Yi Sun-sin equaled Washington's character regarding truthfulness with his own character regarding perseverance in the face of hardship and his loyalty to defend, his homeland. When he broke his leg in a fall from his horse during his military exam-ination at age twenty-eight, he bound the leg with a tree branch and fin-ished the course. He failed the examination because of the fall, but that did not daunt him. He persevered and prepared for another four years and passed the examination at age thirty-two. After winning all of his naval battles during the first Japanese invasion and being appointed chief admiral of the Korean fleet, Yi was demoted to deckhand as the Japanese planned the second invasion. Nevertheless, his loyalty remained strong, and he accepted back the tattered Korean fleet of twelve ships along with his command post. With this remnant, Yi still was able to defeat the Japanese during their second invasion of Korea. As a result of these episodes, Yi Sun-sin's character became legendary in Korea.

Beyond these character traits, his strategic genius was apparent in his conception of the naval blockade as the source of ruin for extended Japanese lines of supply, and his tactical genius exhibited itself time after time during his undefeated naval battles. His tactical bag of tricks was extensive, including his development and use of turtle ships, his use of tides and currents during battle, and his development of overwhelming flanking maneuvers such as the crane's wing formation.

Japanese military leadership was extremely competent and effective in the blitzkrieg-style land movement from Busan to Seoul to Pyongyang during the first invasion, but it could not move beyond Pyongyang toward its goal of conquering China for two reasons. First, because of Yi Sun-sin's naval blockade, the Japanese could not resupply their extended forces, and second, sizable Chinese forces finally crossed the Yalu River to join the fight as allies of the Koreans, who had fought alone against the Japanese up to that point. Although Hideyoshi had proved himself to be a great military genius by unifying Japan through military victories in the home islands, he suffered his only military failure in his invasions of Korea while attempting to incorporate the Asian mainland under his rule.

RELATIVE POWER RELATIONS

Thucydides said, "It was the rise of Athens and the fear that this instilled in Sparta that made war inevitable." Similarly, it might be said, that the rise of Hideyoshi's Japan and the fear that this installed in Ming China that made war inevitable. Athens was a rising power, and Sparta was the established, status quo power. Likewise, Japan was a rising power, while China was the established, status quo power. In *Destined for War*, Graham Allison examined sixteen cases of rising powers confronting established powers between the years 1500 and 2000. This study was meant to be comprehensive, looking at all significant cases during the most recent five hundred years of human history. In twelve of the cases reviewed, the powers went to war, indicating a high probability, though not "inevitability," that rising and established powers will go to war. The problem of the "Thucydides trap" is to determine how war might be avoided amid the tension between rising and established great powers. The work gives some clues for avoiding war, including opposite poles of accommodation and mutual assured destruction. The study did not include the case of the Imjin War, which arguably is as important in scope and scale as the European cases reviewed during the same sixteenth-century period. A rising Japan and stagnant China appeared again during the early twentieth century, again resulting in war. This case was included in *Destined for War*.

ALLIANCE RELATIONS

Hideyoshi made a mistake when he assumed that the Korean state, Joseon (Choson), which had a tributary relationship with China, would become Japan's ally in attacking China. Instead, Korea allied with China. As allies, Joseon Korea and Ming China had different goals. Korea's goal was to prevent Japan from ruling the Korean peninsula. Being militarily weaker than Japan, Korea sought China's help to save its sovereignty, though Korea was under Chinese suzerainty regarding foreign relations. China's goal, was to prevent Japan from invading and conquering China. Thus China was interested in using Korea as a buffer zone to keep Chinese losses low while Korea put up the first line of defense. On land, China's alliance with Korea had positive effects, while on the sea it had minimal impact.

During the first invasion of Korea by Japan, China offered no naval support to the Korean navy under the command of Yi Sun-sin. After Yi's success at the Battle of Myeongnyang early during the second invasion, the Chinese navy under Chen Lin came from the eastern coast of China to join the efforts of the Korean navy in resisting the Japanese. While Chen Lin held back Chinese naval forces from front-line action, perhaps to limit losses, Korean naval success continued. In spite of fraught personal and professional relations, Korean and Chinese naval forces did work together during the final naval battle at Noryang. Ultimately, the Chinese navy did not demonstrate that it was a significant contributor to military success on the naval front. The case of the Imjin War, with its mixed army-navy alliance results but final success of the overall Korea-China alliance, provides evidence to support Winston Churchill's observation that "There is only one thing worse than fighting with allies, and that is fighting without them."

RELATIONSHIP OF MARITIME ECONOMIC SUCCESS TO MARITIME MILITARY SUCCESS

In the case of the Imjin War, maritime economic success accompanied Korea's maritime military success during the war. In fact, the Japanese forcibly took Korean potters back to Japan to start important pottery works in Kyushu, thereby negatively affecting Korea's ceramics capabilites. Through its So clan intermediaries in Tsushima, Japan subsequently reaped maritime trade benefits even though it had lost the Imjin naval war.

IMPORTANCE OF HISTORICAL AND CURRENT KNOWLEDGE

It appears that Hideyoshi lacked key elements of information before embarking on his invasions of Korea. In hindsight, it seems clear that he was not prepared for how the lack of cooperation by Koreans on the peninsula would make his invasion difficult, how the vast geographic scope of the continent would not even begin to open itself up to him, or how his lack of naval capacity would put him in jeopardy. Such were the limits of his geographic sense of possibility that he had visions of conquering India as well as China. The samurai were fearsome and fearless warriors, but they were not equipped to overcome these fundamental oversights. Hideyoshi became bogged down in Korea and in fact never made it to China. Centuries ago, Hideyoshi was exposed to the problems of fighting a land war in Asia, a lesson that had to be relearned by the Japanese during the twentieth century in their attempt once again to control China. They got further with their objective this time than they did during the Imjin War, but in the end they failed again.

Admiral Yi's sources of intelligence led him to believe that the Japanese were leading the Korean navy into a trap at the beginning of the second invasion attempt. Thus he refused to attack the Japanese as the Korean king demanded. Yi was demoted and Won Gyun was appointed in his place. Won Gyun fell into the Japanese trap and lost most of the Korean naval fleet. Sunzi would have been proud of the Japanese disinformation effort, but he would have been even more proud of Yi Sun-sin, whose intelligence information prevented him from being duped by the disinformation. This early "info war" had profound ramifications. Fortunately for Korea, Admiral Yi was able to bounce back using the twelve-ship fragment of the Korean navy, and still went on to forge ultimate naval victory. Yi used luck and chance, Clausewitz-style, as well as shrewd naval acumen to achieve success. A better lesson than using luck and chance, difficult things to control, was to believe better information and avoid being duped by misinformation, as the Korean king and Admiral Won Gyun had been.

MONGOL AND JAPANESE INVASIONS COMPARED

The Mongol invasions of Japan by way of Korea occurred toward the end of Mongol unification of the mainland. Before attempting to invade Japan, the Mongols had already subjugated Korea and were able to use it as a base for stepping off to Japan. The Mongols used Korean military assistance, especially their sea experience and technology. The first Mongol invasion, a short probe less than two months long, took place in 1274, five years before the final defeat of the Song Dynasty in 1279. The second invasion in 1281 included a larger force and lasted about three months before its devastation by the great kamikaze divine wind. The Mongols were not sufficiently knowledgeable to have understood the severe storm season.

The Japanese attempted invasions of China by way of Korea also occurred toward the end of a period of unification, in this case of the Japanese main islands. The first invasion, an extensive drive lasting fourteen months, had China as its goal, but it was repulsed in Pyongyang before it reached China. The second invasion, lasting fifteen months but less successful in its penetration of Korea, collapsed completely with the decision to withdraw following the death of Hideyoshi. Yi Sun-sin played the role of *kamikaze* "divine wind" for the Koreans during both invasions. Later, during the Meiji era, the Japanese understood that controlling Korea was the first order of business during both the 1894–1895 Sino-Japanese War and during the 1904–1905 Russo-Japanese War. After formally annexing Korea in 1910, Japan pursued its continental ambitions for about three decades with moderate success, as compared to its inability to penetrate China during the 1590s.

The Mongol amphibious landings in Japan and Vietnam have left a historic consciousness of the possibility of a Chinese invasion of Japan and Vietnam. Likewise, the Japanese invasions of Korea have left a historic consciousness of the invasion of the Asian continent into Korea and China by Japan. These episodes of northeast Asian maritime history are part of the fabric of Asian historic consciousness.

SEVEN

Ming Expulsion of the Dutch from Taiwan

Koxinga, Seventeenth Century

Core and Periphery: Chinese Dynastic Change, Europeans on the Coast

Geopolitics of Taiwan in Asia was a minor factor prior to the seventeenth century, as the island lay beyond coastal maritime trade paths. In 1600, the island was occupied by about 100,000 aboriginal peoples and a few hundred lost fisherman, shipwrecked sailors, and occasional pirates from China, Japan, and the Ryukyu Islands. The geostrategic value of the location of the island became prominent during the seventeenth century, and its significance has persisted until today.

Since the demise of aboriginal control in the seventeenth century, Taiwan has been occupied in sequence by the Dutch, Spanish, Ming, Qing, British, Japanese, and Nationalist Chinese, prior to the current Taiwanese democracy. The flags of each of these entities flutter in chronological sequence over Spanish- and Dutch-built Fort San Domingo in Danshui, northwest Taiwan, as a reminder of the complex series of changes that have occurred on Taiwan. The long-term fate of Taiwan remains uncertain during the current period of Taiwanese democracy and its quasi-state status. Mainland China has insisted that there is only one China and that Taiwan is a part of the People's Republic of China.

This case study revolves around the maritime history of the Ming to Qing transition, interactions with Europeans on the scene at the time, and the role of the powerful Zheng clan on the Fujian coast. Although many of the Zheng clan were involved between the 1620s and 1680s, the primary focus will be on Zheng Chenggong, known more widely in the West as Koxinga.[1] During the late 1650s, Koxinga led two major offensives that failed against the Qing in Nanjing. These expeditions were followed by an attack on the Dutch in Taiwan in the early 1660s, which succeeded in driving the Dutch off Taiwan after a military victory that surprised Europeans at the time. The Dutch returned to their base in Batavia on Java in the East Indies. After defeating the Dutch, the Ming ruled Taiwan for two decades until the last Zheng family Ming loyalists were defeated in a naval battle at the Penghu Islands in the Taiwan Strait in 1683. Following this defeat, the last holdout loyalists of the Ming on Taiwan were subjugated to Qing rule. It was a defector from the Zheng family navy, Shi Lang, who was ultimately successful in defeating the Zheng navy at Penghu.

The maritime saga of the end of the Ming Dynasty is both a story of domestic Chinese dynastic change involving transfer of power from the Ming to the Qing, and the story of an international triumph of Chinese over Europeans, including the last strategic military victory of the Chinese over a Western power up to the present.[2]

EUROPEANS IN THE CHINA SEAS

In 1495, Portugal and Spain agreed to the division of the Atlantic proposed by Pope Alexander VI by signing the Treaty of Tordesillas. But what about the other side of the world, where conflict developed after Portugal went all the way east across the Indian Ocean and Spain went all the way west across the Pacific Ocean? To address this problem, the two parties signed the Treaty of Saragossa in 1529. This additional treaty ran a meridian that cut through Japan and Australia, leaving mostly blue Pacific water to Spain. According to these tidy division lines, Portugal had approximately 190 degrees of the world's surface and Spain had about 170 degrees. Although the two treaty lines were clear on maps, they were murky when ships met at sea or when explorers met in the jungles of the Amazon. The treaty provisions were put into effect more

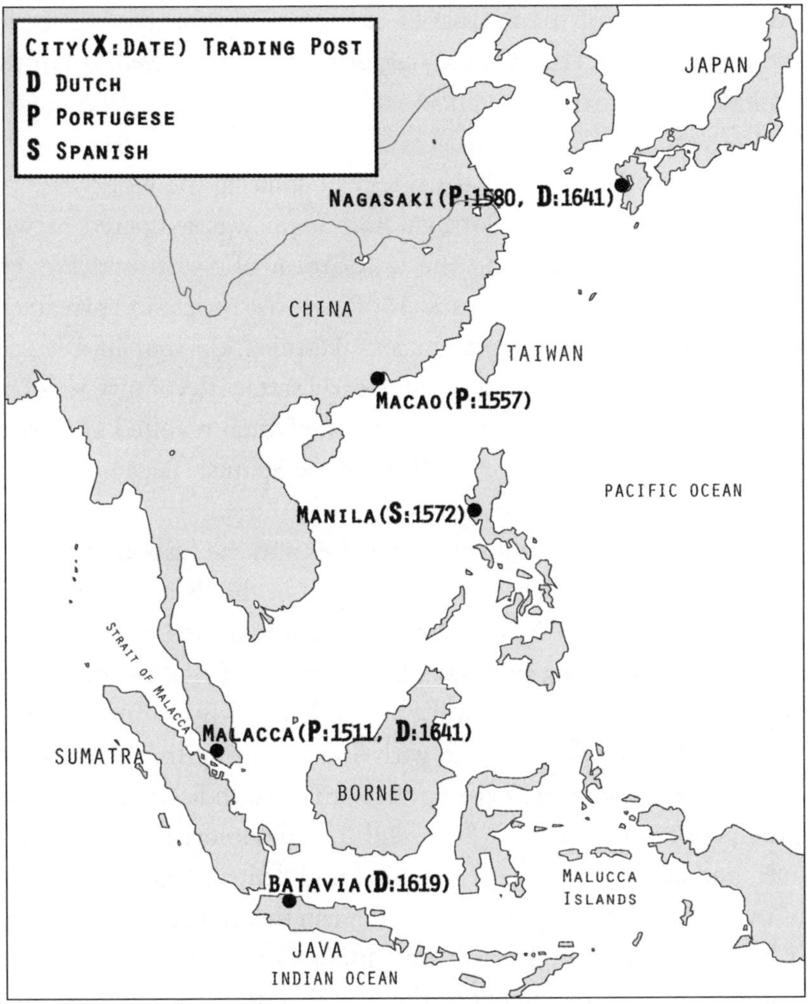

MAP 7.1 European arrivals in Southeast and East Asia
Adapted by Jamie Rhode from Warren Cohen, East Asia at the Center: Four Thousand Years of Engagement with the World *(New York: Columbia University Press, 2000), 203*

by action and occupation than by survey. Eventually, the Treaties of Tordesillas and Saragossa were superseded by other agreements.

In the interim, Portugal and Spain used the treaties to form basic rules of engagement to guide their division of the world, until the Dutch, English, and French challenged the idea that the world belonged only to Portugal and Spain. Dutchman Hugo Grotius wrote his essay *Mare Liberum* in 1609, laying out the concept of freedom of the seas for everyone, not just for the Portuguese and the Spanish.[3] During the sixteenth century, however, the treaty agreements worked well as Portugal became dominant in the Indian Ocean, and Spain focused on colonizing the Americas.

Pope Alexander VI's global strategy of splitting the world into two hemispheres controlled by Portugal and Spain was tempered between these superpowers following the unification of Spain and Portugal under one king between 1580 and 1640, which rendered the treaties of Tordesillas and Saragossa meaningless. Domination that had worked well for Spain and Portugal during the early sixteenth century was challenged in the seventeenth century when the Dutch revolted against the Spanish in Europe and disputed Portuguese-Spanish hegemony in the international arena.

The Dutch had been cut off from spices and the Lisbon markets by King Philip II of Spain. Their revolt resulted in the Dutch War of Independence, or the Eighty Years War, which lasted from 1568 to 1648. As Protestants, the revolting provinces had religious as well as political and economic differences with Catholic Spain. The newly established Dutch Republic carried on the struggle with Spain. During the 1590s, Dutch merchants sent exploratory expeditions to the East Indies, notably to Banten, the pepper port of west Java, and to the Moluccas, the source of nutmeg and cloves, cutting off Javanese middlemen. Profits for expeditions ran as high as 400 percent. The English threatened Dutch competitors by establishing the English East India Company in 1600. Not to be outdone, Dutch merchants of the Republic founded the Vereenigde Oostindische Compagnie in 1602. It was known as the VOC or Dutch East India Company by English speakers, in order to distinguish it from the English East India Company (EIC).[4] The VOC issued shares of stock to the general public, making it the forerunner of modern global corporations as the world's first publicly traded company. It was created to push forward Dutch interests outside of Europe. In addition to having the power to trade, the VOC also possessed quasi-governmental powers to negotiate treaties, maintain armies and forts, wage war, imprison and execute convicts, establish colonies, and issue coins. It established trading posts in Banten in 1603 and at Ambon in 1610 before establishing an adequate permanent trading center in Jayakarta, renamed Batavia in 1619 when it came under Dutch control. Batavia became Jakarta with the Japanese occupation in 1942.

From their Batavia base, the Dutch built their eastern empire during the 1620s. Through clearing for plantation development, they decimated the population of the Banda Islands. Unable to force the Portuguese out of Macao in an attack in 1622, the VOC nevertheless followed the Portuguese string-of-pearls strategy by establishing a trading center on the Penghu Islands in 1622 before being forced by the Chinese to move to Taiwan in 1624. From this mid-China coast location with access to Chinese silk and porcelain, the Dutch moved north to force the Portuguese out of Nagasaki, establishing in 1641 the only Japanese-sanctioned European trading post on the artificial island of Dejima in Nagasaki Bay.[5] The Dutch also supplanted the Portuguese in Malacca in 1641. Thus by the 1640s, the Dutch had replaced the Portuguese as the predominant European trading entity in the China Seas. The Spanish contested control of Taiwan by establishing the forts of San Salvador at Jilong (Keelung) in 1626 and San Domingo at Danshui (Tamshui) in 1629, thereby opposing the Dutch forts at Zeelandia and Provintia established in 1624. But the Dutch forced the Spanish to abandon Taiwan by 1642.[6] Thus the Portuguese were reduced to Macao and the Spanish to Manila in terms of their substantial presence in East Asia, while the Dutch, through their presence in Batavia, Malacca, Zeelandia, and Nagasaki, clearly now dominated East and Southeast Asia in terms of European influence during the middle and latter half of the seventeenth century.

The English had contested the Dutch in the East Indies during the 1620s, but later they pulled back to India. The English anticipated better trading success in India than in the East Indies after the Amboyna Massacre of 1623 in the Molucca Islands drove them to redirect their competition with the Dutch from Southeast Asia to South Asia. The Dutch, however, continued to contest the settled Portuguese and the arriving British in the Indian Ocean. They established VOC Ceylon ports at Galle in 1640 and Colombo in 1658, expelling the Portuguese and driving them from the Malabar coast of India, except for Goa. The

VOC became a huge operation during the seventeenth century, with a merchant fleet that exceeded the size of the combined fleets of Portugal, Spain, England, France, and Germany. By the late 1660s, it was the richest private company in the world, with deep pockets that nearly bankrupted the English EIC during the 1680s over their head-to-head Asian competition. The Dutch loss of Zeelandia during the Sino-Dutch War of 1661–1662 marked the beginning of the demise of the lucrative Dutch China trade, especially in silk. Although the VOC was flush with other success, the Sino-Dutch War of the early 1660s foreshadowed the eighteenth-century decline of the VOC and its ultimate dissolution in 1799.

Unsuccessful Ming Attempt to Repel the Qing in Nanjing, 1658–1659

Ming loyalist Koxinga determined that he would challenge the Manchu Qing farther north by engaging in a northern expedition to push them out of south China.[7] Departing from his Fujian base late spring 1658 for the mouth of the Yangzi River on his way to Nanjing, his large expeditionary force included women and children intended to populate Nanjing after the Manchus were removed. Dominican Vittorio Riccio wrote that "It was the most powerful fleet that had ever been seen in the China seas."[8] The expedition consisted of about 100,000 soldiers and a thousand ships, a force more than three times the size of the largest of Zheng He's great sea expeditions during the early Ming dynasty.[9] Despite its size, the 1658 expedition was unsuccessful due to storms at sea.

In 1659 Koxinga headed north along the coast with even larger forces than in 1658, having an estimated 200,000 men and 2,000 ships. Outside the walls of Nanjing, against the counsel of his commanders, Koxinga delayed attacking the city, allowing Manchu troops to reinforce the city. In the ensuing battle, the Manchu Qing force drove Koxinga's forces back down the Yangzi River and ultimately back to Fujian Province. Koxinga sailed south to his base at Xiamen (Amoy), pursued by a Manchu naval force of eight hundred vessels.

Although Koxinga had not distinguished himself in the north, he demonstrated that he was still commander of the sea in the south. The following summer, on June 17, 1660, he decisively defeated the Manchus in a sea battle in Jinmen Bay off Xiamen, taking four thousand Manchu prisoners and slaughtering them.[10] The Manchus retaliated by instituting a draconian scorched-earth policy along the coast, prohibiting coastal residence and moving all coastal inhabitants several miles inland so that maritime Ming loyalists like Koxinga would have no local sources of food to sustain military operations on land or at sea.[11]

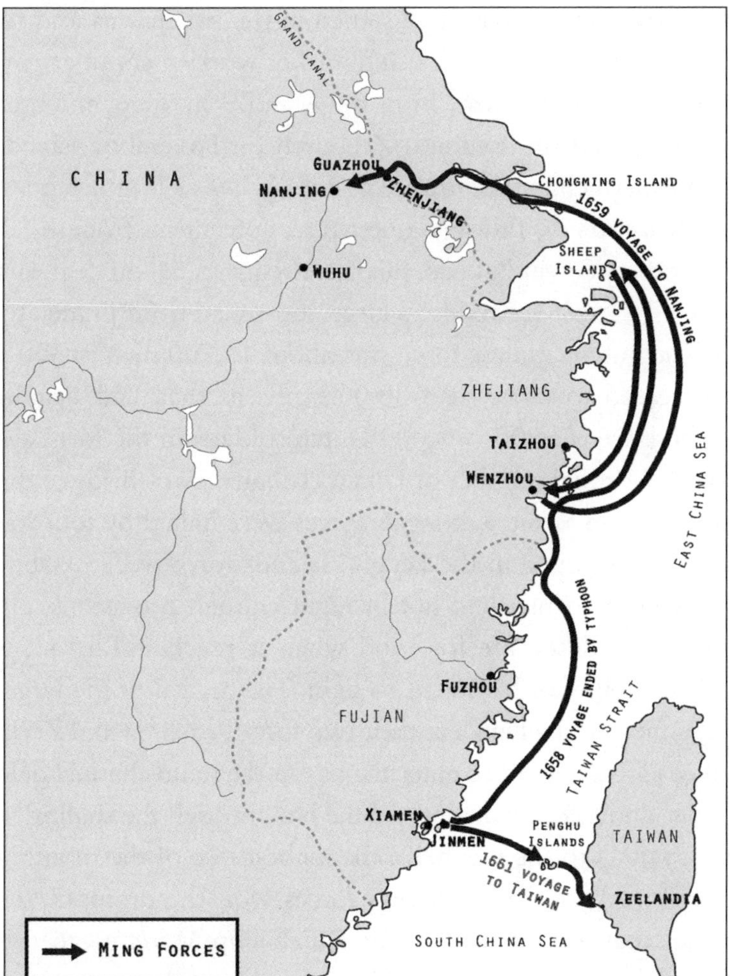

MAP 7.2 Koxinga's expeditions, 1658–1661
Adapted by Jamie Rhode from Tonio Andrade, Lost Colony: The Untold Story of China's First Great Victory over the West *(Princeton, NJ: Princeton University Press, 2011), 88, 105*

Successful Ming Attempt to Drive the Dutch from Taiwan, 1661–1662

The Qing coastal prohibitions pressured Koxinga to move his base of operations to Taiwan, called Formosa by the Portuguese and Dutch, despite objections by his commanders that the island was too wild and disease-ridden.[12] Lack of space and security on the Fujian coast could be solved by the larger, more securely defensible territory on Taiwan. Being accessible only by sea, it was a position Koxinga favored, given his seafaring prowess. In 1652, there had been a revolt of the Chinese on Taiwan against the Dutch who had settled in the two towns and forts at Tai Bay, resulting in the Dutch being further worried about attempts of the Chinese to remove them from the island.[13] In 1656, an enormous typhoon destroyed the Redoubt Zeeburch on Baxemboy Island, such that the northern channel entrance to Tai Bay was left undefended. The Dutch at their forts on Taiwan requested reinforcements from the administration of the VOC in Batavia, but these requests fell on deaf ears.

On April 21, 1661, Koxinga's large fleet sailed from Jinmen toward Taiwan. The initial Chinese force was about 11,700 men in 300 junks, which increased to more than 30,000 men as they laid siege to the forts.[14] There were 2,000 to 3,000 Dutch soldiers in the forts, with an approximately equal number of Dutch civilians. Two-thirds of the way across the Taiwan Strait, Koxinga's forces were halted by foul weather, and they were trapped in the Penghu Islands for a week. Assuming a quick passage, Koxinga had not brought enough provisions, and the expedition was desperate for food when it reached Taiwan, which inhibited the ability of his forces to fight. The arrival of the large fleet, however, unnerved the Dutch at their two forts, Provintia and Zeelandia, on Tai Bay. Choosing not to enter the bay at the main channel defended by Fort Zeelandia, Koxinga entered the bay through the shallow Deer's Ear Gap channel to the north, on the highest tide of the month at the new moon on April 30. Koxinga's forces won the dramatic sea and land battles that took place, but the Dutch ship *Maria* escaped to sail to Batavia for reinforcements. Koxinga demanded the surrender of the smaller fort, Provintia, from its commander, Jacob Valentine, offering to let the Dutch go free in exchange for territorial control of the Dutch area. Valentine's superior, Dutch governor Frederic Coyett seated at Zeelandia, suggested Dutch and Chinese coexistence, a proposal rejected by Kox-inga. Fort Provintia surrendered on May 6, a short but eventful week after Koxinga's arrival. The Dutch at the more substantial Fort Zeelan-dia, however, raised the red war flag of resistance over the fort, setting the stage for a prolonged siege.

As at Nanjing two years earlier, Koxinga appeared to be in no hurry, thinking that the limited Dutch troops in Fort Zeelandia would be unable to sail south against the summer monsoons to request reinforcements from Batavia. He was incorrect. Dutch sailors could tack more closely against the wind in their ships than Chinese junks could. The Dutch messenger ship *Maria* made it to Batavia. In the meantime, Koxinga attempted to starve the Dutch, who had stored provisions in the fort sufficient for several months. Instead, the Chinese suffered a shortage of provisions, as ships did not arrive as expected with rice and other supplies due to the evacuation of the Fujian coast by Qing decree, as well as to cracks in Zheng family loyalties among the general populace. That summer Koxinga's sailors and soldiers in Taiwan became farmers to supply food for the numerous Ming loyalist forces. In this war of attrition, many of Koxinga's forces died of illness.

On August 12, 1661, a Dutch relief fleet of twelve ships arrived from Batavia under the command of Jacob Cauw, made landing, and restocked Fort Zeelandia with food and men. Cauw was sent to replace Coyett as governor and commander, but he thought better of the idea and later sailed away, leaving Coyett and his men in increasingly difficult circumstances.[15] Both sides faced the specter of starvation, with the Chinese in even worse shape than the Dutch, with many more mouths to feed with few provisions to go around. Chinese defectors aided the Dutch side during the summer, while Dutch defectors to Koxinga played a significant role toward the end of the year.[16] On December 16, some defectors left Fort Zeelandia. Among them was rice-wine-drinking sergeant Hans Radis, who gave Koxinga advice on how to attack Fort Zeelandia from the Utrecht redoubt position. Damage to the fort was so severe that on January 27, 1662, Coyett and his council decided to negotiate surrender. Agreement was reached on February 1, 1662. The Dutch were allowed to leave with their personal arms and possessions, but they abandoned the fort's weapons and the company's wealth. The siege had gone on for nine long and bitter months, from May 1661 to February 1662, longer than either of the sieges of Rhodes or Malta. Casualties were similar to those on Malta, fewer on the Dutch side and heavier on the Chinese side. As an order of magnitude estimate, perhaps half of the 5,000 Dutch and a third of the 30,000 Chinese died during the siege. Sickness and starvation caused many of the deaths, in addition to those lost in battle.

In an analysis intending to shed light on the historical military revolution debate from both Euro-centric and Asia-centric positions, Tonio Andrade compares the seventeenth-century military capabilities of the Chinese with those of the Dutch. He does this on four levels: guns, military discipline, ships, and forts. His conclusions are that first, the technology of guns was about equal; second, the military discipline of the Chinese was better than that of the Dutch, whose military discipline was considered the best in Europe at the time; third, the ability of the Dutch ships to sail toward the wind gave them an edge over Chinese warship capability, and the construction strength of the Dutch ships and their broadside cannons gave the Dutch ships an advantage in deep-water engagements; and fourth, although the Chinese outnumbered the Dutch by a large margin, the renaissance fortress configuration with corner battlements allowed the Dutch to hold out for many months before surrendering. That was long enough for Koxinga to study and absorb the technology of the renaissance fort and incorporate it into his own counterstrategy, albeit with the help of a Dutch defector. In summary, each side had elements of relative strength, and the elements were not static in terms of relative advantage. Thus, Andrade proposes that during the seventeenth century, China was fairly similar to Europe in terms of military capabilities, but that the Dutch had a slight advantage in technology overall. Environmental factors, especially storms but also tides, were wild cards that affected the ebb and flow of the siege.

The deciding key difference that led to Chinese victory, according to Andrade, was stronger leadership by Koxinga and his commanders, compared to what he considered poor Dutch leadership. This judgment contains some irony, as it is inconsistent with the judgment about Koxinga's poor leadership during the failed siege of Nanjing.

ZHENG RULE ON TAIWAN AND THE FALL OF TAIWAN TO THE MANCHUS, 1683

Before the Dutch left Taiwan, Koxinga had renamed the island Ming Eastern Capital. With the demise of the Yongli emperor in early 1662, Koxinga began to treat the island as an independent realm from the Qing. In name, the island regime maintained loyalty to the Ming, but it was difficult to ascertain what this meant since there was no generally accepted Ming sovereign following the death of Yongli. Less than five months after the Dutch surrender, Koxinga himself passed away, burdened by both physical and psychological illness. He was succeeded by his son Zheng Jing, who for another eighteen years successfully implemented the Ming bureaucratic structure and Zheng business program that his father had begun before his premature death at thirty-eight. At the same time, Zheng Jing prevented the Qing from conquering Taiwan despite several attempts from the mainland. The Zheng clan company continued to be so strong that its revenues typically exceeded those of the powerful Dutch VOC.[17] Although his leadership was stable, Zheng Jing did not leave a strong succession plan in place after he died in 1681. Zheng Jing's seven-year-old son Zheng Keshuang served as the Zheng successor, overseen by a regent. The weakened Zheng ruling authority withstood ongoing Qing pressure for only two years. The Zheng demise on Taiwan was brought about by Koxinga's former naval commander turned nemesis, Shi Lang.

In 1651, eleven years before taking Taiwan, Koxinga had rejected the advice of Shi Lang, one of his naval commanders considered to be wise and brave, to protect their base at Xiamen while the Zheng forces attacked Guangdong. The Qing plundered unprotected Xiamen. Shi Lang flaunted his prescient counsel to protect Xiamen. This appeared to be arrogant to Koxinga, who imprisoned him. Shi Lang escaped and defected to the Qing, bringing detailed knowledge to the Manchus of Zheng plans and organization along with him. After Koxinga captured Taiwan from the Dutch in 1662, the Dutch engaged Shi Lang to take back the island from Zheng Jing in 1663. The threat of typhoons stopped two invasion dates scheduled by Shi Lang. The following year, the Qing appointed Shi Lang chief of the Fujian navy and directed him to capture Taiwan, but his fleet was destroyed by a typhoon. In 1667, Zheng Jing requested that the Qing recognize his Taiwan regime as an equal and separate state. Shi Lang lobbied the Qing emperor to attack Taiwan, but the suspicious Qing treated him like other defectors, such as Koxinga's father Zheng Zhilong, and placed Shi Lang under house arrest, taking him to Beijing in 1668. At the time of the transition following Zheng Jing's death in 1681, Shi Lang was released from house arrest by the Qing, and he resumed his post as chief of the Fujian navy. After disagreement with the governor of Fujian Province over how to attack the Zhengs on Taiwan, Shi Lang was granted total authority over military decisions by Emperor Kangxi. In spite of opposition within the Beijing court arguing that Taiwan was too remote, too unproductive, and too expensive to maintain, Shi Lang was authorized by the emperor to conquer Taiwan for the Qing.

On July 7, 1683, Shi Lang sailed from Fujian for two days to reach the Penghu Islands, seventy miles from the Fujian coast, in order to attack the Zheng navy stationed in the islands.[18] His fleet included 300 junks and 21,000 men, a force similar in size to the one that Koxinga had brought to Taiwan to evict the Dutch twenty-two years earlier in 1661. Initially his fleet was deflected south by a storm. The Zheng navy under the command of Liu Guoxuan was unprepared because it believed an attack during typhoon season would be unlikely. After a hurricane force wind delay, the Qing forces returned north and made a devastating naval attack. Bolstered by superior guns provided by the Dutch, the Qing navy sank 169 Zheng junks with the loss of 12,000 men, but with little loss to Shi Lang's forces. A Qing landing force completed the takeover of the islands. Zheng naval superiority was shattered. At the proclamation of surrender on August 26, 1683, thirteen-year-old Zheng Keshuang handed over the Ming emperor Yongli seals in his family's possession. In September 1683, Zheng Keshuang shaved his head Manchu style as a sign of submission. In October, Shi Lang proclaimed a general amnesty for all who recognized Qing rule. Then in November, Shi Lang visited Koxinga's shrine. A few Zheng sympathizers committed suicide, but most agreed to the generous terms offered by Shi Lang.

Meanwhile, debate in Beijing raged about whether to incorporate Taiwan into the state. Many advocated abandoning the island and moving its population to the mainland. Desiring to replace the Zheng commercial enterprise on Taiwan with his own monopoly, Shi Lang counseled Emperor Kangxi to incorporate Taiwan into China to prevent any further possibility of a base for continued Ming insurgency. In February 1684, Shi Lang petitioned the throne to annex Taiwan. Emperor Kangxi decided to incorporate Taiwan as a prefecture of Fujian Province in March 1684. The new Taiwan Prefecture consisted of 3 counties with a garrison of 11,000 men. As pleased as Shi Lang must have been by incorporation of Taiwan into the Qing state, he was frustrated when Kangxi lifted the maritime trading ban on the coast in November 1684, opening competition and ending Shi Lang's dream of a trade monopoly. Subsequently Shi Lang's influence declined until his death in 1696.

The strategic importance of the Penghu Islands (Pescadores), as well as Jinmen (Quemoy) and Xiamen (Amoy) in relation to Taiwan is notable. All three invasions of Taiwan during the seventeenth century used the Penghu Islands as a staging ground for amphibious operations. The Dutch had established a fort in the Penghus in 1622 before being forced to Tai Bay by the Chinese in 1624. Koxinga, representing the Ming, came through the Penghus in 1662 to conquer the Dutch on Taiwan. Shi Lang, representing the Qing, came through the Penghus in 1683 to conquer the Ming loyalist Zheng clan on Taiwan. During the nineteenth century, the French navy attacked Taiwan by way of the Penghus in the 1880s. In March 1895, the Japanese took the Penghus as the last battle of the Sino-Japanese War, paving the way for Taiwan to become a Japanese colony pursuant to the Treaty of Shimonoseki, a situation that lasted for the next fifty years. With a large, deep natural harbor thirty miles from Taiwan and seventy miles from the coast of China, the islands provide a significant logistical shortening of the final attack distance to Taiwan. The importance of the twin islands of Xiamen and Jinmen to control both the southeast coast of China and the Taiwan Strait was clearly demonstrated by the struggle between the Ming and the Qing to control these islands.

Although close together near the coast, Xiamen is currently a Chinese island, while Jinmen belongs to Taiwan. The mid-twentieth-century struggle for Jinmen is documented by Michael Szonyi in *Cold War Island: Quemoy on the Front Line*. The role Jinmen played in 1958 during the Taiwan Strait crisis brought China and the United States to the brink of nuclear war.[19] The geographical facts surrounding Taiwan, the Penghus, Jinmen, and Xiamen have implicated these islands in larger geopolitical struggles to the present day. The struggles of the nineteenth and twentieth centuries mirror those of the seventeenth century and point to the continuing importance of these islands in the twenty-first century.

DUTCH VS. MING SHIPS

Although Koxinga's attack on the Dutch at Provintia and Zeelandia required an amphibious operation involving the transfer of more than 20,000 Chinese troops across the Taiwan Strait by ship, and supply of these troops partially by ship, the battle itself involved little ship-to-ship naval conflict. But Koxinga's lack of understanding of the Dutch ships' superior ability to sail toward the wind nearly resulted in a disaster that might have changed the course of the campaign. When Koxinga attacked Provintia, the small ship *Maria* had escaped and sailed south to Batavia to notify the VOC authorities that the Dutch were under siege in Taiwan. Koxinga had not worried about the escaped ship because the summer monsoon had arrived, blowing hard from the southwest. Based on his extensive knowledge gained while sailing Chinese junks, Koxinga felt it would have been impossible for a ship to sail to Batavia during the summer monsoon season.[20] But the *Maria* did make it to Batavia in a

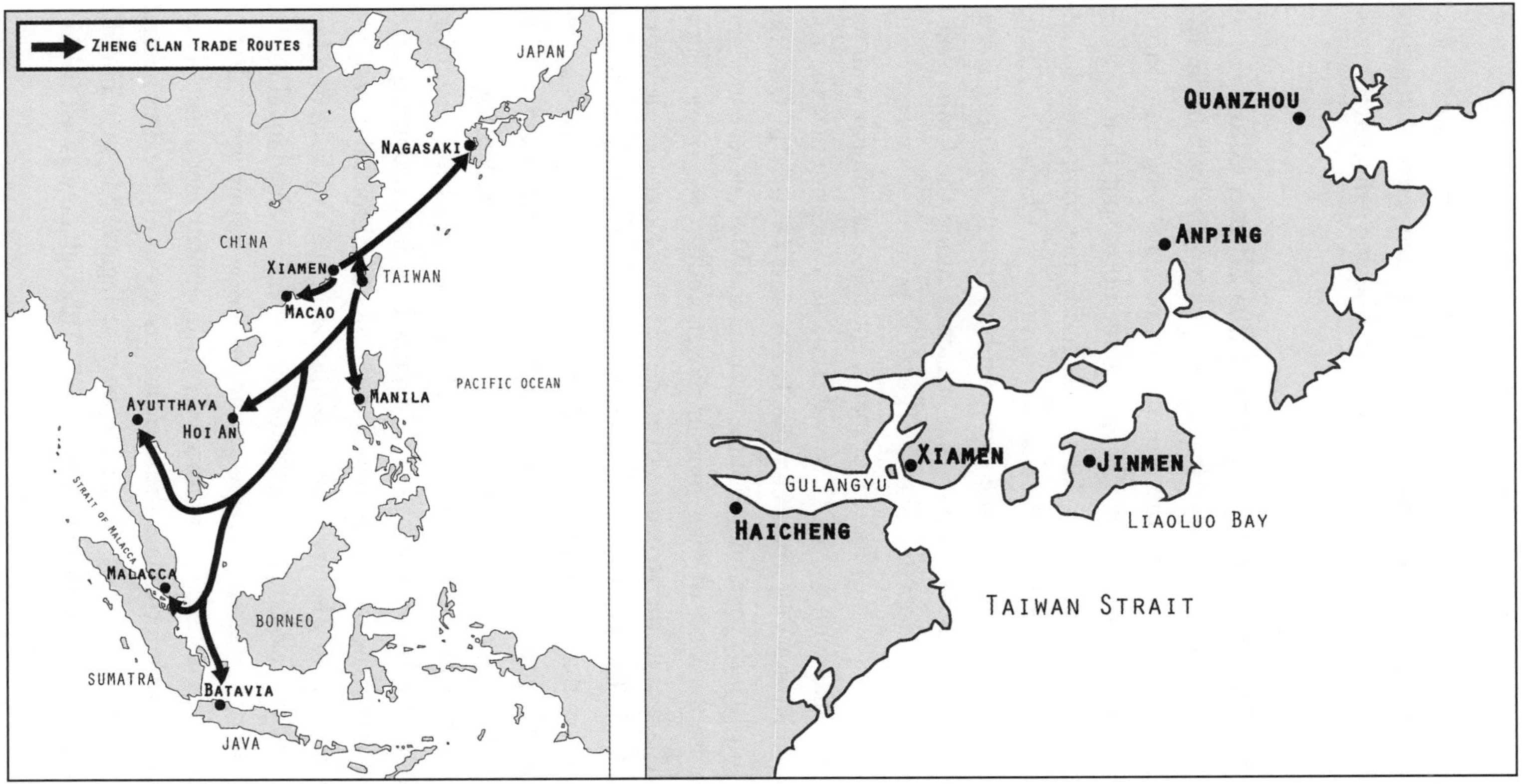

MAP 7.3 Zheng clan maritime world, 1620s–1680s, Xiamen and Jinmen home ports
Adapted by Jamie Rhode from Andrade, Lost Colony, *41, and Xing Hang,* Conflict and Commerce in Maritime East Asia: The Zheng Family and the Shaping of the Modern World, c. 1620–1720 *(Cambridge: Cambridge University Press, 2016), xi–xii*

seven-week voyage lasting from May 6 to June 24, 1661. Koxinga was completely surprised and unsettled when twelve Dutch warships appeared in Tai Bay in August in response to the *Maria* having delivered the message in Batavia.

Koxinga/Zheng Chenggong and the Zheng Clan

Koxinga, hero of the Chinese defeat of the Dutch on Taiwan in the seventeenth century, was a member of the renowned Zheng clan on the southeast coast of China. The Zheng clan members split their loyalties between the Ming and Qing Dynasties during the complicated mid-seventeenth-century period of dynastic transition in China. The Zheng organization (ZO) refers to the clan members' family business, a seaborne maritime trading empire that stretched along the China coast from Japan to Malacca and Siam.[21] The ZO's primary competitor was the VOC, the Dutch East India Company. For those unfamiliar with the ZO but familiar with the VOC, it will come as a surprise that the ZO outperformed the VOC between the 1620s and 1670s: "In fact, the Zheng consistently matched or outperformed the VOC in revenues and profitability for most of their time in power, and proved more adaptable to changes in the structure of trade."[22] Thus Koxinga's defeat of the Dutch on Taiwan was not only a political-military victory. It was also a victory that consolidated the Zheng business enterprise's access and control in the China Seas. Table 7.1 brackets Koxinga's life within the context of the Zheng clan over four generations, including his father, Zheng Zhilong, his son Zheng Jing, and his grandson, Zheng Keshuang. These four generations of Zheng leadership will be discussed in sequence before assessing the place of Koxinga in East Asian historical narratives.

The decades of Zheng Zhilong's eclipse were years of fame and fortune for his son, Koxinga, who, unlike his father, remained loyal to the Ming. The basic facts of Koxinga's life are known, but many details have been embellished and interpreted by subsequent accounts.[23] Thus a great deal of myth overlays the known facts about his life. It is agreed that he was initially named Zheng Sen, born to Tagawa Matsu in Hirado near Nagasaki, Japan, during August 1624. Although he was left behind

TABLE 7.1
Leadership of the Zheng clan and the Zheng organization

Zheng Zhilong b. 1590s, d. 1661, Zheng Organization head: 1622–1646; born in modest Fujian circumstances; became the wealthiest, most powerful figure on China's southeast coast; defected from the Ming to the Qing (1646)
Zheng Sen later Zheng Chenggong/Koxinga b. 1624, d. 1662; Zheng Organization head: 1646–1662; born into joint Chinese/Japanese heritage followed by Fujian wealth and power; maintained loyalty to the Ming; lost to the Qing (1659), defeated the Dutch (1662)
Zheng Jing b. 1642, d. 1681; Zheng Organization head: 1662–1681; born into Fujian wealth and power; from dissolute beginnings became the stable head of an emerging Taiwan maritime state
Zheng Keshuang b. 1670, d. 1707; Zheng Organization head (under regent): 1681–1683; too young to rule, his regents lost Taiwan to the Qing navy under Shi Lang (1683)

in Japan as an infant during his first year when his father returned to Fujian, he was Zheng Zhilong's eldest son, serving the important function of carrying forward his father's surname. He was raised by his mother in Japanese tradition for the first six years of his life. As part of a samurai family, he received early instruction in swordsmanship and archery. When he was brought to Fujian to be with his father in 1630, his mother was left behind in Japan, most likely managing Zheng Zhilong's business interests in Japan. She had a second son, Shichizaemon, with a different father four years later. This stepbrother remained close to Koxinga throughout their lives. Zheng Zhilong took a Chinese wife in Fujian, the daughter of one of merchant Li Dan's business partners. Such multiple family arrangements occurred among those involved in far-flung maritime trade. Koxinga lived in Fujian amid newly acquired family wealth and power at the family mansion in Anhai. He exhibited academic talent and was sent at age nineteen to Nanjing in 1643 to study classics such as *The Spring and Autumn Annals* and Sunzi's *The Art of War*.[24] He became a student of the famous Ming scholar Qian Qianyi, a poet, historian, and, less usual for the time, a supporter of independent women. Reports indicate that Zheng Sen excelled in his studies with this master. His studies were terminated in 1644 when the Ming capital in Beijing fell to the Qing who established their dynastic capital in Beijing while still embroiled in quelling Ming loyalists in the south of China. The Ming resistance had difficulty maintaining a sustained head of state, as the seventeenth Ming emperor Chongzhen died in Beijing in 1644, and the eighteenth Ming emperor Hongguang died in Nanjing in 1645.

Driven from Nanjing, the Ming prince of Tang set up as the nineteenth Ming emperor Longwu in Fuzhou on the Fujian coast. Longwu took a personal interest in the promising Zheng Sen. He granted him new names including both Guoxingye "lord of the imperial surname," romanized as Koxinga in most Western accounts, and Chenggong "achievement." Using his family name with this latter given name, he was known as Zheng Chenggong. Koxinga is used here more often, since he himself liked the Ming loyalty implied by being given the Ming imperial surname Zhu by Emperor Longwu. Koxinga's father Zheng Zhilong moved in the opposite political direction, away from loyalty to the Ming. He made a deal with the advancing Qing armies to switch to their side in 1646. The Ming emperor Longwu was killed in 1646 in a campaign to the interior of Fujian. Although Zheng Zhilong wished to remain in Fujian to rule on behalf of the Qing and had made a deal with the Qing to be governor of Fujian, he was instead removed to Beijing, where he lived for a decade under increasingly uncomfortable house arrest. The great struggle of Koxinga's life was between his loyalty to his Ming sovereign and the Confucian requirement that he have loyalty and filial piety toward his father. Accounts describe the son Koxinga tearfully remonstrating his father Zheng Zhilong for abandoning the Ming cause and trusting the Qing. On Taiwan, there are many statue depictions of Koxinga with his mother, but none with his father. Koxinga considered him to be a traitor to the Ming cause after his father agreed to support the Manchus in 1646, the same year his mother died at the hands of the Manchus during an attack on the Zheng family home. Thus the year 1646 was a year of triple tragedy for Koxinga that included the defection of his father to the Qing, the death of the Ming emperor Longwu, who had treated him as an adopted son, and the death of his mother Tagawa Matsu in particularly tragic circumstances. Shortly after she moved from Hirado to the Zheng family compound in Anhai, the compound came under Qing attack. In most accounts, her demise took place by suicide following rape by Manchu soldiers. Koxinga is said to have slit her belly to purify her body before he burned his Confucian robes as a sign that he was giving up the scholar's life.

Unlike his father, Koxinga remained loyal to the Ming, in spite of many offers of titles and property from the Qing. The moment of his father's defection in 1646 was a turning point for Koxinga. Beginning then, he gradually took a few Zheng loyalist supporters and turned them into a formidable naval force supporting the Ming. During the late 1640s and early 1650s, Koxinga consolidated control along the Fujian coast in the face of Qing opposition. Following the death of Longwu in 1646, he again was loyal to a Ming prince, Guei Wang, who established himself as the Yongli emperor in Guangdong. In 1650, at age twenty-six, Koxinga wrested control of Xiamen from his uncle Zheng Lien and beheaded him before establishing bases on the key islands of Xiamen and Jinmen, twin strategic islands that became the center of his maritime empire that stretched from Japan to Southeast Asia. While the Qing concentrated on pursuing the Ming Yongli emperor into southeast China and Burma, Koxinga fought brilliant campaigns in 1652 to capture the areas of Zhangzhou and Quanzhou, expanding his coastal control from Guangdong to Zhejiang. The Qing emperor Shunzi unilaterally proclaimed a southeastern coast cease-fire in 1653 in order to negotiate with Koxinga. The Qing were willing for Koxinga to rule four provinces in exchange for recognizing the Qing through the symbolic act of cutting his hair and shaving his head, citing the Korean example as precedent for a tributary state. Koxinga stalled and continued to consolidate his gains, entertaining plans for a northern expedition to force the Qing from south

China. In the meantime, he consolidated wealth, power, and territory, having mixed results on land but controlling the sea north to the mouth of the Yangzi River. Koxinga established effective administration using the same board structure that had come to characterize Ming bureaucracy. During these years Koxinga's Zheng organization competed successfully with the Dutch VOC from Nagasaki to Hoi An in Vietnam, where Zheng junks were the dominant presence. Xing Hang summarizes their success between 1650 and 1662: "To put it in today's terms, the Zhengs took in some 91 million in US 2014 dollars every year."[25] By 1657, Koxinga felt emboldened enough by his success to make the northern expeditions he had been contemplating for some time. As already described, in 1658–1659 Koxinga failed in his attempts to take Nanjing from the Qing, but he successfully drove the Dutch from Taiwan in 1661–1662 and transferred his Ming-style administration there.

Koxinga died on Taiwan in June 1662, only a short time after his successful expulsion of the Dutch in February 1662. He did not rest on the laurels accorded to him following his Taiwan victory, but rather immediately turned his focus toward the Philippines. His new goal was to drive the Spanish from the Philippines, just as he had driven the Dutch from Taiwan. To that end, he sent a mission to Manila headed by Vittorio Riccio, a Dominican priest and translator, with a letter dated April 21, 1662, demanding surrender by the Spaniards. Koxinga's conception of his position was made clear in the phrase "that every foreign nation recognize celebrated princes chosen by heaven, and that it pays them tribute." The Spaniards in Manila reacted much as Coyett and the Dutch had reacted when issued an ultimatum by Koxinga, angrily rejecting demands of surrender and threatening to kill all of the Chineses in Manila. Riccio returned to Taiwan, evacuating some of the Chinese on junks, but before he arrived, stories reached Koxinga of thousands of Chinese killed. Koxinga did not live long enough to put in place an invasion and siege plan for the Philippines as he had done on Taiwan. While the Philippines venture was going poorly, he also received much other bad news.

A perfect storm of personal grief swept over Koxinga during early 1662 as he learned of the death of the Ming sovereign Yongli in Yunnan, the death of his own father Zheng Zhilong in Beijing, and the incest of his son Zheng Jing in Xiamen. For Koxinga, all three of these events tore the fabric of Confucian piety that structured relations between subject and ruler and between father and son. Although Koxinga is said to have burned his Confucian scholar's robes when overcome by grief at the time of his mother's death at Anhai in 1646, the power of Confucian filial values over him prevailed, as it does widely throughout Asian societies influenced by China. In the end, Koxinga's loyalty to his Ming sovereign was stronger than loyalty either to his father or to his son.

Koxinga never met Yongli, the nineteenth Ming emperor, who fled progressively into the southwest interior of China and then into Burma, pursued by the Qing Manchus, while Koxinga stayed on the coast, attacking Nanjing and then Taiwan. Despite the geographical separation from his emperor, Koxinga remained loyal to his Ming sovereign. Thus, when Yongli was captured, brought from Burma to Yunnan, and executed in a marketplace there on June 11, 1646, news of his capture likely reached Koxinga in Taiwan, where he was setting up a Ming-style administration after his defeat of the Dutch. This was devastating news to Koxinga, as the Ming imperial line came to an end with Yongli's demise.

Koxinga's commitment to his Ming sovereign overshadowed loyalty to his father, Zheng Zhilong. With his father, the conflicted filial relationship never resulted in severed communication or total abandonment, but rather in continued correspondence and soul searching for more than a decade following Zheng Zhilong's defection to the Qing in 1646. Koxinga lived in Fujian while Zheng Zhilong lived in Beijing, where he was taken by the Manchus for safekeeping as well as to be used as bait to lure Koxinga to join the Manchu cause as his father had done. Zheng Zhilong lived comfortably in Beijing from the time of his defection to the Manchus in 1646 until 1656, when a letter to Koxinga was intercepted that had not been registered by the Qing in the usual censoring process. Zheng Zhilong's comfortable house arrest turned into harsh imprisonment and increased binding with chains. Spanish accounts say that a brother and another son were imprisoned with Zheng Zhilong. Because he had been baptized in Macao as Nicholas Iquan, Jesuit priests tried to ease his captivity by slipping him gold pieces to buy favors. Accounts of Zheng Zhilong's death vary widely, from beheading to death by slow slicing to being "blown to the clouds" on a pile of gunpowder. Whatever the actual specifics, all accounts point to a violent and disturbing death scenario. Dates of Zheng Zhilong's death vary between late 1661 and early 1662. News of the death would have reached Koxinga approximately the same time as news reached him regarding the demise of the Ming emperor and complications in the Philippines venture.

Further bad news reached Koxinga regarding his own son, Zheng Jing, who had been born in 1642 while Koxinga was a student in Nanjing. At the time that Koxinga drove the Dutch from Taiwan, Zheng Jing continued to live on the coast in Xiamen, where he had intimate relations with his younger brother's wet nurse, who subsequently gave birth to Zheng Jing's child. When Koxinga heard this story during the late spring of 1662, during the same period he heard the news of the emperor and his father's deaths, he ordered his brother Zheng Tai to kill Zheng Jing, along with the baby, the wet nurse, and his own first wife, who should have kept better order in the household. Zheng Tai killed the baby and the wet nurse, but not Zheng Jing and the wife. Koxinga was infuriated by what he perceived as incest and the lack of a complete response to his command. He reiterated his commands but was ignored by his generals, who prepared to recognize Zheng Jing as their leader.[26]

Caught in the perfect storm of emotional response to the Ming emperor's death, his father's death, his son's incest coupled by refusal of some of his generals to obey his orders, and the unwillingness of the Spanish to capitulate in Manila, Koxinga died in late June 1662.[27] Accounts of his death in Tainan vary even more than those of his father's death in Beijing. Some simply say he died of a fever resulting from a cold, malaria, or syphilis. Many accounts include what appear to be descriptions of madness or insanity for several days, including crying out about hallucinations of seeing beheaded men, weeping that he had neither fulfilled his obligations regarding loyalty or filial piety, gnawing his fingers and biting his tongue resulting in bleeding to death, while scratching his face and eyes violently. Other accounts attribute his death less to madness and suggest that he had ruined his formidable constitution with wine and women or died from fatigue of his military service in Taiwan, or even was killed by his own son.[28] In any event, he outlived his own father by only a few months, dying after a highly eventful and busy life at the early age of thirty-eight.

Zheng Jing's choice of successor was his son, Zheng Kecang, who was killed shortly after Zheng Jing's own death, and the thirteen-year-old Zheng Keshuang was put in place.[29] It was only two years later when the Tai-wan Zheng Dynasty fell to Shi Lang's Qing naval forces in the Battle of Penghu in 1683. Keshuang was brought to Beijing, where he lived until his death from illness in 1707.

Reflections on the Ming-Qing Transition Naval Experience

The Ming naval factor was an important part of the difficulty the Qing had in subduing the remnants of the Ming in southeastern China, a struggle that took them four decades after their capture of the Ming capital in Beijing. The Qing could not rely on their weaker naval experience to defeat the strong forces of the Ming loyalist Zheng family fleet in Fujian. In the end, it was a Zheng family fleet commander, Shi Lang, who defected and became the Qing admiral with enough experience and skill to defeat the Zheng fleet.

Maritime Strategic and Tactical Lessons

Lessons can be learned from a review of the case study material on how Koxinga failed against the Qing and prevailed against the Dutch, and how his descendants ultimately succumbed to the Qing, who replaced the Ming.

LOCAL KNOWLEDGE OF NATURAL PHENOMENA

Although the Dutch were knowledgeable and competent sailors, the Chinese who sailed the coast of Fujian were in more familiar home waters, which they used to their advantage. The Zheng family established their base in the complicated area of Jinmen and Xiamen islands, where they knew the intricate passages and seaways. Local sea knowledge helped them to protect their Fujian base for decades. Although familiar with the coast and having deep Zheng family experience with the East and South China Seas, Koxinga did not predict the typhoon that caught him unaware in 1658 at Sheep Island, causing him to abandon his attack on the Qing at Nanjing and postpone that expedition for another year. The Qing never claimed they were saved by a *kamikaze*, or divine wind, but the Japanese may have seen it that way.

Koxinga knew enough to have his ships avoid the passage into Tai Bay, which was covered by the heavy guns of Fort Zeelandia. He also knew the local tides well enough to plan passage through the shallow strait to the north at Deer's Ear Gate on the high tide. From there he was able to capture Fort Provintia and lay extended siege to Fort Zeelandia. He thanked the sea goddess Mazu for success at Deer's Ear Gate by establishing a Mazu temple there. Although he knew the sea conditions, gratitude to the assisting sea goddess was always in order.

ADVANTAGES IN MILITARY TECHNOLOGY

In a useful comparison, Tonio Andrade estimates that there was overall parity in military technology between Ming China and the Dutch at the time of the Sino-Dutch War in the 1660s. Andrade suggests that both parties were equal in gun technology and use, while the Ming had the edge in military discipline, and the Dutch had the edge in sailing craft that could point closer to the wind, making their ships more maneuverable. The Dutch had an edge in fort technology, but Dutch fort design was understood by Koxinga during the siege of Zeelandia, indicating the nature of technology transfer during wartime.

After the Dutch defeat by Ming loyalists in 1662, the Qing completed its conquest of the Ming by taking Taiwan in 1683. China entered a long period of relative peace under Qing rule that lasted until the nineteenth century. Meanwhile Europe engaged in continuous warfare and related development of warfare technology during these subsequent two centuries. Thus when the Europeans fought with the Chinese on the China coast during the nineteenth century, European military technology superiority quickly overcame Chinese military resistance. Indeed, the Sino-Dutch War of the 1660s, when there was rough military parity, was the last strategic defeat of a Western power by the Chinese up to the present day.

CONTINENTAL VS. MARITIME IDENTITIES

There is a prevalent view that the Chinese "pulled back from the sea" following Zheng He's final voyage to the Indian Ocean in 1433, implying a complete withdrawal from maritime identity. It is true that the Chinese state organized no further expeditions to the Indian Ocean after Zheng He until the Chinese antipiracy patrols beginning in 2008, a lapse of 575 years. During the Ming, however, the Chinese continued to trade with both northeast and southeast Asia using major large-scale shipping routes. During the Imjin War of the 1590s, the Ming sent a larg naval force to assist the Korean navy against the Japanese. This Ming force had been honed in the antipiracy battle involving the *wako* on the Chinese coast. During the early and mid-1600s, the Zheng family had a fleet of hundreds of merchant ships trading in northeast and southeast Asia, indeed competing successfully for revenues equal to those of the Dutch East India Company, the famed VOC. It seems prudent to temper the concept of China having "pulled back from the sea" during the early Ming by recognizing that significant Chinese state naval operations continued in practice until Qing admiral Shi Lang's defeat of the remaining Ming navy in the Penghu Islands in the Taiwan Strait in 1683.

Despite being based on the European continent, Dutch consciousness turned toward the sea, and the Netherlands developed a profound maritime identity. After establishing the VOC as the world's first publicly traded stock company in 1602, the Dutch quickly became the wealthiest nation in Europe. The Dutch string of forts and trading posts in Asia, supported by the VOC and the Dutch navy, was centered in Batavia, Java, with extensions to Zeelandia and Nagasaki in the China Seas, and to Malacca, Galle, and Kochi in the Indian Ocean.

The enormous wealth returning to the Netherlands resulted in Amsterdam's becoming the center of the Dutch Golden Age. The remains of the Golden Age are visible not only in Amsterdam architecture and museums, but also in the built environment of Leiden, Delft, and Rotterdam. As lowlands, the sea constantly threatens survival in the Netherlands, but the sea remains the source of Dutch wealth. Rotterdam is the largest container port by volume in Europe. Although traumatized during the Golden Age by the loss of their colony at Zeelandia, the Dutch and the VOC survived and thrived following the Sino-Dutch War of the 1660s. The Dutch became the only European *persona grata* in Japan, operating through their facilities in the Nagasaki Bay island of Dejima. Their East India islands spice trade remained strong with their presence in Batavia. They penetrated much of the Indian Ocean "Portuguese lake" by taking over Malacca, Galle, and Kochi from Portugal. Later the Dutch were replaced in all three places by the British in the European Portuguese-to-Dutch-to-British revolving door in Asia. At the same time the Dutch East India Company was operating in Asia, its West India Company was operating in the New World through its colonies at Surinam in South America and New Amsterdam in North America. While Koxinga was planning his attack on the Dutch in Taiwan in 1660, the Dutch released their map of New Amsterdam, the Castello Plan, clearly laying out their settlement at the southern tip of Manhattan. The Dutch maritime identity during the seventeenth century was truly global, including both the Old and New Worlds.

DEEPLY FELT NATIONAL IDENTITIES

During the seventeenth century there was a general struggle taking place between European and Asian identities, but the more relevant aspect in this case study is the struggle during Chinese dynastic change that took place between the Han identity of the Ming Dynasty loyalists and the Manchu identity of their Qing Dynasty successors. Han identity, referring to the core identity of the majority of Chinese in the current era, took its name from the people settled along the Han River in central China, who established the Han Dynasty (206 BCE–220 CE). Ethnic successors to the Han ruled China during the long Tang (618–906), Northern and Southern Song (960–1279), and Ming (1368–1644) Dynasties, while ethnic Mongols ruled during the Yuan Dynasty (1279–1368), and ethnic Manchus ruled during the Qing Dynasty (1644–1911). Thus, the recent two millennia of Chinese history during major dynasties involve rule by Han Chinese majority for 1,310 years. The Mongols and Manchu, western and northern tribes identified as "barbarians" by the Han, ruled for 356 years. These major dynasties were interspersed with some shorter periods of warring states and short-lived dynasties. Taken from the point of view of dynastic longevity, Han identity has been the core identity for China for much of two millennia. Han national identity was threatened during the mid-seventeenth century as the Qing encroached from the north and took the Ming capital in Beijing in 1644. Koxinga's father, Zheng Zhilong, defected to the Qing, while Koxinga remained loyal to the Ming successors who fled to the south to escape the Qing. Koxinga's national identity remained Ming, as did the identity of his son Zheng Jing and grandson Zheng Keshuang. In their national struggle, the Zheng clan extended the remnants of the Ming Dynasty from 1644 to 1683, until their base on Taiwan was taken by the Qing navy under Shi Lang. Koxinga was deeply loyal to the Ming and is revered to this day in both China and Taiwan for his unwavering loyalty to Han culture and Ming rule, as well as for his patriotic expulsion of the Dutch from the Chinese sphere of influence.

Koxinga's personal story of national identity has another fascinating dimension. His father was a Chinese man who fathered Koxinga with a Japanese mother from a samurai family while trading in Hirado on Kyushu in Japan. In statue depictions of Koxinga in both Kyushu and Taiwan, Koxinga stands only with his mother, never with his father, who is perceived as a disloyal defector. During the mid-seventeenth century, the Japanese were sympathetic to the Ming, not to the Qing, so there is an element of Japanese pride in the fact that Koxinga remained a Ming loyalist, fidelity being the prime samurai virtue. Called Tei Seiko in Japan, Koxinga became a hero in Japanese literature and plays during the seventeenth century, sometimes fictionally winning rather than losing in his struggle against the Qing.[30]

MILITARY LEADERSHIP

Koxinga was trained during his early years in the samurai arts of loyalty, discipline, archery, and swordsmanship, and during his adolescent years in the Mandarin arts of scholarship and historical and philosophical thought. This combination of disciplines, coupled with a family background that included wide travel, worldly experience, and wealth, gave him a platform to become the outstanding Ming leader of his age. He understood the sea better than his Ming military contemporaries and was unafraid to confront the seafaring Dutch across the daunting Taiwan Strait. Despite fierce Dutch resistance, he succeeded in his final goal of expelling the Dutch from Taiwan, carefully studying and learning from the Dutch as he laid siege to Zeelandia.

But Koxinga also had leadership flaws. Most telling, he did not heed the advice of his commanders in Nanjing who advised him to strike the city quickly once he was in the shadow of its walls. In the period of delay, Qing reinforcements arrived and drove Koxinga's Ming forces away. What shape would history have taken if Koxinga had taken Nanjing and been able to repel the Qing from Nanjing's impregnable walls? Might he have established a Southern Ming Dynasty like the Southern Song Dynasty, which extended Song power for more than 150 years?

Koxinga died young of mysterious causes at thirty-eight years of age. What if he had survived and established an even firmer Ming base on Taiwan than his son Zheng Jing managed to do? He was not the military leader that Alexander the Great was during his thirties, but his passing was a great loss to Ming loyalist leadership at the time.

RELATIVE POWER RELATIONS

The Dutch were a powerful maritime power, but in Zeelandia they were separated from their primary source of maritime assistance by the long sea lane between Batavia and Taiwan, about 2,200 miles as the crow flies. The sea forces of the late Ming also had power, largely due to the Zheng family trading organization. Although crossing the Taiwan Strait is hazardous during typhoon season, the distance is relatively short compared to the longer Dutch supply route to Southeast Asia. Koxinga's base in Jinmen was about one hundred miles from the Penghu Islands, with a good harbor for reconnoiter, and a day sail of about fifty miles to Tai Bay, the location of the Dutch settlements. Clearly, the Chinese had the advantage of position and strength of numbers in this conflict, while the major Dutch advantage was having a strongly prepared defensive position.

In the bigger picture of relative power relations, Chinese power was tempered by its internal conflict involving dynastic change from the Ming to the Qing Dynasties. European powers were on the rise, and in the mid-seventeenth century Dutch power was the greatest of the European powers. In that sense, the outcome of the Sino-Dutch War of the 1660s is surprising. Once the Manchus established strong dynastic control in China, the continued rise of Europe's power in relation to China was not to be determinative until the nineteenth century. The Sino-Dutch war fits less well into the paradigm of Allison's Thucydides trap analysis because it was a localized war considerably smaller in scope and scale than the Ottoman-Hapsburg conflict or the Imjin War, which were general wars over broader geography.

ALLIANCE RELATIONS

During a time when Ming cohesion was fracturing in the face of the Qing onslaught, Koxinga was able to draw tens of thousands of Ming forces together both to attack the Qing at Nanjing in 1658–1659 and to attack the Dutch on Taiwan in 1661–1662. His was not so much an exercise in building alliances as in finding enough Han support to carry on with these campaigns. He did, however, negotiate with the Japanese, who were sympathetic to the Ming and considered the idea of assisting the Ming against the Qing. Unfortunately for the Ming, the Japanese policy of seclusion from the late 1630s onward inhibited Japanese decisions to become actively involved in the conflict. Koxinga was on his own.

The Dutch had a natural ally in the Qing, since the Qing were also enemies of the Ming under Koxinga. Communication with the Qing was difficult for the Dutch, however, due to Koxinga's successful blockade of Taiwan. The brief periods of cooperation between the Dutch and the Qing were too little, too late, and the alliance did not realize its potential. The Dutch were ousted from Taiwan before the Dutch-Qing alliance could bear fruit.

RELATIONSHIP OF MARITIME ECONOMIC SUCCESS TO MARITIME MILITARY SUCCESS

During the Sino-Dutch War of the 1660s, maritime economic success was intimately tied up with maritime military success for both the Chinese and the Dutch. The Zheng family created the greatest Asian trading operation in the China Seas, while the Dutch had forged the VOC into Europe's largest corporation, dependent on Asian trade for its wealth. In terms of scope and scale, Zheng family firm revenues and profits competed favorably with VOC revenues and profits during the 1640s through 1680s.[31] In order to protect and support the economic benefits of trade, both the Zheng firm and the VOC developed powerful fort and naval capability along the China coast, which resulted in the armed clash of Koxinga's invasion of Taiwan. The military expulsion of the Dutch from Taiwan led to further trade opportunities for the Zheng family, opportunities made good by Zheng Jing after Koxinga's passing in 1662. Due to Koxinga's early life connections in Kyushu, opportunities for trade with Japan continued even after the Japanese implemented their policy of *sakoku*, seclusion, by 1640. In fact, in spite of their seclusion policy, the Japanese considered assisting Koxinga militarily in his fight against the Qing. In the end, they decided against offering this assistance, although they continued to be open to Zheng trading vessels operating in Nagasaki, where a Chinese trading community operated in a Chinatown parallel to the Dutch on the island of Dejima.

IMPORTANCE OF HISTORICAL AND CURRENT KNOWLEDGE

Koxinga used the Chinese settlers on Taiwan to good effect to obtain knowledge about the position and strength of the Dutch on Taiwan. This information allowed him to plan to avoid the Dutch guns of Fort Zeelandia, strike the weaker Fort Provintia first, surround Fort Zeelandia, and then reduce it by siege. The information was good enough to develop a plan that was workable and ultimately successful.

Koxinga took care to prevent the Dutch from sailing from Taiwan to seek help of reinforcements in Batavia. Nevertheless, he did not worry much when the sloop *Maria* escaped the blockade. His experience sailing Chinese junks was that a ship could not sail south during that season against the prevailing southwesterly monsoon winds. He did not realize how much closer to the wind a Dutch ship could sail. In this case, Koxinga's knowledge base led him to a faulty assumption. The *Maria* did make it to Batavia and sent back reinforcements, surprising Koxinga. Ultimately, these reinforcements did not save the Dutch due to issues of divided command between the Dutch ship and fort commanders.

Once engaged in the siege, Koxinga was able to obtain cooperation of Dutch defectors to help him, especially during the later stages of the siege. It was intelligence from a Dutch defector that allowed him to execute a plan to force the Dutch to surrender the Zeelandia fort. By comparison, the Dutch had little intelligence collection capability and had to rely on weaker local sources. Historically, there was nothing in their experience to prepare them for Koxinga's fierce and well-organized attack.

Koxinga's military leadership prevailed in the seventeenth century Sino-Dutch War. Ultimately, it was a hollow victory following the Ming collapse to the Qing two decades later. Europe's rise was to come back to haunt China during the mid-nineteenth century.

KOXINGA'S LEGACY AND MEANING IN HISTORY

Koxinga's early death poses the question "what if" he had lived to age sixty-eight as Barbarossa had, instead of dying prematurely at age thirty-eight. Could he have died peacefully in a palace on the sea as Barbarossa had? Would he have had the strength, will, and cunning to have extended Ming resistance more successfully? Or would he have established a successful independent kingdom on Taiwan since there were no more Ming successors? Certainly he might have been more successful than his heirs as a naval match for Shi Lang, who was three years older than Koxinga. The Zheng-Shi clan rivalry continues to the present time. A Zheng will not marry a Shi and vice versa. In another family development, descendants of Koxinga's half-brother Shichizeamon changed their name from Tagawa to Zheng and served as Meiji diplomats who oversaw Japanese control of China.

Although honored by subsequent historical accounts, Koxinga left a mixed legacy subject to several interpretations. He was loyal to the Ming, but ultimately failed to reinstitute the Ming Dynasty on the mainland. He successfully added Taiwan to the realm of Chinese geography, an important point in the development of Chinese historical narratives. Without Koxinga's program to drive out the Dutch, the chances are good that Taiwan would never have become a part of the territory of the Chinese empire.[32] In any event, due to Koxinga's efforts, Taiwan did not become a Dutch-ruled island similar to the Philippines that was ruled by the Spanish. This was a possible outcome for Taiwan until Koxinga arrived. Thus the results of the Sino-Dutch War substantially changed the path of East Asian politics.

The story of Koxinga's life has proven useful in supporting a variety of historical narratives, adding to his luster as a historical character not to be forgotten. At least as important as the facts of Koxinga's life are the interpretations of the meanings of his life by subsequent groups important in China's history. There are at least five differing interpretations, four of which are Chinese variants, including the Ming, the Qing, the Chinese communist, and the Chinese nationalist interpretations, while the fifth involves Japanese politics and culture. First, to the Ming loyalists who established temples to worship Koxinga after his death, he was the founder of Chinese society and administration on Taiwan and was a revered loyalist to the Ming. Second, after defeating the Zheng family on Taiwan two generations after the death of Koxinga, the Manchu Qing eventually built a shrine to commemorate Koxinga on Taiwan in the nineteenth century, since he exemplified the values of Confucian loyalty that the Qing wished to encourage. Third, for the current Chinese Communist Party rulers on the mainland, Koxinga personifies Chinese strength in throwing off imperialist European power and control, symbolized by the fifty-foot-high granite statue of Koxinga on the headland gazing out over the Taiwan Strait from Gulangyu in Xiamen. Fourth, for Chinese nationalists driven to Taiwan in the late 1940s, Koxinga represents the obvious symbolism of a government in exile on Taiwan. An exercise in the politics of memory similar to the identification in Korea of Park Chung-hee with Yi Sun-sin has taken place in Taiwan, where Chiang Kai-shek associated himself during the 1960s with Zheng Chenggong, the liberator of Taiwan from the Dutch, as well as the Ming loyalist on Taiwan fighting mainland domination.[33] Fifth, when the Japanese took Taiwan in the aftermath of the Sino-Japanese War in 1895, they made Koxinga a Shinto god and claimed Japanese descent for him through his mother.

Debate continues among historians as to Koxinga's ultimate motives. Was his primary objective to establish Taiwan as a Ming loyalist outpost, or as a base for a more personal maritime empire that he intended to expand by driving the Spanish from the Philippines as he had driven the Dutch from Taiwan? His early, unexpected, and sudden demise at age thirty-eight prevents this question from having a definitive answer.

EIGHT

Maratha Naval Resistance to the British on the Konkan Coast

Kanhoji Angre, Eighteenth Century

Asymmetrical Naval Warfare along the Konkan Coast

The Maratha navy, commanded by Sarkhel Kanhoji Angre and his sons, won many asymmetrical naval victories against the British along the Konkan coast during the eighteenth century.[1] Tactically, these encounters replicated the asymmetrical naval victories that the Kunjali Marakkar had achieved against the Portuguese along the Malabar coast during the sixteenth century. As a result of the successful naval resistance of the Maratha to the British, Dutch, and Portuguese, Kanhoji Angre continues to be revered today as the greatest of Indian naval commanders during the premodern period. The Angre clan learned from the earlier Marakkars and modified their strategy and tactics, most notably by incorporating a series of powerful sea forts, to cope with the new waves of Europeans, the Dutch and the British, who had arrived and diminished the power of the Portuguese in the Indian Ocean two centuries after Portuguese sixteenth-century ascendancy.

During the seventeenth and eighteenth centuries, Dutch and British naval forces limited Portuguese influence on the west coast of India to the area around the Portuguese forts and headquarters at Goa, located at the midpoint between the southern Malabar coast and the northern Konkan coast.[2] The Dutch headquarters were in Cochin, well south of

Goa, while the British established their trading and naval operations in Bombay, well north of Goa. While the Maratha navy fought all three of these European powers during the seventeenth and eighteenth centuries, its locus was the Konkan coast, which created an antagonistic relationship with the nearby British in Bombay.

Sweeping Changes on the Indian Subcontinent

Following the domination of the Indian Ocean by the Portuguese during the sixteenth century, great changes took place both in the role of the Europeans off the coasts of India, and within India itself. These dual changes provided the setting for the exploits of the Maratha navy and its admiralty. The major features of historical development within India during this period include the rise of the Mughal Empire in the interior beginning in 1526, while Kunjali Marakkar resistance was occurring on the coast. The Mughal Empire was to become the largest political entity in Indian history after the Maurya Empire fifteen hundred years earlier. The struggle of the Maratha to replace the Mughals in the seventeenth and eighteenth centuries resulted in widespread Maratha control of the subcontinent by the mid-eighteenth century.

The maritime aspect of the story, rather than in the central land mass where the Mughals met Marathas, is the history of Europeans encountering Marathas, not Mughals. The Europeans included primarily the Portuguese, Dutch, and British, but also involved the French and Danish. Maratha maritime history centered on the Konkan coast of India, which faces west toward the Arabian Sea. This coastal region had more conflict between Marathas and Europeans than between Marathas and Mughals. Although the focus here is the maritime history between Marathas and Europeans, it must be noted that the Maratha were successful in expanding their control of the subcontinent against the Mughals following the death of Aurangzeb in 1707.[3]

The Maratha in Indian History

The Maratha as a power in Indian history began with Shivaji's revolt and early successes against the Mughal Empire in the late 1650s and culminated with greatest expansion of the Maratha Empire by 1760.

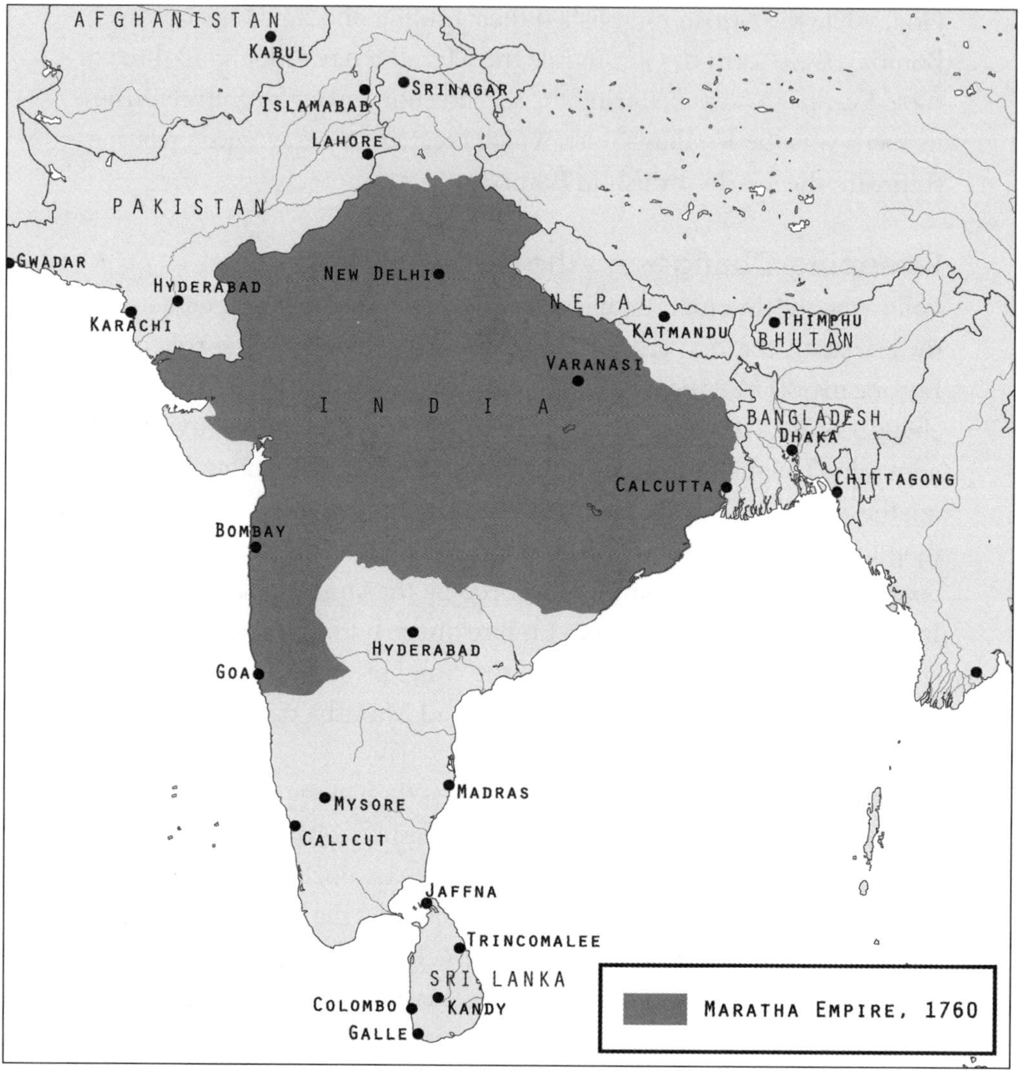

MAP 8.1 Maratha Empire, 1760
Adapted by Jamie Rhode from https://commons.princeton.edu/mg/marathas/, accessed May 31, 2022. This image has been released into the public domain by its creator Deepak Gupta

This is the century in which Maratha maritime power grew and was finally eclipsed with the fall of the sea fort at Vijaydurg, the "Gibraltar of the East," in 1756. Although the Maratha Empire was no longer a power on the sea after this event, it continued its land battles against the British East India Company under their peshwa, prime minister, during the first, second, and third Anglo-Maratha wars between 1775 and 1818. At the end of these conflicts, the peshwa surrendered to the British. Thus the Maratha lost control of their territory in 1818, as they had lost control of the sea along the Konkan coast in 1756.

RISE OF SHIVAJI, BEGINNING OF THE MARATHA NAVY

To the east of Mumbai, formerly Bombay, the wide Kalyan Creek curves below a temple site. On the bank ships were built by Shivaji along the creek's shores during the mid-seventeenth century. Today, there is no sign of construction remains to verify the story, but it has been commemorated in the temple on the hill. Shivaji built his first ship here around 1658, had about eighty-five ships by 1665, and gradually built a naval maritime force including about two hundred large and small warships and perhaps another two hundred merchant ships.[4] In spite of its quiet appearance today, Kalyan Creek was a busy shipyard 350 years ago.

Within the broader historical struggle between the Maratha, the Mughals, and the Europeans, who was Shivaji and why was he building ships? Shivaji Bhonsale, also known as Chhatrapati Shivaji Maharaj after he was crowned Maratha emperor in 1674, was an Indian warrior-king and member of the Bhonsale Maratha clan. He became the military and political leader of the Maratha, west coast Hindus who fought against the continental power of the Muslim Mughals. The Mughals ruled much of central India beginning in the early sixteenth century, while Kunjali I was fighting naval battles against the Portuguese for the zamorin of Calicut. In addition to fighting the Mughals on land, Shivaji fought simultaneously against the rising maritime power of the Dutch and English in India during the seventeenth century while Portuguese power in India was fading. The hundreds of ships that were built on the Kalyan Creek banks were constructed primarily to defend against the British, who had come to India to seize trading rights from the Portuguese and the Dutch. The British established Bombay port on the islands on the northwest side of the broad harbor into which the Kalyan Creek flows. Charles II granted the islands in a charter to the British East India Company (EIC) in 1668, after acquiring possession from Portugal in

1661.[5] Bombay was advantageous to Britain because it was an independent territorial holding that included a spacious, deep harbor.

During the mid-seventeenth century, Hindu Marathas in the west of India began to oppose the Muslim Mughals who ruled the central area of the subcontinent. Shivaji came to lead the Marathas in battle beginning with his attack on the Mughal fortress of Junnar in 1657, and he maintained his leadership role until his death in 1680. When Aurangzeb became Mughal emperor in 1659, he sent a large force to punish Shivaji, who was intent on establishing a Maratha Empire independent from the Mughals. The Hindu Maratha military elite had served the Deccan sultans, switching sides as convenient. The core area of residence for Marathi-speaking people was the area now known as the state of Maharashtra, which includes Mumbai and the Konkan coast on the west side of the Indian subcontinent north of Goa facing the Arabian Sea. Although Shivaji founded a navy to serve Maratha coastal interests, he is better known for his land campaigns, establishing the Maratha capital inland at Pune. While Aurangzeb was a Mughal Muslim who assessed special taxes on non-Muslims, Mughal-Maratha conflict was less about religion than about territorial control, political domination, state formation, and regional identity.[6]

Notwithstanding Shivaji's legacy as a military leader best known for his success in land battles, he is also remembered for founding the Maratha navy with the hundreds of ships built in Kalyan Creek, as well as for his program to reinforce numerous vast sea forts along the coast of Maharashtra.[7] In 1665, Shivaji was forced to cede twenty-three forts to Mughals supported by Maratha rivals. He had to present himself to Aurangzeb in Agra, where he was humiliated and detained. The story of his escape from Agra is the theme of Maratha heroic narrative. War resumed in 1670 when Shivaji raided the port city of Surat and exacted revenge tribute. In 1672, Shivaji defeated a Mughal army of 25,000, so in 1674 he was crowned Maratha *cchatrapati*, "emperor," a title he held until his death in 1680.

After Shivaji died, a succession struggle took place between his sons Sambhaji and his half-brother Rajaram, which ended when Sambhaji was captured and killed by the Mughals in 1689. Rajaram successfully fled from the Mughals and became a symbol of Maratha resistance. Rajaram died in 1700 and was succeeded by his widow Tara Bai, regent for their infant son Shivaji II. Tara Bai appointed Khanhoji Angre as commander of Maratha naval forces along the Konkan coast, a career he pursued vigorously and successfully.

Aurangzeb continued the Mughal struggle against the Maratha until he died of an illness in 1707, which began the disintegration of the Mughal Empire. The Marathas emerged from the vacuum left by the Mughals and strove to dominate eighteenth-century India. On the coast, Kanhoji Angre achieved steady victories until his death in 1729. After that, his five sons competed to lead the Maratha navy, until the Angre family's final naval defeat at Vijaydurg in 1756.

As Mughal power faded on the continent during the first half of the eighteenth century, the saga of Angre clan dominance of the Maratha navy unfolded as it struggled to control the long Konkan coast against the Portuguese, Dutch, French, and, most notably, British opponents. The pattern of Konkan coast clashes during the eighteenth century bore similarities to the more southerly Malabar coast conflict between the zamorin of Calicut, his Kunjali Marakkar admirals, and the Portuguese during the sixteenth century. Thus the problems of European incursion along the Indian seaboard were historically familiar to the Maratha. By the 1660s, the Dutch had replaced the Portuguese along the Malabar coast. In Cochin, the Portuguese Mattancherry Palace, built in Malabar courtyard style and gifted to the raja of Kochi in 1555, was taken over, expanded, and renovated by the Dutch by 1663. This Portuguese-built structure was subsequently known as the Dutch Palace, since it served as a center of trade for the Dutch East India Company (VOC), founded in 1602.[8] The Portuguese, although limited in their activity along the Malabar coast, maintained their stronghold in Goa on the northern end of the region until 1961. While the Dutch controlled the southern part of the west Indian coast and the Portuguese controlled the center, farther north, along the Konkan coast, English traders acquired a stable port at Bombay. Aside from their trading ships being armed themselves, the British founded the Bombay Marine to protect British ships traveling along the coast. The Maratha considered this coast to be part of the Maratha state and took exception to the rights assumed by the British, resulting in an ebb and flow of armed conflict at sea between the Maratha and the British for nearly a century between the 1660s and the 1750s.

During the latter seventeenth century, the English and the Dutch sought alliance with the Mughals, who were foes of the Maratha.[9] The Mughals had established a port at Surat in Gujarat, the gateway to Mecca for pilgrims leaving from India on the Hajj north. Before obtaining Bombay, the EIC traded in Surat, where the Portuguese were also active during the early seventeenth century. The Mughals at Surat possessed a small number of fighting craft, called grabs (ghurabs) and gallivats, like those that had been used by the Kunjali Marakkar. During the early 1600s, this fleet worked closely with the EIC's maritime force. Later in the 1600s, Aurangzeb expanded the Mughal navy, although it remained a coastal, brown-water power.[10] In his struggle against the Maratha, Aurangzeb gained a coastal ally in the Siddis, who controlled the massive island sea fort at Janjira.[11]

SEA FORTS: KHANDERI, KOLABA, JANJIRA, SUVARNADURG, VIJAYDURG

Shivaji established a program of reinforcing existing and building new sea forts along the Konkan coast. The most strategically located and active sea forts along the Konkan coast during the Maratha resistance to the British included, from north to south, Khanderi, Kolaba, Suvarnadurg, and Vijaydurg. Shivaji gained control of each of these islands between 1653 and 1680 and built forts on them that were later enlarged and refortified by subsequent Maratha admirals of the Angre clan during their period of naval dominance.[12] The only sea fort along the Konkan coast not controlled by the Maratha was Janjira. In spite of many attempts by the Maratha to take Janjira, the powerful Siddis maintained control, often allying with the enemies of the Maratha, including the Mughals, British, and Portuguese.

MAP 8.2 Konkan coast: Maratha navy theater, 1660–1760
Adapted by Jamie Rhode from Manohar Malgonkar, The Sea Hawk: Life and Battles of Kanhoji Angre *(New Delhi: Orient Paperbacks, 1979), 2*

KHANDERI

Khanderi lies ten miles south of Bombay, near the southern entry to the mouth of the bay leading into Bombay Harbor. About a mile long and half a mile wide, kidney-shaped Khanderi supports a fort well-positioned to survey and control ship traffic along the coast of India into and out of Bombay Harbor. A smaller island, Underi, lies nearby. Thorns in the side of EIC shipping, the British referred to Khanderi as Kennery, or the pair of islands as "Hunarey and Cunarey."[13] Khanderi fell under Shivaji's control in 1679, while the neighboring island of Underi was controlled by the Siddis and used as an outpost of the fort at Janjira, until Sambhaji captured Underi in 1700.[14] A fort was built by Shivaji's forces on Khanderi to control approaches to the more southerly Siddi-held fort at Janjira, as well as to dominate approaches to northerly Bombay Harbor.

After Maratha admiral Kanhoji Angre obtained the fort at Khanderi as one of the ten sea forts and sixteen land forts he was awarded when he swore allegiance to the Maratha king Shahu in 1714, his attacks on British shipping became increasingly onerous.[15] Unhappy with the disruption of EIC ship traffic so close to their home base, Charles Boone, the British governor of Bombay, decided to personally lead an attack on the fort at Khanderi, an island clearly visible from the harbor. In order to put the island fort out of commission as a base imperiling British shipping, Boone organized a fleet of about twenty heavily armed ships with many smaller supporting gallivats, manned by about 2,500 sailors and soldiers. Following the summer monsoon season, the ships made the short trip to Khanderi within a few hours on November 1, 1718. The British fleet established a blockade around the island to prevent ammunition supply to the fort. The British ships began shelling the Maratha fort before dawn on November 3. In an early action, two Maratha ghurabs made a break from Khanderi harbor and were pursued by three British frigates. Fourteen Maratha gallivats pursued the frigates and forced them to fall back, allowing the sixteen Maratha ships to sail on to Kolaba, the next sea fort to the south.[16] The fort, under the command of Kanhoji Angre's local lieutenant, Mankoji Suryawanshi, was brilliantly defended by about 250 men, about one-tenth of the British force.[17] Short of ammunition, the Maratha did not return fire until the British were lured close enough for the effects of fire to be devastating. EIC commanders were not hardened military men used to laying siege and conducting landing parties. Sepoys, Indians pressed into military service, refused to serve behind or ahead of these commanders. British landing parties were surprised that the current was too strong for landing, with the tide capsizing their boats. Those who made it to shore came under fire from conserved ammunition from the fort, such that dozens were killed before the assault began. The siege went on without British progress for less than two weeks. Governor Boone returned to Bom-bay on November 14, his ships having exhausted their ammunition, and a squadron of Kanhoji Angre's ships arrived from Vijaydurg to reinforce the Maratha defenders of Khanderi. In the seventy-five-year period between 1679, when Shivaji established a fort on Khanderi, and 1756, when Vijaydurg fell, this abjectly failed siege was the closest the British came to controlling the Khanderi "choke point" in their trading route along the coast of India.

Khanderi and the adjacent Underi Island, sitting at the southern entry to Bombay/Mumbai Harbor, are easily visible from Kolaba Fort in Alibag. In fact, most of the forts along the Konkan coast operate on a line-of-sight basis, in which each fort may be seen from the next fort along the coast.

KOLABA

Kolaba is the southern district of Mumbai as well as the name of the island fort along the coast six miles south of Khanderi.[18] Kanhoji Angre used the fort as his primary base against the British and as the family home. He died in 1729 of natural causes at Kolaba Fort, and his sons took over Maratha command at sea, remaining based at Kolaba.

Many of the walls of Kolaba Fort are more than twenty-five feet tall and up to seventeen feet thick.[19] Although the fort is on an island surrounded by the sea, it contains three freshwater wells. Tanks of water have been taken from the largest of the well pools in recent years to supply fresh water to the town of Alibag during droughts.[20] Thus, although located on an island, the fort could maintain a self-sufficient water supply for an indeterminate length of siege. Inside the fort is a temple, construction of which has been attributed to Kanhoji Angre's son Raghoji Angre in 1759, indicating that Kolaba Fort and Alibag continued to be the family seat of the Angre clan, even though they lost their overall control of the Konkan coast in their defeats at Suvarnadurg in 1755, and at Vijaydurg in 1756.

Although Kanhoji Angre fought several battles in the vicinity of Kolaba Fort during his three decades as admiral of the Maratha fleet, the most significant battle at Kolaba took place at the end of 1721. Both the British EIC in Bombay and the Portuguese in Goa were exhausted by Kanhoji Angre's successful forays against their merchant shipping. In a treaty signed in August 1721, the two European powers allied to create a "springboard for the Anglo-Portuguese conquest of the Konkan," uniting them to form a force they thought would overwhelm Maratha resistance led by Angre.[21] According to the terms of the treaty, they would only offer peace to the Maratha if both parties agreed, and the spoils would be divided evenly, with the fort at Gheria (Vijaydurg) going to the British and the fort at Kolaba going to the Portuguese. Strange bedfellows in history, the British and Portuguese developed a plan that appeared sound but turned out to be good strategy poorly executed.

After the debacle in attempting to take the Angre fort at Khanderi in 1717, Governor Boone was pleased with the arrival of Royal Navy forces in August 1721 to supplement the gunships of the EIC's Bombay Marine. Navy Commodore Thomas Matthews and Governor Boone got along imperfectly, beginning with a dispute about whose salute would take priority. Nevertheless, the British put together a force of 2,500 land forces with some artillery, along with five heavily armed ships. The Portuguese supplied 4,000 land troops with more artillery than the British, and also included five heavily armed ships. The core of the plan was for the two armies to meet at Portuguese-held Chaul, sixty-two miles south of Kolaba, then for the combined armies to march north and surprise Kolaba Fort from the land side, while the ships fired on the fort as decoys on the seaside. The first problem with this plan was that Kanhoji Angre had intelligence scouts who followed the path of the European joint force, eliminating any possibility of surprise. In fact, Maratha forces twice attacked the joint force after they began their journey on December 10, 1721. These two Maratha attacks, led by Angre's appointed commander Pilaji Jadhav, were not successful, so the joint Anglo-Portuguese forces moved forward. Dragging their heavy artillery, the Portuguese arrived at the headland to the northeast of Kolaba Island, while the British set camp on the shore southeast of the island. The powerful British and Portuguese ships blockaded Angre ships in the harbor behind the island and prevented Maratha reinforcement from entering the harbor by sea. The ships' bombardment of the fort proved to be insufficient to deter the Maratha defense.

On December 24, the two sides squared off against each other. The defensive position in the fort required about half the troops that might be required to take the fort, but the numbers of the forces were fairly evenly matched. Nevertheless, the joint Anglo-Portuguese forces decided that the British would make the first attack, while the Portuguese remained in reserve. The attack did not take place until 4 p.m., probably due to the timing of low tide to make crossing easier. One thousand British soldiers attacked the main fort gate in the northeast but were unable to break through. Others scaled ladders and went over the top of the fort walls but were cut down by long Maratha curved swords. The ferocious attack was repelled, with the British suffering more than one hundred casualties. Seeing the British retreat, Kanhoji Angre calculated that the best defense was a good offense. He sent fort defenders to follow the British to the southeast camp to wreak havoc, while at the same time ordering Pilaji's cavalry to swoop down on the Portuguese who had been stunned by the British retreat. Fifteen hundred Maratha "exulted" in a wild cavalry horse charge against the stationary enemy.[22] The Portuguese retreated to their former base camp in Alibag, while the British retreated to their ships to be carried back to Bombay. It was a sudden, unexpected, and decisive victory for the Maratha. On the following Christmas morning, Kolaba was clear of the Anglo-Portuguese invasion force. The Portuguese sued for peace, which Angre granted on generous terms. Commodore Matthews blamed Portuguese treachery for the loss but accepted the peace terms under protest. Maratha peshwa Prime Minister Bajirao arrived with 25,000 reinforcements, putting to rest any thought of reviving the joint expedition. Less than a month later, in January 1722, Governor Boone returned to London, leaving a failed military record behind him, although he had been regarded as a fine administrator of Bombay. Kanhoji Angre's decisive victory at Kolaba in 1721 averted other serious attacks against him by any Europeans, whether British or Portuguese, until his death eight years later.

JANJIRA

The great fort on Janjira was built by Malik Ambar in the sixteenth century.[23] The Siddis were Ethiopians who came to India by sea, having survived by "excellent seamanship and sturdiness . . . on the sea they were a deadly enemy."[24] The name Janjira likely derives from the Arabic word *jazeera*, meaning island. The island is just over 124 miles south of Mumbai and is covered entirely by the fort. The fort has twenty-six intact rounded bastions of similar appearance, each approximately forty feet high, creating an impression of massive strength and impregnability. The main gate of the fort faces west toward the shore and can only be seen from about forty feet away because of the manner in which the gate is tucked into the walls. An image of a tiger trampling elephants is carved in a stone at the entrance.[25] A second small postern gate for escape faces south. Although the exterior of the fort retains its solid structure, the interior is largely ruined, with many native Indian and European cannons sitting on the stone decks pointed out to sea, remnants of the 572 cannons that the fort held when fully armed. These cannons successfully repelled all attackers. Some of the cannons are massive, weighing more than twenty tons each. The many interior buildings include officers quarters, a mosque, and the exterior walls of an impressive three-story palace, now without floors or roof. The palace was built for the Siddi rulers of the fort, who maintained allegiance to the Mughals. A separate palace of the Mughal Nawab of Janjira sits on a mainland hill overlooking the island fort. The large deep wells with tank pools in the fort are still functional, features that allowed resistance to long-term siege like the wells of Kolaba Fort. Portuguese accounts of the Ottoman fleet that sailed to Aceh led by Kurtoglu Hizir Reis mentions that two hundred of the expedition's sailors came from Janjira.

Shivaji led the Marathas in many unsuccessful attempts to scale the forty-three-foot-high walls. Shivaji's son Sambhaji attempted to tunnel his way into the fort, also unsuccessfully. In 1676, Shivaji built Padmadurg sea fort northeast of Janjira to challenge the Siddi fort, but this effort ultimately failed to help Shivaji, nor were any of his successors able to drive the Siddis from Janjira. In 1725, the Siddi Rasul Yakut Khan, encouraged by the British and Portuguese, besieged Kolaba with more than one hundred frigates and gallivats manned by six thousand soldiers, a larger naval force than had ever attacked Kolaba. Kanhoji Angre had fought and won control of the coast, and now in his fifties and desirous of peace, he concluded a pact with the Siddi, buying them off with an offer that the British and Portuguese could not match.[26]

Tensions between the Siddis and the Maratha continued after Kanhoji's death in 1729. In 1733, Maratha peshwa Baji Rao and Sarkhel Sekhoji, one of Kanhoji's sons, began a campaign against the Siddi. Sekhoji was unable to successfully blockade Janjira. He died in August 1733, creating confusion in which two of his brothers, Sambhaji and Manaji, disputed succession. The naval aspect of the Maratha conflict with the Siddi was unsuccessful in its attempt to take Janjira. Not surprising given earlier patterns, the Siddi were assisted in their island defense by the British.[27] But the Maratha were more successful on land. In 1736, the Siddi army was defeated by Marathas on the mainland at Rewas near Bombay Harbor. The loss considerably reduced Siddi power, although Janjira Fort remained unconquered. Janjira finally became part of Indian territory in 1947 after the British departed. Janjira Fort was the only spot along the Konkan coast that neither Shivaji nor Kanhoji nor any of their combined seven sons were able to defeat, capture, control, or administer.

SUVARNADURG

Suvarnadurg, the "Golden Fort" pride of the Maratha Konkan coast sea fort system, was originally built by the Bijapur kings in the sixteenth century.[28] Credit for reconstructing the fort is given to Shivaji after he took control of the island in 1660. The fort is impressively large, covering about eight acres. Many of the walls of the fort have been cut from the solid rock on the island, creating an impregnable façade.[29] Although the island is ringed with stone walls, the appearance is less "constructed" and more natural looking than the walls at Janjira. The fort has many bastions. Boat access is achieved via a small beach rather than through a water gate as at Janjira. Suvarnadurg was originally connected to the land by a tunnel, which is now defunct. The fort had great defensive strength, but also maintained a shipbuilding capacity. Opposite Suvarnadurg on the mainland, Harnai port remains an active, colorful seaport with a large fishing fleet.

Kanhoji Agre was born in 1669 and spent his childhood split between Pune and Suvarnadurg, where his father Tukoji was the deputy commander of the fort. As a teenager, Kanhoji impressed those at the fort with his strength and diligence. He demonstrated his leadership potential before he was twenty. In 1688, Siddi archenemies of the Maratha surrounded the fort with ships on three sides and land forces across the harbor. Inside the fort, Mughal clerks convinced the fort commander to surrender. Unhappy with the plan to capitulate, Kanhoji led a coup and arrested the commander, some accounts saying with the blessing of the Maratha king Sambhaji, others reporting that he did not wait for approval. Initially, Kanhoji attacked the land forces. His reckless first foray resulted in his capture. Somehow he escaped and swam back to the island. His second plan was to mimic the turtle deity over the front entry gate. He ordered retirement to the shell of the fort and began a waiting game. Not willing to incur the heavy costs of attacking the fort of solid rock, the Siddis eventually retreated before the monsoons began. The king recognized Kanhoji's achievement of maintaining control of the fort by making him commander. Thus, Suvarnadurg was the fort where Kanhoji Angre began his military successes, which would continue for another forty years.

In 1714, in recognition of his fealty to the Shivaji family, Kanhoji Angre was granted control of twenty-six forts, including Suvarnadurg. Sambaji, Kanhoji's son, was given control of Suvarnadurg following Kanhoji's death in 1729. Sambaji's stepbrother Tulaji later took control of the fort before finally losing it in battle with the British in 1755.

During the 1740s, succession problems plagued the Maratha, resulting in schisms both within the Angre clan between brothers Tulaji and Manaji, and with Shahu, the Maratha king who was in poor health, and the peshwa, his prime minister. Tulaji won control of the southern forts of Suvarnadurg and Vijaydurg but did recognize the superior role of the peshwa, who allied with the British to oppose Tulaji after the death of Shahu in 1749.[30] The peshwa concluded a formal agreement of alliance with the British governor of Bombay in March 1755. In it, the peshwa agreed to attack Suvarnadurg by land, while a combined British and Maratha fleet was to attack the fort by sea. Tulaji's smaller fleet slipped anchor and escaped from the harbor inside the island of Suvarnadurg as Commodore William James arrived with the combined peshwa and British fleet. Heavy British guns unsuccessfully pounded the west coast walls carved from solid rock but had success on the eastern side facing the shore when shells set thatched houses on fire inside the fort. The fire spread to the powder magazine, causing a great explosion. Those who fled the fort by boat were captured. Two smaller forts on land were seized along with Suvarnadurg, the main large fort. Some tried to escape the fort through the tunnel connecting it to the mainland but were caught and killed. The fort surrendered at the beginning of April 1755, when Commodore James returned to Bombay ahead of the monsoons.

VIJAYDURG

Vijaydurg, "Victory Fort," was originally constructed by Bijapur kings, but it was named by Shivaji in the seventeenth century after he captured it from the Mughals. Shivaji expanded the fort and added triple walls, including seaside walls cut from the solid rock as part of his coastal defense plan.[31] The fort was built on an island although today the water channel on the eastern side has been filled and buildings in the town of Girye occupy the space. The Angres continued to refine the fort during the eighteenth century. An undersea wall was constructed to the western side of the fort to ground ships attacking from the sea. The island fort is located south of the mouth of Waghotan Creek, capable of shielding views of Angre ships that anchored in the creek, a natural port that is still used by local fishermen. The creek is shallow, ideal for Maratha ships but difficult to enter for larger deep draft English or Portuguese ships. The ruins of the Rameshwar dockyard are farther up the creek on the south bank where Maratha ships were built and repaired. The impressive stone-built entry walls of the dockyard remain, with holes drilled through large stone blocks for mooring ships. Ships would enter on the high tide, to be grounded at low tide for repairs and cleaning, while the gate at the entry kept the next high tide from rushing in, a natural form of dry dock.[32] This fort was put firmly under Kanhoji Angre's authority as one of the forts ceded to him in 1713. During Kanhoji Angre's period as admiral, the British attacked Vijaydurg twice, considering it to be a key to control the Konkan coast. In the first of these attacks, Governor Boone of Bombay planned an expedition to Vijaydurg at the beginning of the monsoon season in 1718.

While Kanhoji Angre was preoccupied with his daughter's wedding in Kolaba, and the bulk of the Maratha fleet was tied up for the monsoon in the creek behind Vijaydurg, Boone sent an expedition with fireships on June 9, 1718, to burn the Maratha fleet while it was packed and tied together.[33] Unfortunately for the British, the Maratha had taken a simple precaution that frustrated the launching of fireships into the Maratha fleet. They had placed a boom across the mouth of Waghotan Creek that blocked passage into the creek. Although the British blockaded the harbor and shelled the fort without result, little fire was returned from the fort. A British landing party intending to set fire to the ships going overland was not opposed by the fort. The landing party's progress was halted by a swamp, and the fort's guns felled about one hundred attackers. By June 18, the British were back in Bombay, having failed in their mission. It was later discovered that the fort had few defenders, perhaps one hundred, accounting for the sparse return fire.

In the second of the attacks on Vijaydurg by the British during Kanhoji's command, a British fleet sailed to Vijaydurg in September 1720. In this confrontation, both offense and defense were so cautious that neither side committed to a decisive battle. The British introduced a new weapon, a floating gun platform that failed to deliver results. One small landing party also was unsuccessful. Lack of focus permeated the British ships, one observer commenting that "Onboard ship there was no discipline but plenty of hard drinking."[34] The British withdrew in mid-October after this weak effort to take Vijaydurg and did not return for another twenty-five years, long after Kanhoji Angre's passing in 1729.

Following the fall of Suvarnadurg in April 1755, the British and the peshwa focused on a plan to capture Vijaydurg, the fort to which Sarkhel Tulaji Angre had fled from Suvarnadurg. In October 1755, a British naval squadron commanded by Admiral Watson arrived in Madras, accompanied by Captain Clive and his troops. They sailed on to Bombay. Governor Bourchier of Bombay concluded an agreement with the peshwa to split the gains once Vijaydurg was taken, while Commodore James sailed from Bombay to the southern Konkan to survey the waters around Vijaydurg in November 1755.[35] Tulaji continued the Maratha civil war with the peshwa by deciding not to surrender to him. Instead, he sought to ally with the Portuguese against the peshwa and the British, but he came to another dead end when the Portuguese said they would refuse to fight the British.

On February 7, 1756, Watson and Clive sailed from Bombay, joined by about fifty of the peshwa's ships. Arriving at Vijaydurg on February 11, the British forces blockaded the Maratha fleet in the Waghotan Creek with a row of ships on each side of the creek entry, forcing any Maratha ships wishing to escape to run a gauntlet between two opposing lines of British ships. The bombardment released on February 12 set fire to the Maratha fleet. The fire spread to the shipyard on the shore, as well as to the town and the fort, burning through the night. The fort surrendered on February 13, and Clive entered it with his five hundred marines on February 14.[36] The British and peshwa had built a road to the end of the peninsula facing the island fort Vijaydurg, so that the peshwa forces and British marine forces could attack the fort from the land while the British ships attacked from the sea. Not waiting for the Maratha, the British raised their flag and collected substantial spoils, including 250 cannon and a substantial treasury of cash and valuable items. The British did not hand over the fort immediately to the peshwa as per treaty, but eventually exchanged it for Bankot Fort. The peshwa naval commanders who replaced the Angre family were from the Dhulap family.

Tulaji went to the peshwa camp to enter negotiations, but he was arrested and taken prisoner. Rather than handing Tulaji over to the British, he was imprisoned in a series of the peshwa's forts until he died in 1786. Tulaji's armada was destroyed, and the Dhulap family peshwa's admirals replaced the Angres as the Maratha admirals on the Konkan coast. The 1756 battle of Vijaydurg marked the end of a potent Maratha navy, although Dhulap admirals subsequently were active on the coast. These later Maratha naval forces, however, were no longer able to systematically limit the movement of British ships along the west coast of India. Command of the Konkan coastal waters had passed to the EIC.

The alliance between the British and the peshwa that was established to fight the chief Maratha admiral Tulaji Angre resembled the alliance between the Portuguese and the zamorin to fight Admiral Kunjali IV a century and a half earlier in Calicut. In both cases, internal division between Indian forces, with one party in each case allying with a European power, led to Indian collapse and European domination. In the first case, the Portuguese dominated in the early seventeenth century, and in the second case, the British dominated in the late eighteenth century and on through the nineteenth century.

MARATHA SHIPS: GRABS AND GALLIVATS

Several ship carvings in stone remarkably similar to those at Borobudur and Angor Thom have been found at Borivali in northern Mumbai and in Goa.[37] These carved drawings in stone, dated between the eleventh and thirteenth centuries, are the last ship drawings available in India until the Maratha period, during which European travelers and historians produced drawings recording the shapes and details of Maratha ships.[38]

Apte distinguishes between two primary ship types, roundships and longships, in which structure gives clues regarding function. Broad roundships typically were better for cargo as merchant ships, and narrower longships were faster and better suited as warships. Roundships, however, could be adapted for war as necessary.

Maratha shipbuilding became more sophisticated as time passed: "Bigger ships constructed by the Angres were more seaworthy than the light ships of Shivaji."[39] EIC official and historian Robert Orme provided a brief, accurate account of the Angre fleet, indicating that the ships primarily fell into two types, grabs and gallivats, which were well-suited to sailing the west coast of India.[40]

The larger grabs had the capacity of 150 to 300 tons with two or three good-sized masts. They were broad in proportion to length, drawing little water, with a sharp prow for cutting into the wind. The two grab bow-cannons were nine to twelve pounds while the broadside cannons were six to nine pounds.

The smaller gallivats had a capacity of less than seventy tons, with a mainmast supporting a large triangular sail and a small mizzen mast, which sometime appears in drawings to be a flagpole rather than a sailing mast. The gallivat hull shape is similar to that of the grab, but lower to the water so that it could also be effectively rowed at up to four knots, with a complement of forty to fifty oars. This was fast enough to catch EIC merchant ships moving slowly in low wind conditions. Gallivats carried six to eight lighter cannons, two to four pounds, sometimes mounted on swivels. The din of battle was also part of the Maratha strategic arsenal. Maratha warships carried military bands, including a form of large brass trumpet and skin and brass tom-tom drums, which made an "amazing noise."[41]

Gallivats have sometimes been referred to as warboats while grabs have been called warships. During later periods, the Maratha also built three-masted ships even larger than the largest three-masted grabs. Called pals, these ships had crews of about two hundred, as opposed to about one hundred for the grabs. Records of pals, which had less ability to maneuver in shallow creeks than gallivats and grabs and required small boats to transport crews, appear in the registers kept by the Dhulap admirals after the fall of Vijaydurg.[42] The repair dockyards in Waghotan Creek near Vijaydurg appear to have been expanded to accommodate these larger pals.

DASHTAKS: MARATHA PASSPORTS ON THE KONKAN COAST

The EIC issued passports for a fee to non-British ships trading on the west coast of India, not dissimilar to the *cartaz* system that the Portuguese instituted in India in the sixteenth century. The Portuguese continued to use *cartaz* during the seventeenth and eighteenth centuries, although they were relatively weaker and less able to enforce the system than during the sixteenth century.

In response to these European impositions of costs on shipping, the Maratha navy under Kanhoji Angre and subsequent Maratha admirals instituted their own system of passports for European ships, called the *dashtak* system. A merchant ship carrying a Maratha *dashtak* could travel unhindered by the powerful Maratha navy along the Maratha-held Konkan coast as far north as Gujarat.[43] Enforcement of the *dashtak* was the primary situation in which the Maratha navy engaged in its successful asymmetrical guerrilla actions against both the EIC and Portuguese ships. Along the Konkan coast, *dashtak* became more sought after than EIC passports due to Angre control of the coast.[44] Although correspondence shows that EIC officials recognized the role of Kanhoji Angre as an agent of the Maratha king, the EIC referred to him as a pirate in a propaganda war meant for the public and Parliament in England. A difference between the Portuguese *cartaz* system and the Maratha *dashtak* system was that the Portuguese applied the *cartaz* throughout the Indian Ocean, while the Maratha applied the *dashtak* only along the Konkan coast. It was not just Kanhoji Angre, however, who successfully enforced the *dashtak*. His sons who succeeded him as *sarkhel*, including Tulaji until his capture at Vijaydurg in 1756, also successfully enforced the *dashtak*. In fact, the Dhulap admirals also enforced the *dashtak* after the restructuring of the Maratha navy following Tulaji's loss of Vijaydurg to the British and peshwa forces.[45]

The Life and Legacy of Kanhoji Angre

During the first three decades of the eighteenth century, Kanhoji Angre controlled the Konkan coast of India between British Bombay and Portuguese Goa, operating his navy from a series of vast sea forts, most notably at Kolaba, Suvarnadurg, and Vijaydurg. He strengthened Shivaji's seventeenth-century Maratha consolidation of the western region of India in their struggle against the Mughals, the Siddis, and the Europeans. He passed on control of the coast to his sons, who finally succumbed to the British allied with the peshwa at Vijaydurg a quarter-century after his death. The Portuguese likened Kanhoji Angre to the Ottoman admiral Hayreddin Barbarossa. British newspapers printed lurid stories of his life as a pirate, although the East India Company knew Kanhoji was an admiral fighting on behalf of the Maratha king. Kanhoji's seal stated, "by the pleasure of King Shahu, the seal of Kanhoji *Sarkhel*, the son of Tukoji, is always victorious."[46] The seal clearly noted that Kanhoji was operating on behalf of the Maratha state. Although his ships were smaller than those of the Europeans, they were fast and numerous. In asymmetrical naval warfare, he ruled supreme on the Konkan coast, remaining feared and undefeated against Europeans in spite of sustained efforts against him by a variety of capable enemies.

KANHOJI ANGRE'S EARLY YEARS AND MILITARY CAREER

Records are scarce regarding Kanhoji Angre's early life. The probable year of Kanhoji's birth was 1669. A myth that surrounds his youth involves a five-headed cobra, which forecasted his becoming a great leader.[47] Born into a warrior caste family, Kanhoji's early education was with a Brahmin in Harnai village overlooking the massive brooding fort of Suvarnadurg, located on an island off Harnai harbor. Folklore surrounding Kanhoji's relationship with his Brahmin tutor indicates that he granted the Brahmin his wish for a field and an orchard once he became acknowledged ruler of the Konkan region two decades later. At the time of Kanhoji's birth, his father Tukoji Angre was posted at Suvarnadurg during the war-torn era of Shivaji's consolidation of the Konkan coast for the Maratha.[48] Tukoji had shown great valor in naval battle against the Portuguese in 1640 at Chaul, serving Shivaji's father, and he later served Shivaji during the 1660s, eventually rising to become deputy commander of Suvarnadurg. Thus Kanhoji's family, including his father before him and his sons after him, had a long and successful family tradition of naval service to the Maratha state and political leadership. The name Angre became the symbol of naval might along the west coast of India.

Following his early Brahmin instruction and with his teacher's recommendation, Kanhoji began working at Suvarnadurg. He carried out successful raids on Siddi territory but was also captured by the Siddi for a brief period.[49] It was during this time that Kanhoji developed a friendship with Balaji Vishwanath, later to become chief minister of the Maratha kingdom.[50] After Shivaji died in 1680, Maratha rule passed to his son Sambhaji, who became king of the Marathas. Although courageous, Sambhaji lacked his father's strategic vision and military success. His narrow focus turned to attempts to capture the Siddi fortress of Janjira, not least by attempting to build a causeway to the island where the fortress was located. Like his other attempts at taking the fort, this one failed. Kanhoji Angre likely did not participate in this action during the early 1680s, but he joined Sambhaji's forces while in his mid-teens, strong and confident with sword, and serving on ships. In 1688, at age nineteen, he took his first command by coup, defending Suvarnadurg from an attack by the Siddi fleet, to whom the Maratha fort commander had defected.[51] Kanhoji was captured, escaped, and then returned to Suvarnadurg. Mimicking the carving of a turtle deity over the entry gate of the fort, his forces withdrew behind the strong walls of the fort like a turtle retreating into its shell, and they held out until the monsoon drove away the Siddi fleet. His friend Balaji Vishwanath was working as a clerk for the Siddi while also serving as a spy for Kanhoji, informing him of Siddi moves. For saving the fort, the Maratha king rewarded Kanhoji, not yet twenty, by giving him command of Suvarnadurg, the Golden Fort where his father had previously served.

In his struggle against the Mughals, Maratha king Sambhaji was defeated and beheaded in 1690, beginning a seventeen-year period of Maratha succession crises. In addition to killing Shivaji's eldest son Sambhaji, the Mughals captured the Maratha capital fort at Raigad and imprisoned Sambhaji's wife and infant son Shahu. Shivaji's second wife's son Rajaram took charge of the Maratha Empire and fought back against the Mughals. Rajaram appointed Kanhoji Angre to be admiral of the Maratha navy. Kanhoji made Vijaydurg capital of his territory along the coast in 1698. When Rajaram died in 1700, his widow Tara Bai ran the Maratha Empire until 1707. During this period, Kanhoji's power expanded as Tara Bai recognized him as *sarkhel*, "admiral" of the west coast of India.[52] When Mughal leader Aurangzeb died in 1707, Sambhaji's son Shahu was released and competed successfully to take the Maratha throne from Tara Bai, who was given a small fiefdom and later imprisoned. Despite great internal struggle concerning his allegiances, Kanhoji shifted his loyalty from Tara Bai to Shahu. In exchange, Kanhoji was confirmed by King Shahu as commander of the Maratha fleet and was granted twenty-six forts with their dependent villages. Kanhoji was always loyal to and served the Maratha monarch, but during this period of succession crisis, he had problems determining which Maratha monarch should be considered legitimate.

Nevertheless, from the moment he was recognized as *sarkhel* by Tara Bai in 1700, Kanhoji was the chief naval leader for the Maratha along the Konkan coast, a position competing monarch Shahu reconfirmed. In the Treaty of Kolaba in 1714, Kanhoji Angre accepted the suzerainty of Shahu in exchange for control of the coast from Bombay to Goa, including control of Khanderi, the strategic island at the mouth of the entrance channel to Bombay Harbor. Balaji Vishnawath had become peshwa, chief minister, for King Shahu, and he negotiated the treaty on behalf of the king. A common bond was that both Balaji Vishnawath and Kanhoji Angre had become disciples of the charismatic religious leader Brahmendra Swami. Shahu was grateful and invited Kanhoji to celebrate Holi, the spring festival of color, with him.[53]

Kanhoji had remarkable success as chief admiral in naval engagements against Maratha enemies, including the British, Siddi, Portuguese, and Dutch between 1700 and his death in 1729. During this three-decade period, Kanhoji reigned supreme over the waters of the Konkan coast between Bombay and Goa, on behalf of the Maratha state. During the 1720s, late in his life, Kanhoji Angre became less of a firebrand and more temperate, even though he was at the peak of his power. He desired peace and negotiated from a position of strength. Kanhoji resisted entreaties by both King Shahu and the swami to attack the Siddi during his final two years.

Reflections on the Maratha Maritime Experience

Guerrilla tactics were usually executed by smaller Maratha ships, which would appear by surprise from behind an island or from a hidden anchorage in an estuary along the coast. Typically, the attack was on a larger EIC ship, or sometimes on a Dutch or Portuguese ship. The Maratha swarm tactics were effective, from the time Kanhoji became *sarkhel* in 1698 to his son Tulaji's loss of Vijaydurg in 1756. During this period, the Maratha navy was able to enforce the *dashtak* permit system along the coast from Bombay to Goa.

The success of the Angre admirals in the use of asymmetrical naval warfare against the British and other European powers on the Konkan coast during the eighteenth century paralleled the success of the Kunjali Marakkar in the use of asymmetrical naval warfare against the Portuguese on the Malabar coast during the sixteenth century. The Maratha, however, added the dimension of formidable stone fortresses, many built on islands. These forts are impressive legacies of the Maratha period. Their brooding silhouettes still provoke thought about the naval events that took place around them three hundred years ago.

Maritime Strategic and Tactical Lessons

Useful lessons can be learned from a review of the case study material on the maritime interactions of the British and Maratha during the seventeenth and eighteenth centuries, specifically, how the Maratha managed their naval resistance to the British along the Konkan coast of India during the century between 1660 and 1760.

LOCAL KNOWLEDGE OF NATURAL PHENOMENA

The Maratha understood the contours of the coastline and how they might be used effectively in asymmetrical naval encounters with the British, their main adversary, and with secondary adversaries including the Dutch, Portuguese, and Siddi. The core of the Maratha naval defense plan involved controlling the coast with a series of line-of-site coastal forts, often situated on islands at the mouths of small rivers where smaller ships could hide undetected. By building and maintaining forts in such situations, the Maratha had the ability to use the protected waters behind the islands and in the river estuaries to prepare fleets of small attack craft and keep them hidden until a British ship target sailed by along the coast. The deeper draft British ships could not follow them into the shallow estuary waters. If the British target appeared vulnerable to the Maratha, their ships would attack. The Maratha used their local knowledge of the "terrain," as Sunzi called it, in this case referring to the Konkan coastline, to establish positions and use them to their advantage.

ADVANTAGES IN MILITARY TECHNOLOGY

The British had heavier, stronger ships than the Maratha, with cannons set up for broadside battle. When attacking, the Maratha counteracted the British big-ship advantage by offering to fight only when their small ship numbers were greater. Preferably such attacks would be on the stern of the British ships, where boarding parties were not confronted by cannon fire. Maratha boarding parties were noted for being particularly fierce. Long curved swords would be used for fighting in man-to-man combat. Short straight swords would be used for slashing at the standing rigging, cutting it through and eliminating the supports needed for keeping the masts upright. Once the ship was dismasted and the British crew subdued, the British prize was taken. When defending, the Maratha exploited their massive forts along the coast. This effective defensive fort technology with its heavy wall construction, combined with careful placement of the forts, allowed the Maratha to hold the Konkan coast until internal dissension and treachery allowed the British to take Vijaydurg in 1756, after one hundred years of effective fort use.

CONTINENTAL VS. MARITIME IDENTITIES

Like the Portuguese before them, the British developed a maritime identity, maritime capability, and maritime interest to project themselves across the globe in pursuit of their trading interests. From the time of the successful defense against the Spanish Armada in 1588, the British grew to become a global naval power. The dowry gift of Bombay in 1662 gave the British a secure location on the Indian coast from which to compete with the Portuguese, who had established themselves in Goa 150 years earlier. By the early 1660s, the identical time that the British occupied Bombay, Shivaji was beginning his successful Maratha resistance against the Mughals on the subcontinent. The Maratha identified themselves as having continental interests, but Shivaji also began Maratha naval traditions by building ships and refurbishing and building new sea forts. In the generation after Shivaji and his son Sambhaji, Maratha maritime identity became tied up with the emergence of the Angre clan as Maratha admirals, first with *sarkhel* Kanhoji Angre and then with his sons who succeeded him as *sarkhel*. Thus, a branch of the Maratha developed a strong maritime identity, despite the more general continental identity of the Maratha under the leadership of the peshwa.

DEEPLY FELT NATIONAL IDENTITIES

The British had a strong national as well as maritime identity. Their encounter with the Maratha on the west coast of India took place over a span of about one hundred years from the establishment of their port in Bombay in 1662 to the fall of Vijaydurg in 1756.[54] Over the course of this century, Maratha national identity, often tied in with Hindu consciousness, grew as they successfully reduced the power of the Muslim Mughals. Mughal leader Aurangzeb was defeated by the Maratha in 1706, followed by his death a year later. Thus British nationalism was competing with a rising local Maratha nationalism during the century of interaction between the two nationalities. In the end, the British were able to ally with forces of the Maratha peshwa to defeat the Maratha forces who controlled the coast under Angre family leadership, a classic case of successful British "divide and rule" strategy.[55]

MILITARY LEADERSHIP

Shivaji Bhonsale's broad strategic vision of pursing both continental and maritime military preparedness set the stage for subsequent Maratha dominance of the Konkan coast for over half a century by Kanhoji Angre and his sons. In fact, Angre clan involvement in Konkan coast protection began with Kanhoji's father Tukoji, who held several posts assigned by Shivaji, and was most notable for Kanhoji, as deputy commander of the great sea fort at Suvarnadurg. In 1698, Kanhoji was appointed *sarkhel*, "admiral" of the Maratha fleet, a title he held until his death in 1729. In his many sea battles with the British, Portuguese, and Dutch, he never suffered any defeats. This unbroken success enabled him to control the Konkan coast of Maharashtra from Alibag near Bombay to Vengurla near Goa. Although undefeated at sea by the Siddis, allies of the Mughals and British, Kanhoji was unable to capture the Siddi fort at Janjira, the one spot on the Konkan coast over which he never had control. Despite his appointment as admiral by the Maratha state, he was called a pirate by EIC officials, a label that gave license to attack the Angres. If the British Parliament had known that Kanhoji Angre was an admiral of a foreign state rather than a pirate, they could not have allowed attacks on him without declaring a formal state of war between the British and Maratha states. Kanhoji demonstrated courage when he was young while defending the Suvarnadurg fort. His careful execution of tactics and unbroken record of success led to his legacy as the greatest of India's naval heroes during the premodern period. Since Kanhoji never lost a battle to the British on the west coast of India, there is no British naval commander of the period who is remembered today as Kanhoji Angre's equal. It should be remembered, however, that Lieutenant Colonel Robert Clive was involved in the capture of the fort at Vijaydurg in 1856 that ended the rule of Angre admirals on the Konkan coast. Subsequently, the Maratha were never a threat to the British at sea, even though the Dhulaps replaced the Angres as Maratha admirals. In 1757, a year after helping take Vijaydurg from Tulaji Angre, Clive's more famous reputation was made at the Battle of Plassey, after which the British established military supremacy in Bengal, and Clive became the first British governor of the Bengal presidency.

RELATIVE POWER RELATIONS

European power dominance in Asia shifted from Portuguese and Spanish pre-eminence in Asia in the sixteenth century to Dutch and British pre-eminence during the latter half of the seventeenth century. Meanwhile, during the same period, Indian power relations were shifting from Mughal toward Maratha dominance, coinciding with the rise of Maratha power under Shivaji's leadership on the Indian sub-continent during the seventeenth century. In the maritime realm, the Maratha navy under Angre leadership competed favorably with the EIC and Royal navies, as well as with Portuguese and Dutch sea power on the west coast of India. The British, however, were an emerging world power and had much with which to contend aside from the west coast of India. Caribbean islands, American colonies, Canada, and Sumatra were all contested areas between the British and the Spanish, Dutch, and French. Although the British were much stronger militarily than the Maratha or the Mughals, British resources in India were limited by military, especially naval, commitments in all these other parts of the globe. Maratha naval success between 1660 and 1756 was in good part dependent on the relatively small proportion of its total naval capability that Britain put into place along the coast of India. Aside from India, the British had to defend their European homeland, as well as protect their American and Asian colonies.

ALLIANCE RELATIONS

The British developed alliances of convenience with both Europeans and Indians. For instance, Britain formed an alliance with Portugal to send a joint Anglo-Portuguese force to attack the Maratha fort of Kolaba in Alibag, the family seat of the Angre clan. The alliance was motivated by the consternation of both the British and the Portuguese with the success of the Maratha navy against their trading ships sailing out from Bombay and Goa respectively. Despite their best efforts, the joint Anglo-Portuguese attack on Kolaba failed. In a different instance, British alliance with an Indian ally bore fruit. The British allied with the Maratha peshwa to organize a joint force to confront the Maratha navy under the command of the Angres at Vijaydurg. This effort, unlike the Anglo-Portuguese effort, was successful and led to the demise of the Maratha navy as an opposition force to EIC shipping along the coast of

India. The Maratha navy did not develop alliance partners to help it during its fight with the British, but Kanhoji Angre brought many nationalities together to operate his ships during his tenure as admiral. These included English and Portuguese as well as Muslims from Egypt and Arabia. The portrait of Kanhoji Angre that was done during his lifetime was drawn by a European sailor in his own ship's crew.

RELATIONSHIP OF MARITIME ECONOMIC SUCCESS TO MARITIME MILITARY SUCCESS

Portuguese motivations in the Indian Ocean had been driven by a combination of religious and economic goals. On the religious side, these goals included finding and building relations with existing Christians, as well as converting new Christians. On the economic side, the goal was to develop a monopoly over the spice trade. They were only partially successful on both fronts. Neither the British nor the Dutch were particularly concerned with Christian conversions. Both were more interested in building wealth through trade. The British established the EIC in 1600, and the Dutch established the VOC in 1602. The new VOC stock ownership system led to the wide distribution of profits and to the Dutch Golden Age in Amsterdam, where both art and architectural gems became widely available among the populace. The EIC began as a private company and only later became a joint stock company open to all. In terms of profits, the VOC outshone the EIC during the seventeenth century, while the EIC trade volume and profits surpassed those of the VOC during the eighteenth and nineteenth centuries, coming to account for about half of the world's trade. Thus, both the VOC and EIC were, successively, the economically most successful firms based in Europe from 1600 to 1874, a period of more than 250 years. In a structure not replicated by businesses in later centuries, both the VOC and EIC through their initial charters had the right to "wage war" if it was required to maintain their economic objectives. Thus, the EIC established the Bombay Marine squadron as a private navy to counter any Maratha meddling in their trading activities along the coast of India. The VOC was given not only the power to wage war, but also to make treaties, execute criminals, create colonies, and issue coins. Thus the EIC and VOC could be considered "states outside of states," doing the work of Britain and the Netherlands in Asia. The military capability of the companies could make trade routes more secure for cargo carrying trade ships. In India, the EIC under Clive became the controlling power during the 1760s, immediately after the naval power of the Marathas had been crushed at Vijaydurg in 1756. Britain's EIC economic maritime success was closely linked to EIC military maritime success in Indian waters.

IMPORTANCE OF HISTORICAL AND CURRENT KNOWLEDGE

Knowledge of the Konkan coast was passed down from Shivaji's early sea fort commanders to Kanhoji Angre's father at Suvarnadurg. Family experience was transferred to Kanhoji, who then transferred it to his sons, who also became Maratha admirals. The Angre clan's knowledge of the Konkan coast was unsurpassed by other Indian groups or by Europeans.

FACTIONALISM IN MARATHA POLITICS AND THE DEMISE OF THE MARATHA EMPIRE

The Maratha sought freedom and independence from both the Mughals and the British. With the death of the Mughal Aurangzeb in 1707, the Marathas positioned themselves as a successor empire to the Mughals on the Indian subcontinent. Within a few years, Maratha Empire landholdings came to include most of what had once belonged to the Mughal Empire.

In the end, the Maratha were less successful against the British. The demise of the Maratha navy at Vijaydurg resulted in establishing British power on the west coast of India, a disastrous national development from the perspective of Indian control of their own subcontinent. The feudal system of the Marathas had helped create the factionalism that fueled this problem. The Marathas led by the peshwa assisted the British in defeating the Maratha faction led by Tulaji at Vijaydurg.

Like the zamorin and Kunjali IV relationship 250 years earlier, the peshwa and Tulaji were not on good terms, which resulted in the zamorin-Portuguese alliance in the sixteenth century and the peshwa-British alliance in the eighteenth century, respectively. These alliances brought about the destruction of the naval power of both the zamorin and the peshwa, in the face of major European sea powers. There is a parallel between Kunjali IV and Tulaji. Certainly, there is a historical echo of the adage "divide and rule," successfully employed first by the Portuguese and later by the British. Both the zamorin-Kunjali period and the Shivaji-Angre period lasted about a century before Europeans came to dominate, the Portuguese in the first instance and the British in the second.

LEGACY AND COMMEMORATIONS

Many public tributes to Shivaji Bhonsale and Kanhoji Angre may be seen in Indian public life today. Both are regarded as heroes of Indian independence due to their resistance to European encroachment, even though they ultimately were not successful in their resistance. In this respect, they also echoed the earlier zamorin-Kunjali resistance.[56] Kanhoji Angre's naval legacy, as the lustrous central period of the Maratha navy, is celebrated with numerous statues and memorials to Kanhoji in various places along the Konkan coast. Most notable of these commemorations is the naming of India's Western Naval Command Headquarters in Mumbai, Indian Naval Station INS Angre, which sits on the harbor opposite the Angres' home fort at Kolaba about a mile away.

CONCLUSION

Lessons from Eurasian Maritime History

Looking Back to Lean Forward

The past is never dead. It's not even past.

—William Faulkner

The Eurasian Maritime Rimland: From Malta to Tsushima

Malta and Tsushima, geostrategically situated islands at choke points in critical sea lanes of communication, mark the western and eastern ends of the Eurasian maritime rimland, the geographic scope of this study. Contemporary strategic thinkers remember Malta as the vital Allied base in the Mediterranean, which held out against German and Italian air attacks and in 1943 served as the stepping stone for Operation Husky to take Sicily and move on to the Italian peninsula. Strategists remember Tsushima as the place where Admiral Togo sank the Russian Baltic fleet in 1905, creating a watery grave for Russian aspirations in the Far East.

What may be less well remembered are the Ottoman siege of Malta in the 1560s and the use of Tsushima as a stepping stone by the Mongols in the 1270s, and later by the samurai in the 1590s. The enduring geostrategic importance of these islands as critical geographic bases has shown itself throughout history. What if the Allies had lost Malta to the Axis powers in 1943? What if the Knights had lost Malta to the

Ottomans in 1565? In each of these situations, the course of history likely would have been different, for Europe would have had vastly different subsequent rulers in each of these periods. What if the Japanese fleet had been sunk by the Russians at Tsushima in 1905, instead of vice versa? What if the Mongols had been turned back at Tsushima in 1274? In each of these examples, the course of history would have been drastically altered. Malta and Tsushima are tips on the horns of geostrategic dilemmas across the sweep of maritime Eurasia, dilemmas that have produced many clashes throughout history.

The cases discussed in this work illustrate historical conflicts anchored in enduring tensions that continue to affect regional competitions and the global balance of power today. Over the past decade, American maritime policy views have been expanding from an Asia-Pacific concentration toward a broader Indo-Pacific focus. The cases in this study contribute historical background for understanding the past, thereby illuminating the present and the future of the Indo-Pacific region. China's current maritime policy views embodied in its Maritime Silk Road hark back to the historical significance of its ancient silk road narrative. This is the maritime component of China's broader Belt and Road Initiative involving the restoration of the ancient silk roads by both land and sea, a conscious connection of current policy to a grand historical precedent. China's Maritime Silk Road includes a sweep broader than the American Indo-Pacific conception, for it includes a significant presence in the Mediterranean and noteworthy connections in Africa and Latin America, not just in Asia, the Middle East, and Europe.

India's involvement in the Indo-Pacific is pivotal in counterbalancing China in the Indian Ocean. India stands aloof from China and currently has not joined China's Belt and Road Initiative. Meanwhile, China courts Sri Lanka and Pakistan, India's neighbors. The central prize for both of these Asian giants are links to the neighboring economies of the ten Association of Southeast Asian Nations (ASEAN) countries. India's recent Look East Policy echoes that of the eleventh-century Chola, while China's emphasis on its "Peaceful Rise" in the Indian Ocean echoes the fifteenth-century voyages of Ming admiral Zheng He. Southeast Asia became known as Indochina for good reason, given the extensive historical patterns of influence by both India and China.

To understand the present and future of Southeast Asia, it is useful to understand that India and China have been involved for many centuries in shaping the region, especially through trade and diffusion of religious ideas, aspects often linked in temple institutions and their constructions. The design of these monuments relates strongly to the architectures of India and China. For example, the Borobudur and Prambanan temple complexes in central Java reflect the Buddhist and Hindu beliefs of their Indian founders. Relief carvings of the trade ships they sailed are carved in stone on temple friezes there, as well as on the walls of the Bayon Temple in Angkor Thom in Cambodia. Temples to the Chinese goddess of the sea, Mazu or Tianfei, mark the Southeast Asian ports of Chinese sailors, especially those from Fujian, in places still containing vibrant Chinese communities, such as Hoi An, Jakarta, Singapore, and Malacca. These surviving Indian and Chinese temple structures vividly indicate the ancient presence of both India and China in the region and set the stage for their continuing presence.

India and China have long played roles in their projection of power and influence in the Eurasian maritime rimland between the furthest points of the arc between Malta and Tsushima, and they will continue to do so now and into the future. Of the case studies included here, three involve India (the Cholas, the Kunjali Marrakkar, and the Maratha), while four involve China (the Mongols, the early Ming voyages, the Imjin War, and the Sino-Dutch War). Other regional powers, such as Japan and Korea in the northeast of the Eurasian rimland arc, will be significant going forward, as they have been in the past, as will certain European powers, including Russia, on the western end of the arc. The United States is a relatively new player on the stage of power politics in Eurasia, challenging China as an Asian maritime power as it formerly contested Japan, and engaging with India in subtle ways since the Second World War. A discussion follows of selected conflicts in the China Seas, Indian

Ocean, and Mediterranean Sea. They illuminate dimensions of Eurasia's maritime history and provide perspectives on patterns of events that are useful to consider when assessing the dynamics of regional and global relationships today.

China Seas

Ghosts of maritime history and theory haunt much of the maritime activity in the South China Sea, arguably one of the world's most important bodies of water today. It is a sea where great power competition threatens dangerous conflict. Who are these ghosts? Some are evocatively portrayed by political analyst Daniel Yergin.[1] Peering through the fog over the politically roiling waters, one can see apparitions of Zheng He sailing his treasure fleet to Champa, Sumatra, and Malacca; Hugo Grotius providing Dutch justification for freedom of the seas for the VOC; Alfred Mahan arguing for sea power based on equal doses of commercial and naval prowess; and Norman Angell cautioning that the costs of war will be far outweighed by the benefits of peace in the economically interdependent and booming nexus of Southeast Asian regional states with the great powers. While the ghostly shades of Zheng He, Grotius, Mahan, and Angell loom large, other ghosts from the past also inhabit the China Seas. These include figures who thought sea power was key to hegemonic power, like Kaiser Wilhelm, who built a navy to compete with Britain's, and Teddy Roosevelt, who sent the Great White Fleet around the world to demonstrate his commitment to a modern navy. And there are ghosts that worry us about an incident that might spark a larger conflict, like Archduke Ferdinand, whose assassination by a single bullet sparked a conflagration that led to the demise of the Ottoman, Austrian, and Russian Empires within a period of four years. Others still living enter Yergin's ghostly conversation: Robert Kaplan characterizes the South China Sea as *Asia's Cauldron*, remarking that "The Chinese are Mahanians now."[2] China's Admiral Wu Shengli punctuates the point, stating, "History reminds us that a country will not prosper without maritime power."

Many others continue the conversation about the South China Sea. Among them, Adm. James Stavridis, USN (Ret.), projects a disturbing fictional scenario during the 2030s in which the South China Sea becomes the flashpoint for a great war.[3] Clearly, such a haunting scenario is one to be avoided. By understanding the ghosts of the past, Stavridis suggests a cautionary approach that could lead us toward a less catastrophic future than the imaginary war his novel describes. Can we avoid a flashpoint event today like the assassination of Archduke Ferdinand in 1914? Can we avoid a strategy in relation to China like the oil embargo of Japan in 1941, which some analysts contend forced Japan to fight on death ground, a scenario Sunzi counseled against twenty-five hundred years ago? The novel implies that we must be well-informed about these earlier scenarios so as not to repeat disastrous mistakes of the past.

Understanding Chinese maritime history is relevant to U.S.-China global competition today. Premodern Chinese maritime history from the thirteenth through the eighteenth centuries is a rich field for understanding China's present trajectory and dreams of international leadership. For naval strategists, the lessons of maritime history are pertinent to guiding future action. Sun Tzu's advice to "Know your enemy, know yourself; your victory will never be endangered" is particularly relevant for American naval strategists in relation to China.[4]

Four of the cases of premodern Chinese naval endeavors in this work offer lessons for American strategists. The Yuan Dynasty Mongol invasions of Japan and Southeast Asia during the 1270s and 1280s are striking examples of ambitions and aggression of an earlier Chinese dynasty. The early Ming Dynasty voyages to the Western Ocean led by Zheng He between 1405 and 1433 demonstrate a historical Chinese effort to pursue a "string of pearls" strategy in the Indian Ocean, that is, developing a series of ports that provide logistical support for a fleet operating across the breadth of the ocean. Hideyoshi's invasion of Korea during the Imjin War is an instructive example of a Japanese invasion repulsed by Korean forces with Chinese backing between 1592 and 1598, with an important naval component. The Sino-Dutch War, in which Koxinga drove the Dutch from Taiwan in 1661–1662, illustrates China's ability to defeat one of the West's most powerful navies within the first island chain running from Japan south through the Ryukyu Islands and Taiwan to the Philippines. Most Chinese—both in popular culture as well as among naval strategists—know these events within the China Seas inside the first island chain well, though they are less often studied in the West. American naval strategists are at a disadvantage in applying the lessons of Chinese maritime history to the current geostrategic competition if they have not studied these cases.

Grand strategic lessons can be drawn from these four case studies. First, the Yuan Dynasty Mongol case is a cautionary tale: a great continental power does not necessarily make a successful transition to being a maritime power. Second, the Zheng He case is more encouraging for China: China has been, and thus can be again, a far-seas maritime power. A limiting note, however, is that Zheng He's enterprise proved relatively short-lived. His efforts were not sustained after the Ming emperor lost interest in maritime expansion and discontinued voyages to the Western Ocean. Third, the Imjin War case is encouraging for China, as it was able to project its power and influence through its Korean ally in their defeat of Japan in the late sixteenth century. This case illustrates the importance of China's partnership with Korean forces in a proxy conflict with Japan, using the Korean peninsula as a buffer. Fourth, the Sino-Dutch War case is also encouraging for China by way of its defeat of the Dutch navy, which was the greatest European maritime power of its time. Thus, by implication, China could extrapolate that it can achieve maritime supremacy over a Western power again.

The trajectory of the Ming Dynasty, with its rapid rise, is a strong precedent for the meteoric rise of China today, and it provides an encouraging precedent for Chinese strategists as they assess their country's possibilities for current and future naval dominance.[5] Western scholarship tends to focus on the decline of Chinese maritime capability after Zheng He. In contrast to this conventionally accepted analysis, Ming experience shows that China was strong at sea throughout that period. Thirty-seven years after the founding of the Ming Dynasty in

1368, Zheng He set sail on his first voyage to the Arabian Sea, an astonishing development. During this short period of less than four decades, the Ming threw off the Mongol yoke, built the world's largest ships, loaded 200 of them with 30,000 men, and dispatched a state-sponsored expedition to the far reaches of the Indian Ocean. In some ways, China's current rise in the maritime realm is more modest. It took fifty-nine years, almost six decades, from the founding of the Peoples Republic of China in 1949 for China to launch its first naval foray beyond local waters to the Arabian Sea in 2008. This antipiracy patrol was heralded as a sign of Chinese naval expansion into the "far seas."[6] If the Chinese are confident about their ability to move quickly, they are backed up in this view by the Ming example of their rapid development of maritime power even more quickly than China has accomplished today.

From a budget point of view, China's naval development efforts may be more sustainable now than during the early Ming. Compared to the expense of the huge fleets led by Zheng He, the cost of recent Chinese antipiracy patrols, consisting of two warships and one supply ship, are relatively modest. Although the Chinese navy has grown rapidly in the past decade, the burden of naval expenditure on the Chinese national treasury is significantly less now than it was during the early Ming period, implying that the current effort may be more sustainable. Attacks against the Ming by northern and western tribes diverted the military budget away from continued naval development and expeditions. Today China has more settled land borders, except with India, which allows greater budget focus on the maritime arena than was possible over the course of Ming history.

China remains extremely sensitive to perceived international efforts to impose limits on its maritime territorial ambitions, such as in the South China Sea. In earlier conflicts in the sixteenth and seventeenth centuries, China won two wars against the Japanese and Dutch, respectively. The Imjin and Sino-Dutch Wars are precedents for contemporary Chinese optimism that it can be successful in confronting competition in regions defined within its sphere of influence and interest. In those conflicts,

China has successfully opposed both an Eastern and a Western power in the past, and thus can do so again in the future. Both the Imjin and the Sino-Dutch Wars demonstrate the possibility of Chinese victory in the "near seas," along with Zheng He's earlier achievements in the "far seas."[7]

The Ming period, although premodern, is fresh enough to have great salience for China today. Chinese president Xi Jinping's Belt and Road Initiative, what some observers consider an integrated national strategic plan, consciously uses the Zheng He precedent as the rationale for establishing the policy of the twenty-first-century Maritime Silk Road, embodying what President Xi presents as the "peaceful rise" of China. American strategists would do well to note the lessons from China's maritime history in order to understand with greater nuance the motivations and confidence driving Chinese endeavors at sea. These lessons derived from understanding Chinese maritime history, primarily within the China Seas, remain relevant today. Some of the lessons emerging from an analysis of premodern Chinese maritime history in this work follow.

LOCAL KNOWLEDGE OF NATURAL PHENOMENA

Knowing the local sea conditions is the naval equivalent of Sun Tzu's emphasis on knowledge of terrain for armies. Storms played a key role in the negative outcome of the Mongol invasions in Japan, and tidal change had important effects in the defeat of the Mongols in Vietnam. Zheng He began his expeditions in December, riding the fresh northeast monsoon winds, and returned two years later on the southwest monsoons. Against great odds, Yi Sun-sin won the battle of the roaring currents at Myeongnyang through his understanding of how to use the tides to his advantage. Koxinga found his way into Tai Bay by using the tides through shallow Luermen channel to divide and conquer the two Dutch forts, Provintia and Zeelandia.

ADVANTAGES IN MILITARY TECHNOLOGY

The Mongols had riverine naval success with the ship-mounted trebuchet, but they were ill-prepared for ocean invasions of Japan and

Southeast Asia. Relying on Song and Korean ships and naval technology, essentially "bought" navies, was unsuccessful. Zheng He's ships were technological wonders of their age in terms of scale and the use of watertight compartments, needle compasses, the stars, and cartography. Korean admiral Yi Sun-sin used "turtle" ships, the first armored ships, to defeat the Japanese. Koxinga used superior military discipline and gun power parity that ultimately were enough to overcome superior Dutch ship sailing ability toward the wind.

CONTINENTAL VS. MARITIME IDENTITIES

The Mongols attempted major maritime adventures while remaining continental in their identity, even bringing their continent-conquering horses on board their ships to Japan. Zheng He's voyages were a strong attempt by the early Ming to establish a maritime identity, but the dynasty's continental identity prevailed as decisions made in the capital ultimately prohibited further great state-sponsored maritime voyages and treasury allocations went to continental defense instead. During the Imjin War, the Japanese navy was much like that of the continental Ottomans. Ships were platforms for opponents to engage in boarding-party combat similar to land combat. The samurai were more comfortable once on land on the Korean peninsula. Koxinga's Ming forces had a maritime identity that grew out of the maritime trading empire of the Zheng clan, which allowed them to challenge Europe's most successful maritime state, the Dutch Republic, in their China Seas operations. With the loss of Taiwan to the Qing, Chinese maritime identity receded for the remainder of the Qing Dynasty.

DEEPLY FELT NATIONAL IDENTITIES

National pride can play a key role in outcomes and so must be considered in evaluating an adversary, even if that adversary is relatively small. Tiny Vietnam united with common will to resist the mighty Mongols in the thirteenth century. Malacca developed stature through its relationship with the Ming and grew in regional stature. Korean admiral Yi Sun-sin's loyalty to his country and naval skill led to Korea, the "shrimp between whales," driving the Japanese off the Korean peninsula and back to Japan. His story remains highly inspirational to Koreans today. Mainland Chinese today are proud that Koxinga drove the Dutch from Taiwan in the seventeenth century. Modern Taiwanese take heart from Koxinga's setting up an entity on Taiwan that was independent from the Qing although it had limited short-term success and the island was eventually taken under Qing control.

MILITARY LEADERSHIP

Effective naval leadership matters. During the Mongol invasion of Vietnam, Tran Hung Dao successfully used a combination of historical precedent, local tidal knowledge, and clever asymmetrical tactics to overwhelm and destroy the much larger Mongol naval force. Zheng He not only commanded his huge expeditionary fleets efficiently, he also successfully subdued opponents in Sumatra and in Sri Lanka. Yi Sun-sin's naval leadership capability far exceeded that of other Korean commanders, but also that of the Japanese commanders. Koxinga's military leadership record was mixed, though he learned from his loss to the Qing in Nanjing to exercise more wily and aggressive leadership against the Dutch on Taiwan. In a situation of approximate technological parity, Koxinga's military leadership appears to have been the deciding factor in driving the Dutch from Taiwan.

RELATIVE POWER RELATIONS

Preponderant power of the Mongols on the continent translated poorly into maritime power. Zheng He's "shock and awe" voyages limited aggressive responses, and when aggressive responses occurred, they were dealt with quickly and effectively by overwhelming Ming force, demonstrating that preponderant maritime power can be an effective deterrent to regional conflict. Like the Mongols, Japan also lacked preponderant maritime power when attacking Korea, whose navy defeated them in battle and cut the supply lines for their more effective land armies. Maritime prowess and power of Koxinga and the Zheng clan were instrumental both in driving the Dutch from Taiwan and keeping the Qing away from Taiwan for decades.

ALLIANCE RELATIONS

There are many examples that demonstrate the wisdom of developing and keeping good relations with allies. The Mongols subjugated the Koreans and the Song and conscripted their navies for their maritime expeditions to Japan and Southeast Asia. Having little sympathy for the Mongols, the Koreans and Song seafarers had little stake in the Mongols' aims of maritime expansion, thus they had no alliance commitments based on common war aims, leaving the Mongols weakened in their ability to execute maritime policy. Zheng He developed a number of partners in his voyages to the Western Ocean, most significantly with the king of Malacca, who returned with Zheng He to meet the Yongle emperor in Nanjing. Although this was an important tributary acknowledgment toward the Ming emperor, the relationship was perhaps even more important to the Malacca king, Paramesvara, who was threatened by stronger powers in Siam and Java. Having Zheng He as a protective ally set up the basis for development of an independent Malacca, which arguably became the most important trade port in the Indian Ocean during the fifteenth century before the Portuguese arrived there in 1511. During the Imjin War, Korea could have allied with either Japan or China. By siding with China, Korea's tough fighting forces subsquently became the deciding naval factor in the victory over Japan in the Imjin War, with the two countries surmounting tensions in their alliance relationship. During the Sino-Dutch War, alliance possibilities between the Ming and the Japanese and between the Qing and the Dutch were implemented weakly, hence they were not decisive in the outcome of events.

RELATIONSHIP OF MARITIME ECONOMIC SUCCESS TO MARITIME MILITARY SUCCESS

Mongol sea trade was important and was documented by Marco Polo, among others. But it was short-lived because the Mongol Yuan Dynasty was brief within the scope of Chinese history, and trade with Japan and Southeast Asia was frustrated by the lack of Mongol maritime military success. Zheng He had no serious maritime military competitors during his voyages. Although the potential was there for long-haul transactional trade, the best foundation for maritime power was removed with the withdrawal of Ming support of major maritime expeditions in 1433, thereby producing weakened commercial and military success, especially in the far seas of the Indian Ocean. During the Imjin War, the Japanese were repulsed, and Japan subsequently turned inward for over two centuries of seclusion. This left trade with Korea to the So clan on Tsushima, which limited both Japanese maritime commercial and military success. The military loss of Taiwan by the Dutch in 1662 was the beginning of the decline of the commercial Dutch VOC giant trading firm, which was eventually eclipsed by the English East India Company.

IMPORTANCE OF HISTORICAL AND CURRENT KNOWLEDGE

In 1288, Vietnamese forces led by Tran Hung Dao successfully opposed the Mongols in the Bach Dang River estuary by using the same ruse that was used in 938, in which stakes planted in the tidal flats caught enemy ships attempting to retreat on the outgoing tide. The Vietnamese knew this history and the Mongols did not. Zheng He used the knowledge of earlier Chinese traders in the Indian Ocean to select ports of call before he arrived, and he also used Muslim networks familiar to the Arab traders. The So clan on Tsushima were purveyors of historical knowledge, including the use of Tsushima during the attempted Mongol invasions of Japan. The Japanese commander Yukinaga married a So daughter to solidify Japanese presence and control in Tsushima because it was such a valuable strategic asset. The extensive experience of the Zheng clan on the Fujian coast provided Koxinga with extensive knowledge of the value and use of the Penghu Islands as a staging ground.

Indian Ocean

For two thousand years the Indian Ocean has been a maritime meeting place for representatives of great civilizations, including Mediterranean, Arab, Indian, and Chinese. Its traditional role as a maritime crossroads continues today, as 80 percent of global seaborne trade passes through the Indian Ocean.

Panikkar's descriptive image of the Indian subcontinent as the roof over the Indian Ocean provides a context for Sanyal's long essay "The

Ocean of Churn," on the influence of Indian culture on the littoral polities of Africa and Arabia to the west and especially on the societies of continental Southeast Asia and the insular Indies to the east.[8] Many of these societies became Indianized because of their physical proximity and the consequent cultural and religious diffusion made possible by their geography. A free trade system developed early in the Indian Ocean, with the knowledge of how to use the prevailing monsoon winds to facilitate trade going back even earlier than what was documented in ancient Greek and Roman reports. Indeed, Asians in antiquity knew these routes well, with Gujarati traders sailing west and Arab traders sailing east, and with Chinese traders sailing west and Chola traders sailing east. They met in ports along the coasts of the Indian subcontinent, such as in Nagapattinam in the eleventh-century Chola period, and in Calicut in the fifteenth-century period of Zheng He's early Ming voyages. Ships carved in stone appear on many Indian monuments in Southeast Asia, indicating the importance of maritime capabilities for establishing these outposts with Indianized influence.

The Indian Ocean case studies reviewed in this work have included those of the Chola, Kunjali Marakkar, and Maratha. But they also have included the early Ming voyages connecting the China Seas to the Indian Ocean in the fifteenth century, and the Ottoman maritime ventures connecting the Indian Ocean to the Mediterranean Sea. Indeed, the Indian Ocean has been a broad maritime crossroads both historically and increasingly today. Following are some of the lessons that these conflicts illustrate.

LOCAL KNOWLEDGE OF NATURAL PHENOMENA

Chola eleventh-century development of ports to control the east coast of India was based on detailed knowledge about it from the southern tip of India to the mouth of the Ganges. Zheng He's fifteenth-century Ming voyages to the Indian subcontinent relied less on local knowledge than on the "shock and awe" effect of the overwhelming force evident in the massive flotilla arrangements of his treasure ships. Knowledge of the seasonal variation of the monsoon winds, however, was central to the success of these early Ming voyages. Kunjali Marakkar sixteenth-century and Maratha eighteenth-century knowledge of Indian west coast geography, tides, and winds gave them advantages in conducting asymmetrical naval warfare against stronger Portuguese and British naval forces. Their asymmetrical tactics included building forts on islands at the mouths of rivers so that the smaller Indian vessels could gather in large numbers in the shallow estuary harbors behind the mangrove swamps lining the coastal banks and the forts. From there they could sweep out to attack single large European vessels from behind to avoid broadside gunnery. Thus the specific configuration of local terrain and sea conditions were critical for the asymmetrical naval success of the Indian forces. Sixteenth-century Ottoman forays into the Indian Ocean were facilitated by the knowledge obtained through alliances with Indian forces but was limited by long logistical supply routes and sailing vessels that were less capable of blue-water voyages than those of the Portuguese.

ADVANTAGES IN MILITARY TECHNOLOGY

The significance of technological advances playing a factor in military success is evident by the innovations in Chola ships and navigational techniques that surpassed those of others deployed in the eastern Indian Ocean in the eleventh century. In the fifteenth century, Zheng He's ships set higher world standards for size and technology. Bulkhead compartments made sinking less likely, and the use of the magnetic compass and detailed charts improved navigation. Indian ship technology was adequate for asymmetrical coastal defense during the Kunjali and Maratha periods but could not compare with the blue-water capabilities of Portuguese caravels and carracks, or later EIC armed Indiamen or Royal Navy frigates. Ottoman galley adaptations were never equal to the sea capabilities of the Portuguese ships in the Arabian Sea. In each of these cases, superior technology ultimately prevailed, although for the Kunjali Marakkar and Maratha, their more limited technology was effectively offset for several decades by highly successful asymmetrical naval tactics.

CONTINENTAL VS. MARITIME IDENTITIES

Under the leadership of Rajaraja Chola followed by Rajendra Chola, an Indian kingdom transformed continental identity within the subcontinent toward a maritime identity. Chola trade and naval dominance ranged throughout the Bay of Bengal to the Java Sea by 1025, before the Chola's continental neighbors, the Pandyan Dynasty, brought about the demise of the Chola Dynasty in 1279. During the period of Rajaraja and Rajendra, the Chola were strong and successful on both the subcontinent and on the sea, and for a few decades in the eleventh century demonstrated a successful hybrid continental/maritime identity. Similarly, Zheng He established a Ming maritime identity for three decades during his seven voyages ending in 1433, creating a successful continental/maritime hybrid model until the emperor chose to end support for maritime endeavors. The Zheng clan operation on the Fujian coast during the seventeenth century demonstrated that Ming maritime identity was not entirely in eclipse, as maritime prowess allowed Ming loyalists to fend off Qing control for forty years until 1683 in maritime southeast China, though the capital in Beijing was lost in 1644.

By comparison to the Chola, the zamorin and Kunjali Marakkar, and the Maratha had less focus on a blue-water maritime identity by prioritizing the coastal defense of India. The development of an Indian maritime identity has been complicated by the Hindu taboo against traveling across the sea. Called the *kala pani*, crossing the seas to foreign lands could result in losing *varna*, caste, and social respectability. The Ottoman focus in both the Mediter-ranean and the Indian Ocean was concentrated primarily on controlling the land in order to control the sea. This worked reasonably well in the Mediterranean and the Red Sea and in the Persian Gulf, all areas with limited distances over water, but it did not allow the Ottomans to compete successfully against the Portuguese, who developed a deep-seated blue-water maritime identity through their Atlantic voyages around Africa. Insular Britain also developed a profound maritime identity, which eventually allowed them to dominate the Indian Ocean as they replaced the Portuguese and Dutch European influence there.

DEEPLY FELT NATIONAL IDENTITIES

Chola identity was strongly tied to the Hindu belief system and worship of Shiva. The impressive temple complexes built by Rajaraja Chola and Rajendra Chola in the Tamil area of southeastern India express the cultural flowering of their identity, and they brought both their religious and trade ideas to Sri Lanka, Sumatra, and the Malay Peninsula through their temple-based commercial guild system. Zheng He disseminated ideas about the role of the Ming emperor Yongle as the moral center of the Chinese worldview, where all others were expected to present tribute to the emperor. He was largely successfully in bringing back tribute missions from Southeast Asia, Sri Lanka, and Africa. Local pride and the spunk of the underdog were present in the resistance of both the Kunjali Marakkar to the Portuguese and of the Maratha to the British. Both were adequate to prevent subjugation by the militarily superior Europeans until local divisions between the zamorin and the Kunjali, and between the Maratha navy and Maratha peshwa, led to fracturing of national pride as the glue holding together political and military resistance.

MILITARY LEADERSHIP

The Chola expedition of 1025 cleverly and effectively planned an unexpected "Sunda surprise" by traveling southeast down the west coast of Sumatra and attacking the Srivijayan center of power at Palembang from the eastern Sunda Strait rather than from the expected usual route along the northern coast of Sumatra through the Malacca Strait. Zheng He capably commanded the many resources under his control for each of his seven voyages, whether peacefully negotiating with local leaders and carrying them back to Nanjing to present tribute to Emperor Yongle, or successfully quelling armed opposition, as he did in Sumatra and Sri Lanka. Kunjali Marakkar and Maratha naval leadership was effective until the zamorin joined forces with the Portuguese to defeat the Kunjali Marakkar and, similarly, when the Maratha peshwa joined forces with the British to defeat the Maratha Angre navy.

RELATIVE POWER RELATIONS

There was an ebb and flow of power as the entities involved in these cases balanced domestic economic strength and political cohesion with their international economic and political goals, coupled with and reinforced by their naval capabilities. The Cholas' rising power in the tenth century allowed its dynasty to expand beyond its consolidation of the subcontinent from the tip of the Indian subcontinent to the waters of the Ganges delta in the northeast. Growing trade interests in Sri Lanka and Southeast Asia led to maritime expeditions that were reinforced by naval capabilities and to subsequent Chola domination in those areas for about a century during the Song Dynasty, which was a desired Chola trading partner. Four centuries later, following Mongol trading activity in Southeast Asia and failed naval expeditions there, Zheng He projected rising Ming power in the maritime dimension all the way across the Indian Ocean, before contracting back into the China Seas. Within a few decades, early Ming maritime influence in the Indian Ocean was replaced by European maritime power, first by the Portuguese, then by the Dutch and the British. This power was opposed with modest success by the Ottomans, by the zamorin of Calicut with his Muslim Kunjali admirals during the sixteenth century, and later by the Maratha during the seventeenth and eighteenth centuries.

ALLIANCE RELATIONS

Overall, alliance relations through history in the Indian Ocean were fluid and dynamic, leading to differing results in successive periods and situations. The Chola successfully relied on Javanese help in moving through the Sunda Strait in their surprise attack on the Srivijayans. Zheng He developed close relations with Parmeswara in Malacca in order to establish a forward base of operations for all seven of his forays into the Indian Ocean. This alliance between Parmeswara and Zheng He, and by extension the Ming emperor, enabled the development of Malacca into an important Indian Ocean port in spite of threats from stronger kingdoms in Java and Siam, who were kept in check by fear of Chinese retaliation. The Portuguese allied with the king of Cochin to fight the zamorin of Calicut and his Kunjali Marakkar admirals, but this alliance failed until a rift developed between the zamorin and his Kunjali naval leaders. Joint Portuguese and British forces were unsuccessful against the Maratha navy until the Maratha navy was divided from the Maratha prime minister, called the peshwa, who sided with the British. The Ottomans developed alliances of convenience with Indian forces but were unable to compete with Portuguese blue-water capability in the Arabian Sea.

RELATIONSHIP OF MARITIME ECONOMIC SUCCESS TO MARITIME MILITARY SUCCESS

Chola trading interests drove the empire's expansion toward Sumatra, where the Srivijayans limited the Indian trade with China with excessive tolls on ships, considered by the Chola to be piracy. Rajendra Chola's successful military raid on the Srivijayans in Palembang and Kedah in 1025 broke up the Srivijayan monopoly over the Malacca and Sunda Strait trade routes. Zheng He's voyages were based less on geoeconomic trade interests than on the geopolitical goal of expansion of the Chinese tribute system requiring recognition of the primacy of the Chinese emperor. Militarily, Zheng He was successful through overwhelming force and leadership when required in Sumatra and Sri Lanka. Portuguese motivations were trade-based as they sought to break the Venetian monopoly on the spice trade to Europe and establish their own spice trade monopoly. In spite of Portuguese naval superiority on the high seas, the zamorin of Calicut and Kunjali Marakkar managed to limit the control of the Portuguese to a small percentage of the total spice trade through control of coastal ports and hinterland trade. The Ottomans assisted the Kunjali in this effort by their presence and control in the Red Sea and Persian Gulf. Trade drove Dutch and British interests following the establishment of the Dutch VOC and English EIC, leading to ascendency in trade of the Dutch in the seventeenth century and the British in the eighteenth century. The ships of both of these companies had strong military capabilities, including cannon, to protect their primary function, trade. The Maratha navy under Angre clan leadership successfully limited the development of British trade on India's west coast for more than half a century despite the British navy's presence and attempted protection, until the fall of the Vijaydurg sea fort in 1756.

IMPORTANCE OF HISTORICAL AND CURRENT KNOWLEDGE

Knowledge of the long history of mutually beneficial trade provided a moderating influence on premodern Eurasian relationships in order to keep trade corridors open. Chola maritime expansion followed earlier patterns of Indianization of Sri Lankan and Southeast Asian cultures through long-established networks, including the flow of travelers to centers of learning. Knowledge of the Arab and Muslim world was an important aspect that enhanced Zheng He's capabilities in the Indian Ocean, whether with Muslim traders in Malacca, at Beruwala in Sri Lanka, or on the Arabian Peninsula, where fellow Muslim members of Zheng He's expeditions went on pilgrimage to Mecca, as his father had when he had been a Mongol administrator. Maratha naval forces looked back at successful Kunjali Marakkar asymmetrical naval resistance to the Portu-guese and developed similar patterns against the British.

Eastern Mediterranean Sea

Sea trade took place from the Mediterranean into the Indian Ocean and China Seas from the earliest periods of history and was documented in classical Greek and Roman texts, thus locating the western end of premodern Eurasian maritime connectivity to European destinations. This maritime connectivity was enhanced during the nineteenth century by the Suez Canal, not an option for Zheng He's fifteenth-century ships, but a key dimension of maritime commerce today, carrying more than 10 percent of global sea trade. China's current conception of its Maritime Silk Road extends China's premodern maximum extent, reached during the early Ming, to include the Mediterranean and direct access to European markets, initially through its activity in Greece to develop and use the port of Piraeus.[9]

From the sixteenth century onward, the Ottomans became a significant land power, having control of much of the Mediterranean coastline and a part of the Arabian Sea coastline through their presence on the Red Sea and on the Persian Gulf. During the sixteenth century, the Ottomans developed a dominant maritime presence in both the eastern Mediterranean and Indian Ocean theaters, offering instructive lessons for understanding Eurasian maritime history.

LOCAL KNOWLEDGE OF NATURAL PHENOMENA

Knowledge of the late-season winds was critical in the Mediterranean, while tides played less of a role in strategic considerations. Ottomans lost the siege of Malta but saved their fleet by returning to Constantinople before the winter storms. Although retreat from the winter storms may have been the best tactical choice, the question remains whether this was the best strategic choice for the Ottoman navy.

ADVANTAGES IN MILITARY TECHNOLOGY

The Ottomans ultimately matched the Venetians in galley technology but failed to compete with the Portuguese in sailing ship technology, although their gunnery capability was approximately equal to that of the Portuguese.

CONTINENTAL VS. MARITIME IDENTITIES

The Venetians and Portuguese developed deep maritime identities, while the Ottomans stretched their primary continental identity with a maritime component and did not become a true continental/maritime hybrid power.

DEEPLY FELT NATIONAL IDENTITIES

In the Ottoman period, the identities associated with the conflicts described here were more about religion rather than place. Muslim versus Christian identities, deeply felt, invoked memories of the Crusades.

MILITARY LEADERSHIP

Suleiman chose wisely in appointing Barbarossa as his naval commander. Barbarossa's strength and success are still revered today. Andrea Doria has a more tarnished record.

RELATIVE POWER RELATIONS

Ottoman power rose quickly in the period from 1453 to 1560, then stalled as the Holy League alliance pushed back. A geographic stalemate in the eastern Mediterranean took place for two hundred years before the Ottoman decline in the nineteenth century.

ALLIANCE RELATIONS

During the sixteenth century, the Ottomans had no alliances in the Mediter-ranean, while the Holy League was a five-party alliance including the Papal State, Hapsburg Spain, and the Knights on Malta, Genoa, and Venice. Attempted Ottoman alliances with Egyptians and Indians were largely unsuccessful.

RELATIONSHIP OF MARITIME ECONOMIC SUCCESS TO MARITIME MILITARY SUCCESS

Maritime economic success was linked to maritime military success through control of trade routes, whether Ottoman or European.

IMPORTANCE OF HISTORICAL AND CURRENT KNOWLEDGE

Cartography was developed as an effective discipline by both the Ottoman and European powers. Ottoman cartography by Piri Reis was an outstanding tool for Ottoman expeditions. The historically minded Knights incorporated the earlier experience of the Crusades into their planning.

Within the Mediterranean, Ottoman victory in the siege of Rhodes in 1522 and loss at the siege of Malta in 1565, as well as their victory in the naval battle of Preveza in 1538 and loss at the naval battle of Lepanto in 1571, indicate that leadership and logistics matter a great deal. Where the Ottomans had competent unified leadership under Suleiman at Rhodes, they succeeded. Where they had divided leadership under Mustapha, Piyali, and Dragut at Malta, they failed. The inverse was true for the Holy League during the naval battles. At Preveza, differences between Genoese and Venetian leadership led to disaster, whereas Don Juan of Austria united the Holy League for victory at Lepanto.

Assessing Theoretical Explanations

Though each of the theories considered in the introductory chapter provides insight into dimensions of the eight case studies presented, Spykman's formulation of the Eurasian maritime rimland and Mahan's formulation of the relationship of sea power to economic competition have the most consistent relevance and applicability to the historical cases reviewed. The concepts of Alexander VI's bipolar division of the world, Grotius' freedom of the seas, Mackinder's heartland, Angell's economic interdependence, Huntington's civilizational clashes, and Allison's power transition all illuminate dimensions of the cases, but on a less comprehensive basis than Spykman's or Mahan's theories.

Regarding Spykman, the strength of his theory lies in the fact that a high percentage of the world's social and economic interaction takes place over the sea rather than over land. He asserted that the maritime rimland of Eurasia is the most populous of the world's continents, so is most likely to be the locus of the most tension and conflict in the post–World War II era. In fact, the eight cases discussed in this book demonstrate that conflict has taken place along the Eurasian maritime rimland for at least the past millennium, setting a precedent for more recent developments. The primary region on the globe today where conflict has taken place since World War II, as Spykman presciently predicted, is the Eurasian maritime rimland including North Africa, the Middle East, Vietnam, and Korea, and the South and East China Seas. This list of post–World War II conflict has obvious geographic parallels to the arc of conflict of the Eurasian maritime history cases analyzed here, which include, from west to east, the Ottoman Empire with the Holy League, the Kunjali with the Portuguese, the Maratha with the British, the Chola with Srivijaya, the early Ming with Sumatra and Sri Lanka, the Ming with the Dutch, the Mongols with the Vietnamese and Japanese, and the Japanese with the Koreans and Chinese. All these cases fit within Spykman's formulation of the Eurasian maritime rimland as a zone of potential conflict. Clearly the Eurasian maritime rimland conflict of the past is not dead; rather it has lived on into the twenty-first century.

The strength of Mahan's theory lies in the universality of the need to satisfy economic imperatives, which Mahan recognized leads to competition, which in turn drives the need for naval strength to protect trading interests on the "wide common" of the open seas. In the cases discussed herein, the seas included are the China Seas, Indian Ocean, and eastern Mediterranean. The Chola and the Ottomans developed strong navies to protect their trade, and they did so in the greater Bay of Bengal and the Mediterranean, respectively. The early Ming concept of maritime activity and dominance was related to prestige rather than trade, with tribute trade and the exchange of gifts in the Western Ocean taking precedence. The Chinese at that time largely felt that it contained and produced most of the goods it desired, both necessary and for luxury. The early Ming under Zheng He built the greatest navy of its era to implement and protect its tribute trade. The later Ming under Koxinga also developed an efficient and profitable trading fleet of hundreds of junks that operated all the way from Japan to Java. Koxinga led his navy to victory over the Dutch in Taiwan, securing the centrally located East China Sea and ejecting a major competitor, a Mahanian stroke of genius. Once Europeans arrived in the Indian Ocean, the Portuguese and the English controlled the blue water with their navies and ultimately prevailed with military domination that allowed the Europeans to create immense trade wealth. The Kunjali Marakkar and Maratha navies successfully resisted the Portuguese and English for a few decades despite an asymmetrical power balance, but that only occurred in the brown-water coastal regions along the west coast of India. The least Mahanian players in this series of case studies are the Mongols and the samurai. Both had geopolitical dominance on their minds, although geoeconomic motives were also involved. Both the Mongols and samurai failed in their invasion attempts going in opposite directions across the Tsushima Strait in different eras, largely because they did not have adequate navies and were unable to maintain robust supply lines in order to make a success of their invasion attempts.

Alexander VI's division of the world into Portuguese and Spanish halves, essentially a bipolar concept of international relations with two approximately equal and balanced parties, has no application to any of the eight Eurasian cases surveyed.

The Grotius scheme of freedom of the seas has much more applicability. By eliminating Srivijayan trade interference, the Cholas were practitioners of the principle of freedom of the seas long before Grotius developed it to rationalize a place for Dutch traders in the Portuguese-Spanish division of the globe. Similar to Chola naval action to open the trade route to China, Zheng He removed pirate Chen Zuyi from his role as controller of the Strait of Malacca, thus opening free passage between the China Seas and the Western Ocean. The zamorin of Calicut and others had promoted free trade in the Indian Ocean as a tradition for centuries before the Portuguese arrived and tried to eliminate free trade by monopolizing the spice trade. The Kunjali Marakkar and Maratha were partially successful in maintaining traditionally open trade patterns through asymmetrical naval resistance. In the China Seas, the free trade mantra played less well, with the Mongols, Dutch, late Ming, and Japanese all having a greater desire for hegemonic control of the seas.

As the proponent of the idea that the heartland would control the world island, Mackinder used the Mongol Empire as his primary example from world history. But as shown in the Mongol encounters with Japan, Vietnam, and Java, dominance over the heartland did not lead to control in the maritime realm, as all of the naval ambitions of the Mongols failed along the perimeter of the Mongol Yuan Dynasty. In the current era, China is too far east to dominate the heartland. Whether Mackinder's heartland theory is ultimately revived depends on the future relationship of Russia and China, which is growing closer in recent years after their dramatic split in the Cold War. Thus, Mackinder's heartland theory has little relevance for the maritime case studies of the premodern era. The 2021 crisis in Ukraine, however, sparks new consideration of Mackinder's theory, though the Odessa and Black Sea component has a Spykman dimension.

Angell's argument for economic interdependence as a deterrent to conflict appears logical and compelling. The main example of this theory would be the mutually beneficial trade and relative lack of conflict in the Indian Ocean before the arrival of Europeans in the sixteenth century. After 1500, trade and conflict went hand in hand as Portuguese interest in monopolistic trade increased, thereby incensing competitors. The costs of war did not deter either the Mongols or the samurai, both of whom were prosperous enough before their invasion attempts to contemplate and launch maritime invasions. To the Mongols and samurai, the benefits of conquest outweighed the benefits of economic interdependence.

Huntington's clash of civilizations theory is based on differences in culture and values, and the Ottoman case is a good example of this conflict, in which the rise of the sixteenth-century Ottoman navy provoked a maritime response by the Holy League alliance. The clashes between Ottoman and European forces hark back to the conflicts associated with the Crusades, because religion played a major role in the vitriol between the parties involved. In the other cases reviewed, economic and geopolitical factors were more important to the outbreak of violence than cultural factors, although several of the later clashes between European and Asian forces involved a clash of values. Examples of these situations include the Portuguese and English interactions with the Kerala and Maharashtra Indians. The case of the Japanese banning the Portuguese, but not the Dutch, from Japan is an interesting example of the role of religion in these relationships. The Japanese banned the Portuguese to prevent them from spreading Christianity in Japan, but they did not ban the Dutch, who valued and promoted trade, not religion.

In Allison's theory of power transition in which violence is caused by rising powers that threaten established powers, the conflict between the Ottomans and the Holy League is one of his twelve cases that produced war from a sample of sixteen cases over the past five hundred years. The rising Ottoman Empire challenged established Europeans, in what Allison calls the Thucydides trap, and war erupted. In a similar fashion, although not one of Allison's examples, a rising Japan challenged the established Ming Dynasty in China through their vassal tributary state Korea, and the Imjin War broke out. Allison's theory has strong explanatory power for these two cases but does not seem particularly relevant to the other six cases.

Thus, theories of Spykman and Mahan provide the most relevant analytical frameworks for the eight cases of Eurasian maritime conflict contained in this work. The ideas of Grotius are applicable in several cases, and Mackinder's and Angell's concepts can be applied in selected cases. Meanwhile, the theory of Huntington is relevant where there are substantial cultural differences, and that of Allison is valuable in situations of rising power scenarios.

Leaning Forward: Policy Implications of Eurasian Maritime History

The analysis of Eurasian maritime history cases and associated details are relevant for foreign policymakers and practitioners when developing and implementing twenty-first-century policy for the Eurasian maritime rimland. In addition, those who want to understand the complexities of the region and their impact on global affairs will find this history to be significant. Knowing the Eurasian maritime past illuminates the present, facilitating in a more informed way perspectives about what may happen in the future. The following are examples of how knowledge of the cases discussed in this work will help in understanding the present and provide a pathway for considering potential future outcomes.[10] These examples are presented geographically rather than chronologically and offer brief food-for-thought suggestions in relation to potential policy responses as opposed to providing concrete policy suggestions.

BARBAROSSA/TURKEY'S BLUE HOMELAND POLICY

In recent years, Turkey has reasserted maritime claims in the eastern Mediterranean under a policy rubric called Blue Homeland. One consequence of those claims was the Maritime Boundary Treaty signed with Libya in November 2019. It establishes north-south economic claims that interrupted the east-west undersea pipeline plans of Israel, Cyprus, and Greece, who regarded the Turkey-Libya deal as highly aggressive. At the time, the Turkish foreign minister proclaimed, "Barbaros is back!" His reference is a reminder to Turkey's populace, and as well as to friends and competitors, of the Turkish government's pursuit of an assertive neo-Ottoman foreign policy, which explains why the Turkish navy has recently begun firing gun salutes when passing Barbarossa's tomb in Besiktas on the Bosphorus Strait. Knowing Barbarossa's story and the sixteenth-century Ottoman posture in the eastern Mediterranean goes a long way toward understanding current Turkish policy direction. Indeed, some of Turkey's neighbors in the eastern Mediterranean are fearful of Turkey's reassertion of Ottoman maritime dreams and are shaping their foreign policies accordingly.

RAJENDRA CHOLA/INDIA'S LOOK EAST POLICY

Ongoing prospects for conflict with Pakistan have drawn India's attention west since postwar independence, but the potential value of stronger relations with Southeast Asia resulted in a Look East policy in the early 1990s. This transformed into a more activist Act East policy under Prime Minister Narendra Modi in 2014. The deep historical involvement of India in Southeast Asia and its related competition with China have focused greater attention on India as a global factor in foreign affairs generally, and India's becoming a major player in Southeast Asia is producing heightened attention on strategic events in the Indo-Pacific region. It is relevant to know the ancient history of the Chola and the dynasty's regional maritime exploits under Rajendra Chola, which amounted to an eleventh-century Look East/Act East policy a millennium before India's current policy focus. The purpose of the current policy is to cultivate extensive economic and strategic relationships with Southeast Asian nations in order to bolster India's position as a regional power and as a counterweight to the strategic influence of the People's Republic of China. These objectives echo the goals of the Chola's regional maritime exploits of the tenth century.

ZHENG HE/CHINA'S MARITIME SILK ROAD POLICY

Chinese president Xi Jinping's announcement of the twenty-first-century Maritime Silk Road (MSR) in 2013—the sea portion of China's signature foreign policy Belt and Road Initiative—references the history of the early Ming maritime expeditions in the fifteenth century and Zheng

He's role as a proponent of China's quest for peaceful relationships via sea throughout the world. The MSR accounts for a much larger proportion of trade goods to and from China than does the BRI's overland Silk Road Economic Belt. The *guanchang* warehouse logistical bases that Zheng He established in Malacca, Samudera, Calicut, and Hormuz echo China's MSR Indian Ocean port strategy of today, which is labeled its "string of pearls" in Kyaukpyu, Hambantota, Gwadar, and Djibouti. A difference today is that China has extended the MSR to China's dramatic port developments in Piraeus in the eastern Mediterranean as well as to other regions around the world, including Africa and Latin America. Policy dramas related to the MSR's expansion will play out over decades to come and will continue to reference the early Ming period and its narratives as an aspirational template for China's global ambitions.

KOXINGA/CHINA'S TAIWAN POLICY

Taiwan today is the most important vestige of what China refers to as its "century of humiliation," and one of the most humiliating blows of that period was the cession of Taiwan to Japan under the terms of the Treaty of Shimonoseki in 1895. A prouder moment for China occurred when the Ming loyalist Koxinga drove the Dutch from Taiwan in 1662. This historical moment provides China with a model of successful resistance to foreign domination of Taiwan, whether European, Japanese, or American. Following the expulsion of the Dutch, Taiwan became a pawn in the civil war rivalry between the Ming and the Qing, just as control of Taiwan today is still fraught with the outcome of the Chinese civil war and the intense rivalry between the Nationalists and the Communists. Admiral Shi Lang, a defector from the Ming to the Qing, invaded Taiwan through amphibious warfare in 1683 to put the island under mainland Qing control. The situation in the twenty-first century is ominously parallel to that in the seventeeth century.

YI SUN-SIN/KOREA'S SURVIVAL POLICIES

The challenges for Korea and its survival as a "shrimp between whales" are as profound today as they have been for centuries. Examples are numerous, from the seventh-century struggle of China and Japan over

Korea's Three Kingdoms to the way the Mongols co-opted Korea in the thirteenth century to invade Japan, to the sixteenth-century Korean bloodbath during the samurai invasions, and to the twentieth-century Korean War. That most recent conflict continues to divide the Korean peninsula, and the map of Korea today is eerily similar to the seventh century map. Korea's peaceful coexistence with its more powerful neighbors is perennially in doubt. Yet Koreans, a proud and culturally rich people, have continued to survive, supported by leaders like the great and profoundly capable Yi Sun-sin, whose naval leadership ultimately turned back the Japanese in 1598, at the cost of his life in the final sea battle of the war. In East Asia, Admiral Yi's story transcends Admiral Nelson's. It is a need-to-know story for all those interested in why and how Korea may endure going forward.

Eurasian maritime history cases are fascinating on their own terms. Crucially, they offer much to inform frameworks for thinking about the present and future of regional and global affairs.

ACKNOWLEDGMENTS

After thirty years in business, I was welcomed back into the world of international relations discussions by many old and new colleagues and friends who have respected and supported my work over the past decade, much of it in relation to the work presented in this volume. I wish to acknowledge and thank them deeply for their support and friendship. Acceptance back into this community discussing global affairs has profoundly enriched my life.

Tufts Fletcher School colleagues Erik Goldstein and John Maurer encouraged me to re-enter the academic world at Boston University and at the U.S. Naval War College, for which fundamental thanks are required and are gratefully given. Longtime member of the European Parliament from Greece George Dimitrakopoulos provided entrées not only for the sixteenth-century Mediterranean research included in this work, but also for guidance regarding twenty-first-century echoes of this earlier history. Author Ellen Beth Lande provided both encouragement and practical advice in developing the manuscript.

At the Boston University Pardee School of Global Studies, Bill Grimes and Joe Fewsmith organized and found a place for me at the Center for the Study of Asia, where subsequent directors Eugenio Menegon, Cathy Yeh, and Thomas Berger have all been unfailingly supportive of my work. My great thanks go to each of them. Pardee School colleagues ambassadors Vesko Garčević and Jorge Heine, as well as Kevin Gallagher and Min Ye, have illuminated my way on many occasions, and it has been a great pleasure to have them as academic colleagues. Mike Corgan kindly made arrangements for me to teach his course on the Sea in International Relations. I greatly value having been accepted as part of the Pardee School family.

At the U.S. Naval War College, Toshi Yoshihara encouraged me to develop an Asian maritime history syllabus and recommended that the van Beuren Foundation help underwrite this work. I am grateful that the foundation funded my teaching of the resulting course, which was also supported by Dean Tim Schulz. Admiral Nirmal Verma of the Indian navy encouraged me to broaden the course beyond the China Seas, and he lent his network to me for organizing related field research in the Indian Ocean. Tonio Andrade from Emory University and Michael Szonyi from Harvard University came to Newport to support the Eurasian maritime history course program with guest lectures. Naval War College faculty Jeff Shaw and Dex Wilson also generously shared their related research and publication work in guest lectures. Most recently, Lyle Goldstein supported my efforts enthusiastically by coteaching the Eurasian maritime history course with me. Mike Pavković generously advised me in the effort to put together the book proposal for the publisher.

Oxford colleague David Bradshaw has been my British intellectual sounding board and sailing partner for decades. Our fellow Oxford housemate Gan Kong Hiok shared my research travels for this book in Japan, Taiwan, Vietnam, Malaysia, Thailand, and Sri Lanka. What could be more satisfying than seeing the world and reflecting on it with such trusted old friends?

Additionally, I would like to acknowledge and thank those who not only assisted me in the academic institutional world, but also those who made my Eurasian field research fascinating and fruitful. U.S. Foreign Service officer Alexander Suderow opened doors and provided guidance in Japan and Oman. U.S. Army Foreign Area officer Dave Wilkinson introduced us to well-informed guides in Indonesia. Scholars Ron

Suleski of Suffolk University and Jonghyun Lee of Bridgewater State University provided guidance for trip planning in Korea and Japan as well as the translation of a sixteenth-century poem by Admiral Yi Sun-sin. Japanese scholar Chihiro Narita and Indian scholar Afzal Ahmed Khan accompanied us on the south coast of Korea.

A Taiwan Fellowship award made it possible for me to spend several months in Taiwan, where I visited the sites of the seventeenth-century Sino-Dutch War. The award was the result of initial contact with Bruce Chen at a Boston University talk discussing East China Sea issues, which led to subsequent contact with the Bos-ton branch of the Taipei Economic and Cultural Office. I am grateful for this support, which enabled me to meet with many scholars, officials, and hosts in Taiwan, including Chun-chieh Huang, Kirill Thompson, Yuming Shaw, Weiping Lin, Yubin Ma, Amanda Liao, Dustin Wang, Chang Liao, Hiroshi Kakazu, Hui-Ming Tsai, Yongwook Ryu, Chi-Ting Tsai, Karyn Wang and her uncle C. T. Chi, J. C. Chang, Ryo Irei, Chou-tien Yao, and Tuo Liu. Their help was essential to the success of my research, and I thank them with gratitude.

Our invaluable guides in India were Sachin Sawant and Swati Gosavi, who traveled with us to sites along the extensive Konkan, Malabar, and Coromandel coasts. They unstintingly shared their deep knowledge, good cheer, and great artistic talent for portraying India's maritime heritage. On the west coast of India, they introduced us to the Mumbai Maritime History Society research and literature and to key scholars including Odakkal Johnson, Oliver Noone, and Ramesh Babu. On the Konkan coast between Mumbai and Goa, they introduced us to current descendants of eighteenth-century Maratha admirals from competing naval clans, Raghujiraje Angre and Amit Raje Dhulap. On the east coast of India, they introduced us to Professors Jayakumar, Neelkantam, and Selvakumar at Tamil University. We were welcomed at the Indian Naval War College in Goa during the festival of Holi by Admiral Monte Khanna and Captains Guarav Mehta and Dhiraj Sareen. I learned much from each of these distinguished students of Indian maritime affairs and am very grateful for both their hospitality and guidance.

I am grateful too for the publisher's acquisition of peer review comments by Bernard Cole and Robert Haddick on the manuscript, which have made this a better book. Naval Institute Press acquisitions editor Glenn Griffith and production editor Brennan Knight have been a pleasure to work with in the process of turning the manuscript into a book.

I have been inordinately blessed by family and friends that not only tolerated my work on this ten-year-long research and writing project, but also grabbed the galley oars and rowed along with me. I especially value the support of my siblings and the keen editorial eye of brother-in-law Peter Brinch. On the home front, my wife Judy was my intrepid and long-suffering travel companion to many remote and difficult corners of Eurasia, where her consistent vivacious social energy created friendships that have endured. Her Arabic skills proved useful not only in the Arabian Sea, but also, amazingly, in both Malta and Xi'an. Her careful work as first, and as last, reviewer of the manuscript has been a profound sustained labor for which I am forever grateful. My daughter Lauren continuously supports and inspires me through both her intellectual and athletic skills, not to mention business acumen, as well as her irrepressible vision and determination. My daughter Jamie has added a wonderful visual dimension to this particular endeavor by creating sixty maps for me to use in teaching Eurasian maritime history, twenty of which appear in this book. I am grateful for her graphic talent, perseverance, and patience in our work together. Judy, Lauren, and Jamie's support and participation in this project have been a source of joy for me. My core thanks and book dedication go to them.

NOTES

INTRODUCTION

1. The characters *yi dai yi lu* (一带一路) are used for the "One Belt One Road" in Chinese, but the preferred English translation "Belt and Road Initiative" better captures the many subroutes that both the land and sea paths follow.
2. Efforts to understand the BRI include the Assessing China's Belt and Road Initiative at Boston University's Pardee School of Global Studies, directed by Grant Rhode, and the Reconnecting Asia project at the Center for Strategic and International Studies in Washington, DC, directed by Jonathan Hillman.
3. Peter Frankopan, *The Silk Roads: A New History of the World* (New York: Vintage Books, 2015).
4. Much of the BRI literature focuses on land-based rather than sea-based dimensions. For a sea-based analysis, a useful work is Richard Griffiths, *The Maritime Silk Road: China's Belt and Road at Sea* (Leiden: International Institute for Asian Studies, 2020).
5. Pope Alexander VI, "Inter Caetera: Division of the Undiscovered World between Spain and Portugal," Papal Encyclicals Online, May 4, 1493.
6. He was also known as Hugo de Groot, a different rendering of his family name, meaning "the great."
7. Hugo Grotius, *Mare Liberum: The Freedom of the Seas, or The Right Which Belongs to the Dutch to Take Part in the East Indian Trade* (Clark, NJ: Law Book Exchange, 2001), 16.
8. Grotius, *Mare Liberum*, 16–75.
9. The Treaties of Tordesillas and Saragossa are discussed in their relation to Grotius' *Mare Liberum* "freedom of the seas" concept in Francois Gipouloux, *The Asian Mediterranean: Port Cities and Trading Networks in China, Japan and Southeast Asia, 13th–21st Century* (Cheltenham, UK: Edward Elgar, 2011), 125.

10. Martine Julia van Ittersum, "The Long Goodbye: Hugo Grotius Justification of Dutch Expansion Overseas, 1615–1645," *History of European Ideas* 36 (2010): 386–411.
11. Van Ittersum, "The Long Goodbye," 406.
12. Van Ittersum, "The Long Goodbye," 407–9.
13. A. T. Mahan, *The Influence of Sea Power upon History, 1660–1783* (New York: Dover Publications, 1987, first published 1890).
14. Information in this section relies on lectures about Mahan by John M. Maurer, current A. T. Mahan Professor of Strategy at the U.S. Naval War College, Newport, RI.
15. Mahan, *The Influence of Sea Power upon History,* 25.
16. Nicholas Lambert, "Classical Theories of Sea Power and World Economic Systems," U.S. Naval War College, EMC Chair Symposium Working Paper, 2017.
17. Mahan, *The Influence of Sea Power upon History*, 26.
18. Mahan, *The Influence of Sea Power upon History*, 28–88.
19. Mahan, *The Influence of Sea Power upon History*, 329.
20. Norman Angell, *The Great Illusion: A Study of the Relation of Military Power to National Advantage* (New York: G. P. Putnam's Sons, 1913); Cornelia Navari, "The International Theory of Norman Angell," *Review of International Studies* 15, no. 4 (Oct. 1989): 341–58.
21. Navari, "The International Theory of Norman Angell," 341–58.
22. Navari, "The International Theory of Norman Angell," 352.
23. Paul Krugman, "The Great Illusion," *New York Times*, Aug. 15, 2008.
24. Halford John Mackinder, *Democratic Ideals and Reality: A Study in the Politics of Reconstruction* (New York: Henry Holt and Company, 1919), 38–89.
25. Halford Mackinder, "The Geographical Pivot of History," *Geographical Journal* XXIII, no. 4 (April 1904): 421–37.
26. Mackinder, *Democratic Ideals and Reality*, 169.
27. Mackinder, *Democratic Ideals and Reality*, 170.
28. Mackinder, *Democratic Ideals and Reality*, 186.
29. Mackinder, *Democratic Ideals and Reality*, 197–99.
30. Mackinder, *Democratic Ideals and Reality*, 171–72.
31. Mackinder, *Democratic Ideals and Reality*, 256.
32. Mackinder, *Democratic Ideals and Reality*, 215.
33. Nicholas John Spykman, *The Geography of the Peace* (New York: Harcourt Brace and Company, 1944), 43. For a map depicting Spykman's view of the rimlands, see map I.1, which also gives more insight about Spykman's work.
34. Nicholas J. Spykman, *America's Strategy in World Politics: The United States and the Balance of Power* (New York: Transaction Publishers, 2008; first published by Harcourt Brace and Company, New York, 1942).
35. Spykman, *The Geography of the Peace*, 41.
36. Spykman, *The Geography of the Peace*, 60–61.

37. See Henry Bergen's review of *The Geography of the Peace: "Geopolitical Fallacies," The New Masses* (June 6, 1944), 26–27. https://www.unz.com/print/NewMasses-1944jun06–00026/.
38. Samuel P. Huntington, "The Clash of Civilizations?," *Foreign Affairs* 72, no. 3 (Summer 1993): 22–49.
39. Samuel P. Huntington, *The Clash of Civilizations and the Remaking of World Order* (New York: Simon & Schuster, 2011; first published 1996).
40. Huntington, "The Clash of Civilizations?," 22.
41. Huntington, *The Clash of Civilizations*, map 1.3, 26–27. Based on a comment by Fernand Braudel, *On History* (Chicago: University of Chicago Press, 1980), 210–11.
42. Kishore Mahbubani coined the phrase "the West and the Rest," Huntington, "The Clash of Civilizations?," 41.
43. Huntington, "The Clash of Civilizations?," 48–49.
44. Huntington, "The Clash of Civilizations?," 49.
45. Huntington, *The Clash of Civilizations*, 321.
46. Huntington, *The Clash of Civilizations*, 209–18.
47. Graham Allison, *Destined for War: Can America and China Escape Thucydides's Trap?* (Boston: Houghton Mifflin Harcourt, 2017). The book expands Allison's earlier article presenting his argument, "The Thucydides Trap: Are the U.S. and China Headed for War?," *The Atlantic*, Sept. 24, 2015.
48. A. F. K. Organski developed his theory of power transition in *World Politics* (New York: Alfred A. Knopf, 1958).
49. Allison, *Destined for War*, 215.
50. Allison, *Destined for War*, 286.
51. Allison, *Destined for War*, 287. Regarding the question of missing cases, Allison adds that "The Thucydides' Trap Case File is incomplete" and "is open" since the publication of *The Atlantic* article (2015) presenting a preview of the book's argument.
52. John Maurer, "Thucydides and the Tragedy of Athens: A Parable for America," *Foreign Policy Research Institute*, June 26, 2017. https://www.fpri.org/article/2017/06/thucydides-tragedy-athens-parable-america/.
53. Ian Buruma, "Dance with the Dragon: Are the United States and China on a Collision Course?," *The New Yorker*, June 19, 2017, 61–65.
54. Jeremy Black, ed., *Great Military Leaders and Their Campaigns* (London: Thames & Hudson, 2008), 8–11. Suleyman, 108–11; Hideyoshi, 124–31; Peter the Great, 152–57.
55. Black, *Great Military Leaders and Their Campaigns*, Nelson, 192–97; Togo, 234–37; Nimitz, 274–79.
56. For a consideration of the great man explanation of history versus a complex adaptive system theory in Asia, see Sanjeev Sanyal, *The Ocean of Churn: How the Indian Ocean Shaped Human History* (New Delhi: Random House India, 2016), 11.

CHAPTER 1. CHOLA MARITIME EXPANSION TO THE GANGES, SRI LANKA, AND SRIVIJAYA

1. A. Yudhistira, trans., *Borobudur and Temples of Java* (Borobudur: Aiaz Rajasa, 2017), 1, 14.
2. K. M. Panikkar, *India and the Indian Ocean: An Essay on the Influence of Sea Power on Indian History* (London: George Allen & Unwin, 1951), 19.
3. The broad role of the Indian Ocean in history is lucidly presented by Sanjeev Sanyal in *The Ocean of Churn: How the Indian Ocean Shaped World History* (Haryana, India: Penguin Random House India, 2016). For the pre-Chola trade period, see 39–130.
4. A periplus is a logbook record of sailing itineraries containing commercial, political, and cultural details of voyages. The Erythraean Sea was the Greek name for the Indian Ocean.
5. B. Arunachalam, "Navigation Environment of Ports of Indus Valley Civilization," in *Essays in Maritime Studies Vol. III*, ed. Sachin Pendse and Odakkal Johnson (Mumbai: Maritime History Society, 2016), 3–10.
6. Joseph Needham, *Science and Civilization in China, Volume IV:3* (Cambridge: Cambridge University Press, 1971), 583.
7. Panikkar, *India and the Indian Ocean*, 27.
8. Sanyal eloquently tells the story in *The Ocean of Churn*, 82–102.
9. A thalassocracy is a state with primarily maritime realms that controls power by using the sea, literally a "sea power" from the Greek *thalassa* "sea" and *kratien* "power."
10. Coedes uses the term Indianized States in the title of his seminal work on the subject. G. Coedes, *The Indianized States of Southeast Asia*, trans. Susan Brown Cowing (Honolulu: University of Hawai'i Press, 1968).
11. Paul Michel Munoz, *Early Kingdoms of the Indonesian Archipelago and the Malay Peninsula* (Singapore: Editions Didier Millet, 2006).
12. Coedes, *The Indianized States of Southeast Asia.*
13. N. Susanti, T. Pudjastuti, and D. Trigangga, eds., *Inscribing Identity: The Development of Indonesian Writing Systems* (Jakarta: National Museum of Indonesia, 2015), 116–20.
14. D. G. E. Hall, *A History of Southeast Asia*, 4th ed. (London: Macmillan, 1981), 47–73.
15. Tansen Sen, "The Travel Records of Chinese Pilgrims Faxian, Xuanzong, and Yijing," *Education About Asia* 11, no. 3 (Winter 2006), 24–33.
16. Hall, *A History of Southeast Asia*, 64.
17. Lo Jung-pang, *China as a Sea Power 1127–1368: A Preliminary Survey of the Maritime Expansion and Naval Exploits of the Chinese People during the Southern Song and Yuan Periods*, ed. Bruce A. Elleman (Singapore: National University of Singapore Press, 2012), 129–208.
18. B. Arunachalam, *Chola Navigation Package* (Mumbai: Maritime History Society, 2004), 20.
19. B. Arunachalam, *Indian Boat Designs and Forms* (Mumbai: Maritime History Society, 2009), 82–93.

20. Arunachalam, *Indian Boat Designs and Forms*, 82–83.
21. Arunachalam, *Chola Navigation Package*, 79–99.
22. Arunachalam, *Chola Navigation Package*, 25.
23. Rajaraja is used here to refer to Rajaraja Chola I, and Rajendra is used to refer to Rajendra Chola I. Subsequent leaders of the Chola use the same names but are distinguished by the suffixes II and III.
24. Sanyal, *The Ocean of Churn*, 132–33.
25. The account here relies primarily on the thin material evidence, mostly Tamil temple inscriptions with a Chola point of view, about Chola relations with Srivijaya, including Rajendra's maritime missions there, which has been collated and analyzed into a coherent picture in Hermann Kulke, K. Kesavapany, and Vijay Sakhuja, eds., *Nagapattinam to Suvarnadwipa: Reflections on the Chola Naval Expeditions to Southeast Asia* (Singapore: Institute of Southeast Asian Studies, 2009).
26. Panikkar in *India and the Indian Ocean*, 34, refers to this as a "nearly 100 years" naval rivalry.
27. In addition to his temple, coins commemorated the reign of Rajaraja.
28. The three temples are known as the "Great Living Chola Temples."
29. In this work, the term "national identities" is not used in the context of modern nationalism in which popular sovereignty of the people is associated with the nation-state and its geography. Instead, it is used to indicate pride of place and common loyalties to an ethnic polity that played a key role in one of these conflicts.
30. Hall, *A History of Southeast Asia*, 73

CHAPTER 2. LIMITS ON MONGOL MARITIME EXPANSION TO JAPAN, VIETNAM, AND JAVA

1. Annam and Champa are roughly the areas of current northern and central Vietnam, respectively.
2. Typhoon is one of the few words in English borrowed from Chinese. In Chinese, *tai feng* means "greatest wind" or "supreme wind."
3. *Kamikaze* (神風 "divine wind") may be pronounced either as *kamikaze or shinpu*. *Shinpu* is closer to the Chinese pinyin pronunciation of these characters, *shen feng*.
4. Accounts containing more detail on Mongol continental expansion include Jack Weatherford, *Genghis Khan and the Making of the Modern World* (New York: Broadway Books, 2004); Paul Khan, *The Secret History of the Mongols: The Origins of Chingis Khan* (translation of a thirteenth-century account) (San Francisco: North Point Press, 1984); and Robert W. Strayer and Eric Nelson, *Ways of the World: A Brief Global History with Sources*, 4th ed. (Boston: Bedford/St. Martin's, 2019), 520–67.
5. For an account of Korea's Three Kingdoms period and relations with the Japanese, see Nakaba Yamada, *Ghenko: The Mongol Invasions of Japan 1274–81* (London: Leonaur, 2012), 15–31.
6. Lo Jung-pang, *China as a Sea Power 1127–1368: A Preliminary Survey of the Maritime Expansion and Naval Exploits of the Chinese People during*

the Southern Song and Yuan Periods, ed. Bruce A. Elleman (Singapore: National University of Singapore Press, 2012), 48–54.

7. Lo, *China as a Sea Power*, 54.
8. These sections on the Mongols in Korea and Japan rely on Grant Rhode, "Mongol Invasions of Northeast Asia: Korea and Japan." This online supplement case study accompanied "China, Global History, and the Sea: Pedagogical Perspectives and Applications," by Grant Rhode, lead author, with coauthors Thomas Kennelly, Eytan Goldstein, William Grimes, Eugenio Menegon, and Robert Murowchick, in Association for Asian Studies, *Education About Asia* 25, no. 2 (Fall 2020). Portions here are reprinted with permission of the Association for Asian Studies, Inc., www.asianstudies.org/EAA.
9. Ishii Susumu, "The Decline of the Kamakura Bakufu," in *The Cambridge History of Japan, Vol. 3: Medieval Japan*, ed. Kozo Yamamura (Cambridge: Cambridge University Press, 1990), 131–35. A translation of Kubilai's letter to the Kamakura *bakufu* is included.
10. Lo, *China as a Sea Power*, 254.
11. Masan Bay is sometimes called Happo Bay.
12. Lo, *China as a Sea Power*, 252–59.
13. Lo, *China as a Sea Power*, 260–79.
14. A picul equals approximately sixty kilograms, as much as a man could carry on a pole.
15. Lo, *China as a Sea Power*, 271.
16. Chinese dynasties exerted power over Vietnam for much of the past two thousand years.
17. *Some Historic Battles in Vietnam* (Vietnam: The Gioi Publishers, 2013), 37–64.
18. *Some Historic Battles in Vietnam*, 1–10.
19. Kawazoe Shoji, "Japan and East Asia," in *The Cambridge History of Japan, Vol. 3: Medieval Japan*, ed. Kozo Yamamura (Cambridge: Cambridge University Press, 1990), 419–20.
20. Lo, *China as a Sea Power*, 323–43.
21. Sun Tzu, *The Art of War*, trans. Samuel B. Griffith (Oxford: Oxford University Press, 1963), 124–40.
22. A. T. Mahan, *The Influence of Sea Power upon History 1660–1783* (New York: Dover Publications, 1987), 25–89 (based on fifth edition, 1894, originally published 1890).
23. Carl von Clausewitz, *On War*, trans. Michael Howard and Pater Paret (Princeton, NJ: Princeton University Press, 1976), 100–112.
24. Clausewitz, *On War*, 85.
25. Sun Tzu, *The Art of War*, 129.
26. Yamada, *Ghenko*, 11–12.

CHAPTER 3. EARLY MING VOYAGES TO THE WESTERN OCEAN

1. For lucid, informed accounts of Zheng He's voyages, including descriptions of his ships, see Edward Dreyer, *Zheng He: China and the Oceans in the Early Ming Dynasty, 1405–1433* (New York: Pearson Longman,

2006); and Louise Levathes, *When China Ruled the Seas: The Treasure Fleet of the Dragon Throne, 1405–1433* (Oxford: Oxford University Press, 1994), 80. For an article-length account, see Yang Wei, "Admiral Zheng He's Voyages to the 'West Ocean,'" *Education About Asia* 19, no. 2 (Fall 2014): 26–30.

2. See the rudder discussion in Joseph Needham, *Science and Civilization in China*, vol. 4: *Physics and Physical Technology*, Part III: *Civil Engineering and Nautics* (Cambridge: Cambridge University Press, 1971), 481.
3. Detailed arguments with counterarguments and citations for the shorter length are put forward by Sally Church, "Zheng He: An Investigation into the Plausibility of 450-ft Treasure Ships," *Monumenta Serica* 53 (2005), 1–43.
4. Dreyer, *Zheng He*, 113.
5. Lo Jung-pang, *China as a Sea Power 1127–1368: A Preliminary Survey of the Maritime Expansion and Naval Exploits of the Chinese People During the Southern Song and Yuan Periods* (Singapore: National University of Singapore Press, 2012), 342–43.
6. Ming sea power extending later than voyages of Zheng He is a point made by Professor Andrew Wilson in lectures at the US Naval War College.
7. Zhu Di is the given name, while Yongle is the reign name.
8. Dreyer, *Zheng He*, and Levathes, *When China Ruled the Seas*, are good works to consult for overviews of Zheng He, both with much interesting detail.
9. For Dreyer's translation of the Changle inscription, see Dreyer, *Zheng He*, 195–99.
10. For Dreyer's translation of the Liujiagang inscription, see Dreyer, *Zheng He*, 191–94.
11. For a translation of the Galle inscription, see E. Backhouse in *Spolia Zeylanica*, accessed May 31, 2022, https://sangam.org/wp-content/uploads/2020/09/TRILINGUAL-INSCRIPTION.pdf. The Galle inscription is trilingual, written in Chinese, Tamil, and Persian. It is assumed to have been carved in China in 1409 and placed on the south coast of Sri Lanka during Zheng He's third voyage.
12. For a translation of this biography of Zheng He in the *Ming Shi* by Edward Dreyer, see Dreyer, *Zheng He*, 187–91.
13. Suzerainty implies a tributary relationship with a greater power that controls foreign relations while the vassal controls internal affairs.
14. Gavin Menzies, *1421: The Year China Discovered the World* (London: Bantam Books, 2002).
15. Ma Huan, *Ying-Yai Sheng-Lan: "The Overall Survey of the Ocean's Shores (1433),"* introduction and notes by J. V. G. Mills (Cambridge: Cambridge Univer-sity Press, 1970), published for the Hakluyt Society.
16. Ma Huan, *Ying-Yai Sheng-Lan*, 35–36.
17. Tan Ta Sen, *Cheng Ho and Malaya* (published jointly by Singapore: International Zheng He Society and Melaka: Cheng Ho Cultural Museum, 2014), 73–86.
18. Geoff Wade, "The Zheng He Voyages: A Reassessment," *MBRAS: The Malaysian Branch of the Royal Asiatic Society* 78, no. 1 (2005): 38.

19. See Wade, "The Zheng He Voyages," 47–59, for more details about this point of view and the three examples given here regarding "major military actions."
20. Dreyer, *Zheng He*, 50.
21. Dreyer, *Zheng He*, 67–70.
22. Wade, "The Zheng He Voyages," 50.
23. Dreyer, *Zheng He*, 79–81.
24. Wade, "The Zheng He Voyages," 50.
25. Wade, "The Zheng He Voyages," 49–51.
26. Beiping, "northern peace," became Beijing, or the "northern capital," when the city officially became the Ming capital in 1521, replacing Nanjing, the "southern capital."
27. John King Fairbank, *The Chinese World Order: Traditional Chinese Foreign Relations* (Cambridge, MA: Harvard University Press, 1968). In this study, Fairbank used the term "tributary system" to describe China's foreign relations, especially during the Ming and Qing Dynasty periods.

CHAPTER 4. KUNJALI MARAKKAR NAVAL RESISTANCE TO THE PORTUGUESE ON THE MALABAR COAST

1. Vegetable fiber was more durable than iron in salt water, but hulls were less stiff and solid than later European metal-fastened hulls.
2. See Venetian Marco Polo's account of Calicut during his return from China via sea to India and Persia, and the later accounts of Calicut by Moroccan Ibn Battuta and by Chinese Ma Huan, Zheng He's chronicler of the fourth, sixth, and seventh of Zheng He's seven voyages.
3. For this remarkable story, see Roger Crowley, *Conquerors: How Portugal Forged the First Global Empire* (New York: Random House, 2015), xix–xxv, 3–49.
4. Crowley, *Conquerors*, 85–134; Gaspar Correa, *The Three Voyages of Vasco da Gama, and His Viceroyalty* (Brookline, MA: Adamant Media Corporation, 2001). Facsimile reprint of an 1869 edition by the Hakluyt Society, London.
5. Crowley, *Conquerors*, 160.
6. Sebastian R. Prange, "'Measuring by the Bushel': Weighing the Indian Ocean Pepper Trade," Institute of Historical Research, University of London School of Advanced Study, *Historical Research* 84, no. 224 (May 2011), 219–20.
7. Prange, "Measuring by the Bushel," 229–30.
8. K. M. Panikkar, *India and the Indian Ocean: An Essay on the Influence of Sea Power on Indian History* (London: George Allen & Unwin, 1945), 43.
9. Panikkar, *India and the Indian Ocean*, 41.
10. Peter Padfield, *Tide of Empires: Decisive Naval Campaigns in the Rise of the West: Volume One: 1481–1654* (London: Routledge & Kegan Paul, 1979), 49–53. See also Oliver Noone, "Changes in Technology and War Tactics: Reinterpreting the Naval Battle of Calicut, 1503" (unpublished paper, 2017), 20–25.

11. This made it possible to sail due north, as Sodre and da Gama had to do to hold their course per the chart of the 1503 battle.
12. Padfield, *Tide of Empires*, 52.
13. Padfield, *Tide of Empires*, 62–63.
14. Panikkar, *India and the Indian Ocean*, 43.
15. Crowley, *Conquerors*, 123–323. Auguste Toussaint, *History of the Indian Ocean*, trans. June Guicharnaud (Chicago: University of Chicago Press, 1966).
16. See Crowley, *Conquerors*, 119–20; K. S. Mathew, "Trade in the India Ocean and the Portuguese System of Cartaz," in *The First Portuguese Colonial Empire*, ed. Malyn Newitt (Exeter, UK: A. Wheaton & Co. Ltd., 1986).
17. O. K. Nambiar, *The Kunjalis: Admirals of Calicut* (New York: Asia Publishing House, 1963), 75.
18. The fort is a remnant of what it once was, but a diorama of the fort layout in juxtaposition to the waterways gives a clear idea of the protected and defensible situation of the sixteenth-century fort.
19. At the beginning of each of the text sections of the four Kunjali Marakkar, a quote appears in italics. These quotes are the inscriptions for each of the Kunjali Marakkar on the stone memorial column in the garden of the Kunjali Marakkar Museum. The museum is the former location of the Kunjali Marakkar fort in Iringal north of Calicut, visited by the author in March 2017. Dates on the text headings vary between those included here from the memorial stela, and a range of dates included in the literary accounts.
20. Nambiar, *The Kunjalis*, 77.
21. Nambiar, *The Kunjalis*, 77.
22. The zamorin passed away in 1522 but was succeeded by another leader without disruption of the Kunjali Marakkars's attention to the coastal trade.
23. Nambiar, *The Kunjalis*, 79.
24. Nambiar, *The Kunjalis*, 80.
25. Nambiar, *The Kunjalis*, 84–91.
26. Nambiar, *The Kunjalis*, 96–101.
27. Nambiar, *The Kunjalis*, 109–11.
28. Nambiar, *The Kunjalis*, 111.
29. See Nambiar, *The Kunjalis*, viii–ix. Nambiar translates *Kunjali* as "Ali, the beloved," making a parallel to the affectionate term *amigo*; he translates *Marakkar* as "navigator of ships."
30. Nambiar, *The Kunjalis*, 114.
31. Nambiar, *The Kunjalis*, 118.
32. Prange, "Measuring by the Bushel."
33. Dan Gauvin, "Kunjali Marakkar and the Malabar Spice Trade" (unpublished paper, Newport, RI, U.S. Naval War College), 2017. Gauvin points out that the Kunjali legacy was not only one of resistance, but also of perseverance.
34. Details about the stamp may be found at http://www.istampgallery.com/kunjali-marakkar/.
35. For instance, see the film *Marakkar: Lion of the Arabian Sea*, 2020.

CHAPTER 5. LIMITS ON THE OTTOMAN NAVY IN THE MEDITERRANEAN SEA

1. Jakub Grygiel develops the idea of these maritime theaters in his chapter "Ottoman Sea Power and the Decline of the Mediterranean World," in *China Goes to Sea: Maritime Transformations in Comparative Historical Perspective*, ed. A. Erickson, L. Goldstein, and C. Lord (Annapolis, MD: Naval Institute Press, 2009), 90–119.
2. A study that examines Ottoman naval power after Lepanto is Daniel Panzac's *The Ottoman Navy: From the Height of Empire to Dissolution, 1572–1923*, trans. Peter R. Gillespie (Oxford: Oxford University Press, 2020).
3. Lateen sails are triangular sails on a long yard at an angle of about 45 degrees to the mast.
4. The Knights of St. John, known as the Knights Hospitaller during the Crusades for their care of the sick and wounded in Jerusalem, subsequently were also known as the Knights of Rhodes and the Knights of Malta, due to these islands being their primary homes for a period of almost five hundred years, from 1310 to 1798.
5. Methoni is also known as Modon; Coroni is also known as Coron.
6. Also known as the battle of Sapienza for the nearby island or the first battle of Lepanto for the fortified town.
7. E. Brockman, *The Two Sieges of Rhodes: The Knights of St. John at War, 1480–1522* (New York: Barnes & Noble, 1996), 29–37. He provides a fine description of the island in general terms and the port, harbor, and fortifications in more detail.
8. Brockman, *The Two Sieges of Rhodes*, 111–59. Brockman describes in detail the second siege of Rhodes.
9. The walls still stand and are preserved as a UNESCO World Heritage site. A dry moat surrounds the walls, making a walk around the walls easy as well as instructive.
10. Langues were named for the various European languages that the Knights spoke.
11. Brockman, *The Two Sieges of Rhodes,* 123–55. He includes details of Tadini and 1522 siege proceedings.
12. Charles V granted Malta, to the Knights of St. John in exchange for an annual gift of a live falcon.
13. Accounts of the naval battle of Preveza appear in Ernle Bradford, *The Sultan's Admiral: Pirate and Empire Builder* (London: Tauris Parke Paperbacks, 2009), 161–85; and Crowley quotes the chronicler Katip Chelebi.
14. For a detailed account of the dramatic sequence of the siege of Malta, see Ernle Bradford, *The Great Siege: Malta, 1565: Clash of Cultures, Christian Knights Defend Western Civilization Against the Moslem Tide* (London: Open Road Integrated Media, 2014), and his translation of Francisco Balbi di Corregio's eyewitness account as a soldier fighting for the Knights from the Spanish edition of 1568, in *The Siege of Malta, 1565* (London: Boydell Press, 2011). Another useful account of the siege wrapped into the larger story of the sixteenth-century Mediterranean is in Roger Crowley,

Empires of the Sea: The Siege of Malta, the Battle of Lepanto, and the Contest for the Center of the World (New York: Random House, 2008), 85–187. For helpful summary maps of the siege sequence, see Tim Pickles, *Malta: 1565: Last Battle of the Crusades* (London: Osprey, 1998).

15. Janissaries were elite Ottoman infantry troops, including the sultan's bodyguard, created from a slave corps of kidnapped Christian boys forcibly converted to Islam. They were noted for their discipline including celibacy, cohesion, and loyalty to the sultan.
16. Lepanto, the Venetian name, is called Nafpaktos in Greek. Much has been written on the Battle of Lepanto, and accounts vary; the summary here draws from these works. See Notis Botzaris, *The Battle of Lepanto* (Athens: Demetrius and Egle Botzaris Foundation, 2001). Other detailed accounts include Hugh Bicheno, *Crescent and Cross: The Battle of Lepanto 1571* (London: Phoenix Orion Books, 2004), and Niccolo Capponi, *Victory of the West: The Great Christian-Muslim Clash at the Battle of Lepanto* (Cambridge, MA: DaCapo Press, 2006).
17. Lepanto was an Ottoman naval station at the time of the battle in 1571, and the battle was fought about thirty-one miles west of the fortified town of Lepanto, near Oxia Island and Scrofa Point at the opposite end of the Gulf of Patras.
18. Fleet numbers vary slightly in the sources.
19. Grandnephew of noted admiral Andrea Doria.
20. Barbarossa is often remembered in the West as a "pirate" rather than as the chief naval officer of a major world power. Ernle Bradford offers the alternative point of view of Barbarossa as an admiral in *The Sultan's Admiral* (2009), the best twentieth-century biography of Barbarossa in English. A fine nineteenth-century sketch of Barbarossa's life appears in Edward Creasy, *History of the Ottoman Turks*, originally published in 1878 (reissued by Beirut: Khayats, 1968), 173–78.
21. Oruc is also Romanized as Aruj in the literature. Khizr is sometimes Romanized as Khidr or Hizir.
22. Hayreddin is Romanized many other ways in the literature, including Heyreddin, Kheir-ed-Din, etc.
23. Bradford, *The Sultan's Admiral*, 77–78.
24. Reis is a title equivalent to captain.
25. The name Barbarossa used here should not be confused with Frederick Barbarossa, Holy Roman Emperor Frederick I, or Operation Barbarossa, the Axis invasion of the Soviet Union during World War II.
26. See the early chapters of Bradford, *The Sultan's Admiral*, for details on this encounter and Oruc's remarkable career.
27. Moriscos were former Muslims who converted or were coerced into converting to Christianity, after Spain finally outlawed the open practice of Islam by its sizable Muslim population in the early sixteenth century.
28. Ilyas and Ishak are sometimes Romanized as Elias and Isaac.
29. *Beylerbey*: In Ottoman usage, where the rank survived the longest, it designated the governors-general of some of the largest and most important provinces, although in later centuries it became devalued into a mere honorific title.

30. Corsair is a term usually given to pirates on the south coast of the Mediterranean between the sixteenth and eighteenth centuries.
31. Also known as Turgut Reis.
32. Bradford, *The Sultan's Admiral*, 146.
33. For instance, George Leonardos, a Greek journalist, has portrayed Barbarossa primarily as a pirate in his recent historical novel *Barbarossa: The Pirates*, 2nd ed. (Scotts Valley, CA: CreateSpace Independent Publishing Platform, 2018).
34. Bradford, *The Sultan's Admiral*, 185.
35. Bradford, *The Sultan's Admiral*, 123–29.
36. "Turkish Navy Revives 500-Year-Old Salute for Renowned Ottoman Sailor Barbarossa," *Daily Sabah Istanbul*, Sept. 3, 2019, accessed May 31, 2022, https://www.dailysabah.com/istanbul/2019/03/09/turkish-navy-revives-500-year-old-salute-for-renowned-ottoman-sailor-barbarossa.

CHAPTER 6. JAPAN'S THWARTED MARITIME INVASIONS OF KOREA

1. Because Hideyoshi died a premature death in 1598 and further civil leadership struggles ensued, the closing date of Japan's warring states period is considered to be 1600, the year that Tokugawa Ieyasu assumed leadership after the Battle of Sekigahara.
2. Qin, in pinyin romanization, is pronounced Chin in English. Thus, the name "China" comes from Emperor Qin's name, as does the name of the short-lived Qin Dynasty (221–206 BCE).
3. So clan residences and tombs can still be visited in Tsushima. A shrine to Konishi's daughter, wife of the So clan head, remains well-tended in Izuhara.
4. Chong Pal's memorial statue now stands next to the Japanese consulate in Pusan. His concubine committed suicide next to his dead body.
5. Given names are used in this description rather than clan names, following the more usual use of Hideyoshi rather than Toyotomi for Toyotomi Hideyoshi.
6. Tongnae (Dongnae) contains the Chungryolsa (Chungnyeolsa) Shrine, established to soothe the souls of Koreans who died during the invasion.
7. Named locations on the routes may be found on map 6.2.
8. The Imjin War, the Korean name for the war, refers to a calendar date, not the Imjin River. This discussion of the Imjin War relies heavily on three works based on Chinese, Korean, and Japanese sources, respectively: Kenneth Swope, *A Dragon's Head and a Serpent's Tail: Ming China and the First Great Asian War, 1592–1598* (Norman: University of Oklahoma Press, 2009); Samuel Hawley, *The Imjin War: Japan's Sixteenth Century Invasion of Korea and Attempt to Conquer China* (Seoul: Conquistador Press, 2014); and Stephen Turnbull, *The Samurai Invasion of Korea, 1592–1598* (Oxford: Osprey Publishing, 2008).
9. One report also mentions that 40,000 Jurchens under Nurhaci had joined the Chinese and Koreans during the siege of Pyongyang.

10. *Wajo* are Japanese defensive fortresses built in the Japanese style with heavy stone foundations.
11. A useful discussion of the *wajo* is undertaken by Stephen Turnbull, *Japanese Castles in Korea 1592–98* (Oxford: Osprey, 2007).
12. Swope, *A Dragon's Head*, 273.
13. Unpublished translation of poem by Dr. Jonghyun Lee.
14. Proof of a Korean death required that a Korean head be brought back to Japan. Due to the size of the cargo, the requirement was reduced to a nose or an ear.
15. Disease played a major role, up to half of the deaths in the American Revolution according to some estimates.
16. Jo Seong-do, *Admiral Yi Sun-sin: A National Hero of Korea* (Seoul: Naval Academy Museum and Sinseowon, 2005), 227.
17. Yi Sun-sin, *Nanjung Ilgi: The War Diaries of Admiral Yi*, trans. Tae-hung Ha (Seoul: Yonsei University Press, 1977), 117.
18. Mearsheimer argues that the presence of oceans in the world prevents any state from achieving world hegemony. John Mearsheimer, *The Tragedy of Great Power Politics* (New York: W. W. Norton, 2001).
19. Saeyoung Park, "National Heroes and Monuments in South Korea: Patriotism, Modernization, and Park Chung Hee's Remaking of Yi Sunsin's Shrine," *Asia-Pacific Journal* 8, no. 24 (Article ID 3374, June 14, 2010), 1–27, https://apjjf.org/-Saeyoung-Park/3374/article.html.

CHAPTER 7. MING EXPULSION OF THE DUTCH FROM TAIWAN

1. Alternatively spelled as Coxinga, western pronunciation of Guoxingye (pinyin) "he of the royal surname."
2. In this war, the Ming achieved strategic victory over the Dutch by taking control of the island of Taiwan. Although the Chinese later had a tactical victory over the French in the Battle of Zhennan Pass in Guangdong in March 1885, the results of the Sino-French War of 1884–1885 did not result in a strategic Chinese victory, as it included Chinese naval losses at Fuzhou and unfavorable peace terms that included ceding control of the Gulf of Tonkin to France.
3. The Treaties of Tordesillas and Saragossa are discussed in their relation to Grotius' *Mare Liberum* "freedom of the seas" concept in Francois Gipouloux, *The Asian Mediterranean: Port Cities and Trading Networks in China, Japan and Southeast Asia, 13th–21st Century* (Cheltenham, UK: Edward Elgar, 2011), 125.
4. Gipouloux, *The Asian Mediterranean*, 126–37.
5. Warren I. Cohen discusses European engagement with the Japanese in *East Asia at the Center: Four Thousand Years of Engagement with the World* (New York: Columbia University Press, 2000), 194–200.
6. Substantial remains of Forts Zeelandia and Provintia are in Tainan. For those interested in the European-Ming saga, they are worth visiting, as are the fort in Danshui and the fort that remains in Jilong.

7. English accounts worth consulting on the Sino-Dutch War include Tonio Andrade, *Lost Colony: The Untold Story of China's First Great Victory Over the West* (Princeton, NJ: Princeton University Press, 2011); Jonathan Clements, *Coxinga and the Fall of the Ming Dynasty* (Gloucestershire: Sutton Publishing, 2004); Ralph Crozier, *Koxinga and Chinese Nationalism: History, Myth, and the Hero* (Cambridge, MA: Harvard University Press, 1977); Xing Hang, *Conflict and Commerce in Maritime East Asia: The Zheng Family and the Shaping of the Modern World, c. 1620–1720* (Cambridge: Cambridge University Press, 2016; Donald Keene, *The Battles of Coxinga: Chikamatsu's Puppet Play, Its Background and Importance* (London: Taylor's Foreign Press, 1951).
8. Andrade, *Lost Colony*, 86.
9. Hang, *Conflict and Commerce in Maritime East Asia*, 121.
10. Keene, *The Battles of Coxinga*, 52.
11. For a description of the Qing coastal prohibitions, see Michael Szonyi, *Practicing Kinship: Lineage and Descent in Late Imperial China* (Stanford, CA: Stanford University Press, 2002), 81.
12. The name Formosa, "beautiful" in Portuguese, was chosen by early Portuguese seafarers sailing the east coast of the island, where spectacular wooded mountains plunge into the sea. The name Taiwan comes from Tai Bay, the body of water where the Dutch settled on the west coast in 1624. The name was eventually taken to designate the entire island, not just the bay. Bay is pronounced *wan* in Chinese.
13. Tonio Andrade has persuasively argued the thesis that the Dutch as administrators and the Chinese as merchants and farmers co-colonized Taiwan during the 1620s through 1650s in *How Taiwan Became Chinese: Dutch, Spanish, and Han Colonization in the Seventeenth Century* (New York: Columbia University Press, 2009).
14. Hang, *Conflict and Commerce in Maritime East Asia*, 132–37.
15. Andrade, *Lost Colony*, 204.
16. Andrade, *Lost Colony*, 228. Andrade provides a defectors' graph showing many more defectors to the Dutch side between August and October 1661, and more defectors to the Chinese side between November 1661, and January 1662.
17. Hang, *Conflict and Commerce in Maritime East Asia*, 146–230. See the analysis of Zheng market share in Hang, *Conflict and Commerce in Maritime East Asia*, 263–94.
18. More details of the 1683 battle of Penghu are in Hang, *Conflict and Commerce in Maritime East Asia*, 230–34.
19. Michael Szonyi, *Cold War Island: Quemoy on the Front Line* (Cambridge: Cambridge University Press, 2008), 64–78.
20. For sailing toward the wind under various sailing rigs, including Chinese junks, see Joseph Needham, *Science and Civilization in China*, Vol. IV:3 (Cambridge: Cambridge University Press, 1971), 588–620. Also see C. R. G. Worcester, *The Junks and Sampans of the Yangtze* (Annapolis, MD: Naval Institute Press, 1971).

21. Malacca is more usually spelled Melaka in Malaysia.
22. Hang, *Conflict and Commerce in Maritime East Asia*, 244. Xing Hang's thorough study of the Zhengs, especially the detailed appendices with relative Zheng organization and VOC trade and revenue figures, challenge Eurocentric views of seventeenth-century international business.
23. See Ralph Crozier's review of primary sources in chapter 2 of *Koxinga*, 6–11.
24. Sunzi is also romanized as Sun Tzu.
25. Hang, *Conflict and Commerce in Maritime East Asia*, 99.
26. Andrade, *Lost Colony*, 301, 393. Some accounts say that the baby survived and was a candidate for succession in the early 1680s.
27. June 23 is often given as his date of death, although there is confusion between lunar and Gregorian accounts.
28. For more specific discussion of possible causes of death, see Andrade, *Lost Colony*, 301–2, or Keene, *The Battles of Coxinga*, 69–73.
29. Clements, *Coxinga*, 255–59.
30. Keene, *The Battles of Coxinga*, 1–2.
31. See statistics comparing the VOC with the Zheng firm in Hang, *Conflict and Commerce in Maritime East Asia*, 263–94, app. 3.
32. Crozier, *Koxinga*, 19. He points out that it is an irony of history that Koxinga's last campaign was forced on him due to his failure to oust the Ming from Nanjing, yet this campaign became "his only lasting historical achievement."
33. Jeremy E. Taylor, "The Production of the Chiang Kai-Shek Personality Cult, 1929–1975," *China Quarterly* 185 (March 2006): 96–110.

CHAPTER 8. MARATHA NAVAL RESISTANCE TO THE BRITISH ON THE KONKAN COAST

1. *Sarkhel*, a Marathi word, is usually translated as admiral.
2. The Malabar coast is the coastal area of present-day Kerala and Karnataka, and the Konkan coast is the coastal area of present-day Maharashtra, sometimes configured as overlapping with the Malabar coast in Karnataka.
3. See Stewart Gordon, "The Marathas, 1600–1818," in *The New Cambridge History of India* (Cambridge: Cambridge University Press, 1993); C. A. Kincaid and D. B. Parasnis, *A History of the Maratha People*, vol. I (London: Henry Milford, 1919); A. R. Kulkarni, *The Marathas (1600–1848)* (Delhi: Books and Books, 1996); G. S. Sardesai, *New History of the Marathas*, vol. I (Bombay: Phoenix Publications, 1946).
4. B. K. Apte, *A History of the Maratha Navy and Merchant Ships* (Bombay: State Board for Literature and Culture, 1973), 71–73. K. M. Panikkar, *India and the Indian Ocean: An Essay on the Influence of Sea Power on Indian History* (London: George Allen & Unwin, 1951), 59, cites Shivaji's contributions to Indian naval development.
5. Philip MacDougall, *Naval Resistance to Britain's Growing Power in India, 1660–1800: The Saffron Banner and the Tiger of Mysore* (Woodbridge, Suffolk, UK: Boydell Press, 2014), 46–47. The transfer of Bombay from Portugal to Britain was part of the dowry of Catherine of Braganza, daughter of King John IV of Portugal, who married Charles II, king of England, in 1661.

6. Eugenia Vanina, *Medieval Indian Mindscapes: Space, Time, Society, Man* (New Delhi: Primus Books, 2012), and Eugenia Vanina, "Mughal Maratha Wars (1659–1707)," in *War and Religion: An Encyclopedia of Faith and Conflict, Volume 2*, ed. Jeffrey Shaw and Timothy Demy (Santa Barbara, CA: ABC_CLIO, LLC), 571–74.
7. M. S. Naravane, *The Heritage Sites of Maritime Maharashtra* (Mumbai: Maritime History Society, 2001) provides sketches, photographs, maps, and stories about Maharashtra's sea forts. Amit Chilka, *Sea Forts of India* (Osmora Inc., eBook Publisher, 2014), available on Google, Apple, and other sites, describes India's remarkable stock of one hundred thirty sea forts along the east coast, and thirty sea forts along the west coast.
8. The Dutch Palace now serves as a museum, with displays of seventeenth-century life in Kochi.
9. MacDougall, *Naval Resistance*, 21.
10. MacDougall, *Naval Resistance*, 30.
11. This impressive structure was never taken from the Siddis by force, despite many attempts. The Siddis were Abyssinian Muslims who came to India, some as slaves, as early as the seventh century.
12. Apte, *A History of the Maratha Navy*, 62.
13. Apte, *A History of the Maratha Navy*, 18.
14. For an account of Shivaji's wresting of Khanderi from the Bombay Marine allied with Siddi forces, see MacDougall, *Naval Resistance*, 55–59.
15. Apte, *A History of the Maratha Navy*, 76.
16. Manohar Malgonkar, *The Sea Hawk: Life and Battles of Kanhoji Angrey* (New Delhi: Orient Paperbacks, 1979), 208–9.
17. Malgonkar, *The Sea Hawk*, 210–16.
18. Kolaba means "sea-land," an appropriate name for places where the land meets the sea. Kolaba is often also spelled Colaba.
19. Apte, *A History of the Maratha Navy*, 18. Apte includes an instructive schematic map of the Kolaba region drawn during the eighteenth-century period of Angre dominance along the Konkan coast.
20. Historic and current use of the fort was explained to the author in conversation on March 10, 2017, in Alibag by the current descendant of the Angre clan Sarkhel Raghujiraje Angre.
21. Malgonkar, *The Sea Hawk*, 255.
22. Malgonkar, *The Sea Hawk*, 260.
23. Chilka, *Sea Forts of India*.
24. Apte, *A History of the Maratha Navy*, 54.
25. Apte, *A History of the Maratha Navy*, 18.
26. Malgonkar, *The Sea Hawk*, 282.
27. Apte, *A History of the Maratha Navy*, 107–9.
28. The suffix "durg" means fort.
29. Apte, *A History of the Maratha Navy*, 20.
30. Apte, *A History of the Maratha Navy*, 97–100.
31. Apte, *A History of the Maratha Navy*, 21.
32. Fishing boats still use the old stone anchors as mooring bits.
33. Malgonkar, *The Sea Hawk*, 197–203.

34. Malgonkar, *The Sea Hawk*, 235.
35. Apte, *A History of the Maratha Navy*, 100.
36. Apte, *A History of the Maratha Navy*, 101–4.
37. Apte, *A History of the Maratha Navy*, 43–47.
38. Apte, *A History of the Maratha Navy*, 119.
39. Apte, *A History of the Maratha Navy*, 120. Apte's work on Maratha ships, 119–63, is thorough and accessible, providing much of the detail in this section.
40. In the related literature, grab is also spelled gurab or ghurab; gallivat is also spelled galbat or gallibat.
41. Apte, *A History of the Maratha Navy*, 121.
42. Apte, *A History of the Maratha Navy*, 244–63; see Dhulap records from Vijaydurg, 1764–1780.
43. MacDougall, *Naval Resistance*, 42–43.
44. MacDougall, *Naval Resistance*, 87–91.
45. MacDougall, *Naval Resistance*, 122.
46. Apte, *A History of the Maratha Navy*, 76.
47. Malgonkar, *The Sea Hawk*, 9–15.
48. The Angre family took their name from the village of Angarwadi near Pune (Poona); see Malgonkar, *The Sea Hawk*, 11.
49. In an unflattering English account, Kanhoji is given Zanzibar roots, as an ally of the Siddi.
50. Malgonkar, *The Sea Hawk*, 15.
51. Malgonkar, *The Sea Hawk*, 51–56.
52. Malgonkar, *The Sea Hawk*, 88–171.
53. Malgonkar, *The Sea Hawk*, 174–78.
54. While 1662 was the year that the British gained Bombay, it was also the year that the Dutch lost Taiwan.
55. Shashi Tharoor, "The Partition: The British Game of 'Divide and Rule,'" *Aljazeera*, August 10, 2017.
56. Public images of Shivaji appear throughout Maharashtra, both in statues and in popular public art like motorcycle cowlings and cell phone cases.

CONCLUSION

1. Daniel Yergin, "The World's Most Important Body of Water: More Than Most, Four Men Shaped the Oft-Cited 'Strategic Tensions' over the South China Sea," *The Atlantic*, December 15, 2020.
2. Robert Kaplan, *Asia's Cauldron: The South China Sea and the End of a Stable Pacific* (New York: Random House, 2014).
3. James Stavridis and Elliott Ackerman, *2034: A Novel of the Next World War* (New York: Penguin Press, 2021).
4. Sun Tzu, *The Art of War*, trans. Samuel Griffith (Oxford: Oxford University Press, 1963), 129.
5. See Paul Cohen, *History and Popular Memory: The Power of Story in Moments of Crisis* (New York: Columbia University Press, 2017), on how complex histories are transformed into myth-like stories that become the basis for action many years later, especially during crises.

6. In terms of Chinese state-sponsored naval voyages to the Indian Ocean, there was a gap of 575 years between the last Zheng He voyage in 1433 and the first Chinese antipiracy voyage in 2008.
7. These three positive cases are from the Ming Dynasty, a native Han ethnicity dynasty. Han Chinese pride in these victories contrasts with naval failures during the earlier Yuan and later Qing Dynasties, in which the Mongols and Manchus asserted themselves over the Han Chinese. Subjection of China to the Treaty of Nanjing in 1842 began what China calls its "century of humiliation." This is perhaps the most powerful example of how past foreign intervention has shaped current Chinese thinking.
8. K. M. Panikkar, *India and the Indian Ocean: An Essay on the Influence of Sea Power on Indian History* (London: George Allen & Unwin Ltd., 1951); Sanjeev Sanyal, *The Ocean of Churn: How the Indian Ocean Shaped Human History* (Haryana, India: Penguin Random House, 2016).
9. Grant Rhode, "China's Emergence as a Power in the Mediterranean: Port Diplomacy and Active Engagement," *Diplomacy & Statecraft* 32, no. 2 (June 2021): 395–415.
10. An insightful analysis regarding the use of history by policymakers is Richard Neustadt and Ernest May, *Thinking in Time: The Uses of History for Decision Makers* (New York: The Free Press, 1988), 232–72.

BIBLIOGRAPHY

BOOKS AND DISSERTATIONS

Allison, Graham. *Destined for War: Can America and China Escape Thucydides's Trap?* Boston: Houghton Mifflin Harcourt, 2017.

Allsen. Thomas. *Culture and Conquest in Mongol Eurasia.* Cambridge: Cambridge University Press, 2001.

Andrade, Tonio. *How Taiwan Became Chinese: Dutch, Spanish, and Han Colonization in the Seventeenth Century.* New York: Columbia University Press, 2009.

———. *Lost Colony: The Untold Story of China's First Great Victory over the West.* Princeton, NJ: Princeton University Press, 2011.

Angell, Norman. *The Great Illusion: A Study of the Relation of Military Power to National Advantage.* New York: G. P. Putnam's Sons, 1913.

Apte, B. K. *A History of the Maratha Navy and Merchant Ships.* Bombay: State Board for Literature and Culture, 1973.

Arunachalam, B. *Chola Navigation Package.* Mumbai: Maritime History Society, 2004.

———. ed., *Essays in Maritime Studies.* Mumbai: Maritime History Society, 1998.

———. *Heritage of Indian Sea Navigation.* Mumbai: Maritime History Society, 2002.

———. *Indian Boat Designs and Forms.* Mumbai: Maritime History Society, 2009.

Atil, Esin. *The Age of Sultan Suleyman the Magnificent.* Washington, DC: National Gallery of Art, 1987.

Balasooriya, J. *The Glory of Ancient Polonnaruva.* Polonnoruva, Sri Lanka: Parakum Books, 1999, 2nd ed., 2004.

Balbi di Corregio, Francesco. *The Siege of Malta, 1565.* Translated from the Spanish edition of 1568 by Ernle Bradford. London: Boydell Press, 2011.

Barbosa, Duarte. *An Account of the Countries Bordering on the Indian Ocean and Their Inhabitants, 1518*. Translated by Mansel Longworth Dames. London: Hakluyt Society, 1921.

Barfield, Thomas J. *The Nomadic Alternative*. Hoboken, NJ: Prentice Hall, 1993.

Beng, Ooi Kee. *The Eurasian Core and Its Edges: Dialogues with Wang Gungwu on the History of the World*. Singapore: Institute of Southeast Asian Studies, 2015.

Berry, Mary Elizabeth. *Hideyoshi*. Cambridge, MA: Harvard University Press, 1982.

Bicheno, Hugh. *Crescent and Cross: The Battle of Lepanto 1571*. London: Phoenix Orion Books, 2004.

Black, Jeremy, ed. *Great Military Leaders and Their Campaigns*. London: Thames & Hudson, 2008.

Blair, Sheila S. *A Compendium of Chronicles: Rashid al-Din's Illustrated History of the World*. London: Nour Foundation in association with Azimuth Editions and Oxford University Press, 1995.

Botzaris, Notis. *The Battle of Lepanto*. Athens: Demetrius and Egle Botzaris Foundation, 2001.

Boxer, Charles R. *Four Centuries of Portuguese Expansion, 1415–1825: A Succinct Survey*. Los Angeles: University of California Press, 1961.

———. *The Portuguese Seaborne Empire 1415–1825*. New York: Alfred A. Knopf, 1969.

Bradford, Ernle. *The Great Siege: Malta, 1565: Clash of Cultures, Christian Knights Defend Western Civilization Against the Moslem Tide*. London: Open Road Integrated Media, 2014.

——. *The Sultan's Admiral: Pirate and Empire Builder.* London: Tauris Parke Paperbacks, 2009.

Braudel, Fernand. *On History.* Chicago: University of Chicago Press, 1980.

Brockelman, Carl. *History of the Islamic Peoples*. New York: Capricorn Books, 1960.

Brockman, E. *The Two Sieges of Rhodes: The Knights of St. John at War, 1480–1522*. New York: Barnes & Noble, 1996.

Brummet, Palmira. *Ottoman Seapower and Levantine Diplomacy in the Age of Discovery.* Albany: State University of New York Press, 1994.

Burton, Richard F. *The Arabian Nights: Tales from a Thousand and One Nights*. New York: Modern Library Random House, 2004.

Campbell, William. *Formosa under the Dutch: Described from Contemporary Records*. London: Kegan Paul, Trench, Trubner & Co. Ltd., 1903.

Capponi, Niccolo. *Victory of the West: The Great Christian-Muslim Clash at the Battle of Lepanto*. Cambridge MA: DaCapo Press, 2006.

Casale, Giancarlo. *The Ottoman Age of Exploration*. Oxford: Oxford University Press, 2010.

Chesterton, G. K. *Lepanto with Explanatory Notes and Commentary*. Edited by Dale Ahlquist. San Francisco: Ignatius Press, 2004.

Chia, Lin Sien, and Sally K. Church. *Cheng Ho and the Afro-Asian World.* Melaka: Perbadanan Muzium Melaka and International Zheng He Society, 2012.

Chilka, Amit. *Sea Forts of India*. Osmora Inc., e-Book Publisher, 2014.

Chong, A., and S. Murphy, eds. *The Tang Shipwreck: Art and Exchange in the 9th Century*. Singapore: Asian Civilizations Museum, 2017.

Cipolla, Carlo M. *Guns, Sails, and Empire: Technological Innovation and the Early Phases of European Expansion, 1400–1700*. New York: Pantheon Books, 1965.

Clausewitz, Carl von. *On War*. Translated by Michael Howard and Peter Paret. Princeton, NJ: Princeton University Press, 1976.

Clements, Jonathan. 2004. *Coxinga and the Fall of the Ming Dynasty*. Gloucestershire: Sutton Publishing, 2004.

Coedes, George. *The Indianized States of Southeast Asia*. Edited by Walter F. Vella. Translated by Susan Brown Cowing. Honolulu: University of Hawai`i Press, 1968 (1964 in French).

Cohen, Paul. *History and Popular Memory: The Power of Story in Moments of Crisis*. New York: Columbia University Press, 2017.

Cohen, Warren I. *East Asia at the Center: Four Thousand Years of Engagement with the World*. New York: Columbia University Press, 2000.

Conlan, Thomas. *In Little Need of Divine Intervention*. Ithaca, NY: Cornell University Press, 2001.

Correa, Gaspar. *The Three Voyages of Vasco da Gama, and His Viceroyalty*. Facsimile reprint of an 1869 edition by the Hakluyt Society. London: Adamant Media Corporation, 2001.

Creasy, Edward S. *History of the Ottoman Turks*. Beirut: Khayats, 1968.

Crowley, Roger. *Conquerors: How Portugal Forged the First Global Empire*. New York: Random House, 2015.

———. *Empires of the Sea: The Siege of Malta, the Battle of Lepanto, and the Contest for the Center of the World*. New York: Random House, 2008.

Crozier, Ralph C. *Koxinga and Chinese Nationalism: History, Myth, and the Hero*. Cambridge, MA: Harvard University Press, 1977.

De Silva, Nimal, et al. *Maritime Heritage of Lanka: Ancient Ports and Harbours*. Colombo: National Trust of Sri Lanka, 2013.

De Silva, Raja. *Archaeological Guide to Sigiriya*. Nawala, Sri Lanka: Bibliotheque Ltd., 2004.

———. *Distortions in History. The Dossier on Nissamka Malla, Prince in India, King of Lanka (1187–1196)*. Nawala, Sri Lanka, 2016.

———. *Polonnaruva. An Archaeological Guide and Related Matters*. Nawala, Sri Lanka, 2013.

Delgado, James P. *Khubilai Khan's Lost Fleet: In Search of a Legendary Armada*. Oakland: University of California Press, 2010.

Dreyer, Edward L. *Zheng He: China and the Oceans in the Early Ming Dynasty, 1405–1433*. New York: Pearson Longman, 2006.

Fairbank, John King. *The Chinese World Order: Traditional Chinese Foreign Relations*. Cambridge, MA: Harvard University Press, 1968.

Findley, Carter Vaughn. *The Turks in World History*. Oxford: Oxford University Press, 2005.

Frankopan, Peter. *The Silk Roads: A New History of the World*. New York: Vintage Books, 2015.

Freedman, Maurice. *Chinese Lineage and Society: Fukien and Kwangtung.* London: Athlone Press, 1966.

———. *Lineage Organization in Southeastern China.* London: Athlone Press, 1958.

Gallupini, Gino. *Warships of the World.* New York: Random House Times Books, 1983.

Gipouloux, Francois. *The Asian Mediterranean: Port Cities and Trading Networks in China, Japan and Southeast Asia, 13th–21st Century.* Cheltenham, UK: Edward Elgar, 2011.

Glete, Jan. *Warfare at Sea: 1500–1650 Maritime Conflicts and the Transformation of Europe.* London: Routledge, 2001.

Griffiths, Richard. *The Maritime Silk Road: China's Belt and Road at Sea.* Leiden: International Institute for Asian Studies, 2020.

Grotius, Hugo. *Mare Liberum: The Freedom of the Seas, or The Right Which Belongs to the Dutch to Take Part in the East Indian Trade.* Clark, NJ: Law Book Exchange, 2001.

Guilmarten, John Francis Jr. *Gunpowder & Galleys: Changing Technology & Mediterranean Warfare at Sea in the 16th Century.* London: Conway Maritime Press, 2003.

Hall, D. G. E. *A History of Southeast Asia.* 4th ed. London: Macmillan, 1981.

Hang, Xing. *Conflict and Commerce in Maritime East Asia: The Zheng Family and the Shaping of the Modern World, c. 1620–1720.* Cambridge: Cambridge University Press, 2016.

Hang, Xing, and Tonio Andrade, eds. *Sea Rovers, Silver, and Samurai: Maritime East Asia in Global History, 1550–1700.* Honolulu: University of Hawai'i Press, 2016.

Hawley, Samuel. *The Imjin War: Japan's Sixteenth Century Invasion of Korea and Attempt to Conquer China.* Seoul: Conquistador Press, 2014.

Helles, K. *Tranquebar under Danish Rule 1620–1845.* Tranquebar: Tranquebar Maritime Museum, 2013.

Hoon, Hum Sin. *Zheng He's Art of Collaboration: Understanding the Legendary Chinese Admiral from a Management Perspective.* Singapore: Institute of Southeast Asian Studies, 2012.

Hori, Kyotsu. "Mongol Invasions and the Kamakura Bakufu." PhD dissertation, Columbia University, 1967.

Hummel, A. ed. *Eminent Chinese of the Ch'ing Period (1644–1912).* Washington, DC: U.S. Government Printing Office, 1943.

Hung, C. "Taiwan Under the Cheng Family 1662–1683: Sinicization After Dutch Rule." PhD dissertation, Georgetown University, 1981.

Huntington, Samuel P. *The Clash of Civilizations and the Remaking of World Order.* New York: Simon & Schuster Paperbacks, 2011.

Imber, C. *The Ottoman Empire.* New York: Palgrave Macmillan, 2002.

Iyer, Krishna. *The Zamorins of Calicut.* Calicut: Norman Press, 1934.

Jayne, K. G. *Vasco da Gama and His Successors, 1460–1580.* New York: Barnes and Noble, 1970.

Jo, Seong-do. *Admiral Yi Sun-sin: A National Hero of Korea.* Seoul: Naval Academy Museum and Sinseowon, 2005.

Juvaini, Ata-Malik. *Genghis Khan: The History of the World Conqueror*. Translated by John Andrew Boyle. Manchester: Manchester University Press, 1997.

Kaplan, Robert. *Asia's Cauldron: The South China Sea and the End of a Stable Pacific*. New York: Random House, 2014.

———. *Monsoon: The Indian Ocean and the Future of American Power*. New York: Random House, 2010.

———. *The Revenge of Geography: What the Map Tells Us about Coming Conflicts and the Battle against Fate*. Random House: New York, 2012.

Keene, D. *The Battles of Coxinga: Chikamatsu's Puppet Play, Its Background and Importance*. London: Taylor's Foreign Press, 1951.

Ketkar, D. R., and Ravindra Ramdas. *Sarkhel Kanhoji Angre . . . Maratha Armar*. Mrunmayi Rugvedi Prakashan, 1997.

Khan, Paul. *The Secret History of the Mongols: The Origins of Chingis Khan*. San Francisco: North Point Press, 1984.

Kincaid, C. A., and D. B. Parasnis. *A History of the Maratha People*. Vol. I. London: Henry Milford, 1919.

Korean Spirit and Culture Promotion Project. *Admiral Yi Sun-sin: A Brief Overview of the Life and Achievements*. Seoul: Samjun Munhwasa, 2005, 2nd ed., 2010.

Kouwenhoven, Arlette. *Siebold and Japan: His Life and Work*. Leiden: Hotei Publishing, 2000.

Krishnamurthy R., and S. Wickramasinghe. *A Catalogue of the Sangam Age Pandya and Chola Coins in the National Museum, Colombo, Sri Lanka*. Colombo: Department of the National Museums, 2005.

Kulkarni, A. R. *The Marathas (1600–1848)*. Delhi: Books and Books, 1996.

Kulke, Hermann, K. Kesavapany, and Vijay Sakhuja, eds. *Nagapattinam to Suvarnadwipa: Reflections on the Chola Naval Expeditions to Southeast Asia*. Singapore: Institute of Southeast Asian Studies, 2009.

Kurup, K. K. N., ed., *India's Naval Traditions (The Role of the Kunhali Marakkars)*. New Delhi: Northern Book Centre, 1997.

Laine, James W. *Shivaji: Hindu King in Islamic India*. Oxford: Oxford University Press, 2003.

Leonardos, George. *Barbarossa the Pirate*. CreateSpace Independent Publishing Platform, 2013.

Levathes, Louise. *When China Ruled the Seas: The Treasure Fleet at the Dragon Throne, 1405–1433*. Oxford: Oxford University Press, 1994.

Lewis, James B. ed. *The East Asian War, 1592–1598: International Relations, Violence, and Memory*. London: Routledge, 2015.

Lo Jung-pang. *China as a Sea Power 1127–1368: A Preliminary Survey of the Maritime Expansion and Naval Exploits of the Chinese People during the Southern Song and Yuan Periods*. Edited by Bruce A. Elleman. Singapore: National University of Singapore Press, 2012.

Ma Huan. *Ying-Yai Sheng-Lan "The Overall Survey of the Ocean's Shores (1433)."* Translated by Feng Ch'eng-Chun. Introduction and notes by J. V. G. Mills. Cambridge: Published for the Hakluyt Society at the University Press, 1970.

MacDougall, Philip. *Naval Resistance to Britain's Growing Power in India, 1660–1800: The Saffron Banner and the Tiger of Mysore*. Woodbridge, Suffolk, UK: Boydell Press, 2014.

MacIntosh-Smith, Tim, ed. *The Travels of Ibn Battutah*. Abridged from translation by H. Gibb and C. F. Beckingham. Published in four volumes by the Hakluyt Society, 1958–1994. London: Macmillan, 1958.

Mackinder, Halford John. *Democratic Ideals and Reality: A Study in the Politics of Reconstruction*. New York: Henry Holt and Company, 1919.

Mackintosh-Smith, Tim. *The Travels of Ibn Battutah*. London: Picador, 2003.

Mahan, A. T. *The Influence of Sea Power upon History, 1660–1783*. New York: Dover Publications, 1987.

Malgonkar, Manohar. *The Sea Hawk: Life and Battles of Kanhoji Angrey*. New Delhi: Orient Paperbacks, 1979.

Marshall, Robert. *Storm from the East: From Genghis Khan to Kubilai Khan*. Oakland: University of California Press, 1993.

Matius, L., trans. *Prambanan*. Jakarta: Perpustakaan Nasional, 13th edition, 2007.

Mearsheimer, John J. *The Tragedy of Great Power Politics*. New York: W. W. Norton & Co., 2014.

Menegon, Eugenio. *Ancestors, Virgins, and Friars: Christianity as a Local Religion in Late Imperial China*. Cambridge, MA: Harvard University Press, 2009.

Menzies, Gavin. *1421: The Year China Discovered the World*. London: Bantam Books, 2002.

Miyamoto, Kazuo. *Vikings of the Far East*. New York: Vantage, 1975.

Mote, Frederick W., and Denis C. Twitchett, eds. *The Cambridge History of China: Volume 7, The Ming Dynasty 1368–1644*. Cambridge: Cambridge University Press, 1988.

Munoz, Paul Michel. *Early Kingdoms of the Indonesian Archipelago and the Malay Peninsula*. Singapore: Editions Didier Millet, 2006.

Murphey, Rhoads. *Ottoman Warfare, 1500–1700*. New Brunswick, NJ: Rutgers University Press, 1999.

Nambiar, Odayamadath Kunjappa. *The Kunjalis, Admirals of Calicut*. Delhi: Asia Publishing House, 1963.

Naravane, M. S. *The Heritage Sites of Maritime Maharashtra*. Mumbai: Maritime History Society, 2001.

Needham, Joseph. *Science and Civilization in China*, vol. 4, *Physics and Physical Technology*, Part III: *Civil Engineering and Nautics*. Cambridge: Cambridge University Press, 1971.

Neustadt, Richard E., and Ernest R. May. *Thinking in Time: The Uses of History for Decision Makers*. New York: The Free Press, 1988.

Organski, A. F. K. *World Politics*. New York: Alfred A. Knopf, 1958.

Ozukan, Bulent. *The Book of Bahriye*. Istanbul: Boyut Publishing, 2013.

Padfield, Peter. *Tide of Empires: Decisive Naval Campaigns in the Rise of the West, Volume One: 1481–1654*. London: Routledge & Kegan Paul, 1979.

Panikkar, K. M. *India and the Indian Ocean: An Essay on the Influence of Sea Power on Indian History*. London: George Allen & Unwin, 1951.

Panzac, Daniel. *The Ottoman Navy: From the Height of Empire to Dissolution, 1572–1923*. Translated by Peter R. Gillespie. Oxford: Oxford University Press, 2020.

Pathmanathan, S., ed. *Tamil Inscriptions in the Colombo National Museum*. Colombo, Sri Lanka: Department of National Museums, 2005.

Pearson, Michael. *The Indian Ocean*. New York: Routledge, 2003.

Pickles, Tim. *Malta: 1565: Last Battle of the Crusades*. London: Osprey, 1998.

Polo, Marco. *The Customs of the Kingdoms of India*. Translated by Robert Latham. London: Penguin Books, 2007.

———. *The Travels of Marco Polo*. Translated by Ronald Latham. New York: Penguin Books, 1958.

Prematilleke, P. L. *Nalanda: A Short Guide to the* "Gedige" *Shrine*. Sri Lanka: Ministry of Cultural Affairs, 1985.

Pryor, John H. *Geography, Technology, and War: Studies in the Maritime History of the Mediterranean, 649–1571*. Cambridge: Cambridge University Press, 1988.

Ranawella, S., ed. *Sinhala Inscriptions in the Colombo National Museum*. Colombo, Sri Lanka: Department of National Museums, 2005.

Reischauer, Edwin O., and John K. Fairbank. *East Asia: The Great Tradition*. Boston: Houghton Mifflin Company, 1958.

Sanyal, Sanjeev. *The Ocean of Churn: How the Indian Ocean Shaped World History*. Haryana, India: Penguin Random House India, 2016.

Sardesai, G. S. *New History of the Marathas*. Vol. I. Bombay: Phoenix Publications, 1946.

Sarkar, Jadunath. *Shivaji and His Times*. Calcutta: M. C. Sarkar and Sons, 1919.

Seong-do, Jo. *Admiral Yi Sun-sin: A National Hero of Korea*. Seoul: Naval Academy Museum and Sinseowon, 2005.

Sezgin, Fuat. *Piri Reis & The Pre-Columbian Discovery of the American Continents by Muslim Seafarers*. Istanbul: Boyut Publishing, 2013.

Some Historic Battles in Vietnam. Vietnam: The Gioi Publishers, 2013.

Soucek, Svat. *Piri Reis: Turkish Mapmaking after Columbus*. Istanbul: Boyut Publishing, 2013.

Spence, Jonathan D., and John E. Wills Jr. *From Ming to Ch'ing: Conquest, Region, and Continuity in Seventeenth Century China*. New Haven, CT: Yale University Press, 1979.

Spencer, George W. *The Politics of Expansion: The Chola Conquest of Sri Lanka and Sri Vijaya*. Madras: New Era Publications, 1983.

Spykman, Nicholas J. *America's Strategy in World Politics: The United States and the Balance of Power*. New Brunswick, NJ: Transaction Publishers, 2008.

———. *The Geography of the Peace*. New York: Harcourt Brace and Company, 1944.

Sridhar, T. S. *Select Inscriptions of Tamil Nadu*. Chennai: State Department of Archaeology, 2006.

Sridharan, K. *A Maritime History of India*. New Delhi: Government of India, 1982.

Stavridis, James. *Sea Power: The History and Geopolitics of the World's Oceans*. New York: Penguin Press, 2017.
Stavridis, James, and Elliott Ackerman. *2034: A Novel of the Next World War.* New York: Penguin Press, 2021.
Strassler, Robert B., ed. *The Landmark Thucydides: A Comprehensive Guide to the Peloponnesian War.* New York: Simon & Schuster, 1996.
Strayer, Robert W., and Eric Nelson. *Ways of the World: A Brief Global History with Sources*. 4th ed. Boston: Bedford/St. Martin's, 2019.
Struve, Lynn. *The Ming-Qing Conflict, 1619–1683: A Historiography and Resource Guide*. Ann Arbor: Association for Asian Studies, 1998.
———. *Southern Ming: 1644–1662*. New Haven, CT: Yale University Press, 1984.
Sun Tzu. *The Art of War.* Translated by Samuel B. Griffith. Oxford: Oxford University Press, 1963.
Susanti, N., T. Pudjastuti, and D. Trigangga, eds. *Inscribing Identity: The Development of Indonesian Writing Systems*. Jakarta: National Museum of Indonesia, 2015.
Swope, Kenneth M. *A Dragon's Head and a Serpent's Tail: Ming China and the First Great Asian War, 1592–1598*. Norman: University of Oklahoma Press, 2009.
Szonyi, Michael. *Cold War Island: Quemoy on the Front Line*. Cambridge: Cambridge University Press, 2008.
———. *Practicing Kinship: Lineage and Descent in Late Imperial China*. Stanford, CA: Stanford University Press, 2002.
Tan, Ta Sen. *Cheng Ho and Islam in Southeast Asia*. Singapore: Institute of Southeast Asian Studies and International Zheng He Society, 2009.
———. *Cheng Ho and Malaya*. Published jointly by Singapore: International Zheng He Society and Melaka: Cheng Ho Cultural Museum, 2014.
Tharoor, Shashi. *Inglorious Empire: What the British Did to India*. London: Penguin Random House, 2017.
Toussaint, Auguste. *History of the Indian Ocean*. Translated by June Guicharnaud. Chicago: University of Chicago Press, 1966.
Turnbull, Stephen. *Fighting Ships of the Far East (1), China and Southeast Asia 202 BC–AD 1419*. Oxford: Osprey, 2002.
———. *Fighting Ships of the Far East (2): Japan and Korea AD 612–1639*. Wellingborough, UK: Osprey Publishing, 2003.
———. *Japanese Castles in Korea 1592–98*. Oxford: Osprey, 2007.
———. *The Mongol Invasions of Japan 1274 and 1281*. Oxford: Osprey, 2010.
———. *Pirate of the Far East 811–1639*. Oxford: Osprey, 2007.
———. *Samurai Invasion: Japan's Korean War 1592–98*. London: Cassell & Co., 2002.
———. *The Samurai Invasion of Korea 1592–1598*. Oxford: Osprey, 2008.
———. *The Samurai: A Military History*. New York: Macmillan Publishing Co., Inc., 1977.
Vanina, Eugenia. *Medieval Indian Mindscapes: Space, Time, Society, Man*. New Delhi: Primus Books, 2012.

Vermeer, E., ed. *Development and Decline of Fukien Province in the 17th and 18th Centuries*. Leiden: E. J. Brill, 1990.

Wachman, Alan. *Why Taiwan? Geostrategic Rationales for China's Territorial Integrity*. Stanford, CA: Stanford University Press, 2007.

Wang, Gungwu. *Nanyang: Essays on Heritage*. Singapore: Institute of Southeast Asian Studies, 2018.

Weatherford, Jack. *Genghis Khan and the Making of the Modern World*. New York: Broadway Books, 2004.

Weerasinghe, S. G. M. *A History of Cultural Relations between Sri Lanka and China: An Aspect of the Silk Road*. Colombo: Sri Lanka Ministry of Cultural Affairs, 1994.

Whiteway, R. S. *The Rise of Portuguese Power in India 1497–1550*. New York: Augustus M. Kelley Publishers, 1967.

Williams, Philip. *Empire and Holy War in the Mediterranean: The Galley and Maritime Conflict between the Hapsburg and Ottoman Empires*. London: I. B. Tauris, 2014.

Wills, John E., Jr. *Mountain of Fame: Portraits in Chinese History*. Princeton, NJ: Princeton University Press, 1994.

Worcester, C. R. G. *The Junks and Sampans of the Yangtze*. Annapolis, MD: Naval Institute Press, 1971.

Yamada, Nakaba. *Ghenko: The Mongol Invasions of Japan, 1274–81*. London: Leonaur, 2012.

Yi Sun-sin. *Nanjung Ilgi: The War Diaries of Admiral Yi*. Translated by Tae-hung Ha. Seoul: Yonsei University Press, 1977.

———. *Imjin Changch'o: Admiral Yi Sun-Sin's Memorials to Court*. Translated by Tae-hung Ha. Seoul: Yonsei University Press, 1979.

Yu, Song-Nyong, and Byonghyon Choi. *The Book of Corrections: Reflections on the National Crisis During the Japanese Invasion of Korea, 1592–1598*. Berkeley: Institute of East Asian Studies, University of California, 2002.

Yudhistira, A. trans. *Borobudur and Temples of Java*. Borobudur: Aiaz Rajasa, 2017.

Zheng, Zhenman. *Family Lineage Organization and Social Change in Ming and Qing Fujian*. Translated by Michael Szonyi. Honolulu: University of Hawai'i Press, 2001.

ARTICLES, BOOK CHAPTERS, AND PAPERS

Alexander VI. "Inter Caetera: Division of the Undiscovered World between Spain and Portugal." *Papal Encyclicals Online*, May 4, 1493. https://www.papalencyclicals.net/alex06/alex06inter.htm.

Allison, Graham. "The Thucydides Trap: Are the U.S. and China Headed for War?" *The Atlantic*, Sept. 24, 2015. https://www.theatlantic.com/international/archive/2015/09/united-states-china-war-thucydides-trap/406756/.

Arunachalam, B. "Navigation Environment of Ports of Indus Valley Civilization." In *Essays in Maritime Studies Vol. III*, edited by Sachin Pendse and Odakkal Johnson, Mumbai: Maritime History Society (2016): 3–10.

Barton, Edwarde, and Edwin Pears. "The Spanish Armada and the Ottoman Porte." *English Historical Review* 8, no. 31 (July 1, 1893): 439–66.

Bergen, Henry. "Geopolitical Fallacies." *The New Masses* (June 6, 1944): 26–27. https://www.unz.com/print/NewMasses-1944jun06-00026/

Blusse, L. "Minnan-Jen or Cosmopolitan? The Rise of Cheng Chih-Lung Alias Nicolas Iquan." In *Development and Decline of Fukien Province in the 17th and 18th Centuries*, edited by Eduard B. Vermeer, 245–641. Leiden: Brill, 1990.

Bowdoin College, Asian Studies. *Takezaki Suenaga's Scrolls of the Mongol Invasions of Japan: Interactive Scroll.* https://learn.bowdoin.edu/mongol-invasions/.

Boxer, C. R. "The Rise and Fall of Nicholas Iquan." *T'ien, Hsia Monthly* XI (1941): 401–39.

———. "The Siege of Fort Zeelandia and the Capture of Formosa from the Dutch 1661–1662." In *Transactions and Proceedings of the Japan Society, London* XXIV (1926–27): 16–47.

Buruma, Ian. "Dance with the Dragon: Are the United States and China on a Collision Course?" *New Yorker*, June 19, 2017, 61–65.

Cheng, K. "Cheng Ch'eng Kung's Maritime Expansion and Early Ch'ing Coastal Prohibition." In *Development and Decline of Fukien Province in the 17th and 18th Centuries*, edited by Eduard B. Vermeer, 217–44. Leiden: Brill, 1990.

Chitnis, A. H., and C. S. Patham. "The Naval Tactics of Kunhali Marakkars and Their Relevance to Modern Warfare at Sea." In *India's Naval Traditions: The Role of Kunhali Marakkars*, edited by K. K. N. Kurup, 34–42. New Delhi: Northern Book Centre, 1997.

Church, Sally. "Zheng He: An Investigation into the Plausibility of 450-ft Treasure Ships." *Monumenta Serica* 53 (2005): 1–43.

Gauvin, Dan. "Kunjali Marakkar and the Malabar Spice Trade." Unpublished paper, Newport, RI: U.S. Naval War College, 2017.

Gilbert, Marc Jason. "Admiral Yi Sun-Shin, the Turtle Ships, and Modern Asian History." *Education About ASIA* 12, no. 1 (Spring 2007): 29–35.

Gordon, Stewart. "The Marathas, 1600–1818." In *The New Cambridge History of India*. Cambridge: Cambridge University Press, 1993.

Grygiel, Jakub. "Ottoman Seapower and the Decline of the Mediterranean World." In *China Goes to Sea: Maritime Transformations in Comparative Historical Perspective*, edited by A. Erickson, L. Goldstein, and C. Lord, 90–119. Annapolis, MD: Naval Institute Press, 2009.

Hang, Xing. "Contradictory Contingencies: The Seventeenth-Century Zheng Family and Contested Cross-Strait Legacies." *American Journal of Chinese Studies* 23 (2016): 173–82.

———. "The Shogun's Chinese Partners: The Alliance between Tokugawa Japan and the Zheng Family in Seventeenth-Century Maritime East Asia." *Journal of Asian Studies* 75, no. 1 (February 2016): 111–36.

Henrikson, Alan K. "All the World's a Map." *Wilson Quarterly* 3, no. 2 (Spring 1979): 164–77.

Hess, Andrew C. "The Evolution of the Ottoman Seaborne Empire in the Age of the Oceanic Discoveries 1453–1525." *American Historical Review* 75, no. 7 (Dec. 1970): 1892–1919.

———. "Piri Reis and the Ottoman Response to the Voyages of Discovery." *Terrae Incognitae* 6 (1974): 10–37.

Huber, J. "Chinese Settlers against the Dutch East India Company: The Rebellion Led by Kuo Huai-I on Taiwan in 1652." In *Development and Decline of Fukien Province in the 17th and 18th Centuries*, edited by Eduard B. Vermeer, 265–96. Leiden: Brill, 1990.

Huntington, Samuel P. "The Clash of Civilizations?" *Foreign Affairs* 72, no. 3 (Summer 1993): 22–49.

Ikeda, Yoshifumi, Randy Sasaki, and Jun Kimura. "Recent Underwater Investigations at Takashima: Searching for the Lost Fleet of the Mongol Empire." *Current Science* 117, no. 10 (November 25, 2019): 1635–39.

Jayakumar, P. "Impact of Chinese Trade on the Medieval Chola Economy." *Tamil Civilization Quarterly Research Journal*, no. 19 (September 2008): 9–14.

———. "The Merchants of the West Coast and their Status in Chola Country." In *Studies in India's Maritime Trade through the Ages*, edited by A. Mukherjee, 27–36. Calcutta: Institute of Historical Studies, 1999.

———. "Nagapattinam: A Medieval Chola Port." In *New Trends in Indian Art and Archaeology: S.R. Rao's 70th Birthday Felicitation Volume, Volume 2*, edited by B. U. Nayak and N. C. Ghosh, 429–33. New Delhi: Aditya Prakashan, 1992.

Kawazoe, Shoji. "Japan and East Asia." In *The Cambridge History of Japan, Vol. 3: Medieval Japan*, edited by Kozo Yamamura, 396–446. Cambridge: Cambridge University Press, 1990.

Krugman, Paul. "The Great Illusion." *New York Times*, August 15, 2008. https://www.nytimes.com/2008/08/15/opinion/15krugman.html.

Lambert, Nicholas. "Classical Theories of Sea Power and World Economic Systems." U.S. Naval War College. EMC Chair Symposium Working Paper, 2017.

Lin, R. "Fukien's Private Sea Trade in the 16th and 17th Centuries." In *Development and Decline of Fukien Province in the 17th and 18th Centuries*, edited by Eduard B. Vermeer, 163–216. Leiden: Brill, 1990.

Lin, Wei-ping. "Virtual Recentralization: Pilgrimage as Social Imaginary in the Demilitarized Islands between China and Japan." *Comparative Studies in Society and History* 56, no. 1 (2014): 131–54.

Mackinder, Halford John. "The Geographical Pivot of History." *Geographical Journal* XXIII, no. 4 (April 1904): 421–37.

———. "The Round World and the Winning of the Peace." *Foreign Affairs* 21, no. 4 (July 1943): 595–605.

Maddy. "Hindus and the Ocean Taboo." *Historic Alleys: Historic Musings from a Malabar Perspective* (blog). January 1, 2020. https://historicalleys.blogspot.com/2009/01/hindus-and-ocean-taboo.html.

Majumdar, R. C. "The Overseas Expeditions of King Rajendra Cola." *Artibus Asiae* 24, no. 3/4 (January 1, 1961): 338–42.

Malieckal, Bindu. "Muslims, Matriliny, and a Midsummer Night's Dream: European Encounters with the Mallipas of Malabar, India." *The Muslim World* 95 (2005): 297–316.

"Marathas," Mapping Globalization, Princeton University, https://commons.princeton.edu/mg/marathas/.

Mathew, K. S. "Trade in the India Ocean and the Portuguese System of Cartaz." In *The First Portuguese Colonial Empire*, edited by Malyn Newitt. Exeter: A. Wheaton & Co. Ltd., 1986.

Maurer, John. "Thucydides and the Tragedy of Athens: A Parable for America." *Foreign Policy Research Institute*, June 26, 2017. https://www.fpri.org/article/2017/06/thucydides-tragedy-athens-parable-america/.

Nagel, E. "The Chinese Inscription on the Trilingual Slabstone from Galle Reconsidered." In *Ancient Ruhuna*, edited by H. J Weisshaar, H. Roth, and W. Wijeyapala, 430–36. Philipp von Zabern Mainzam Rhein, 2001.

Navari, Cornelia. "The International Theory of Norman Angell." *Review of International Studies* 15, no. 4 (Oct. 1989): 341–58.

Noone, Oliver. "Changes in Technology and War Tactics: Reinterpretation of the Naval Battle of Calicut, 1503." Unpublished paper, 2017.

Paranavitana, S. "The Tamil Inscription on the Galle Trilingual Slab." *Epigraphia Zeylandia* III, Archaeological Survey of Ceylon (1989): 331–41.

Park, Saeyoung. "National Heroes and Monuments in South Korea: Patriotism, Modernization, and Park Chung Hee's Remaking of Yi Sunsin's Shrine." *Asia-Pacific Journal* 8, no. 24 (Article ID 3374, Jun 14, 2010): 1–27. https://apjjf.org/-Saeyoung-Park/3374/article.html.

Pearson, M. N. "Shivaji and the Decline of the Mughal Empire." *Journal of Asian Studies* 35, no. 2 (Feb. 1976): 221–35.

Po, Ronald C. "'Shi Lang' Hero or Villain? His Evolving Legacy in China and Taiwan." *Modern Asian Studies*, LSE Research Online (June 2017): 1–23. http:/eprints.lse.ac.uk/81309/.

Ponsonby-Fane, R. "Koxinga: Chronicles of the Tei Family, Loyal Servants of the Ming." In *Sovereign and Subject*, 269–330. Kyoto: The Ponsonby-Fane Memorial Society, 1937, reproduced 1962.

Prange, Sebastian R. "'Measuring by the Bushel': Weighing the Indian Ocean Pepper Trade." *Historical Research* 84, no. 224 (May 2011): 212–35.

Rhode, Grant. "Mongol Invasions of Northeast Asia: Korea and Japan." Online supplement. Association for Asian Studies. *Education About ASIA* 25, no. 2 (Fall 2020). https://www.asianstudies.org/wp-content/uploads/Case-Study-Mongol-Invasions-of-Northeast-Asia-1.pdf.

———. "China's Emergence as a Power in the Mediterranean: Port Diplomacy and Active Engagement." *Diplomacy & Statecraft* 32, no. 2 (June 2021): 395–415.

Rhode, Grant, Eytan Goldstein, William Grimes, Thomas Kennelly, Eugenio Menegon, and Robert Murowchick. "China, Global History, and the Sea: Pedagogical Perspectives and Applications." Association for Asian Studies. *Education About ASIA* 25, no. 2 (Fall 2020): 18–24.

Ross, Robert. "The Geography of the Peace: East Asia in the Twenty-First Century." *International Security* 23, no. 4 (Spring 1999): 81–118.

Sangren, P. Steven. "History and the Rhetoric of Legitimacy: The Ma Tsu Cult of Taiwan." *Comparative Studies in Society and History* 30, no. 4 (1988): 674–97.

Sen, Tansen. "The Travel Records of Chinese Pilgrims Faxian, Xuanzong, and Yijing." *Education About ASIA* 11, no. 3 (Winter 2006): 24–33.

Soucek, Svat. "Piri Reis and Ottoman Discovery of the Great Discoveries." *Studia Islamica*, no. 79 (1994): 121–42.

Spencer, George W. "The Politics of Plunder: The Cholas in Eleventh Century Ceylon." *Journal of Asian Studies* 53, no. 3 (May 1976): 405–19.

Stewart P. J., and A. Strathern. "Growth of the Mazu Complex in Cross-Straits Contexts (Taiwan and Fujian Province, China)." *Journal of Ritual Studies* 23, no. 1 (2009): 67–72.

Struve, Lynn. "The Southern Ming, 1644–1662." In *The Cambridge History of China: Volume 7, The Ming Dynasty 1368–1644*, edited by Frederick W. Mote and Denis C. Twitchett, 641–725. Cambridge: Cambridge University Press, 1988.

Susumu, Ishii. "The Decline of the Kamakura Bakufu." In *The Cambridge History of Japan, Vol. 3: Medieval Japan*, edited by Kozo Yamamura, 128–74. Cambridge: Cambridge University Press, 1990.

Swaminathan, London. "Foreign Travel Banned for Brahmins!" In *Tamil and Vedas: A Blog Exploring Themes in Tamil and Vedic Literature*, November 26, 2013. https://tamilandvedas.com/2013/11/26/foreign-travel-banned-for-brahmins/.

Swope, Kenneth M. "Perspectives on the Imjin War." *Journal of Korean Studies* 12, no. 1 (Fall 2007): 154–61.

Taylor, Jeremy E. "The Production of the Chiang Kai-Shek Personality Cult, 1929–1975." *China Quarterly* 185 (March 2006): 96–110.

Tharoor, Shashi. "The Partition: The British Game of 'Divide and Rule.'" *Aljazeera*, August 10, 2017. https://www.aljazeera.com/opinions/2017/8/10/the-partition-the-british-game-of-divide-and-rule.

Thompson, Derek. "The Economic History of the Last 2,000 Years in 1 Little Graph, Parts I, II, and III." *The Atlantic*, June 19–22, 2012. https://www.theatlantic.com/business/archive/2012/06/the-economic-history-of-the-last-2–000-years-in-1-little-graph/258676.

"Turkish Navy Revives 500-Year-Old Salute for Renowned Ottoman Sailor Barbarossa." *Daily Sabah Istanbul,* Sept. 3, 2019. https://www.dailysabah.com/istanbul/2019/03/09/turkish-navy-revives-500-year-old-salute-for-renowned-ottoman-sailor-barbarossa.

"US Anthem Written in Mumbai." *Times of India*, January 24, 2005. https://timesofindia.indiatimes.com/india/us-anthem-written-in-mumbai/articleshow/999652.cms.

Van Ittersum, Martine Julia. "The Long Goodbye: Hugo Grotius Justification of Dutch Expansion Overseas, 1615–1645." *History of European Ideas* 36 (2010): 386–411.

Vanina, Eugenia. "Mughal-Maratha Wars (1659–1707)." In *War and Religion: An Encyclopedia of Faith and Conflict, Volume 2*, edited by Jeffrey Shaw and Timothy Demy, 571–74. Santa Barbara, CA: ABC_CLIO, LLC, 2017.

Wade, Geoff. "The Zheng He Voyages: A Reassessment." *MBRAS: The Malaysian Branch of the Royal Asiatic Society* 78, no. 1 (2005): 37–58.

Watson, James L. "Standardizing the Gods: The Promotion of Tien Hou ('Empress of Heaven') along the South China Coast, 960–1960." In *Popular Culture in Late Imperial China*, edited by David Johnson et al., 292–324. Berkeley: University of California Press, 1985.

Wei, Yang. "Admiral Zheng He's Voyages to the 'West Ocean.'" Association for Asian Studies. *Education About ASIA* 19, no. 2 (Fall 2014): 26–30.

Wills, John. "1500–1800: The Interactive Emergence of European Domination." *American Historical Review* 98, no. 1 (Feb. 1993): 83–105.

———. "Maritime China from Wang Chih to Shi Lang: Themes in Peripheral History." In *From Ming to Ch'ing,* edited by Jonathan Spence and John Wills, 201–38. New Haven, CT: Yale University Press, 1979.

Yang, Mayfair Mei-hui. "Goddess across the Taiwan Strait: Matrilocal Ritual Space, Nation-State, and Satellite Television Footprints." *Public Culture* 16, no. 2 (2004): 209–38.

Yergin, Daniel. "The World's Most Important Body of Water: More Than Most, Four Men Shaped the Oft-Cited 'Strategic Tensions' over the South China Sea." *The Atlantic*, December 15, 2020. https://www.theatlantic.com/international/archive/2020/12/south-china-sea-us-ghosts-strategic-tensions/617380/.

INDEX

ABOUT THE AUTHOR

Grant F. Rhode is senior lecturer at the Pardee School of Global Studies at Boston University, where he directs the Assessing China's Belt and Road Initiative program. He is also an adjunct professor of Eurasian maritime history at the U.S. Naval War College, and a nonresident associate in research at the Fairbank Center for Chinese Studies at Harvard University. Dr. Rhode's research and publications focus on China's role in both historical and contemporary Eurasian maritime affairs. He lives and writes in the historic New England maritime village of Bristol, Rhode Island.

The Naval Institute Press is the book-publishing arm of the U.S. Naval Institute, a private, nonprofit, membership society for sea service professionals and others who share an interest in naval and maritime affairs. Established in 1873 at the U.S. Naval Academy in Annapolis, Maryland, where its offices remain today, the Naval Institute has members worldwide.

Members of the Naval Institute support the education programs of the society and receive the influential monthly magazine *Proceedings* or the colorful bimonthly magazine *Naval History* and discounts on fine nautical prints and on ship and aircraft photos. They also have access to the transcripts of the Institute's Oral History Program and get discounted admission to any of the Institute-sponsored seminars offered around the country.

The Naval Institute's book-publishing program, begun in 1898 with basic guides to naval practices, has broadened its scope to include books of more general interest. Now the Naval Institute Press publishes about seventy titles each year, ranging from how-to books on boating and navigation to battle histories, biographies, ship and aircraft guides, and novels. Institute members receive significant discounts on the Press' more than eight hundred books in print.

Full-time students are eligible for special half-price membership rates. Life memberships are also available.

For more information about Naval Institute Press books that are currently available, visit www.usni.org/press/books. To learn about joining the U.S. Naval Institute, please write to:

Member Services
U.S. NAVAL INSTITUTE
291 Wood Road
Annapolis, MD 21402-5034
Telephone: (800) 233-8764
Fax: (410) 571-1703
Web address: www.usni.org